# Business and Marketing for Engineers and Scientists

# Business and Marketing for Engineers and Scientists

Tony Curtis

*Plymouth Business School*
*University of Plymouth*

## McGRAW-HILL BOOK COMPANY

London · New York · St Louis · San Francisco · Auckland · Bogotá · Caracas
Lisbon · Madrid · Mexico · Milan · Montreal · New Delhi · Panama
Paris · San Juan · Sao Paulo · Singapore · Sydney · Tokyo · Toronto

Published by
McGRAW-HILL Book Company Europe
Shoppenhangers Road, Maidenhead, Berkshire, SL6 2QL, England
Telephone 0628 23432
Fax 0628 770224

British Library Cataloguing in Publication Data

Curtis, Anthony
  Business and Marketing for Engineers and
  Scientists
  I. Title
  658.002462

  ISBN 0-07-707868-3

Library of Congress Cataloging-in-Publication Data

Curtis, Tony (Anthony)
    Business and marketing for engineers and scientists / Tony Curtis.
      p.   cm.
    Includes bibliographical references and index.
    ISBN 0-07-707868-3
    1. Industrial management.   2. Production management.
  3. Marketing—Management.   4. Industrial management—Case studies.
  I. Title.
  HD31.C875   1993
  506.8—dc20                                                      93-49026
                                                                        CIP

12345CL97654

Typeset by Paston Press Limited, Loddon, Norfolk
and printed and bound in Great Britain by Clays Ltd, St Ives plc

# CONTENTS

# WHAT IS AN ENGINEER?

## INTRODUCTION

In engineering science and technology, when we start a subject we begin with some basic definitions. In this book we shall start with the definition of an engineer:

> *An engineer is a person who wants to research, develop or apply technology to make the world a better place. The engineer is an agent of change, attempting to take a selected area from a given state to a better state.*

On your selected engineering course, the technical and theoretical knowledge relevant to your area—electronics, chemical engineering, mechanics or communication—will be covered and this is what you expect. However, what you may not want or expect is that a certain amount of your time will be devoted to management studies, and you may question why you should spend time on this.

The above is a short definition of what an engineer is. The Engineering Council have considered the recommended roles and responsibilities of an engineer and many of these roles and responsibilities involve considerable amounts of management skill. They recommend that posts involving one or more of the duties and responsibilities listed below should be occupied by those registered as Chartered Engineers or Incorporated Engineers.

Chartered and Incorporated Engineers are expected to apply their respective codes of professional conduct, to undertake work within their expertise and to exercise a responsible attitude to society with regard to the ethical, economic and environmental impact of technical need and change.

## RECOMMENDED ROLES AND RESPONSIBILITIES OF CHARTERED ENGINEERS

*(Reproduced with permission of the Engineering Council)*

### 1. Design

- Managerial responsibility for an engineering design function or group.
- Supervising preparation of designs.

- Engineering design outside the scope of established procedures, standards and codes of practice to a competitive level of cost, safety, quality and reliability.
- Promotion of advanced designs and design methods. Continual development of standards and codes internationally.
- Failure analysis and value engineering.
- Design work involving established procedures and the use of Engineering Standards and Codes of Practice to a competitive level of cost, safety, quality, reliability and appearance.

## 2.  Research and development

- Leading research and development effort in engineering resulting in the design, development and manufacture of products, equipment and processes to a competitive level of cost, safety, quality, reliability and appearance.
- Managing engineering research and development groups, planning and execution of research and development programmes, carrying out research and development assignments.
- Evaluation of test results and interpretation of data. Preparing reports and recommendations.

## 3.  Engineering practice

- The exercise of independent technical judgement and the application of engineering principles.
- Application of theoretical knowledge to the marketing, operation and maintenance of products and services.
- Development and application of new technologies.
- Monitoring progress on a worldwide basis, assimilation of such information and independent contributions to the development of Engineering Science and its applications.
- Work involving the need to understand and apply analytical and technical skills and judgement and the use of a range of equipment, techniques and methods for measurement, control, operation, fault diagnosis, maintenance and for protection of the environment.

## 4.  Manufacture, installation, construction

- Managerial responsibility for a production, installation, construction or dismantling function.
- Organization of cost effective manufacturing functions.
- The introduction of new and more efficient production techniques and of installation and construction concepts.
- Organization of quality-driven manufacture, installation and construction factors.
- Day-to-day organization and supervision of manufacturing, installation, and construction functions from raw material input to finished product.

## 5. Operation and maintenance

- Managerial responsibility for an operation or maintenance function of group.
- Providing specifications of operational maintainability standards to be achieved in design and production.
- Determining operational maintenance requirements in terms of tasks to be performed and time intervals between tasks.
- Managing the quality of the output of operational maintenance activities.
- Developing and specifying diagnostic techniques and procedures.
- Developing and specifying repair and rectification methods.
- Assessing the actual and expected effect on performance of deterioration in service.

## 6. Health, safety, reliability

- Making appropriate provision in engineering projects to ensure safety and the required standards of reliability, not only with employees and customers in mind but in the general public interest.
- Responsibility for health, safety, reliability in situations involving engineering plant, systems, processes or activities.
- Accident investigation.
- Supervision of inspection and test procedures.

## 7. Management and planning

- Overall company/commercial responsibility as a director with engineering knowledge.
- Longer range and strategic planning of engineering activities and functions.
- Management of the development and implementation of new technologies with estimation of the cost/benefit of the financial, social and political decisions taken.
- Pioneering of new engineering services and management methods.
- Effective direction of advanced existing technology involving high risk and capital intensive projects.
- Direct responsibility for the management or guidance of technical staff and other resources.
- Supervision of engineering staff and resources and the associated legal, financial and economic practice at a level commensurate with the scale of the activity and size of organization within the constraints of the relevant environment.
- Short-range planning of engineering activities and functions.

## 8. Engineering aspects of marketing

- Management responsibility for a technical marketing function.
- Top-level customer and contract negotiations.
- Setting marketing objectives and policies.
- Territorial or market planning forecasts and targets.
- Management responsibility for the dissemination of accurate technical information.
- Customer technical advisory service.
- Market analysis, contract negotiations.
- Non-standard customer requirements.

- Sales operations, efficient market coverage.
- Preparing cost estimates and proposals.

**9. Teaching, training, career development**

- Academic (teaching) responsibility for engineering courses and activities at first degree and postgraduate level.
- Career development for Chartered Engineers and Incorporated Engineers.
- Responsibility for training and the supervision of experience for those intending to become Chartered Engineers.
- Academic (teaching) responsibility for courses and activities up to BTEC/SCOTVEC Higher National level in Engineering.
- Career development for engineering technicians.
- Responsibility for training and the supervision of experience for those intending to become Incorporated Engineers or engineering technicians.

Every engineer needs to have a significant amount of management skills to succeed in the profession. It is the purpose of this book to provide you with a foundation for the development of these skills. Clearly, in a single book it is not possible to present each and every topic in great depth and this book should instead be regarded as opening doors on topic areas, giving a general overview and understanding, and providing a basis for further reading and skill development where an element is of particular relevance to your further career.

## 1.1 WHAT ENGINEERS DO AND WHAT THEY NEED TO DO IT

Engineers work in a wide variety of organizations: centres of fundamental research; non profit-making services, such as health care and education, the manufacture of products

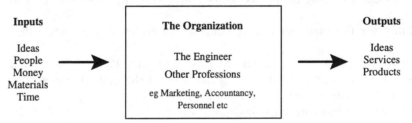

**Figure 1.1** The organization as an input–output device

for sale or the provision of services, such as communications. Whatever the type of organization, it can be considered as an input/output device (Fig. 1.1). The inputs can include time, money, people, materials and ideas from other people. The output may be ideas (fundamental research), services or products. In most businesses there will be profit objectives. In the operation of the organization, wealth is generated and there is a greater valuation of the outputs than the total of the inputs; the organization has added value. In a normal commercial company this added value is used to develop the firm for the future and also taken out by the owners in the form of dividends (profits distributed to owners). These are not the only objectives that an organization may have; for example, universities, hospitals and local authorities all need engineers, but their main objectives are not to make profits. Nevertheless, management skills and insight are just as necessary in the efficient and effective provision of public health care as with the manufacture of VCRs.

The Senior Research Engineer has to prepare budgets (accountancy), motivate and control the research team (human resources management) and communicate the results of research (presentation skills and marketing). The Development Engineer designs products to meet people's needs and wants (marketing), that have to be made efficiently (Operations) to meet given product costs (accountancy). He or she is also responsible for motivating the design team (human resources management). The Production (products) or Operations Engineer (services) is concerned with the effective and efficient operation and development of the organization's main asset, its productive capacity (manufacturing plant) or service provision (for example, the network management in telecommunications). Again, a senior professional engineer is directly concerned with the management of this resource (operations), with producing quality products (Total Quality Management) for customers (marketing), and also needs to motivate and develop the staff (human resources management). Increasingly, engineers are expected not only to work within the organization, but also to market, sell and support products such as local area networks in the field. Such engineers are in direct contact with the source of the organization's existence, its customers, and an intimate knowledge of engineering, the customer's business and marketing, is essential.

From the above we can see that no matter what the specific context of your engineering course and your future role in the world, there will be certain essential tasks that you will need to do to be successful in your engineering career. You will need to set plans in the context of a changing world and with due recognition of your own organization's role and structure. As an agent of change you will need to organize and direct the work of other people. These people will have to be motivated, to identify with your plans and objectives, and will also need to develop and extend their skills to meet the challenges of technological change. No such activity takes place in a vacuum and the Senior Professional Engineer will have to coordinate the unit's activities with that of other parts of the organization and with external people. A Design Engineer who has designed a communication system will have to work with production to ensure the production of the required units and to schedule and liaise with the customer for the firm's field staff to install, commission and hand over the new facility. One of the most challenging areas is that in the real world the only certainty is that plans will not work 100 per cent. The professional engineer has to set objectives and standards and then measure performance against these standards. When deviations are found—for example, connect times starting to get extended in a telephone network—the engineer is responsible for formulating and implementing contingency plans to bring the service or production level back to the target.

To be successful as a full professional you will need skills and competencies in the following areas:

1. *Technical competence as an engineer* It is not suggested in any part of this book that management skills are more important than the specific engineering, scientific and technical skills you have gained and are developing. Rather, it is suggested that unless you develop the additional competencies discussed below you will not be able to effectively exploit your skills fully and make your maximum contribution to society.

2. *People skills* All of us have to work with people and as a senior person you will not

only have to work with others, but be required to supervise and direct the work of others. A key skill for an engineer is to communicate, not only with other professional engineers but with all people in society. To be able to direct and work with people the engineer needs to know what people are, how they develop and what motivates them. Practical answers are required to difficult questions for a particular person. Skills are needed not only to identify and develop the individual staff member's talents but also to do this in the context of developing the total capacity of the organization.

The purpose of this text is to be integrative as motivation issues are not confined within the organization. They affect the way in which the organization is perceived by people in the greater world. In particular, people are motivated by simple needs and more complex desires. An engineer faced with producing a communications system for a hospital will be faced with technical problems but the end result must be to provide a feeling of security, care and love for people who are facing a life threatening situation. These are not trivial issues and the engineer who only focuses on the technical issues may well miss the whole point. In the development of consumer electronics, external design as well as functional design may affect the final consumer selection. Motivation is critical not only in the management of people but also in the marketing of product and services. The most common mistake is to think that all a good sales engineer needs to be is a good talker, to understand the buyer's needs, wants and motivation. However, the skilled sales engineer will also be a good listener.

3. *External analytical skills* All organizations function in the context of society. For the engineer this most often means an international context. Cars, consumer electronics and communications are not made or marketed on a single nation basis, but on a truly global basis. The senior engineer needs to be able to identify and assess the key issues which affect the decisions to be made. In this text, models will be advanced which will assist you in this process.

4. *Internal analytical skills* We have considered above the human resources context of the organization. The senior engineer needs to analyse the organizations, the internal resources and competences (such as the efficiency and effectiveness of the production or service provisions), the flexibility of the firm in responding to the implications of the above with new products or services, possibly produced in entirely new ways and utilizing entirely new technologies. Such an analysis must, of necessity, include an appreciation of the financial consequences.

5. *Imagination and creativity* One of the most difficult aspects of management studies is the fact that there is not a unique 'right' solution. As an engineer, you will often be faced with specific closed questions, such as 'What is the impedance of this circuit under these conditions?' or 'What is the breaking point of this beam?' To this type of question, no matter how complex the differential or linear algebra, there is a single unique and right answer. In the broader context of business studies, the engineer is faced with much more open questions, such as 'How can we make our product more appealing to our customers in the face of competition?' One group of engineers might decide to improve the quality and add features but yet another group might decide to analyse the cost of manufacture in great detail, possibly reduce the features and greatly reduce the price. Which strategy is right? Both, if effectively implemented, might restore the competitive advantage of the firm. The engineer needs to develop

skills to create new and alternative solutions. Structured approaches to this process are given in this text.

6. *Decision making*   The external and internal analysis and process of creativity will generate many alternative options and development opportunities. The senior engineer has the responsibility of deciding which must be rejected and which are to be selected for implementation. Again, structured approaches to this issue are given in this text.

7. *Implementation*   The conduct of any large scale project requires skills of coordination and administration. Tools such as critical path analysis are outlined which will assist you in this task.

8. *Control*   To control, the engineer must first decide what the objectives are and then devise methods of measuring actual performance against these criteria on a day by day basis. Within the organization, this may involve complex computer programs to track production efficiency and cost control. However, the engineer may be faced with much more complex and diffuse problems, perhaps in judging market share in a competitive market or customer satisfaction with a service, such as a postal system, where no simple unique measure is readily to hand.

9. *Empathy and flexibility*   To manage international projects with multi-disciplinary teams to divergent markets with changing social, economic and technical elements, the senior engineer has to relate to the needs and wants of a diversity of human and cultural needs. To track technical advances may require complete flexibility such as the decision to cease manufacture and purchase when the basis of competitive advantage changes.

10. *Ability to see the complete issue*   An engineer was called in to solve the problem of excessive waiting time in a hotel lift service, in response to customer complaints. A thorough mathematical investigation suggested that a new lift, at vast expense, would be required. The solution, however, was to place full length mirrors and menus by each lift, so that people could adjust their hair or ties, check the menu: the actual length of waiting had not been reduced, but the perceived length of time had. The engineer was able to evaluate the real problem, not the apparent problem. The able senior engineer has not only to evaluate the detailed technical complexities but take the holistic, helicopter vision, to see the total dimensions of the issues confronting the organization. In modern civilization these may involve social issues such as meeting the needs and wants of employees, consideration of conservation and environmental issues and ethically acceptable conduct of production and marketing of the firm's services or products. The senior engineer is not a super technician but a key member of society, not only reflecting, but leading the values of society, the deeper meaning of being a chartered engineer.

## 1.2 OBJECTIVES OF THIS TEXT AND HOW TO USE IT

Any of the topics covered in this book (accountancy, human resource management, marketing, operations etc.) can and do form subject areas for full three year degree programmes. Clearly, in a few semester units it is not possible to the cover the full range and depth of all these topics. This book focuses on the key essential principles and broad concepts, to develop understanding of the value, uses and applications of techniques. For example, the mathematics of linear programming is not covered in great depth, but reference is given to various excellent texts should the detail be required. Here, space is devoted to developing the appreciation of the area of use and the strengths and limitations of the models. Engineers are fully aware of the concepts of feedback loops and this is reflected in the treatment of topics such as feedback and control systems in management. Certain topics, an example of which is forecasting, are applicable to more than one area of management, as in operations and marketing. In an integrated text, these subjects are only covered once with back reference to the techniques where appropriate.

Skill in business is like skill in engineering, it is not developed by talking, but by doing. In engineering or science this is done in the laboratory. In business studies, the laboratory is replaced by the case study. This is like the laboratory design experiment, a simplified reflection of real life to develop the full mix of skills for the total complexity of professional life. In this text, various case study examples are given. Where appropriate, case studies and questions are given at the ends of chapters to further develop your skills. These case studies have been selected to demonstrate the application of business principles in technical businesses such as communications and electronics. Given the increasing importance of services, equal emphasis is given to this as well as the manufacturing sector.

This text is intended to form the support for business minor pathways for scientists and technologists and should be taken as an integrated whole over the total, few semester unit, course. Issues, such as quality, cannot be divorced from marketing and it is essential that the overall view of the totality of management should be appreciated as soon as possible before revisiting specific topics in great depth. The text reflects current management thinking as developed on MBA courses, with the presentation of powerful models, such as the value chain and the full development of the service extended marketing mix.

## REVIEW

The engineer is an agent of change at the leading edge of technology involved with design, R and D, manufacture, operation, safety, marketing, managing, planning and training. To succeed, the engineer has to view the specific profession in the broader context of the organization's needs and the needs of the society in which the firm operates. To lead and motivate staff and understand other groups, such as customers, of importance to the firm, the engineer must understand about the nature of people and the skills needed to work, manage and communicate with them. An engineer has to be both analytic in deciding the key issues and finding the facts and then be creative in the search for innovative, competitive, solutions. The engineer must decide among options and then implement and control the entire scope of the operations which he/she is responsible for. In short, to succeed as an engineer you have also to be a manager, even in the research environment.

## QUESTIONS

1. To develop her computer skills in her work placement year, Pat Wilkinson has been asked by her manager to create a database for the telephone directory. Pat is working in a medium size electronics company consisting of production, stores, marketing, sales personnel and accounts departments and the managing director's office, in total some

300 people. What information should Pat include in her database, who would she have to consult to collect and validate the data? What problems could she expect?

2. When you graduate what type of job do you want? What total range of skills will you require to succeed in this job, how will you search for this job?

3. As the student representative of your course, you have been asked to organize an open day for projects in your department. Who might you expect to visit and what would you expect them to want to know and see? Who would you involve in the open day and how would you organize it?

4. As an engineering student you have secured a work placement with the engineering staff in a large oil refinery. What programme would you want and expect on your first day at work there?

## CASE STUDY

The great joy of business studies is that business is all around us, when we shop, when we travel, even when we have a drink in the bar. A case study is an outline of a situation. To complete a case study assignment it is useful to break the activity into a number of steps. The first stage is to gain the overview of the situation and what you are expected to do. Read the case study a few times. Mark what you think are key points with a highlighter pen. Discuss the points with your group members. Decide what tasks need to be completed, what information you will need and how you are to find any additional information required (library research). Decide how you will allocate tasks, agree deadlines and milestones (points where you will check that all is going according to plan).

Having assembled the key information you are in a position to order the information in the appropriate way, decide the outcome of your analysis and formulate your decisions. In many case studies, such as the following one, you will need to formulate action plans and also decide how you would control the plan. After this outline of your response, you have to decide how you will complete your submission.

Over the last 20 years there has been growing interest in 'war games' and 'Dungeons and Dragons'. The popularity is based on the skills needed to play the game, the deep interest that is developed and the escapism. An important dimension of these games is the need for facilitating goods. Complex rule books are required and to play, games players need model armies or other models ('Dungeons and Dragons'). These models have, in their own right, become a major interest. Specialist suppliers will stock them in kit form or ready assembled and painted. People put a high benefit valuation on interests such as these and a good complete army fully assembled and painted is worth several hundred pounds. A specialist small industry has grown to service these customers. New companies have most often entered by researching some particular period (Ancient Greek etc.) and then producing models of better quality in that specific segment.

Graham Cook was a war games enthusiast at university and his final year project was on graphic output and data compression. To illustrate the power of this project software he adapted a war game to be played on the computer for two people who could be linked by network or modem. Moreover, he was able to build in a facility for the player to pit his/her wits against the computer. The key advantage was that with the data compression large amounts of disk space were not needed, yet the graphics were of exceptional quality, with sound effects as well. There was no need to keep the scores, as the computer did this, and all the rules were also available on a help screen.

Graham was persuaded by a local war games club to demonstrate the computer game at a national war games convention. The reaction was outstanding with enthusiastic comments from all types of people at the convention. A few weeks later, Graham had completed his final examinations but was unable to find a job. At the war games club, a local business man suggested to Graham that he could start a business based on his war games software.

How could Graham go about making money out of his idea as a business, what issues would he have to consider, what problems would he encounter?

## FURTHER READING

Harland, R. (1991) 'Engineer or manager – why not both?', *IEE News*.
*Recommended Roles and Responsibilities* (1990) The Engineering Council.
Sampson, A. (1993) 'Stop doing the dirty on Britain's Engineers', *Management Today*.
Sowter, C. (1993) 'Marketing is too important to be left to the marketing department', *IEE News*.

# BUSINESS ENVIRONMENT

Chapter One considers the question 'What is Business?' In this chapter, the context within which the individual technical manager works is considered. This context, the so-called business environment, is best considered in two sections. This process is called environmental analysis. The two sections of the 'Environmental Analysis' are:

1. External (to the organization) environment analysis
2. Internal (to the organization) environment analysis

The purpose of the environmental analysis is to map out the business situations facing the organization, to predict the probable outcome if present policies are continued and the potential outcomes of changes in the organization's strategies.

In this chapter, a broad view is taken and detailed consideration of various issues, such as marketing, are continued and developed in later chapters. The purpose of this chapter is to provide an overview and context for these detailed issues, which must not be considered as unrelated, but rather as varying techniques to understand the anatomy of business. This is no different to understanding the mechanism of the human body, where various disciplines such as biochemistry, physiology etc. are used to develop a full understanding.

The engineer is faced with similar complex practical issues when designing a new electrical device or a new car. Business can be considered to be in some ways parallel to the physical model shown in Fig. 2.1, the business analogy is shown in Fig. 2.2. The particle in Fig. 2.1 has an electrostatic charge and has magnetic properties. It interacts with other objects which have varying magnetic and electrostatic properties.

The particle under consideration has certain characteristics which affect the way it interacts with force fields such as magnetic and electric fields. The outcome of these interactions will be affected by such issues as the mass of the particle and the viscosity of the media. The property of the particle may be modified by the interaction with these forces if, for example, the particle is ferro-magnetic. These forces are not one way, not only will the particle be affected by these influences but also the interacting objects. In addition, the other objects would, of course, be interacting not only with the particle but also with each other, Newton's law that for every action there is an equal and opposite reaction.

Various types of forces are encountered in the physical world, magnetic, electrostatic, gravitational etc. Each type of force interaction has its own laws to measure and predict outcomes. These interactions, for example, will be governed by the distance between a

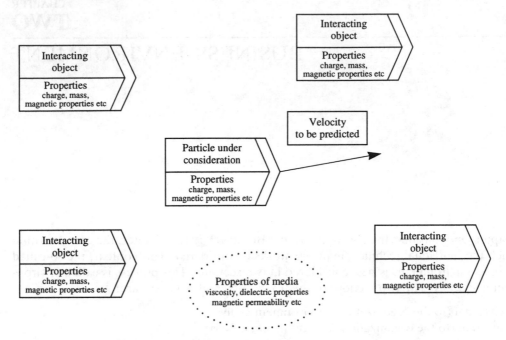

**Figure 2.1**   Movement of a charged magnetic particle

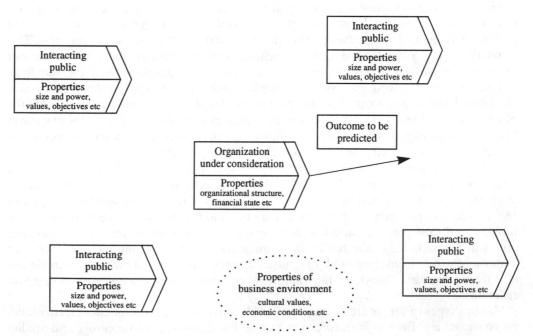

**Figure 2.2**   Predicting the path of an organization in a business

given object and the particle. Moreover, the size and nature of these forces will be influenced by the properties of the media such as magnetic permeability and dielectric properties. The velocity of the particle will be also be limited by the viscosity of the media. The properties of the media may well be changed by small amounts of material, for example, the addition of a small amount of ionic material may cause the dissipation of electrostatic charges and also change the dielectric constant. An engineer faced with this complex problem would decompose the problem into the individual forces to create a complex set of differential equations which might well need a computer for a numerical solution.

The business environment may be considered, in a broad way, to exhibit similar properties to this system. In Fig. 2.2 the particle is replaced by the organization under consideration. The interacting objects are replaced by interacting publics. The concept of a 'Public' is of great use.

## 2.1 PUBLICS

*A Public is any specific, identifiable group, that may have an effect on the organization, either beneficial or adverse.*

A classification of publics is given in Fig. 2.3.

Publics may be classifications of people (for example, customers, users, shareholders etc.). In this case, the people may be considered to be unrelated to each other except by the relationship they have with the organization. Thus the purchasers of a given CD player may be very different people with nothing in common (rock fans, classics, jazz lovers) but they have a single property of critical importance to the organization; they buy the firm's products.

Groupings of people (political parties, pressure groups (Green Peace etc.)) are different in that the individuals are a coherent group who join together for some specific purpose. Such groups may be of critical importance to an organization at the international level (Green Peace) or have dramatic effects at the local level. A company wishing to build a new facility may find a local pressure group forming to oppose its planning application. Failure to contain this might result in a lengthy and costly public enquiry which might delay a major project by years.

Associations are much the same in character to the above groups, but the classification is included to differentiate a pressure group from associations of people who have some common interest and come together to follow this, but not necessarily to change things, as is the case with a pressure group. The institutions are a major feature of the business environment. The whole structure of government can be considered to be an interlocking series of institutions or publics. Thus a large company may be concerned with providing information to a Parliamentary Select Committee which might be considering changes to the regulation of its industry. Organizations are not only faced by the political aspects of government but by the ministries and their agencies. So major companies will be concerned with the influence, regulation and laws enforced by institutions such as the Department of the Environment.

The law agencies are a special class of this type of institution. This not only includes the

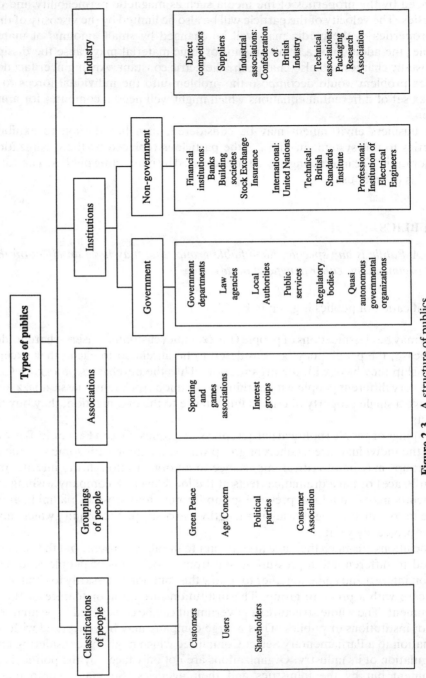

**Figure 2.3**  A structure of publics

police and the law courts but aspects of the work of other ministries. The construction of a new facility may not only involve planning authorities but also the environmental agencies as the details of the building design may have to be considered by the local health and fire regulation authorities.

The power of local authorities is considerable and the issues of local enforcement and planning regulation have been mentioned. However, like the government, the local authorities are major purchasers of goods and services. Such publics are much more likely to exercise political judgements in the placement of their orders, some authorities, for example, may only trade with organizations that will provide an equal employment opportunity statement. The Ministry of Defence is a massive purchaser in the high technology area and also has considerable demands not only on product quality but also on employment policies in areas of defence sensitive contracts. Staff may have to be security screened, the company might need to operate a 'need to know' policy (information only to be given when and where it is essential for the conduct of the project).

These various government bodies do not only provide the structure of administration but, even after privatization, still provide many services to the public. Two of the largest are Health and Education. The emergency services are also major users of high technology equipment. The increasing privatization is tending to move areas such as telephones, energy (gas, electricity, coal), water, transport (road, rail, ports, airports) into the private sector. However, the government still needs to exercise some control over such large, and often essentially monopoly, organizations. Not only will these organizations have to satisfy the general regulations, but may well also have special regulatory and consumer representation bodies.

In the area of business regulation the situation is even more complicated. The ideal situation for a commercial organization is to be in a position of monopoly power. However, the ethos of the market economy is that this is not in the public interest, and for the national and international good, free competition must exist. So, at both the national level (Monopolies and Mergers Commission) and the international level (EC and USA anti-trust laws), there is a heavy structure of regulation to prevent any organization engaging in any activity which is considered to limit free trade to the detriment of the community. The headline news tends to be about the mega mergers but much of the power of these bodies is concerned with issues of inter-company policy. This concerns matters, such as agreements dividing markets or secret price arrangements, which may be illegal both in national and international law. This issue is covered in more depth in Chapter Three, where the issues of competition, free trade and patents are considered.

Another way of classifying government publics is the group known as Quasi Autonomous Governmental Organizations. These can be thought of not only to include some of the independent watch-dog type organizations, but also organizations which are set up, but not controlled, by Parliament. Such organizations as the British Broadcasting Authority and National Parks are typical examples.

Organizations need finance and financial services to trade. These are provided by the financial publics. The banks provide sources of money and mechanisms for payment (cheques and Electronic Funds Transfer). This is a complex role in international trade where varying exchange rates may be involved. Interest rates and bank lending policies are a critical factor in the business environment. The stock exchange provides a mechanism for people to exchange ownership of organizations (trade shares) and also to raise more money (issue new shares or loan stock). Organizations need to protect themselves against risk and insurance is another essential financial service. The insurance groups form another vital public.

The value of the owner's shares may be an important objective so senior managers will be concerned to follow policies that will maintain the value of the firm's shares. Many shares are not owned by the owner but held through occupation pension funds, trusts or insurance investments. The attitudes of these publics have a profound effect on the valuation of the shares in a company and large organizations will go to considerable lengths to maintain the good will of these investment publics.

The international institutions are of increasing importance given the globalization of international trade in industries such as electronics. These bodies are a mechanism for agreeing international standards (for example IATA, International Air Transport Association—air transport standards). The issue of standards is central to the science and engineering-based industries. The British Standards Institute is the focus for the UK activity in the formulation of agreed standards from food to communication equipment. Linked to this are the standards of professional conduct. These issues are regulated by the professional institutions (such as the Institution of Electrical Engineers, Royal Society of Chemistry, etc.) and most now have the recognition of chartered status for their full professional members. These institutions interact with the standard authorities and the national and international regulatory bodies to ensure common professional standards. This international role is most important with the European engineer and the freedom to work within the EC.

Industry itself is populated by publics. The 'Porter 5 Forces' model, discussed later, considers the implications of five key industrial publics to the organization: the direct competitors, the customers and agents/distributors, the suppliers, the threat of new entry and the threat of substitute products. Industry itself needs to have its own voice and organizations and this is achieved through such publics as the CBI (Confederation of British Industry) at the global level, with most industry sectors having their own associations, such as the CIA (Chemical Industries Association). These bodies can provide a framework for industry consultation and for presenting an industry viewpoint. Such associations provide other services for their members, such as information, training for members' staff and sponsored international trade visits. A special need may exist in the technical industries to collaborate in research and development in certain areas, such as the development of standard test methods etc. Thus, many industries have industry research associations, such as the Packaging Industries Research Association.

An organization can be considered to have internal publics, for example, workers (with or without trade union representation), and management. The trade unions are still a major public, not only working within agreements with specific organizations, but also in the pursuit of their members' interests at national levels. Apart from the often-discussed role of furthering the economic aims of their members, trade unions have had a major part to play in the improvement in the standards of health and safety at work, not only by representing their members, but also by sponsoring their own research.

Having considered the replacements of particles in the physical model of Fig. 2.1 with publics, the next matter is to consider the interaction of the publics with the organization. The physical forces in Fig. 2.1 are replaced with business forces: Political (for example, equal opportunity laws), Economic (for example interest rates from banks), Social (Green Power), Technical (such as microprocessors), and Competition. See Fig. 2.4. These forces will be affected by the general business environment in the same way as the forces are

the Engineering Manager needs to consult the appropriate sources and experts to determine the relevant key political and legal issues.

In the physical model of Fig. 2.1 it was noted that the forces in the physical environment could be changed by the properties of the media. This, in turn, could be modified by additions of material such as ionic substances. So it is with the legal framework. Attitudes and ideology do not only express themselves in law, but in the way in which the law is enforced. Thus, if the attitude to the law is that it is important, many people will be engaged in checking if the law is being broken. Once a contravention is identified the level of punishment given out by the courts will be affected by the ideology and attitudes of the time.

### 2.2.2 Economic

A very difficult economic issue for industry has been the cost of energy. The cost of energy can be affected by the political situation in energy producing nations and the relative power between energy suppliers and energy users at any given time as PEST elements are often coupled. An international *political* issue is reflected back into the domestic economy as an *economic* issue, the cost of energy. There may be additional political influences on the use of energy with various rates of taxation on differing types of fuel, such as leaded and unleaded petrol.

The natural gas producers have proposed the use of this energy source for the economic generation of heat and power (in the generation of electrical power about 60 per cent of the available energy is lost). This approach has a number of benefits: it maximizes the use of a non-renewable resource, minimizes the emission of 'green house effect' carbon dioxide, reduces acid rain potential from sulphur oxide emissions and requires no on-site storage of fuel with no road transport (another source of environmental impact). The precise cost/ benefit equation for a given application, of course, depends on the capital cost of the electricity generating and heat recovery equipment and the cost of energy. The wide swings in energy costs have made this a difficult situation to evaluate.

The economics can be further complicated by legislation. The ability to import and export electricity to the general supply and the relative prices and conditions on which this can be done can also have a considerable effect on the viability of such a project. These issues are subject to detailed legislation which can vary from country to country. In the UK, the privatization of the electricity supply industry has made the option of such combined heat and power generation more attractive by providing a more realistic framework for companies to sell and buy marginal electrical capacity to and from the national grid network.

In considering the economic environment, it is not only necessary to consider the present situation, but also the trends. In the physical model of the particle in Fig. 2.1 an engineer would not only be concerned with the velocity of the particle but also its acceleration. For a manufacturer of consumer electronics in the UK, the trends in import penetration in the firm's specific markets, long term exchange rate movements, trends in consumer credit and available income may all be significant factors that the company needs to take into account.

Single factors may affect the organization by more than one mechanism. Interest rates and tax will not only affect the firm's customers (higher interest rates and taxes will result in lower amounts of income available for consumer goods), but will affect the firm itself directly (interest charges and Corporation Tax) and indirectly (pressure for higher wages to offset the effects of high mortgages and tax).

In researching data and economic analysis for a given business situation, considerable care must be taken. In looking at an export market, the engineer may find library figures which give the average income per head for the potential overseas market. However, as always with averages, the average wage may not reflect the complete picture. Thus a company making luxury consumer electronics might consider that a country such as India was not very interesting as a potential market, given the low average earnings. The distribution of wealth is not even, however, and the top one per cent income set of the population may well afford such luxury goods so the market could be of interest after all. It is not only the total wealth, but its distribution, that may affect the potential for a given product in a specific export market.

The Gross National Product (the final sum of goods, services and exports) can be an indicator of general conditions in a given country. It is often useful to adjust figures to a common currency and express on a uniform scale (as a sum per head of the population), to make comparisons and to look at relative trends between nations. The trends in the sizes of imports and exports (the so-called 'trade gap') is also of importance as this will condition government action (such as regional development aid or other forms of subsidies). The scope to limit imports with high duties is governed by the International Free Trade agreements such as GATT (General Agreement on Tariffs and Trade). However, in Chapter Five on Marketing, the tariff and non-tariff barriers to international trade will be discussed in more detail.

### 2.2.3  Social

Both in Europe and the USA there has been a social trend towards more single person households and dual income households. This trend has also been matched with increased valuation of leisure time and higher disposable incomes. The resulting benefit requirement has been for 'exciting food' without the need for long and uninteresting preparation. This has resulted in a number of products and services to satisfy this single increasing benefit demand.

- Increased eating out.
- Increased take-away food market.
- Increasing improvement of microwave ovens and increasing market penetration.
- Ready availability of interesting convenience foods both chilled and frozen, often specifically designed and packed for microwave preparation.

A number of social elements have thus resulted in a single broad benefit requirement, which has lead to developments in the service sector (restaurants and take away), electronics (advanced microprocessor microwave ovens), electrical goods (high freezer ownership) and food technology. Population demographics is an issue which affects some business decisions. In the UK the population is getting older and the number of young people as a proportion of the total population is declining. This has effects on areas as diverse as education and health care.

Social attitudes change with time, and increased foreign travel, better education and international communications have resulted in a general attitude of rising expectations in standards of service. This has been coupled with an increasing concern for personal and consumer rights. In the designing of products or services this is reflected in consumer demands for product features as standard and for higher standards of product safety.

The 80s was the decade when attitudes and values on the environment and conservation changed. Consumption without care is no longer acceptable and this has provided challenges to engineers and scientists to create less environmentally damaging products. This does not just extend to the use of the product, but to the total life of the product. People are not only concerned that a car should have the minimum of environmental impact in use, but that the manufacture should also be conducted in an environmentally acceptable way. Moreover, there is growing concern that products should not add to environmental problems at the end of their useful life. An increasing demand is that products should be able to be effectively recycled after their useful life is completed.

### 2.2.4 Technical

Technical changes can have many influences on a business, on its products, its markets, and its operations. One area for considerable care is in the evaluation of benefit substitution from new technology. The concept of product life cycle will be developed more fully in Chapter 5, Marketing. Products have a natural growth and decay cycle. The time span for this growth and decay can vary from months for some fashion fad to an almost infinite amount of time. Although precise estimates of product life cycle are not possible, the broad concepts are of considerable value in the appraisal of business situations. In the 20s, the introduction of radio generated a vast demand for the amplification of weak electrical signals which was met by the thermionic valve. In the 50s and 60s the world-wide introduction of micro-groove stereo records and TV gave a vast increase in the demand for this type of signal amplification. By the end of the 70s, the valve was essentially dead. Over a space of some 50 years the product had grown to vast production levels and then died.

We need to distinguish between the product life cycle and the benefit life cycle. Has the demand for weak signal amplification in the 70s decreased? The benefit demand for weak signal amplification has continued to grow strongly. The benefit is now provided by product substitution, such amplification being performed by solid state devices. In the evaluation of the environment, through PEST analysis, it is necessary to be sensitive to the position of the firm's product in the total benefit life cycle, not only the position of the product in its own product life cycle.

This type of analysis can require considerable care and creativity. Technical developments can involve substitution of one product by another to give the same benefit (weak signal amplification). However, it is possible for one product to provide more than one benefit, and for there to be differing benefit life cycles. The personal computer can provide very different benefits from entertainment (computer games), to text preparation (authors) to spreadsheet analysis (small trader). Each of these benefit segmentations may require specific evaluation if you are a producer of personal computers. The development of small solid state lasers had a radical impact on communications technology (fibre optic communications). The application of optical/electronic technology in the home has resulted in the substitution of compact discs for home entertainment. The same technology applied in the office has provided the benefit of laser printers and low cost, high capacity, disk storage for small computers. The evaluation of technical change is considered more in the later chapters. The process is not simple and involves a considerable amount of creativity.

## 2.3 COMPETITIVE FORCES

### 2.3.1 Exit and entry barriers

The concept of exit and entry barriers is of value in understanding the precise way the five forces can interact in a given business situation. The term barrier is used rather than costs. Costs are the most frequent and often the most important barrier to be considered, but in some cases, time or some other factor may represent the barrier. Two states for entry and exit can be considered, high and low, yielding a simple $2 \times 2$ matrix. This is shown in Fig. 2.7.

### 2.3.2 High entry–high exit

This is a common situation in the specialist chemical or electronics industry with very high capital investments and very high write-off costs on exit (site clearance can, for example, be a very heavy exit cost). Such plants are often highly specialized and difficult, if not impossible, to convert to the production of other products. A most extreme example would be nuclear power stations. This situation can result in intense internal competition in the sector as once large players have entered they find it difficult to withdraw. In times of over capacity and in recessions this can lead to intense price competition and heavy losses for all engaged in the sector under the worst circumstances. The situation can produce high

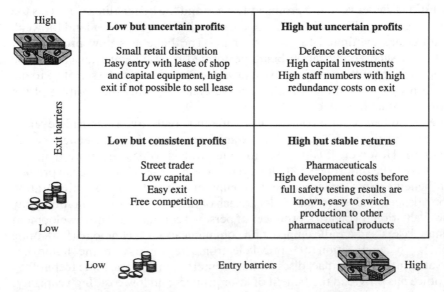

**Figure 2.7**  Effect of entry and exit barriers on competitive environment

profits in good times but in difficult conditions can lead to very unstable profits and even losses.

### 2.3.3 High entry–low exit

This type of situation can be found in products and services where there is a heavy element of up-front investment and/or marketing expenses. A typical example would be the recording of major piece of music. It requires a large initial investment, but on market failure there is no immense additional exit penalty. This is not so damaging as high entry–high exit, as entry is restricted and if competitive pressures are bad, then exit is not too difficult for the weakest competitors. This situation tends to produce high or moderate profits, as when profitability drops the weakest firms exit.

### 2.3.4 Low entry–high exit

This situation can often occur where it is easy to borrow large sums of money or lease property. Many airlines were established not on the investment of large amounts of capital but on the lease of aircraft. When trading conditions were bad they were then locked into a situation where they could not meet the lease payments. This is the most difficult of all competitive situations. It is a very unstable condition as when the market is attractive many firms enter lowering profits even under good conditions. When markets are difficult, then firms are locked in life or death competition and exit may well mean liquidation. The final effect is low unstable profits.

### 2.3.5 Low entry–low exit

This is the situation of pure competition. In good times new firms enter but they find it easy to exit when times are bad. This tends to produce low but stable profits.

### 2.3.6 Final note on exit

It may appear to be a paradox, but on entering a new business venture it is advisable to estimate the exit costs if the venture should fail. If it is a diversification, this may be essential to ensure that the maximum risk is not large enough to endanger the whole firm. Moreover, the exit costs are a guide to the competitive pressures the firm may expect.

### 2.4 Five forces of competitive pressure

The five forces (M.E. Porter, *Competitive Advantage*, 1985) are:

1. Industry Competitors—Segment Rivalry
2. Potential Entrants—Mobility Threat
3. Substitutes
4. Supplier and Supplier Channel Power
5. Buyer and Distribution Channel Power.

(See Fig. 2.8.)

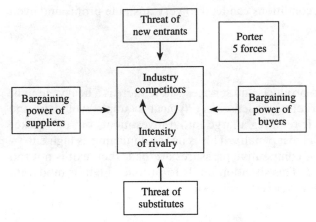

**Figure 2.8**   Porter 5 Forces of competitive pressure.
*Translated and reprinted with the permission of The Free Press, a division of Macmillan, Inc.*

### 2.4.1  Industry competitors

**Segment rivalry**   This is the type of competition which people usually mean when they discuss competitive pressure. This is the simple competition of other firms producing the same product to serve the same benefit set. This occurs in most industries, frozen foods, computers, compact discs etc. The concepts of entry and exit barriers can help estimate the likely competitive reactions in this internal sector competition. This can be modified by the individual characteristics of major competitors.

### 2.4.2  Potential entrants

**Mobility threat**   This is the entry into the sector of new competitors with similar products to satisfy the same benefits. This can often be a geographic effect. In the 80s, many USA and Japanese companies became new, competitors in Europe, as they became attracted by the new unified EC market. Before this, the European market had been too fragmented and difficult to be attractive. Now it represents the most powerful single market area.

A key problem is to determine who might be the new entrants and how and why they might enter. In the UK, a High Street retailer more famous for its sale of underwear and food suddenly became a competitor in financial services. They had launched their own in-store charge card and as a result came to understand much about the financial needs of their customers and had a very useful mailing list. The next step was financial services. A new source of competition not expected by the conventional financial institutions, such as the banks. Note again that the issues of exit and entry barriers will affect this situation.

### 2.4.3  Substitutes

This situation occurs where more than one product or service can be offered to provide the consumer with a given benefit. In the early 90s, the substitution of compact discs with digital audio tape (DAT) was a concern of people who saw their business as the provision of high quality music in the home.

### 2.4.4  Supplier and supplier channel power

This situation can arise in a number of ways. If there are few sources of supply (say for a speciality chemical, enzyme, or microprocessor) then the supplier has considerable power over the firm's business. If there are many alternative sources and the service or product is in free supply, then there is little supplier power.

There are a number of special cases, the most important being in the area of intellectual property—patents, trade marks registered designs, and copyrights. It is easy to see the power of the owner of a patented electronic device or registered design. Without the licence the firm is unable to produce the final product but sometimes the connection is not quite as direct. Some of the major electronic manufacturing firms have been buying up record companies. Why? Well, if you wish to produce digital audio tape equipment and you do not have access to a large library of music copyright, this is of little interest to the consumer. The consumer not only wants the benefit of technical quality but also of quality in the desired area of music.

It should be remembered that the concept should be extended to all goods, services and inputs to the firm's operations necessary for it to conduct its business or market its products, so even organized labour can be considered under this heading.

### 2.4.5  Buyer and distribution channel power

Where there are many firms operating and there is concentration of buying or distribution, then the firm is in a less competitive position. The large swing of consumer buying in the food sector in the UK to a relatively small number of major food distribution groups has shifted power from the suppliers (farming and food processing) into the hands of the distributors. Thus, it is the distributors that shape the markets with authority and not the supplier firms. There can be special situations where channels are controlled by a single or a small number of distributors. The telecommunication companies can therefore exert considerable pressure on what services they are prepared to allow people to offer over their network.

## 2.5  INTERNAL ENVIRONMENT

To consider the internal environment of the organization, two tools are useful, the 'Value Chain' (M.E. Porter, *Competitive Advantage*, 1985) and the McKinsey 7's' model (Peters, T.J. and R.H. Waterman, *In Search of Excellence*, 1982) The 'Value Chain' considers the organization to be an input/output device. The operating characteristics of this input/output system can be altered by such issues as research and development and organizational structure. To consider the organization in such physical terms is rather like considering a computer system without taking into account the software. The 7's' model allows one to consider the 'software' of the organization. In the next sections the external analysis tools are considered in some more detail.

The purpose of the internal environment analysis is much the same as the checks you might make on a car before a long journey in winter. The aim is to evaluate the condition of

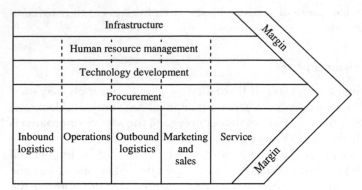

**Figure 2.9**   Porter Value Chain.
*Translated and reprinted with the permission of The Free Press, a division of Macmillan, Inc.*

the firm so that we can assess if it has the capability to achieve its objectives. In the same way as with a car, the check will almost always reveal problems from minor (the oil is a little low) to major (the brakes need to be fixed). Minor problems become major problems if they are not identified early. It is not a good idea to run a car until the oil low warning light appears at 70 mph on the open road.

The internal audit is not a one off, neither is it a total strip down of the company operations every week. Just as with a car, some things need to be checked each journey, while others need less frequent checking. It is important that all issues should be reviewed at appropriate intervals. In checking out the car it is convenient to divide the activity into areas: check the mechanics, check the electrics. For the firm, three dimensions of audit are useful: value chain analysis, the 7's' to check the software, and the money health check.

The 'Value Chain' framework allows us to evaluate the various elements of the company needed to produce the product or service and the support activities that make it possible to do this well. The key asset of a company is its people. A computer is not very much use if you have no software. The 7's' framework allows us to evaluate the relationship of people with the hardware and firmware of the company.

Money is an important issue to a firm. Money in business should be regarded like energy. Energy can exist in various forms, chemical, mechanical, electrical etc., so just as you might audit a physical system for energy, the firm can be audited for money. Money in a company may be just that, cash in the safe or bank accounts. However, it can be in other visible forms such as physical assets (computers, factories), it can be in people (training) or in non-physical assets (patents, copyright, design rights, trade names etc.). Just as in a car, if the energy systems are out of balance (fourth gear is not too good when attempting to climb a 1:4 hill), there will be problems if the money systems in a firm are not appropriate.

### 2.5.1 Value Chain

The Value Chain is a simple concept, rather like the laws of motion. Just like Newton's laws, it can be used to gain insight into a simple system such as the simple pendulum or explain the motion of the planets in the solar system. The value chain is shown in Fig. 2.9. To create the firm's products or services, inputs are required (raw materials etc), some transformations will be needed (manufacturing), then the product or service needs to be physically made available to the customers (distribution). These customers will not be there unless we identify them and make them aware of our product or service (marketing). In many cases, the customer will not be able to make full use of our product or service unless we provide some field support (service).

All this is not possible without some buildings to work in and support activities. People are happy to work but they do expect to get paid. To make all the direct activities possible some support activities are required. An infrastructure such as buildings and computer systems is required. Special skills need to be developed and once people have acquired them they will expect suitable additional rewards. Our products have to be designed, the way in which we make or provide them also has to be developed. The range of inputs necessary has to be acquired, not only direct materials such as chemicals and components, but other inputs such as transport.

The result of all this activity is that the cost of all the inputs is less than the value of the output of product or service. The resulting difference is the added value of the firm, the margin of profitability. The value chain structure allows us to not only to analyse what is relevant for each separate activity but also to see the relationships of each activity to the total firm's objectives and value creation.

**Primary activity**   Primary activities are concerned with the conversion of the input raw materials, services and components to usable products and services (benefits) that are of value to the firm's customers in the field.

**Primary activity—inbound logistics**   In a specialist chemical company, commodity chemical raw materials may come in. These may simply come in sacks or drums. However, such deliveries may not be appropriate for effective and efficient manufacturing. Materials may be highly toxic (sodium cyanide) or dangerously reactive (elemental phosphorus) and in such cases specialist transport would be appropriate, with specialized equipment at the point of delivery to ensure that no escape of harmful materials occurs. Such arrangements are not only necessary for safety and environmental reasons but can also be a highly efficient means of operation.

**Primary activity—operations**   Operations activities are the basic manufacturing operations and are at the heart of the process and engineering industries. In the manufacture of drugs, standard chemical processes can yield racemic (mixed isomers or types) products. A firm that developed an advanced bound enzyme catalyst or had an efficient fermentation process based on genetically manipulated micro-organizms, for example, might be in a much more effective position to make the specific desired compound more profitably.

So, in this area, a whole raft of issues can be considered as to how molecular transformations are completed or how products are purified and then converted into their final form for customer use. It is possible to prepare fertilizers in a number of ways. One particular way is to produce the blend, then prill by melting the mixture and spraying it down a cooled tower. The result is little beads which are much more resistant to dusting in use than normal granules. Such technology may not only have its value in manufacture, but also give added benefits and greater perceived value to end use customers.

**Primary activity—outbound logistics**   One firm's outbound logistics are another's inbound logistics. This activity is concerned with the storage of the finished product and thence its physical distribution to the end use customers. Effective and efficient inventory storage is an important aspect. In certain manufacturing areas this might involve the use of automated warehousing with computer controlled picking of components to satisfy a given specific order. Such a situation may occur in a firm supplying spare parts to retail garages involved in the repair of cars. Any given week's orders will depend on the mix of makes and ages of vehicles in for repair at that time. In the food processing industry it might involve the bulk storage of sugar at a refinery and then bulk transfer by road tanker of the solid to major users such as bakeries.

**Primary activity—marketing and sales**   Two related issues are involved in this area. How does the firm find out what its customers need and want, and having done that and developed the product, how does the firm let the customers know about the product? The activity is not only passive but proactive, with energy devoted not only to informing customers but persuading them this is *the* product to meet their requirements. It also involves the active search to find new customers. The related activity is selling. The marketing communications may have made the consumer aware of the product and aroused interest, but selling may be required to convert that to action (purchase). This activity also includes the mechanisms of regular order entry and collection of money for goods delivered.

   In the food processing industry, this might involve detailed discussions with a major retailing food chain about the development and marketing of a new consumer product and then detailed linking of the two operations systems, with bar coding of the product by the supplier for the food retailing chain's use at their point of sale computer (laser terminals). The order entry can be an equally important issue, with the food chain evaluating in its mainframe the amounts sold that day and the amounts required for re-supply. This interaction can take place in the middle of the night, by direct Electronic Data Interchange (EDI) from major retailers to their suppliers.

**Primary activity—service**   Many products are of little value to the customer unless there is additional field support. This can be simple physical support for an instrument or computer when a component fails and a field engineering call is required to get the equipment back on line. However, many other areas of support may be important to the customer.

   If the product is innovative the customer may need design assistance to build the product into his end-product. With a new resin for encapsulation of electronic components, this could be applications advice. The electronics company may need detailed advice on how to gain the maximum benefit in its specific product range from the new resin technology. The customer may need its staff to be trained on how to maintain, store or use the product. Manufacturers of office technology (photocopiers and word processing software) have to be able to provide appropriate field training for their customer's staff. This can be a direct presence with onsite training or a twenty-four hour help line for software assistance.

**Support activity**   Support activities are those efforts which are directed not at providing the goods or service, but are involved in making it possible to provide these efficiently, effectively and profitably.

**Support activity—firm infrastructure**   This embraces all the major global infrastructures. It can be physical, good buildings and computer systems or it can be software, such as clear management policies and corporate image and brand awareness. By definition, this support activity affects all parts of the firm's operations. In the process industries, it could involve such basic considerations as the efficient and effective provision of energy (heat and electricity) to the various units. This might involve complex networks of cables and pipes and an onsite heat and electrical power plant to supply these requirements, both efficiently and effectively.

**Support activity—human resource management**    Human resource management is one of the four support activities that should be considered in two ways. They may have certain activities that affect all aspects of the firm, just as the firm infrastructure does. However, they may have activities that are focused into just one area of a firm's primary activities, such as operations. Human resource management as a general support activity may be concerned with the selection of new employees, their development within the organization (training), the reward systems (pay) and employee benefits (pensions).

In operations, human resource management within the process industries might be concerned with the special issues of rewards (pay) associated with shift working. This is specific to operations as the sales staff will not be working shifts. The specialized training might involve the development in handling skills for hazardous materials and in the statistical concepts to get the most out of on line test equipment.

**Support activity—technology development**    Technology development might also be general to the whole company but can also be specific to a primary activity. The concept is of use as it is easy without the Value Chain concept to think of technology development in terms of product and process development only. However, it can be just as important to design specialist road tankers or special transport as it is to have an efficient production operation. The product is not much use unless it gets to the customer quickly and in a usable state.

Technology development can involve such activities as writing specialized software to enable rapid costings of customer specific specialist products. It can involve whole sections of development scientists who may work for a major scientific instrument manufacturer, their activity being to develop specific applications methods (sample preparations etc.) such that customers may apply the firm's microprocessor based instrument to their specific field of application.

**Support activity—procurement**    Procurement is as important an activity as sales and marketing. Profit is the difference between the costs of acquiring the input resources and the income generated from the sales of the product or service. Effective procurement is thus one of the key levers of the firm's strategic success.

Procurement is the activity for sourcing all the inputs that the firm needs to conduct its operations. These may be general inputs to the firm infrastructure, such as the provision of telephone and communication systems, or specific to a given primary activity. The concept should be extended to include the buying of financial services (for example, contract payroll services) or even to the purchase of money itself (capital, foreign currency).

---

A business student on industrial placement in a major manufacturing company found that all the computers (accounts, office, manufacturing, design and laboratory) were on individual service contracts placed at the time of purchase. The administration was a nightmare, hundreds of individual contracts with varying annual review dates and differing contractors. After careful investigation a single service contract for all computer equipment was put out for tender. This not only saved a considerable sum on the servicing costs but also reduced the expenses associated with the administration of a multitude of service contracts.

---

The most obvious activity is in the purchase (procurement) of materials (raw materials, components etc) and services (energy, maintenance etc) to the operation's primary activity. Large sums of money can be needed for the provision of other inputs needed outside the operation's primary activity area. The effective purchase of delivery services might be critical. This might involve decisions such as whether to rent a fleet of delivery vehicles or contract out delivery needs completely.

### 2.5.2 Internal Value Chain Links

The above audit of the firm's value chain has enabled us to evaluate the effectiveness of each of the links within the firm's value chain. However, to be effective, the internal value chain links need to be checked. A simple but effective way to do this is to consider three cycles:

1. *The Order–Billing Cycle*   This is the cycle where the customer wishes to order a product, orders, the product is made and shipped, the customer is billed and then pays for the product. Just what systems are used to do this and how effective are they? Simple tests can be applied; if the customer rings up to ask how long before he gets the product, can he be told quickly and accurately? If not, then there are problems that need attention.
2. *The Manufacture–Customer Benefit Cycle*   This is the related interlocking cycle. Need for manufacture is identified, components are made available (ordered or drawn from stock), the product assembled, tested, packed, stored, shipped, delivered, installed and customer field serviced.
3. *The New Product Development Cycle*   This is the cycle where an unmet customer need is identified, a new product formulated, developed, tested, manufactured and introduced into full sales to customers.

By the consideration of these three cycles we can see how effectively the individual value chain elements are linked.

### 2.6 THE 7's'; THE FIRM'S SOFTWARE

The 7's' (see T.J. Peters and R.H. Waterman, 1982) framework is shown in Fig. 2.10. The 7's' analysis should not be regarded as completely orthogonal to the Value Chain. The Value Chain is concerned with both the component parts of the organization and the firm as a single entity. Within that, the people are the force that makes the firm's value chain work. The 7's' structure allows us to look at the people element and their relationships within the firm.

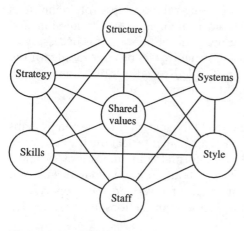

**Figure 2.10**   McKinsey 7's'

**Strategy**   Confusion can be caused when reading about management by the use of the word *strategy*. The word is used in two contexts. When talking about management we consider issues such as strategic orientation, the ability to plan in depth and breadth with a time span beyond the end of the next financial year. The role of the people who conduct the analysis and formulate these strategic plans is often reviewed under the heading 'The business strategist'. In the structure of strategic planning we have a level called 'strategy and programme formulation'. This is the second use of the word. In this context, strategy is the link between the objectives we may desire (increase profits by 10 per cent within the next year) and the detailed set of actions we may need to take to achieve the objective.

Our strategy might be to cut manufacturing costs and the sub-strategies might be to reduce material costs by better procurement, by better and more economical design and by the elimination of waste and re-work. We might also have sub-strategies to reduce assembly time by design for manufacture, improved work flow by better manufacturing operations and gaining more commitment from staff by training, re-structuring work roles and better incentive schemes. Each of these sub-strategies will, in turn, require a complete set of action programmes for implementation.

In the context of the 7's', strategy is the sense of direction given to all in the firm from the complete set of elements of the strategic planning process through clearly formulated and clearly communicated mission, objectives, strategies, implementation programmes and feedback and control systems. Only through this does the firm have the common cause to react with organizational flexibility and coherence. The value chain gives us a view of the organization, but the additional dimension of strategy is required to decide how this value chain system will interact with the changing world, and how the firm's value chain may need to be changed to meet the next set of challenges.

**Structure**   The value chain is a very useful concept with which to view the firm's activities to generate added value. You will not find an organizational structure which is built around it, however, as organizational structure is one of the strategic management variables. If we wish to change the direction of the firm we may well have to revise the organizational structure.

Organizational structure is the framework of reporting relationships, role definitions and accountabilities that are intended to assist the firm in meeting its mission and objectives. There is no single correct structure. In the audit of the firm it is necessary to evaluate how well that is achieved, and if the existing structure will be appropriate for the revised objectives and strategies. There are many detailed variations of organizational structure but at this stage four key variations should be noted.

**Systems**   Systems is most often used with reference to Management Information Systems (MIS) and Marketing Information Systems (MkIS). This is an interlocking framework of hardware (computers, Local Area Networks (LAN), formal communications systems, electronic mail, etc.), of people and procedures. The systems are required to ensure that relevant data is collected and stored, analysed in relevant ways and then reported to people in a way which is timely and pertinent for the decisions and actions that they need to take in their contribution to the firm's activity.

The credit control section will evaluate the financial standing and set a realistic limit on the amount of credit (risk to the firm) that any given new customer might be allowed. The order–billing cycle system will keep track of the state of a given customer's account. In planning sales visits, the salesman will need to check the situation as new orders might bring an account above its 'safe' limit, or even require the salesman to sensitively investigate why the amount owing has increased. Has the customer's business increased quickly with the limit needing revision or is the customer in trouble and the firm at significant risk of allowing a bad debt? The strategic and effective day-to-day running of a business requires the speedy collection, collation and flexible retrieval of information. It is not lightly stated that to manage the future it is necessary to manage information.

Systems apply to many other aspects of the firm. There need to be appropriate systems for the identification of training requirements and career development, with systems of staff appraisal to effect control and feedback, both to the individual and for the control of the firm's programme.

**Staff**   Various positions in the company require differing contributions and this has the implication that different people are needed to fit these various roles. There is no right individual for all roles: people differ in their physical make-up (some jobs may require skilled assembly or special skills such as ability to discriminate odours in the perfume and flavour industries), knowledge and skills (formal knowledge in terms of qualifications and relevant experience).

People also differ in their personality and this is an important consideration. The introverted 'loner' might be ideal in long term fundamental research but would be unlikely to be happy or successful as a salesman, where a more extroverted personality might be appropriate. It is essential that the company attracts, selects and develops the right people for its mix of role requirements. These issues will be further developed in the chapter on implementation.

**Skills**   People in an organization need various skills: specific skills such as engineering, statistics, science, and applications technology are some obvious ones. In the commercial context people will also need business skills, such as marketing, finance and planning. In all organizations, results are not achieved by the individual but by the individual working in a group framework. Thus most people will need appropriate interpersonal skills to succeed.

In evaluating the organization, it is necessary to ensure that the right skill mix is present. This mix will change as the organization's needs and challenges vary. The resulting skill gap needs a continuous programme of identification and training and retraining. In the area of interpersonal skills one of most important factors of business comes into sharp focus. A company is not able to employ an electronics engineer, it can only employ a person who has electronic engineering skills. To develop the person's contribution to the firm, the firm has to develop the person's total capacity, the total person, not just sharpen up the engineering skills.

**Style**    All firms develop a style and culture, 'how things are done round here'. This can relate to dress (should people wear a tie at all times?) or how people work together. In formal organizations people may work together for ten years and still address each other as Mr Wells and Ms Williams in the work situation. In the more 'laid back' informal style of some American companies the Chief Executive Officer may be called by his first name, even by the most junior member of staff. He is still the boss, but the firm's style is different.

Two points need to be remembered. The individuals in the organization need to relate to the style. This may be a consideration in the selection of staff and it is important that new staff quickly know and become comfortable with the firm's given style.

The second key problem in some operations is where differing styles exist in various parts of the organization. Thus the research department may be informal in dress and general styles. The finance administration department might be most formal. Care needs to be taken to reach a common corporate style for the company as differing styles in the firm may result in internal culture clashes ('R and D do not even know how to dress'— 'Finance would not recognize a good idea if they fell over it').

**Shared values**    For the firm to succeed there must be a set of shared values, even of ethics. This is not as easy as it sounds. People engaged in Production might be in love with the product, Marketing with the customer and Finance with the balance sheet. The clear understanding of mission, aims and objectives is central. It is through the process of formulating, reformulating and communicating these that the shared values are understood and accepted by all.

## 2.7 FINANCIAL AUDIT: MONEY—THE ENERGY OF BUSINESS?

The financial analysis of the company is covered in detail in Chapter Nine. To complete the overview of the internal and external audit some financial analysis is required.

### 2.7.1 Accountancy and financial management

There are two distinct roles in industry: accountancy, associated with the 'keeping of the books', and financial management. Accountancy is a specialized activity and has a great value to the firm in areas such as arranging the firm's financial matters in such a way as to minimize tax liability. Financial management is a much more diffuse, generalized and demanding role than accountancy. In industry it is rare to find the role of financial analysis done well by an accountant unless the person also has a relevant technical qualification.

This results from the need to consider what is the actual value of a given situation, not the 'book value'. An extreme example is in the evaluation of patent rights. The firm is considering the purchase of certain patent rights to manufacture a new type of RAM chip. How can the value of these be estimated to evaluate whether this is a suitable investment for the firm? This is a complex issue which requires a total understanding of the firm's present products, how their value might be enhanced with the new technology and, still further, the extent and likely additional sales that might result from the incorporation of this technology. The ideal person to perform this task is an experienced engineer with business skills (operations, marketing and finance). The pure accountant lacks the multi-dimensional perspectives that are required.

### 2.7.2  Balance sheet

In mechanics we have a law that states that 'for each and every action there is an equal and opposite reaction'. Much on accountancy is written on this subject under the heading 'double entry accounts'. The principle is the same. This might be expressed as 'for each and every financial transaction there is an equal and opposite transaction'. If we buy some raw materials the firm's cash is reduced but the firm's value in stock for manufacture is increased by an equal amount. At appropriate times, such as the end of the financial year, the firm will need to take stock of the situation and the way this is done is by the construction of the balance sheet. This represents the company in freeze frame, the state of the company at a single defined time.

The analysis of the firm's balance sheet, Chapter Nine, is important to the firm, but the ability to analyse competitors and customer balance sheets (published for the benefit of the shareholders) is also extremely useful market intelligence. It can enable the firm to consider the resources that a competitor might be able to devote to a competitive response, say a price war. In the case of the new customer it may prevent the company extending too much credit to a company in a poor financial state.

### 2.7.3  Cash flows and profit

Just in the same way that a freeze frame does not give a clear picture of an event, so the balance sheet does not give a complete picture of the company over a period. This insight is given by the cash flow analysis, Chapter Nine, for the period between this balance sheet and the last reported balance sheet.

### 2.7.4  Performance indicators

This analysis has to be taken in the context of the PEST environment and the norms of the industry. The trends over time, as well as the absolute values, are important. One key error in this type of analysis is to fail to take account of inflation. If sales have increased by 6 per cent and inflation is 10 per cent, then in real terms the company has lost sales volume and has problems. This analysis is covered in Chapter Nine. The type of issue that needs to be covered is 'does the firm make effective use of its stocks?' The measure of this is to express it as the number of days of stock cover the company has. If it has many weeks cover, then it may be that the company has too much money held in stock as a buffer for ineffective management control. The comparisons with other companies in the industry enable the company to form a view of its fitness to compete.

## REVIEW

Any business or operation has to work within a context and to succeed the engineer must continue to audit this. Publics are specific, identifiable groups, that may have an effect on the organization, either beneficial or adverse. The engineer needs to evaluate the relevant publics for the situation and then consider the issues and concerns that apply to each established public. The PEST and Porter's 'Five Forces' model give a framework to assess the political, legal, economic, social, technical and competitive issues that confront the engineer in a firm. A particular emphasis emerged in the 80s, requiring specific consideration of environmental and conservation impacts of the manufacture, use and disposal of the firm's products or services. Having looked outside the organization, the value chain and the McKinsey 7's' allow the audit of the primary production activities of the company (Inbound Logistics, Operations, Outbound Logistics, Marketing and Sales and Service) and the support activities needed to ensure the effective and efficient conduct of the firm's primary activities (firm's infrastructure, human resource management, technology development and procurement). A firm is much more than a physical structure of things, to allow the audit of this dimension the McKinsey 7's' (structure, systems, style, staff, skills, strategy and shared values) provides an effective framework for analysis. Any system needs energy to function and money is the energy of business. It was noted that the balance sheet and the cash flow provided a means of checking on the energy equilibrium of the business.

## KEY CONCEPTS AND TECHNIQUES

| | |
|---|---|
| **Entry and exit barriers** | The costs of entering and leaving a business. Important for its effect on competitive behaviour. |
| **Five forces analysis** | A method for the analysis of competitive forces on a company. |
| **McKinsey 7's' analysis** | A way to consider the people issues in a company, the software of the organization. |
| **PEST analysis** | The analysis of the political, economic, social and technical environment within which the company operates. |
| **Product life cycle** | The cycle of introduction, growth, maturity and decline for a product. |
| **Public** | A public is any specific, identifiable group, that may have an effect on the organization, either beneficial or adverse. |
| **Value chain analysis** | A model for the examination of the organization and how it interacts with its environment. |

## CASE STUDY

## MOORTOWN FARM

**General overview**    Jane and David Francis met on an HND Engineering course five years ago. They have been married for two years and have one child just over a year old. They have been working in separate jobs in Plymouth. They have a house with a present market value of £50 000 and a £25 000 mortgage. There are no other outstanding commitments. They have just received the news that a very distant aunt has died and left Jane Moortown Farm and a capital sum of £100 000 in her will. On the open market the farm has a market value of £350 000. Jane and David have decided to run the farm as a business as they do not at present have enough time to spend together.

**Moortown Farm**    Note: the information for this case study has been taken from a number of genuine locations to ensure reality. The information, being amalgamated from a number of authentic locations, does not represent any actual single business or farm.

Moortown farm is located on the edge of Dartmoor in a most beautiful and peaceful environment. Although it is in such a peaceful setting, it is close to the B3357 and only a few miles from Tavistock and the main A386. The farm has excellent road access for the movement of goods on or off the farm. It is also close to the tourist centres (Plymouth, Tavistock, Dartmoor).

The farm consists of some 50 acres of stone walled fields which have been used for grazing sheep, although it has not been run as a real business for some time. The actual work on the farm was done by Andrew Davies who has worked there for 15 years. He is now in his mid 50s. The will indicated that Jane's aunt hoped that his employment would be continued.

The farm consists of a large farmhouse and a number of small and large outbuildings. These are all built in traditional style and have been maintained in reasonable structural order but not modernized to any extent. It should be noted that the farm is within the Dartmoor National Park area and the house and the main outbuildings are considered as grade II listed buildings. With care, these buildings could be used for any number of purposes, from stabling ponies for moor riding to craft work such as wrought iron working. A stream runs through the fields. There is ample room for parking in the old farmyard and this use would not cause any planning problems if done in a sensitive way, given the good local road access. Part of the farm also includes the old quarry. Jane has discovered from the solicitors that limited working of the slate quarry would be permitted.

**Dartmoor**    Dartmoor is a National Park of outstanding natural beauty, located in the south west of England it is a substantial area of land, of about 14 miles diameter. Automatic traffic survey equipment and question surveys have established that about eight million recreational visits a year are made to the park. The area consists of fringe farmland, moorland, high moorland, conifer plantations and wooded valleys. An activity survey in 1985 established that the following activities were engaged in by visitors: picnicking 15 per cent; walking 60 per cent; sightseeing 10 per cent; playing games 10 per cent and 5 per cent other activities (Dartmoor National Park Plan, Second Review 1991).

**Question 1**    On the basis of the above information, complete a brief PEST analysis of the situation. After the completion of the PEST analysis draw up a list of possible potential business ideas that Jane and David Francis could consider for Moortown Farm.

**Cider**    Cider is a traditional West Country drink. Real cider is made from cider apples which have a high sugar content to produce the desired alcoholic content in the finished drink of about 6 per cent. Cider apple orchards take about five years to establish and there are a large number of orchards which produce cider apples which are sold to the cider companies. The manufacture of real cider is a simple process which still requires considerable skill to produce the best product. The apples have to be pulped and quickly pressed to avoid spoiling. Old traditional presses used mechanical screw presses, but more modern facilities use hydraulic operated presses. The harvest of apples takes place over about two months in autumn and the entire crop has to be pressed within this period. Traditional cider, unlike most beer, is deep and slow fermented in large vats over a period of about two months. The cider may be sold on a local basis as alive (still containing some suspended yeast) or bright filtered (all the yeast filtered off). The product is then bottled and distributed.

Jane and David Francis have noted an interest by visitors in traditional cider. They have decided to produce and sell a high quality traditional cider as the business to be developed at Moortown Farm. Their initial plan is to produce about 100 000 litres a year of cider, it takes about two kilograms of cider apples to make a litre of cider.

**Question 2**    Complete a PEST and Porter 5 Forces analysis for Jane and David's proposed Moortown Farm Cider business. A feature of value chain analysis is that it may be used for the analysis of an existing business or for the analysis of the needs of a new business. Complete a value chain audit for the new venture and from this make specific recommendations for the cider manufacturing operations.

## QUESTIONS

1. You are the New Product Development Manager for a company that makes conventional electric light bulbs (filament) for the domestic market. The company is completing a strategic review to decide its policy direction for the next five years. Complete a Porter's 5 Forces model for competition analysis, from the point of view of such a manufacturer.

2. You are the Senior Design Engineer for a company that manufactures electrical and electronic systems for cars. You are completing a strategic review of this business. Complete a PEST analysis of the UK motor industry from the viewpoint of this component supplier.

3. Value chain analysis works both for production and service organizations. Conduct a value chain analysis for your present or last educational establishment. Students in this context are the customers.

4. Within organizations, differing departments or faculties can have differing values, styles and objectives. For your present educational establishment, or your last one, consider two departments or faculties (such as science and languages) and, by using the 7's' framework, evaluate whether there are any differences and if so, what they are.

5. As a technologist with an understanding of business working for a natural gas company, you have been asked to report on the business potential of combined heat and electrical power to your Marketing Director. Draft out the environmental audit report you would give.

## FURTHER READING

Jauch, L.R. and W.F. Glueck (1988) *Strategic Management and Business Policy*, McGraw-Hill. (See Chapters 3 and 5.)

Johnson, G. and K. Scoles (1988) *Exploring Corporate Strategy*, Prentice Hall. (See Chapters 3 and 4.)

Palmer, A. and I. Worthington (1992) *The Business and Marketing Environment*, McGraw-Hill. (See Chapters 4, 5, 9, 11 and 12.)

Peters, T.J. and R.H. Waterman (1982) *In Search of Excellence*, Harper and Row.

Porter, M.E. (1980) *Competitive Strategy, Techniques for Analysing Industries and Competitors*, The Free Press.

Porter, M.E. (1985) *Competitive Advantage, Creating and Sustaining Superior Performance*, The Free Press.

CHAPTER

# THREE

# TECHNOLOGY DEVELOPMENT: CREATIVITY IN A RISK ENVIRONMENT

## 3.1 WHAT IS RISK?

Business is not fail safe, all ventures have a certain risk. If we sell ice-cream on the beach, for example, today sales may be good because the sun is shining but tomorrow it may rain and sales will be poor. To minimize risk we may study the three-day forecasts to make certain that we neither overstock nor run out of ice-cream. Weather forecasts are not perfect and our evaluations will have an element of risk.

The shorter the distance into the future, the more certain we may be of our ability to predict. In the short run, the methods of time series of analysis may enable us to predict the near run future with modest risk. Simple, yet robust, statistical models such as the Holt-Winters will allow the engineer to allow for seasonal and basic trend data. Ice-cream sales may be rising by 10 per cent a year and there will be peaks of demand in the summer months. However, taken into the future, such trends would indicate that we can obtain 110 per cent market shares. This is, of course, not possible so in the more general situation we have to bring other considerations into our analysis. In Chapter Five, marketing models such as the product life cycle, enable us to form a view, taking broader considerations into account rather than simple extrapolation into absurdity. The Ansoff matrix also indicates increasing risk as the firm moves from its known markets and products (market penetration strategy) to new markets for its existing products (market development strategy) and new products for its existing markets (product development strategy). In these two latter cases the firm is entering into one new area. Of course, the strategy of greatest risk is where the firm moves into both new markets and products (diversification strategy). However, if the other options are blocked (for example restricted market size) the company will have to seek new business ventures with risk. This is not to say that the company just accepts the risk. It is necessary to evaluate the risks, their size and nature. By this process the firm will be seeking to manage and minimize the elements of doubt.

This chapter is about the management of risk in a creative environment. We will define business creation as:

*The identification and realization of a new business opportunity.*

This definition in its turn rests upon our definition of a business being to identify and satisfy customers' benefit needs effectively and efficiently with a competitive advantage.

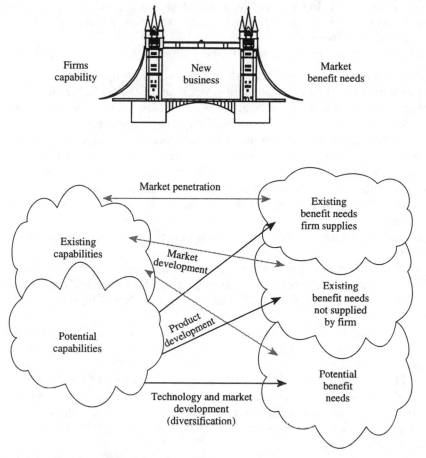

**Figure 3.1**   New products and new markets

The temptation is to say that this process must start with the customer (market orientation) or with the technology (product orientation). Neither philosophy is correct. What we require is a bridge. There must be a capability in the firm and there must be a benefit need from the customers. It does not matter if the initial building of the bridge takes place from the customer or the firm's capability. The critical issue is that after the creative process both elements are in place. If we wish to consider this in more mathematical terms we can consider this as a mapping process as shown in Fig. 3.1.

The 'Walkman' is an example of existing technology needing a creative insight to recognize that there was a potential and unexploited market for a personal stereo. Some 50 organizations are considered to have had the technological capability to develop this product but only one creative person, at first, saw the latent benefit need. Other like examples have been the 'Workmate' and the 'Vax' cleaner. No advance in the boundaries of technology were needed, just new, market driven, engineering insight.

The developing technology of digital signal processing has given CDs and DAT as methods of providing the existing benefit need for high quality sound in the home, with an improved quality. The creative market driven engineer is always alert to the opportunity to map a new business opportunity. In Chapter Five the exploration of products by attribute analysis is opened and the use of this technique for creative new product search and development is continued in Chapter Ten.

Having realized that there is a new potential business what are the risk possibilities?

1. The identification of the need is correct, but the proposed technology is inadequate for the task (for example, the Babbage Calculating Machine) (Chapter Eleven).
2. The technology is sound, but the identification of the benefit need is not correct (for example, the Sinclair C5) (Marketing research, Chapters Five and Eleven).
3. The need and technology is correct, but the customer valuation is not high enough or the market size is too small to recover the R and D investment (Chapter Five).
4. The need and technology is correct, but by the time the firm has commercialized the product the competition has established either an alternative technology (Porter 5 Forces Analysis, Chapter Two) or developed the same or parallel technology (Concurrent Engineering, Chapter Eleven).
5. The need and technology are correct, but the firm fails to protect its inventions and other creative ideas.
6. The quality of the product does not reach the required standard.
7. The firm fails to consider the competitive response of its rivals or the possibility of new entry rivals with lower production costs (Porter 5 Forces analysis Chapter Two and Chapter Six).
8. The firm fails to secure appropriate arrangements for the supply of key inputs (raw materials, components, or software) or to secure appropriate distribution. In the 1950s, it was known that people wanted domestic cookers with a gas hob and an electric oven. However, the distribution of such items were controlled by monopoly organizations; the gas showrooms would not supply cookers with electric ovens, the electricity showrooms would not supply cookers with gas hobs. In effect the suppliers were locked out from their customers by the distributors (Porter 5 Forces analysis Chapter Two, Chapter Five).
9. The firm fails to ensure the availability of the supplementary products or resources for the use of the product or service. For example, a printer company fails to ensure availability of toner cartridges, a consumer electronics company fails to ensure that tape is available for a new recording system or films and music are not available for a new video or digital sound system if the firm fails to secure the necessary copyright licences (Chapter Five).
10. The firm fails to take account of key elements in the PEST environment (Chapter Two). New legislation may make a product illegal, new cost structures may make it uneconomic, social pressures may force its withdrawal (such as the fur trade) and technical developments may make it obsolete.

In the first years of working in industry, the young creative engineer is very likely to start a career in Research and Development. The next section concentrates on the protection of the results gained from this process, the protection of intellectual property.

## 3.2 INTELLECTUAL PROPERTY

A company has physical assets, but its inventions and like property form the most valuable asset in high technology industries. It is not, however, possible to measure the floor area of an invention in the same way as it possible to determine the floor area of a factory. Difficult as it is to value these assets, their protection is even more important than the protection of physical assets, such as money in the company safe. If money is stolen it may be replaced without too much loss of competitive advantage; if an invention is not patented and the know how becomes public property the competitive advantage is lost for ever. Intellectual property can exist in different forms and be protected in differing ways.

### 3.2.1 Know how

The company may have detailed skills knowledge and experience on how to conduct certain operations much better than its competitors. For the reasons given below, it may not be possible to protect by patent or copyright etc. The firm may also elect not to patent, as an element of the patent is to publish the invention and the firm may decide its best protection is not to disclose the invention, but to keep it secret.

This type of commercial information is not limited to the manufacture of the company products but the application technology, the sources of supply of the materials and the key customer and marketing information. It is not possible to patent a list of customers and last year's sales figures. These are of great value to competitors.

The defence for the firm is to ensure reasonable contracts and ethics guidelines for staff so that unauthorized disclosure, once discovered, may be actioned. However, given the open access of computer terminals and photocopiers, it may be very difficult to prevent information loss in the first place and later to identify the source of the loss. Extended computer networks with telephone systems provide a further possible route for unauthorized entry to the firm's commercially sensitive data. In entering into any collaboration with another organization, the firm should ensure that appropriate contracts of know-how disclosure are drawn up. These may provide modest protection.

### 3.2.2 Patents

A patent is a monopoly right to use an invention for a maximum of twenty years after the filing of the original invention. Patents taken out in Europe may be also filed in other countries, such as Japan and the USA, with the priority date and time of the original invention, provided the correct procedures are complied with and the action is taken within twelve months of the original filing. Patents have to be concerned with industrial processes, physical products, methods of construction etc. Mathematical formulae and discoveries may not be patented and a patent must not be obvious to a person who knows the technology. The patent office will apply their standard tests for originality but on publication competitors may lodge objections. Valid grounds might be that the invention was in commercial production in the competitor's company prior to the application for the patent.

A key point is that to be patented, an invention must be novel, that is to say, not described in the literature or already in commercial use. It is possible for an engineer to make an invention impossible to patent if, for example, parts of the invention are discussed at a scientific meeting. The invention may then be held to be in the public literature, even though the disclosure was made by the inventor. Thus, all commercial work which may involve the potential for invention and patents has to be both carefully documented and kept in the utmost secrecy. An issue which calls for skill and judgement is *when* to patent. The patent should be taken out at the earliest time that the process of invention is completed but before commercial production. The difficulty is in deciding when the invention is complete, as the process of making a patent application requires full disclosure of the invention. Once a patent is granted it is in all respects property and may be sold or licensed to other operations.

Patenting is a highly technical area and the services of a specialist Chartered Patent Agent should be sought to ensure both the maximum security and extent of cover from the patent. A simple example serves to illustrate the point.

---

## CROSS PATENTS

London Electronics invent a new powerful LED for use in displays and takes out an immediate patent. However, in commercial use, the product fails to live up to its initial promise.

Birmingham Displays, through marketing intelligence, buys an early model or, through the patent abstracts, learns of the invention. The Development Engineer at Birmingham Displays realizes that the invention will not work in the commercial environment without a special form of encapsulation of the device. This Engineer files an additional patent on this invention.

What is the position for London Electronics and Birmingham Displays?

London Electronics may not make the commercial product as they need to use the additional patented invention from Birmingham Displays. Birmingham Displays may not make the device as they will have to use the original London Electronics patented invention. So why should Birmingham Displays go to the trouble of patenting? The answer is simple; the invention of London Electronics is little use to them without the additional invention. The possession of this patent can then be used to negotiate a cross licence agreement where both companies agree to the use of each other's patents. Without such an arrangement both companies have no advantage; they are, in common language, snookered.

---

It is critical that companies should patent and ensure that the invention is complete. Failure to do this may mean that they have a valid patent but still have to give away the commercial advantage to another. In the complex area of engineering, even competing companies may well find that they need to come to accommodations on licensing arrangements. It should be remembered that this may not be restricted to just patents. A company may have a super device but to use it they may have to licence software from another company (a copyright issue).

From the point of view of the creative inventive engineer, there are some practical strict disciplines. All notes and laboratory records must be kept in an appropriate form. Special books with security paper and page numbers may be purchased for the purpose. Ideas, data and drawings should be recorded, the date and time recorded and the entry signed. At frequent intervals, the record should be countersigned by a senior person such as a chartered engineer. This record may be needed in any litigation over a patent. Such well-documented records can then be used to establish who, when and where an invention was made. If the company elects not to patent but depend on secrecy, then again signed and dated records of production must be held. A defence against a later patent from a competitor will be to prove that the process was commercial prior art, even if the 'new' inventors were not to know this.

At first sight, the obvious answer to the protection of an invention is to patent but there are practical considerations to take into account. The possession of a patent gives the owner the right to enforce the exclusive right to the invention. The key point is that the owner of the patent has to enforce the right, the patent authorities have no part to play. So, to succeed in an action the owner of the patent has to be able to prove that the patent is both valid and has been infringed. If the patent relates to the assembly process for an electronic device, and after assembly it is impossible to tell if the product was made with the use of the invention or by a less good method, then what is the use of the patent? If it is not possible to police the patent, it may be of limited value to deter some companies but still may be infringed by many other firms without possibility of effective action. This is why many inventions are not patented, companies electing to protect their invention by commercial secrecy.

In international businesses, such as electronics, care has to be taken on importing devices to ensure that the imported device does not involve infringement of a patent. A manufacturer may have licence rights in the USA but not in the UK. This may not allow importation of the device or use of the invention, which may have been licensed to another company.

Patents may not be used to protect artistic, dramatic or musical work and neither are patents used to protect computer programs, here the issue is copyright.

### 3.2.3 Copyright

For something to be subject to copyright it does not have to be original but only the result of independent intellectual work. In this respect it is quite different to a patent, where the test of novelty is stringent. Computer programs are protected on much the same basis as literary work (this is a fast developing area). Conversion of a program into another language (say from FORTRAN to PASCAL) will be considered to be an adaptation of the work. To run and display a program involves making a working copy (possibly only in RAM). However, this requires, in strict law, the consent of the copyright holder.

The rights given to a copyright holder are in many ways similar in effect to that of owning a patent. Others may not use, adapt, copy, broadcast or use the work without the owner's permission. Just like a patent, the rights may be sold or licensed.

There is no need to register copyright, which exists as a right in this country. It is essential, however, to be able to prove the date of the creation of the work should it be required. The copyright owner is the creator of the work, except where the work is completed as a part of the creator's normal work, where the owner will be the employer. Most contracts of employment for engineers will make the issue of ownership of patents and copyright quite clear; either they are the property of the employer or the employee agrees to assign rights to his employer. This all appears to be simple but although the drawings of a new device may be copyright, the device itself is not protected, nor is the idea behind the copyright item. This is an area of considerable complexity where computer code can be rewritten using the basic logic flow ideas but not using close code sequences. This is an active area of professional ethic guidance from the professional institutions. Names and the like may not be protected by copyright.

### 3.2.4 Designs

A registered design is much like a patent in that it only has a limited life of an initial five years which may be increased in 5 year increments to 25 years. Just like a patent, the rights can be sold or licensed. Much other material around the design, such as drawings, are automatically protected by copyright. Designs have some of the needs of a patent in that, unlike copyright, certain conditions have to be met. Where the design has no particular qualities (it would not be possible to register the design of a cube) or the object's design is determined by the overall needs of the product, the 'must fit' requirement, it is not possible to protect the design. This protection is concerned with the outward appearance of the product so it does *not* protect the functional products, such as printed circuit boards or microchips.

In many respects, the registered design is much like a patent; it has to be original and not be part of prior art, so the same issues of secrecy and non-commercialization before registration apply. It is essential to maintain records with dates for the development of the design. Again, like a patent, part of the process is the publication of the design. The international conventions on registering in other countries are not so extensive and well developed as with patent designs. Thus international pirating of designs is a real international problem and, in many countries, it is not possible to enforce the rights. If such 'pirate' items are imported into the UK, however, the design owner may take action.

### 3.2.5 Design right

Design right is like copyright in that it is automatic and there is no need to file a registration, but again, there is a need to maintain records to show the date and persons responsible for the origination of the design. The right exists for three-dimensional, objects and must not be for routine objects such as nuts and bolts. Complex three-dimensional, multi-layer circuit boards and microchips are covered.

The life of the protection is limited to five years of full protection and a further five years of limited protection when others have the right to make under licence. This flexibility for competitors to licence after five years does not apply to microchips where the EC directive is that full protection will last for ten years after commercialization. If this represents a strengthening of the designer's rights in another direction, they are reduced with the 'must fit' requirement. Here protection is not given. This limitation on rights is imposed as a support to free trade, otherwise major manufacturers would be able to 'design out' manufacturers of spares who might compete with the original manufacturer.

There is not full international recognition of this type of right and so cover may be very restricted. This can mean that care may need to be taken on the import of equipment to ensure that it does not contain components which are not licensed in the UK.

### 3.2.6 Branding

Many companies wish to use a logo or the like and, in part, advertising material etc. will be protected by copyright. The technical term for registration, is a Trade Mark (goods) or Service Mark (services). For registration a mark must not conflict with an existing mark for similar goods, be of a nature that other traders might normally use or mislead. Once registered, this protection acts rather like registered design and others may not use the mark. The same conditions exist for patents, in the sense that the mark has to be published and people have the right to object. Unlike a patent, the registration may be for an infinite period. The initial registration is for 7 years, but thence the registration has to be renewed every 14 years. Also, the mark may be in commercial use before registration. Firms may often register trademarks before commercialization. Again, the same framework of international agreements that exists for patents is not so well developed in this area and applications may have to be made in each country where protection is required.

It is not the purpose of this book to go into a detailed of account of the law, but the protection of a registered mark is much easier than attempting to take common law action for 'passing off' for an infringement of the firm's position. With a registered mark the simple act of use is all that is required to bring successful action. Without this other elements have to be proved, such as reputation and intention to deceive.

### 3.2.7  Protection of intellectual property

From the above brief discussion it can be seen that the protection of the engineer's intellectual property is both highly technical and very expensive. A simple patent with protection in major countries only (say only 25) may well cost £50 000. Moreover, to keep these protections in place many renewals have to be effected in any countries under differing laws. Most major firms will have patents or intellectual property departments. Within these departments there will be expert engineers who are also qualified in patent law.

However, no matter how professional and well staffed the corporate law departments are, they will not be able to take effective action unless the creative engineer has been professional enough to realize when there is something novel that needs protection. The engineer must also ensure that adequate records are kept of the creative process and that no action is taken before the application for protection that might give grounds to invalidate the protection (such as premature commercialization and disclosure).

### 3.3  SAFETY

It is not the purpose of this section of the book to give a detailed overview of the vast amount of law covering the safety of engineering, the employment of people and the safety of consumers, customers and the public at large. The view is advanced that the chartered engineer is not just concerned with the law. The implication of chartered status is that the engineer will use all professional skill and knowledge to ensure the safety of all concerned, with the manufacture or provision of the service or who will be in contact with the results of his/her work. To say that safety is concerned with the law is to accept the old definition of quality as 'conformance to specification'. Certainly the engineer will ensure all legal compliances are effected. The nature of the innovation in engineering, however, is such that often the engineer, as a result of the advancing boundary of technology and knowledge, will be working 'outside' the law (that is to say, no law is as yet enacted). The law can only be formulated once a body of knowledge has been gained by professional engineers. For example when the first lasers were invented there were no regulations but the dangers existed before the regulations. An engineer is expected to use his/her professional skills to ensure the safety of all, even where the framework of law does not exist. The acceptance of chartered status implies not only the conformance to all laws, but also adds additional layers of professional responsibility. So in this section we take the

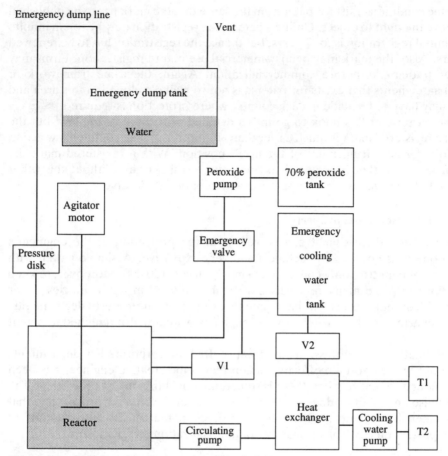

**Figure 3.2**   Simple safety features in a chemical reactor

professional view rather than the legal view, on the basis that this is the more demanding view. It is to be noted that, increasingly, the law is framed on the basis of 'best endeavour' to recognize the fact that any precise code is likely to be out of date before it is published. As always in this book, product can be taken to read product or service.

There are only two aspects that need to be considered in the process of maximizing safety:

1. How can we ensure that the product provides no risk to people, property or the environment in the design, manufacture, distribution, use and disposal of the product? *How do we ensure nothing goes wrong?*
2. In the event of any failure, how can we ensure the minimum danger of death or injury to any person, property or damage to the environment? *What are the provisions when something does go wrong?*

The basic process is illustrated by an example from the chemical industry, a plant built in the 1960s. The safety features built into this plant needed the professional skills of industrial chemists, chemical engineers, electrical engineers, electronic engineers, control engineers, mechanical engineers and civil engineers. A simple outline only is given.

The new process involved the reaction of a natural vegetable oil with hydrogen peroxide. This chemical technology was selected as alternative chemical technologies involving chlorine would give substantial environmental problems (*selection of technology to minimize environmental impact*).

For chemical efficiency 70 per cent peroxide strength was needed. This type of peroxide is about the concentration used in World War Two rocket systems. The potential energy in the reaction system, given a 'run away' reaction, was equivalent to about 1000 kg of TNT. (*The selection of a technology to avoid one problem may well introduce other safety issues.*)

For simplicity the reaction system is only shown in outline. The process was that the oil was charged to the reactor. The peroxide was fed to the reactor through a metering pump. To ensure mixing and reaction of the peroxide the reaction mixture had to be mixed by a high speed agitator as a build-up of unreacted peroxide would represent an extreme danger. The temperature of the reaction mixture was controlled by the circulation of the reaction mixture through the coils of a heat exchanger. The cooling was effected by the circulation of cooling water through the heat exchanger. Failure to remove the heat would represent an extreme danger. The hazard and operability study for this process ran the length of a Dickens novel and below are only some highly selective issues considered in this study. (*An audit of all potential hazard conditions is essential.*)

The storage of the peroxide could represent a hazard. In contact with the wrong metals, the material can decompose with explosive force, the material itself can cause the ignition of oil or other organic material, such as wood. The escape of this material through rupture of the tank, failure of the pump or failure of a pipe join would represent a major risk. It is common standard practice with such tanks that they should be constructed inside a concrete open tank to contain any spillage in the event of a major failure. (*If a failure should occur how can you localize the danger?*)

A critical potential danger is the build-up of unreacted peroxide in the system. This was resolved by the application of elements from a whole range of engineers. The heat given out in the reaction was measured by industrial chemists. Chemical engineers could then calculate the expected heat given out at any given stage of the reaction process. The mechanical and chemical engineers could then design in a metering pump for the hydrogen peroxide. Thus, the amount of peroxide charged to the system could be known by integration of the function {pump rate − time} (control engineering with electronic engineering). The same considerations could be applied to the cooling water pump and the temperature of the cooling water at inlet and outlet of the heat-exchanger be measured (chemical and instrument engineering). The heat output could then could be estimated by the integration of the function {[pump rate − time] × [T1 − T2]}. The integrated function of added peroxide could be compared with the measured output of heat; a significant difference would bring in alarm systems. A major difference would initiate the peroxide emergency cut-off valve and bring the plant into an emergency shut-down procedure. (*Good detection of out of control conditions is essential with thorough understanding of the control operating characteristics of the system*).

In the event of the failure of the cooling water pump, the peroxide emergency valve would close. Circulation of water was maintained by gravity feed from an emergency cooling water tank through valve 2. (*All single element failures should be considered.*)

Apart from specific unit failures, note must be taken of external safety hazards. A major disaster in this system would be possible if there was a general failure of the electricity supply. In this case, the emergency peroxide valve would close, cooling water flow through the heat exchanger would be maintained from the gravity feed. Limited cooling was maintained on the reactor (through a water jacket not shown in the diagram for simplicity). Should the temperature still continue to rise the reaction could be 'drowned out' by the addition of water from the emergency gravity feed tank. The reader will, of course, have noted that the instrumentation needed to be run on an uninterruptible power system with 12 hours' back up battery support. (*General failure conditions must also be considered.*)

All this represents a phase one analysis of the situation 'How do we prevent a "run away" explosive reaction?' After the most extensive analysis to answer this question we move to question two 'What happens if we *do* get a "run away" reaction?'

For example, if the reactor agitator shaft should fracture (most unlikely, but not impossible), none of the above systems might pick up the problem in time. To prevent a pressure explosion a deliberate weak point is constructed in the reaction system with a 'bursting disk' which, given a pressure build-up, will rupture at a precise pressure, allowing the contents of the reactor to vent through a very wide emergency pressure relief dump line. The contents of the reactor would be caught in an emergency dump-tank half full of water with a vent for any remaining gases created in the run away reaction. The final safety feature is that the reactor would be built surrounded by a blast proof wall to contain any explosion should it occur (not shown).

To bring in this new product and process needed the attention and creativity of a whole range of engineers to ensure the safety of the operators, the plant, the general public and the environment. The temptation is to think that, having built all these features in, the role of the engineer is at an end. However, the human element is critical. The uninterruptible power supply will not work unless the batteries are in first class condition and have been subject to frequent inspection. The engineer's role and responsibility is thus not restricted merely to the hardware of the system but also involves considering the training of the staff to operate and maintain the system. Complete programmes must be devised for the testing and maintenance of systems that it is expected should never be used.

> *Hazard and operability studies and safety are not technical issues but general managerial issues with a high technical and professional content and the greatest responsibility an individual can have: the health and safety of others.*

The precise issues to be considered in any given situation are the responsibility of the professional engineers to determine. A key feature of such safety audits on new products and processes is that they need the skills of a whole range of professional people. The greatest care needs to be taken when risks may lie on the fringe areas of several of the professions involved in the project. The final issue will be a major hazard action programme which will link in with major emergency services so that should a major disaster occur there is a well prepared framework for the limitation of the damage and loss of life. The hazard and operability study is one of the most complex, challenging and responsible tasks that the chartered engineer will encounter in his/her working life. Further consideration of related issues are covered in Reliability of Systems in Chapter Six.

### 3.3.1 Product safety and regulatory affairs—liability

In this section, we shall consider the issues that the engineer needs to consider in the provision of products or services to other organizations or individuals. The above section on safety also applies to the user situations. It is unethical for a chartered engineer to be party to the provision of equipment or services into situations where it is known or suspected that the users are unable to install or use with safety. Given the military implications of seemingly mundane equipment, this responsibility is also extended to unauthorized use of the materials, systems or service. The additional complexity is that the supplier does not have managerial control of the user situation.

The engineer is faced with one of the basic laws of engineering 'It is easy to make a system idiot proof, but it is impossible to make a system user proof'. This is linked to another law 'Given there are two ways to use a system the customer will find a third'. The first requirement for the engineer is to make the system as safety resilient as possible, even in the situation of misuse. The second requirement is that the engineer must ensure that full information, instructions and training are available to enable customers and users not only to get full value from their investment but so that they do not put themselves, other people, equipment, buildings or the environment at risk.

From the liability point of view, it is critical that the organization should have documentation and records to show that every reasonable effort has been taken to ensure safety of all who will come into contact with the system. This documentation must embrace the conception, design process, manufacturing operations, installation, customer field service, marketing communications, customer training and even advice, in extreme cases, to local emergency services for procedures in the event of major hazard situations (for example, some science instruments involve the use of radioactive sources and the Fire Service must be aware of such hazards in the event of a building fire). Many major organizations maintain a toll free, 24 hour, emergency line, throughout the year, (not linked to normal commercial lines) direct to a responsible person with full access to all emergency data and the emergency call numbers of all the company experts in various disciplines.

As with safety, the issue is: 'Having done everything to prevent a danger, what do we do if one occurs?' For example, if the company manufactures consumer goods, it must have an emergency product recall plan. If the company has designed a new product line with a new component from a new supplier and it is discovered that a lot of defective components have been built into production units that have been sold to the general public, the defective component could cause the case of the product to become 'live' with real risk of danger to life. The company must have a well considered action plan with responsibilities defined for recall of the product from the distributors. It must also have an action plan for an immediate publicity campaign to get customers to return the units for fault rectification. The issues of total quality management are considered in more detail in Chapter Six.

It is to be noted that in advanced countries there is a movement to strict liability. In the past, it was sufficient for the company to prove that it had taken all reasonable care and any person taking action had to prove that in some way the firm had been negligent. The situation is now more that if the person can prove that the firm, or the firm's products were responsible for the injury, the company may well find itself found held liable, even back to when the hazard was not known to science at the time of manufacture.

In the design of a product, the engineer should draw up a specification covering all relevant issues. This will provide a first line of legal defence in the case of a major dispute. Say, for example, the firm makes electronic components and its customer builds into a system that then fails. If this failure was due to the system manufacturer using the component outside the specification limits, it is essential for the supplying company to be able to prove that it supplied the manufacturer with the design characteristics and specifications showing that the product was not intended to be used under those conditions. Failure to do this could place the component manufacturer with problems in a liability action. This may appear simple, however, with ever-increasing advances and changes in specifications and applications, it is essential that the component company maintains good records of the distribution of specification and design data manuals.

It has to be remembered that the failure of a single component could result in a claim, in real terms, almost without limit. Say it could be proved that a component failed in a flight guidance system that caused an commercial aircraft to crash on an oil refinery.

## 3.4 TECHNOLOGICAL DEVELOPMENT—ENVIRONMENTAL AND CONSERVATION ISSUES

The people who create our future have a heavy responsibility to ensure that they do not create subsequent problems. The electrical and electronics industry was proud of its image as a 'sunrise industry' and that the technology did not have the problems of massive environmental despoilment associated with the old 'smoke stack' industries, such as the manufacture of iron and steel. It is ironic that from this area two of the most massive environmental problems should have largely been created. CFC113 was used in the cleaning of electronic parts as it was by far the most safe solvent that appeared to be available. Polychlorinated biphenyls were used for their stability. How could such a problem have been created without further consideration?

The purpose of this book is not to suggest that the people concerned with the introduction of these products were not well intentioned, nor that they did not exercise all due care as seen by the professionals at that time, but rather that we all learn from the errors of the past. In the case of both of these materials, their reason for use was, in a large part, dependant on their stability (extreme stability in fact). No person asked 'What happens to these materials when they escape into the environment?'. We all know the answer now, for the next 100 years people will have to live with an increased risk of skin cancer from ozone depletion and the contamination of the environment with poly-chlorinated biphenyls with concentration up the food chain, still considered to be a key factor in the low population of otters in some British rivers.

How can professionals protect society from such problems in the future? It is to be hoped that no new product, process or service with a potential environmental and/or conservation issue will be introduced without the consideration of the 'Total Life Cycle'. In Chapter Five, the issue of total cost of ownership is considered for the firm's customers. The total life cycle concept takes this issue to not just the consideration of accountancy costs but with care for the broader issues of concern to society at large. This is not to say that these considerations are not important from the profitability view. They are, as society will not allow operations to continue which pose a threat to resources or the ecological systems.

To consider the total life cycle of a product, we have to consider all the inputs from the primary (often non-renewable) sources (iron ore, oil, etc.), all the conversion processes and resources, such as energy, used in these transformation process. Apart from the inputs to the conversion processes, we need to consider the outputs such as toxic waste, acid rain, noise etc. Moreover, we need to consider if the processes themselves represent the most effective use of non-renewable resources (for example, 'Why do we still generate electricity and waste at least as much energy as we convert to electrical power, when combined heat and power would appear to halve the energy waste?'). Having then considered the manufacture of the product, we have to consider the distribution of the product to the customer and the effect of the product in use. A critical value of the concept of the total life cycle is that our concerns do not stop at this stage. What is the waste and/or environmental impact of the disposal of the product. Here, the power of the new concept is illustrated as this view of innovation would have called into question the use of materials such as CFC113. The question asked is: 'On release to the environment what is the effect of the product and what is the environmental fate?'. In the case of CFC113, the environmental fate was not known and it now appears that it will be well over 100 years before the harmful effects of this product are eliminated.

In the testing of new pharmaceutical products, it is not only essential to test out the beneficial effects and possible side effects, but also to understand how the drug will be broken down and eliminated from the patient. In effect, the same techniques need to be considered in the invention of all new products or the end result may be to create new environmental disasters.

The above is not to be seen as a reason not to seek progress. It must be remembered that the analytical technologies that have given us the understanding to appreciate these risks also required innovation. The key issue is that the process of creative technology development must always carry some element of risk. No product is safe as such, we can only ever say that we have not been able to find any conditions where it is a danger. This does not preclude there being some new conditions or understandings that subsequently do prove that the material is a danger (such as asbestos). To illustrate this, we will consider in the case study the issues that faced electronics manufacturers in 1991.

## 3.5 OTHER ASPECTS OF THE LAW AND THE ENGINEER

The law represents both a protection and a threat if its requirements are not fully understood. In international business, with contracts that have to be implemented more within than one framework of law, the situation is complicated and full of potential risk. Some consideration of these international marketing issues is given at the end of Chapter Five.

Free trade legislation is an area which affects the young professional engineer. The headlines and the economists are most concerned with the mega merger. These are important, but it is unlikely that you will be arranging a billion pound merger in your first five years in industry. Most engineers will be in customer contact, either as the key aspect of their job (technical selling) or, more generally, in technical meetings or in field support.

All companies will state that they believe in free competition. However, the logic of competitive advantage is to gain as strong a market position as possible, which in the end can represent a monopoly position. Society at large takes the view that with a few exceptions (such as patents) such a situation is not in the interests of society. There is an extensive framework of law to ensure that free trade is supported. Given the international character of the science and technology based industries, these provisions must of necessity extend across borders. If they did not, a group of people who wanted to 'rig' the prices in a market such as the USA would only have to fly off-shore to set up the price ring. The complexity is that an engineer working for a UK company which is part of a USA multinational will have to take account of USA, EC and UK law, all of which may apply to a given situation.

The basic motivation of all these laws is to prevent individuals, or groups taking actions which are considered to be unreasonable actions preventing free trade. Such actions may well involve the massive merger but also apply to the most basic levels of trading. A major computer company may wish to sell its systems to a company manufacturing office furniture. The computer company will be a major contractor to buy such furniture. There might be a temptation to suggest that the purchase of the computer systems might result in a favourable consideration of future purchases of office furniture. Such use of the buying power of the company in the discussions of a sale of unrelated equipment might be considered to be an unreasonable restriction of free trade. It might be considered that an overt discussion of prices might be too obvious a way to come to an 'arrangement' to fix prices. A simple way might be to send copies of your price lists to your competitors but, again, this might well be considered to be an attempt to distort prices and be considered an illegal act. Attempts to influence the price at which a distributor sells products to the ultimate consumer may also be considered not to be in the public interest.

The above are general issues relating to trading but there are specific issues which apply to the area of patents and technology development. In particular, the ownership of a 'master patent' with limited life may tempt an eager person into actions which would be considered as unreasonable in terms of free trade legislation. Such areas include attempting to arrange royalty agreements beyond the life of the patent, attempting to link the patent licence with the purchase of unrelated products or services or attempting to restrict the price at which products incorporating the invention are sold. Patent and free trade legislation is most complex and areas such as exclusive grantback, where a company with a master patent requires the company licensing the patent to give exclusive rights to any improving inventions, require most careful consideration. It may well be held that such an attempt is outside the free trade legislation. The result of all these legal complexities is that the inventive engineer is likely to be on first name terms with the people in the head office legal department.

## REVIEW

The development process involves bridging the gap between the firm's capability (or potential capability) and the market benefit needs (or potential benefit needs). Market penetration strategies involve minimum risk as both elements (products and markets) are known. To provide existing products to new customers (market development) or to provide new products to existing customers (product development) involves more risk, as one element of the mix is not well known to the firm. Where the company decides to develop new products to new customers (diversification strategy) both elements are changed and there is even more risk. To minimize risk, the company needs to conduct adequate research.

Technical companies have much of their value in intellectual property. Know how is where the company has skills and information to conduct its business. Where a company invents something novel, it may patent the invention to secure exclusive rights for 20 years. Text, drawings and programs may not be protected by patents but may be protected by copyright. Novel designs may be protected by registering the design, for novel functional products, such as microchips, the intellectual property may be protected by design right.

Given the limited life of the protection and the continual flow of innovation the firm may wish to ensure more long-lasting protection. This can be done by expert marketing and establishing a brand. The trade mark or service mark of the firm can be registered and protected. This protection can be renewed and extended with no time limit. These forms of protection establish a right, but it is the responsibility of the owner to enforce the right, this is not done by the regulatory authorities.

The engineer has the management of safety as one of their major responsibilities. The hazard and operability study provides a framework for this. This rests on the detailed and systematic investigation of two key questions: 'How do we ensure nothing goes wrong?' and 'What are the provisions when something does go wrong?'. With product safety and liability legislation, these questions need to be asked not only about the manufacture but also about the customer installation and use of the product and, with increasing concerns about the environment, the safe disposal of product when it has completed its useful life. In other words, the consideration of the total life cycle of the product from manufacture right through to recycling.

Competition law not only affects the large merger but also the day to day work of the engineer. Disclosure of price information to a competitor or other attempts to limit competition may leave the individual and the company open to action.

## KEY CONCEPTS AND TECHNIQUES

| | |
|---|---|
| **Branding** | The process by which a company gives a distinctive image to its products or services, very often used to provide some competitive protection when a market is, or might become, undifferentiated. |
| **Copyright** | The right of an author, or his employer, to protect independent intellectual work (books, computer programs etc.). This right is automatic and registration is not required, but evidence of the date of production of the work is wise. |
| **Cross patents** | A situation when to operate a master patent, a second 'improver' patent is required which is owned by another. Neither party can operate the process without a licence from the other. |
| **Designs** | Rather like a patent, but for the registration of a design. Again, granted only for a limited time. |
| **Design right** | Registered designs are intended mostly for the protection of products designed for aesthetic reasons. Design right gives protection to functional products such as printed circuit boards. No registration is required. The protection is not as strong as with patents and copyright. This right is for a limited time. |
| **Hazard and operability study** | A systematic process of evaluating all potential hazards to ensure their control, also covers the procedures in the event of a major failure as a second phase. |

| | |
|---|---|
| **Intellectual property** | Those elements of intangible commercial property such as, know how, patents, copyright, designs, design right, trade marks and service marks. This also extends to confidential information, such as mailing lists, marketing and other commercial data. |
| **Know how** | All the special detailed skills needed to make something, such as a manufacturing process, working practice. |
| **Master patent** | Some key invention upon which many other inventions later depend. The original invention of the telephone is an example. |
| **Patents** | A right to have exclusive use of a novel invention for a limited time. |
| **Total life cycle** | The consideration of the environmental issues involved with a product from conception (primary raw materials) through use to grave (ultimate disposal). |
| **Trade, Service mark** | A registered form of words and/or design (often called a logo). Registration must be effected in all countries where protection is required. The registration may be renewed and, in effect, extended without limit. |

## CASE STUDY

## THE IDEAL PROCESS FOR THE CLEANING OF PARTS AND BOARDS

**Overview of the problem**   Many items such as circuit boards, precision metal parts and other items, require cleaning in the course of the manufacturing processes. Present technology has used an inert solvent to effect this process and an alternative water cleaning technology has also been used. In the light of the Montreal Protocol, the use of CFC113 has to be phased out. Extensive work has been undertaken to resolve this problem by the development of improved technologies (improvements to water cleaning), further development of 'no clean' fluxes, the development of partial CFCs with lower ozone depletion potentials and the use of other solvents, such as terpenes.

This problem has been magnified by the developments in technology such as surface mount boards and very high precision mechanical parts. In any case, existing technologies were being tested to the limits and contamination control has become a major issue in the development of certain parts of the industry.

It is to be noted that the ideal invention has to be designed to solve problems in these demanding applications. However, this does not preclude its use where such demands are not required. It is envisaged, given the essential simplicity, safety and near zero environmental impact of such an invention, that extensive use in less demanding applications would be made.

**Limitations of no clean fluxes**   These represent an option for applications of modest demands, such as printed circuit boards for consumer appliances. However, this is not a viable alternative to cleaning for high performance computer applications and/or military applications where very low levels of surface contamination are required (less than ten microgram equivalents of sodium chloride contamination per square centimetre).

**Water cleaning**   By the nature of these items, many require to have a very low surface contamination by water. In fact, CFC113 'cleaning' has been used in the past for the azeotropic removal of water after 'true' water cleaning. Many of the present systems use surfactants. The common ones in use are ionic. Given that the purpose is often to remove ionic contamination to an exceptionally low level this gives considerable problems in final rinsing.

One can envisage how expert surfactant chemistry can improve this situation with the use of non-ionic volatile surfactants. Moreover, the large quantities of water used have to be of exceptional purity, so called 'conductivity' purity water. All these issues taken together mean that the equipment is capital intensive and energy expensive. Moreover, the contaminates (organic, particles, and ionic) that are left in dilution involve either expensive clean-up for recycle or an effluent problem with the possibility of discharge of heavy metals and other potentially toxic and environmentally harmful materials. After all these activities, the parts have to be dried, another energy expensive and capital intensive operation.

It is known that some materials, such as high performance magnesium alloys (used in the aerospace industry—as a specific example of a general class), are susceptible to surface attack and degradation under these types of cleaning conditions. It would appear that water cleaning has many problems.

**Ultrasonic cleaning**   To assist in some cleaning processes, ultrasonic sound is used. Considerable controversy exists as to whether this can cause problems, either by mechanical damage to micro-processor connections or surface damage due to 'cavitation' effects. Certain military specifications exclude the use of ultrasonics in the cleaning processes. An ideal process would be one which avoided the use of a technology with possibly unknown effects.

**Solvent cleaning**   To evaluate the problems of solvent cleaning a number of different but inter-related issues must be considered.

### Environmental issues

*Ozone depletion*   Organic solvents containing chlorine and with a long atmospheric half life will get into the upper atmosphere and cause the problem known as ozone depletion. Thus the extended Montreal Protocol will include some non-CFC solvents, such as carbon tetrachloride.

*Acid rain potential*   All solvents containing chlorine and/or fluorine have an acid rain potential in their ultimate atmospheric fate.

*Greenhouse potential*   All organic solvents to a greater or lesser extent have a greenhouse potential. Though the solvent contribution to this effect may be small compared with the fossil fuel contribution, it still may become a political, environmental, issue.

*Lower atmosphere ozone problems*   It is well known that certain organic materials in their atmospheric degradation pathway give rise to ozone formation in complex interactions with oxides of nitrogen. Such effects are considered harmful to the environment and severe limitations are expected on the release of such materials.

*Contamination of ground water*   Considerable concern is being expressed about the contamination of ground water with low levels of toxic organic solvents from industrial processes.

*The environmental paradox*   The total of the above is that if the organic solvent is stable it may give rise to ozone depletion, ground water contamination or other, as yet unknown, environmental effects.

However, if the organic material is not stable, the atmospheric degradation pathways may give rise to material harmful to the environment and injurious to health (such as enhanced ozone levels in sunlight by photochemical interaction with oxides of nitrogen).

*COSH and human exposure problems*   Great concern is now being converted into explicit legislation to protect workers from exposure to toxic materials. Present systems of tailored CFC113 have profound problems in this respect, with very high vapour pressures and toxic co-solvents (such as Methyl Alcohol with low TLV). The very gravest long term concern exists about the safety of any new material, in the sense that unknown risks may well come to light far into the future (ozone depletion is one example, the very low limits now required for vinyl chloride monomer is another, benzene, asbestos—the list goes on and on).

**Future legislation**   All the above elements will give rise to pressure for VOC emission controls (VOC = Volatile Organic Compounds). Such legislation is already very restrictive in the USA and can give PMN (Pre-Manufacturing Notice—procedures to notify the use of new materials or processes) problems. The European legislation has yet to be framed in total detail, but any solution that does not take account of this could give a very short lived relief from the issue, with all the problems to resurface in the mid 90s. Such comments may well also apply to contamination of ground water.

**Technical problems**   CFC113 is not a good solvent. It is used as it has a high vapour density, good azeotropic properties and is non-explosive in all ratios in air. However, it is such a poor solvent that toxic solvents (such as methyl alcohol) have to be used to improve the cleaning power.

This can give rise to problems. To contain solvent losses, equipment often uses refrigerated cooling coils which causes water to condense out of the atmosphere. This can cause a number of undesired effects, including the disruption of the azeotropic system and corrosion (interaction of the water with the halo-organic solvent at the heating surfaces of the vapour cleaning tank). This can require the introduction of water traps and drying systems which further add to the complexity and cost of these systems. The effects of the partial CFCs under these conditions will take time to fully evaluate. Given their reduced stability (the very reason for their introduction to avoid the ozone depletion problem), however, one might expect increased problems. It is well known that the less stable chlorinated solvents have increased corrosion potentials in this type of equipment.

**Other issues**   In the above brief review of the problems certain other well known problems have not been addressed, such as the need for low viscosity (of particular importance to surface mount technology) and surface tension. A critical problem of other solutions using non-chlorinated solvents is the issue of flammability. Hydrocarbons (such as terpenes) will have considerable problems of flammability and explosion risks requiring expensive, capital intensive, safety provisions. Such provisions may be far from easy in the clean room environments, requiring vastly expensive rebuilding and down time.

**The ideal system**   The above discussion gives us some specification of the ideal cleaning system.

1. No unknown technology or materials should be used.
2. Materials used should have low toxicity where possible.
3. The materials used should be inert to the products being cleaned.
4. The materials should have a known environmental fate and for preference should be 'natural'.
5. It should be possible to recycle the cleaning material with the removal of particles, organic and ionic material for separate, concentrated, safe disposal of the soil material (a key problem with water cleaning). It should be noted that this will become a key problem with the use of proprietary fluxes with unknown (to the user) activators and the potential for heavy metal contamination.
6. The cleaning media should be effective at the removal of soil but inert to the parts to be cleaned and the equipment used in the cleaning process.

7. The cleaning media should have low viscosity and low surface tension.
8. The cleaning media should be low cost and freely available, from sources of little or zero environmental impact.
9. The cleaning media should be inert in the sense that it introduces no flammability hazard.
10. The system should resolve all known, predicted or potential environmental, toxic or safety issues.
11. It should be possible to remove the cleaning media very completely from the cleaned parts.
12. Very low levels of surface water should be left on the cleaned parts.

In conclusion, the most difficult problem in creativity development is not finding the creative answers to questions, but finding the right questions to ask in the first place.

**Question**    The production of a modern motor car requires the manufacture of large numbers of precision parts and electronic components. Many of these are not made by the motor manufacturer, but by subcontractors. Review the issues faced by car manufacturers in the context of the restrictions on products with an ozone depletion potential and volatile organic compound emissions. What specific actions would you recommend they take?

## QUESTIONS

1. Consider yourself in the role of New Product Development Manager in a defence electronics company. Given the problems of the 'peace dividend' for such a company you have turned the world class capabilities of your innovative development team to the consumer markets. Your company has a world class name and identity and you consider it would be good to transfer this image to the domestic sector.

   Recognizing the need for innovative style in the external design of consumer electronics you have recruited a world class Italian designer for the styling of the product.

   You have completed the review of the whole project and have concluded that:

   (a) You can transfer some long established defence manufacturing techniques to this consumer product.
   (b) The external style for the new product from your new Italian designer is excellent.
   (c) Some new technology was needed but your inventive staff have cracked the problems.
   (d) Some new software was needed but it has now been written.
   (e) The company name and image will transfer in customer benefit (branding) terms to the new consumer market segment.
   (f) For rapid exploitation in the international market outside Europe, a licence to manufacture and sell will be necessary with an American consumer electronics company.

   Understanding all the implications you have a meeting for a full review of all the *intellectual property issues* with the corporate legal department at head office.

   In this situation what *intellectual property elements* are involved, what issues would you discuss with the legal department. What actions might result from this meeting?

2. A chemical plant has a number of large storage tanks. These are used to store inflammable and toxic feedstocks. The separate materials will react with explosive

violence outside the controlled conditions of the catalytic reactor system. These liquids are delivered in bulk by road tankers. The pumping of liquids can cause the build-up of static electricity. It is known that such discharges can cause explosions in the cleaning of crude oil tankers with high pressure water jets.

Complete a full hazard and operability study of the operation of accepting a delivery of a road tanker of material into this tank farm.

How would you translate this study into recommendations for the construction of this tank farm and the detailed instructions for the process operators?

3. You are a senior engineer and are now the General Manager of a major factory which produces domestic refrigerators. The parent company is most concerned about environmental and conservation issues, not least of all regarding the use of CFCs in domestic refrigeration compressor systems. You are to discuss environmental and conservation issues at a major head office conference to decide the design brief for the new generation of the company's refrigerators.

Complete a full total life cycle analysis of the domestic refrigerator from the above point of view (Note: in such a conventional factory there is a high VOC emission from the painting processes, such a factory is also a major user of heat, electricity and water).

4. You are the European manager for a range of advanced and innovative electronic equipment in a competitive market. Your company is an operating division of a major multinational with extensive operations in Europe and the USA. There is a major trade meeting in Europe which your suppliers, competitors, distributors/agents and customers will attend. You have intended to use this occasion to start preliminary negotiations with appropriate distributors, joint venture partners and potential patent licensees for an innovative product with patent protection. You have to attend a main board meeting and your able, but young, marketing manager will have to attend in your place. You know that this person has not yet had a full briefing from the company law department on the problems of free trade legislation as they affect the practising manager.

You intend to brief this young manager on the key issues of free trade legislation as they might specifically affect a manager in this situation. Describe what topics you would cover, giving the reasons for your choice.

## FURTHER READING

*Guide-lines on Risk Issues* (1993) The Engineering Council (Appendix 3, Lessons from Past Disasters, Engineers and Risk Issues: Code of Professional Practice).

Clark, A.M. (1989) *Product Liability*, Sweet and Maxwell.

Hodkinson, K. (1987) *Protecting and Exploiting New Technology and Designs*, E & F.N. Spon, New York.

Phillips, J. and A. Firth (1990) *Introduction to Intellectual Property Law*, 2nd edition, Butterworths.

# FOUR

# HUMAN RESOURCE: UNDERSTANDING PEOPLE

## 4.1 IS AN ENGINEER A PERSON?

In this chapter we have to consider issues such as security, fear and love. There are two problems. We can have 2.3852 volts potential but how can we measure security? We have to accept that these personal issues, although the most important matters in our lives, can not be measured with the precision we have come to expect in the physical sciences. The second problem is in part dependent on this first problem, as the first principal of the physical sciences is that to understand, you first have to be able to measure, the more precisely the better. There is no universal theory of motivation and personality in the same way that electronics has quantum theory and a good understanding of how electrons behave. These sciences have not yet discovered the great unifying theories of chemistry and physics. There is no debate that electric current in a wire is a flow of electrons, but there are still many years of active debate ahead before these human sciences attain these levels of understandings. Hence, there is no universal acceptance of any theory, rather the comment you would expect of a science in development, that the only thing that two psychologists can agree on is that a third is wrong. Given all the ambiguity, what is presented is a pragmatic view which enables the practical engineering manager to make better decisions. For further insight and the detailed complexities, controversies and additional theories, references are given at the end of the chapter.

Is an engineer a person? This is, of course, not a sensible question to ask, but so often in industry, managers can talk about chemists, accountants, engineers as if they were like different types of computers. There is one, and only one, thing to remember in the management of human resources: human resources are people. People have skills for which the company employs them, but with these skills they bring their total self, hopes, ambitions, emotions, problems and personalities. If we fail to recognize and respect this, we fail as managers. All the complexities of human resource management come from the fact that people are people. We know ourselves and how complex we are, so we have no real problem in realizing that if we have feelings, then so will others. We also know that our friends each have a different make-up for which we like and respect them. The philosophy of this book is that long term successful management can only be built on total respect for the individual.

We can consider this situation as a mathematical function where maximization depends on a number of factors:

$$Ultimate\ Personal\ Performance = [Capability] * [Motivation]$$

If either the capability or the motivation are low, the outcome will be low and a vastly suboptimal performance of the individual.

Some books will advance the view that 'management by fear' is a realistic option. If you are managing a filling line, you can say to a person 'If you do not fill 2000 cases a day, you will lose your job.' It is suggested that with discretionary knowledge workers (creative scientists and engineers), it is not possible to say 'invent me a replacement for digital communications by the end of the month or you will be out'. Such people may not be 'driven', they require inspiration and leadership. This brings us to the key questions; 'What is motivation?' and 'How are people motivated?' All through this chapter, remember that you have an excellent experimental case study, yourself. Consider whether the models and issues presented are ones that you can relate to your own life experience. We do, however, need some working definition of motivation:

> Motivation is the collection of feelings and manners by which an individual selects personal behaviour to attain personal goals and by which the person may select these personal goals.

The key to successful management is to get to the position where the individual chooses goals that are in harmony with the organization's goals and adopts behaviour acceptable to both the individual and the organization (as well as society at large). Note that this is *not* about manipulation. Good management is not about *control* (as in George Orwell's *1984*) but *a facilitating process to liberate an individual's energy*, *creativity contribution and personal capacity*. It is about leadership rather than driving people. We shall confine ourselves to the two most often used theories of motivation, Herzberg's and Maslow's. It should be noted that in this section we shall consider the issues in relationship to the work experience. These motivational theories are also relevant to buyer behaviour and should be remembered when reading Chapter Five.

Taken from marketing theory, employment is to be seen as an *exchange* process. That is to say, the organization gains a full and total commitment but in return gives financial security and other rewards. It is a process where both parties should be fully satisfied. If not, then effective management has not taken place.

## 4.2 MASLOW

Table 4.1 shows Maslow's hierarchy of needs theory of motivation (Maslow, 1954). This is a pragmatic model which we can see relates to our experience of life. The theory rests on two simple but powerful concepts: that any individual's perception of motivators will change with circumstances and that there is a ranking order of motivators, such that higher order motivators will not come into play until later. We can think of this as a set of gates. If the lower order (first gates) are not open then the issues at the later gates are not relevant.

**Table 4.1**  Maslow's hierarchy of needs

| | |
|---|---|
| *Higher Needs* | Self-actualization |
| | Esteem |
| | Belonging |
| | Safety and security |
| *Lower Needs* | Physiological |

### 4.2.1  Physiological needs

If you have not had food or drink for 24 hours, it is likely that finding something to eat and drink will be your major concern. This motivator should have no place in the work place. In normal working conditions, staff should not be exposed to extreme conditions (for example, high or low temperatures). However, it should be remembered that in the construction and service industries, people will be subjected to extreme conditions, in particular in emergency conditions (for example, the restoration of power and tele-communications after a natural disaster such as a hurricane). The division chief engineer needs to be sensitive to the needs of such people in the field, or head office can be regarded as a bunch of 'fat cats' with no concern for those at the 'sharp end' in the field. The converse is true, if the chief engineer shows concern and sensitivity to the circumstances, mutual respect and commitment is achieved with high levels of motiva-tion, even sometimes under the most appalling conditions. It is the responsibility of the engineer to ensure that staff are not subjected to these conditions when it can be avoided.

### 4.2.2  Safety and security needs

In Chapter Two, Technology Development—creativity in a risk environment, the techni-cal issues of safety were considered. One key issue is repeated here: many accidents occur because people do not have fear. Fear is not a bad thing if it prevents people doing dangerous things. It is the responsibility of an engineer to ensure that staff are aware of hazards. This may create fear (insecurity) if people are not also well briefed that the danger is well understood and well contained (for example, regulations on radioactive sources or lasers). In the technical area, it often appears necessary to take staff through the fear barrier. People must respect the hazards of modern life and then, and only then, can they be given the knowledge and skills to understand how risks are managed. The end result of this process is that in the industries where the highest risks exist, such as chemical processing, people are safer at work than they are at home.

Outside the technical area, people can feel insecure if the job itself appears to be at risk (redundancy). Where technology or economic conditions force the need for some people to lose their jobs, skilled managers will ensure the period of agony is kept to a minimum. Outside this extreme condition, a given individual can feel insecure if they feel threatened at work. The most usual case is when a person is moved to a new job where new skills have to be acquired and new challenges have to be accepted. The skilled engineering manager will recognize this and ensure training before and on assumption of the new responsibili-ties, not six months later. Moreover, the employee in this position should feel supported.

During the transition period, it should be made clear that small errors will be made in developing the required new skills. The atmosphere needs to be open, with the manager and the employee both working for the development of total competence. This takes time, effort and understanding.

### 4.2.3 Belonging needs

People are social beings. Outside our work situation we belong to various social groups, our family, the darts team etc. When people come into work they do not lose their need for a sense of social belonging. Successful companies go to great lengths to gain a sense of corporate culture and a sense of belonging where people feel a sense of identity with their organization. It is the responsibility of top management to set the culture and the mission (Chapter Thirteen), but it is the responsibility of the operational manager to implement and to develop this at the departmental level.

In the 60s, great effort was devoted to work study and how to lay out production lines and work flows to gain the maximum efficiency. It is not suggested that these techniques are not of value, but that if they are applied without the realization that the place of work is also a social structure, then conflict may arise. Even the least qualified staff run complicated lives and face major challenges in their personal lives (they buy houses, bring up families etc.). Good organizations realize that all staff bring creativity and self-reliance into the work place, if they are allowed to. A manager's communications with employees should be two way, with the most difficult skill being not talking, but listening. All employees must feel involved. Some reactionary managers feel that this represents an abdication of management prerogative. The manager has the responsibility to decide, but it must be clear that all people who can contribute have been given the chance to do so. Not all contributions will figure in the final plan so contributors have two legitimate expectations; that their contribution has been reasonably considered, and that there is justification for the adoption of the alternative course of action. Open management is not management by consensus (in the sense that a vote is taken), but is one of willing acceptance of leadership, which depends on trust and mutual respect.

In constructing organizational structures, work flows, teams or even complete factories, care must be taken not only to recognize the need for people to belong, but to use this as a positive strength for the company to build on.

### 4.2.4 Esteem and recognition needs

Over and above the desire to belong, we wish to be recognized and respected. This is often a difficult area to discuss in the UK culture, where the thought of attention getting appears to be over the top. The problem is that in the past some people have read the books and gone through the motions without the sincerity that is needed. If someone makes a suggestion that helps, then the award presentation must be a real event where statements are honestly meant. If there is a difficult project that has been brought in on time, then the note from the managing director and the evening meal (with partners) on the company is not just going through the motions but sincere expression of corporate and personal (the line manager) thanks and appreciation.

There are special needs for technical staff, they not only need to belong to the company community but also to their professional community. The successful company will encourage participation and contributions to technical meetings run by professional and learned societies (IEE etc.). This is not only good publicity for the company, but is also a major source of recognition and esteem, not only at the meeting but, with the agreement to publish, the support of the company (often with significant support with art work, etc., from the marketing department) is seen within the firm as fitting reward for exceptional professional contributions to technical developments.

### 4.2.5 Self-actualization needs

This can appear a diffuse and complex concept. Professional people do not go through the pain and hard work of higher degrees and chartered status just to make money. People do these things because they feel a sense of total self-fulfilment. All the above conditions must be met before we can address this motivator. However, it is suggested in the creative environment of constructing the future now, that the self-actualization needs are essential to releasing the maximum performance of staff.

Thus the fully self-realized engineer will be able to extend his full professional capability in, perhaps, developing better ISDN (Integrated Signal Digital Network) systems and also feel in doing so that a significant contribution is being made to the quality of the society we live in.

### 4.3 HERZBERG

Table 4.2 shows the findings of Herzberg (1966). This classification was originally developed as a result of research into motivation with professional staff. These results are not in conflict with Maslow's theory discussed above.

We can consider this again as a circuit with gates. Motivators can be used to increase the commitment people give to their work and the personal value they draw from that work.

**Table 4.2**   Herzberg—Motivators and hygiene factors

| Motivators | Hygiene factors |
|---|---|
| Achievement | Company policy and administration |
| Recognition | Supervision |
| Work itself | Relationship with supervisor |
| Responsibility | Work conditions |
| Advancement | Salary |
| Growth | Relationship with peers |
| | Personal life |
| | Relationship with subordinates |
| | Status |
| | Security |

Hygiene factors can be seen as the negative gates and if these are open then dissatisfaction is the result. The term hygiene factor can be seen from the following example.

When we go to a five star hotel, enter the wash rooms and find it is clean and well decorated, we do not rush out to reception and ask to see the manager to thank him for the experience. However, if we went in and found the place dirty and there was no paper in the toilet, we might well wish to make a few comments and book into another hotel. A hygiene factor is one where we come to accept a standard (often these days a high standard) as the norm. We accept the norm and a negative deviation will produce a negative reaction. Again this theory, in many ways, not only extends to the work place, but to customer satisfaction in marketing (taken for granted quality) and operations (Just In Time delivery).

We can see this is in harmony with the Maslow theory if we consider the position of a professional in an averagely good company. Such a person will feel secure and, under Maslow's theory, issues such as recognition and achievement will be motivators, lower order factors having been satisfied.

Given this framework, it is no surprise to find that issues such as work conditions are satisfiers rather than motivators. The message is clear. We have to ensure that the satisfiers are satisfied and then we must concentrate on achieving positive motivation with the higher level motivators.

One factor needs to be discussed further. Even though this theory is not new, it is often considered that money is a motivator. Acceptance of this theory and the experimental evidence it is based upon, indicates this is *not* so. People expect to be well paid, that is to say that they expect to be paid the rate for the job. After that, money ceases to be a motivator. The implications of this for financial rewards are profound. Overtime is to be seen not as a motivator but simply as increased fair pay for extended effort. If we are to pay a bonus for special effort, then the theory suggests two factors, the special reward should be closely linked in time and, in an identifiable way, with the effort. Moreover, it is the recognition, rather than the money, which may well be the motivator. So rather than pay through the normal anonymous payroll, a special lunch presentation of a cheque may be a much more powerful motivator for the same expense to the company.

Many companies offer share incentive schemes. Given there is no direct physical link between the personal effort and the final reward, which will in any case be obtained long after any exceptional effort, it is difficult to view this as a simple financial incentive type motivator. That is not to say that it does not have its value, but it may well be associated more with the sense of belonging that share ownership will bring to the employee (sense of real participation in the company).

## 4.4 TEAM WORKING—BELBIN TYPES

Almost all major engineering developments will require a team effort for completion, so it is essential for all the engineers to understand the dynamics of team working. The mechanistic manager will think all he needs is a chemical engineer, a civil engineer, an instrument engineer, a chemist etc., to bring on stream a major new plant. However, we know from our personal life that people appear to adopt role types when they are placed in a group situation. When we go to the pool evening there will be the leader (who decides the order of play etc.) and the resource linker (who lays on the transport and the food, etc.). The essential needs of team building are that we have to not only ensure we have the right mix of professional skills, but also ensure that we have the right mix of team roles being filled. Factors that can influence the performance of teams and the performance of the individual in a team include the person's preferred team role, the person's personality, the person's technical knowledge and, of course, the roles, personality, and knowledge of the other team members. To balance all this needs skills from the senior managers and from the team leader. The management implications and consequences of this are developed further in Chapter Ten. The detailed characteristics of the roles, identified by Belbin in an investigation of effective teams, are described below.

## BELBIN TYPES

**Team worker**   Someone who supports members in their strengths (for example, builds on suggestions); underpins members in their shortcomings; improves communications between members and fosters team spirit generally.

**Shaper**   Someone who shapes the way in which team effort is applied; directs attention generally to the setting of objectives and priorities; seeks to impose some shape or pattern on group discussion and on the outcome of group activities.

**Plant**   Someone who advances new ideas and strategies with special attention to the major issues; looks for possible brakes in approach to the problems with which the group is confronted.

**Monitor evaluator**   Someone who analyses problems, evaluates ideas and suggestions so that the team is better placed to take balanced decisions.

**Resource investigator**   Someone who explores and reports on ideas, developments and resources outside the group; creates external contacts that may be useful to the team and conducts any subsequent negotiations.

**Completer—finisher**   Someone who ensures that the team is protected as far as possible from mistakes of both commission and omission; actively searches for aspects of work which need a more than usual degree of attention; maintains a sense of urgency within the team.

**Chairman**   Someone who controls the way in which a team moves towards the group objectives by making the best use of team resources; recognizes where the team strengths and weaknesses lie; ensures that the best use is made of each team member's potential.

**Team maker**   Someone who turns concepts and plans into practical working procedures; carries out agreed plans systematically and efficiently.

## 4.5 PERSONALITY

There is no neat, one line, definition of this, except to say that each individual has a personal emotional make-up and a personal view of the world. There are many theories, but we will focus on one which has currency in personnel selection and career development areas (most often in the USA multinationals). You may well find yourselves taking this (or some other) personality assessment in your job hunting. This concept of personality was developed by Isabel Briggs Myers (*Gifts Differing*, 1989). The basis of this is that she

**Table 4.3** Personality factors

| Extroversion | Introversion |
|:---:|:---:|
| **E** | **I** |
| Sensing | iNtuition |
| **S** | **N** |
| Thinking | Feeling |
| **T** | **F** |
| Judgement | Perception |
| **J** | **P** |

advanced the theory (on the basis of a vast amount of statistical work) that there were four key personality factors (Table 4.3).

In engineering terms, there is a favoured (ground state) for each person. The person may operate in the non-favoured excited state (to follow out electronic engineering analogy) but this is not the natural state and stress may result. The four factors are shown with their binary states. You can think of this as a 4 bit processor, so there are 16 possible states. This is shown in Fig. 4.1. About this time, you are thinking (as engineering personalities) 'So what?'

Consider the next diagram, this shows the personalities of a large number of finance and commerce students and science students. The light area of the diagram shows the area of preference for engineers, the dark area of preference for accountants. Accountants and engineers not only have differing professions, the chances are that they have differing

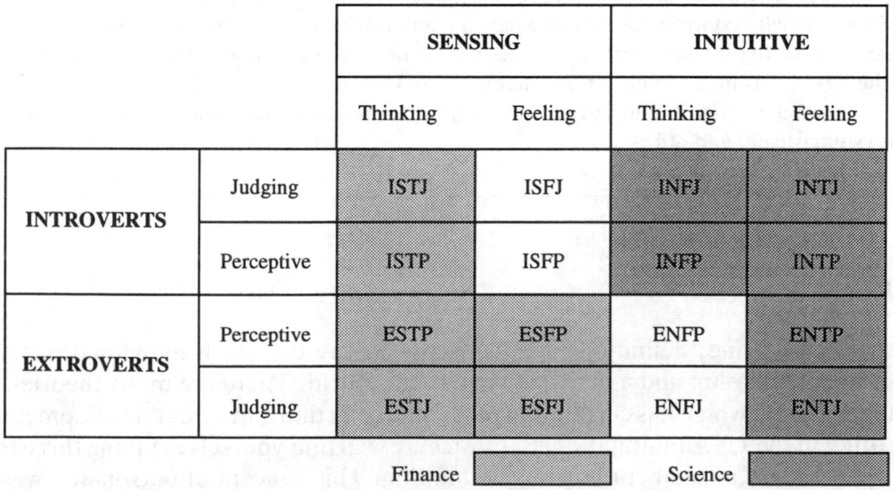

| | | SENSING | | INTUITIVE | |
|---|---|:---:|:---:|:---:|:---:|
| | | Thinking | Feeling | Thinking | Feeling |
| **INTROVERTS** | Judging | ISTJ | ISFJ | INFJ | INTJ |
| | Perceptive | ISTP | ISFP | INFP | INTP |
| **EXTROVERTS** | Perceptive | ESTP | ESFP | ENFP | ENTP |
| | Judging | ESTJ | ESFJ | ENFJ | ENTJ |

Finance ▭      Science ▭

**Figure 4.1** Personality type and career preference

personalities as well. Note of caution: we are talking preferences and inclinations. There will always be exceptions.

In a team, you will have people who have differing perceptions of the world and their place in it (this correlates with the Belbin indicators). Failure to understand this and to consider that rational processes always come into play will cause problems. It is critical to understand and appreciate that there is no right personality, a strength has corresponding weaknesses. In the management of people we need to build to people's strengths, so if we were looking for a marketing manager with a lot of customer contact, we would seek an extroverted personality. Another aspect of business policy is strategy formation and here we might well consider that the deep, insightful, thinking of the introverted personality was acceptable.

**Extroversion–Introversion (E–I)**  The extrovert lives in the 'real' world, is open, and expresses emotions with ease. Extroverts live in the world of people and things; they do not understand life unless they have experienced it. Their weakness is often seen to be their shallow and superficial thinking. The introvert lives in the world of concepts, ideas and understanding, they often do not express their emotions. Their weakness tends to be to be theoretical to the limit of impractibility. They can appear detached from the world but also can be extremely creative.

**Sensing–Intuitives (S–N)**  Sensing types live life for the moment, very dependant on their physical surroundings. Intuitives live life with a sense of inspiration, not very dependant on physical surroundings; they are concerned not so much with what is as what might be. Tend to be restless and inventive.

**Thinking–Feeling (T–F)**  Thinking people are concerned with logic, good at executive decisions, more often men than women.

Feeling people are concerned with sentiment, interested in people rather than things, more concerned with social aspects than executive decisions, more often women than men.

**Judging–Perceptive (J–P)**  Judging types are decisive and live according to plans, they are rational and gain satisfaction from completing things. Perceptive types are investigators rather than decisive. They take things as they come; 'What are plans?' More concerned with new experiences than completing things. Isabel Briggs Myers (1989) outlined the following effects of personality type in the work situation.

## EFFECT OF PERSONALITY AND PREFERENCES IN WORK SITUATIONS

| *Extroverts* | *Introverts* |
| --- | --- |
| Like variety and action. | Like quiet for concentration. |
| Tend to be faster, dislike complicated procedures. | Tend to be careful with details, dislike sweeping statements. |

| Extroverts | Introverts |
|---|---|
| Are often good at greeting people. | Have trouble remembering names and faces. |
| Are often impatient with long, slow jobs. | Tend not to mind working on one project for a long time uninterruptedly. |
| Are interested in the results of their job, in getting it done and in how other people do it. | Are interested in the idea behind their job. |
| Often do not mind the interruption of answering the telephone. | Dislike telephone intrusions and interruptions. |
| Often act quickly, sometimes without thinking. | Like to think a lot before they act, sometimes without acting. |
| Like to have people around. | Work contentedly alone. |
| Usually communicate freely. | Have problems communicating. |

| Thinking types | Feeling types |
|---|---|
| Do not show emotion readily and are often uncomfortable dealing with people's feelings. | Tend to be very aware of other people and their feelings. |
| May hurt people's feelings without knowing it. | Enjoy pleasing people, even in unimportant things. |
| Like analysis and putting things into logical order. Can get along without harmony. | Like harmony. Efficiency may be badly disturbed by office feuds. |
| Tend to decide impersonally, sometimes paying insufficient attention to people's wishes. | Often allow decisions be influenced by their own or other people's personal likes and wishes. |
| Need to be treated fairly. | Need occasional praise. |
| Are able to reprimand people or fire them when necessary. | Dislike telling people unpleasant things. |
| Are more analytically orientated, respond more easily to people's thoughts. | Are more people-orientated, respond more to people's values. |
| Tend to be firm-minded. | Tend to be sympathetic. |

| Sensing types | Intuitive types |
|---|---|
| Dislike new problems unless there are standard ways to solve them. | Like solving new problems. |
| Like an established way of doing things. | Dislike doing the same thing repeatedly. |
| Enjoy using skills already learned more than learning new ones. | Enjoy learning a new skill more than using it. |
| Work more steadily, with realistic ideas of how long it will take. | Work with bursts of energy powered by enthusiasm, with slack periods in between. |
| Usually reach a conclusion step by step. | Reach a conclusion quickly. |

| Sensing types | Intuitive types |
| --- | --- |
| Are patient with routine details. | Are impatient with routine details. |
| Are impatient when the details get complicated. | Are patient with complicated situations. |
| Are not often inspired, and rarely trust the inspiration when they are. | Follow their inspirations, good or bad. |
| Seldom make errors of fact. | Frequently make errors of fact. |
| Tend to be good at precise work. | Dislike taking time for precision. |

| Judging types | Perceptive types |
| --- | --- |
| Work best when they can plan their work and follow the plan. | Adapt well to changing situations. |
| Like to get things settled and finished. | Do not mind leaving things open for alterations. |
| May decide things too quickly. | May have trouble making decisions. |
| May dislike to interrupt the project they are on for a more urgent one. | May start too many projects and have difficulty in finishing them. |
| May not notice new things that need to be done. | May postpone unpleasant jobs. |
| Want only the essentials needed to begin their work. | Want to know all about a new job. |
| Tend to be satisfied once they reach a judgement on a thing, situation, or person. | Tend to be curious and welcome new light on a thing, situation, or person. |

## 4.6 PERSONAL CAPABILITY

Much is made in education of a parameter called 'intelligence'. However, it would appear that this does not correlate directly with what is needed to succeed in business. An alternative parameter has been advanced: capacity. This can be defined as:

> *The way in which a person patterns and orders their experience through life as the basis for making sense of the world and acting upon it.*

In working life we need some indication of the level at which a person is performing. In Chapter Eleven, we shall consider the process of measuring the size of a job (most often for estimating fair pay) by the process of job evaluation. However, the most simple and intuitive way to consider the size of a job, is to consider the time span of the job. A simple working definition of time span is:

> *The length of time it will take for marginal underperformance to be recognized.*

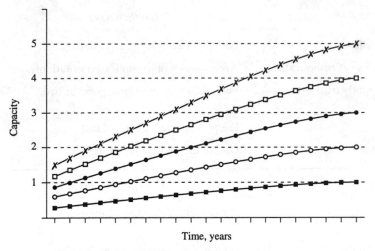

**Figure 4.2**  Schematic capacity growth

If we have a *small* job (in these terms), such as a word processing operator, under-performance will be evident in a matter of weeks. If a creative design engineer or a general manager is underperforming, however, it may take over a year for *marginal* under-performance to become apparent.

In considering these definitions, it is evident that personal capability will grow with time. This is our experience of the real world. As people grow older, they become able to accept bigger, more complex and demanding roles: their capability grows. Figure 4.2 shows this in a schematic way. Real life also tells us that the capacity of differing individuals is not the same. We have a family of capability growth curves which is not unlike the operating characteristics of an amplifier. This framework appears to be common sense and reflect our experience of people in the real world, but can such a framework give us any additional insights or is it just some handy description?

This framework, although simple, can be a potent aid to understanding people in their work situation. In a powerful and witty book *The Peter Principal* a general law of people in work was advanced: 'People rise to their level of incompetence' (L.J. Peter and R. Hull, 1969). This is just what we would expect from the curves in Fig. 4.2 (adapted from *Equitable Payment*, Elliott Jacques, 1970). When a person is promoted to a job demanding a higher level of capability than the person possesses, the person is quite simply unable to perform the role at that level and carries out the job at their actual, and lower, level of capability.

If a person is not matched to their capability level, then stress will result and a person faced with a job that is too big will show signs of strain. If this can be described as the job oversize effect, as engineers we would look for a possible reverse effect. Can a person be stressed by a job that is too small for their capability? The answer is 'yes', if there is no other outlet for this energy. However, a person need not find their real life challenge at work; local politics, the churches, professional societies etc., are run by able people who find that their work does not provide a sufficient challenge. Employers that do not provide a suitably sized challenge to their staff are under using their greatest asset, their people.

A person's capability can be degraded by external factors, such as ill-health or personal problems (bereavement, divorce etc.). Thus, a person who has appeared to be fully competent may find the job too big with the difficulty, for others in the work team, that the problem may have not been shared. When there is some down shift in a person's performance, the engineering manager will need to find out whether there is some hidden reason for the problem.

If we consider reporting relationships, we can quickly spot the problems. People's capability is banded. People are happy to accept direction from a person they perceive as of greater capability than themselves. There are two immediate issues. The senior manager will realize that the young rising star with a great potential capability will outgrow the immediate boss, if this person is of mature and modest ultimate capability potential. When their capabilities begin to match, conflict will start to occur. If we accept that capability is banded then we need to have people reporting to people of greater capability, yet there are not an infinite number of bands. The implication is that if we have too many levels of management, we will have more levels of management than capability bands. We will need to have some people of equal capacity in boss-subordinate relationships. The message is clear; if we wish strong management with acceptance of leadership and low levels of conflict, we require a structure with few levels of management, say no more than four or five from managing director to operation staff. The organization should be lean and mean.

In the above discussion, we have assumed that the growth in capability is a uniform process and that there is no discontinuity in the process. However, as an able engineer you will face an additional factor with your subordinate staff; there is a discontinuity in capability. This is the ability to think not just in terms of the concrete, but to also think abstractly. To consider it in terms of number theory, it is not too difficult to get people to consider the set of integers as 'one orange, two oranges', but some additional intellectual thought is needed to think in terms of 'half an orange' and to move into the set of fractions and decimals. Most people are well able to do this. However, if we consider numbers such as '$e$' and complex numbers, we have much more abstract concepts. An able engineer will be able to order and pattern his thoughts with ease, using such abstract concepts, but many people are not able to do so. The ability to think in both abstract as well as concrete terms represents a major discontinuity in our capability growth. The message is clearly that when presenting complex abstract engineering ideas to people on a level of capability that is unable to think in abstract terms, the theoretical concepts must be made concrete by the use of models or analogy.

## 4.7 ERGONOMICS

People not only have intellectual roles in the work place, they have physical activities. A badly designed office is as much a physical stress as a role demanding heavy physical labour. Poor seating, screens which may not be adjusted to reduce glare can all contribute to stress in the electronic office. The feel of a keyboard is important to the wordprocessing operator. Is it crisp and positive or soggy. The QWERTY keyboard was designed when the early mechanical typewriter was slow and a difficult keyboard layout slowed people down so they did not beat the limited mechanics. In this electronic age we have inherited a keyboard design which maximizes rather than minimizes work stress. In the design of any machine, work station or factory the physical needs of the operators need to be fully considered.

## 4.8 MANAGING PEOPLE–STRESS AND STRAIN–MOTIVATION

In physics, the characteristics of a wire under load can be investigated. Stress is no major problem if we do not exceed the yield point. Remove the stress and the wire returns to its normal length, elastic behaviour. The yield point will depend upon the material. However, pure copper wire, will show a lower yield point than steel wire. The situation with people is more complex in that there are many different forms of stress, as discussed above. The basic principal is the same: what is a challenge to one person may over stress another person, producing strain beyond that person's yield point. In considering personality, we have seen that what would be an opportunity and a challenge to the extrovert might be a threat and severe strain to an introvert. We should take care, both for the company and the individual, to select people for the roles they are fitted for.

If we have a steel wire, we can increase its ability to withstand stress by heat treatment (tempering) and we can improve people's ability to manage stress by appropriate training. The reverse is also true. If we expose a steel wire to adverse conditions, such as corrosion, we reduce the ability to withstand stress and lower the yield point. If we mismanage people, fail to take account of their needs, we can degrade their capability. Similarly, if we are designing an object apart from the devices to withstand stress, we may also design in such a way that we reduce the concentration of stress. Again, in our management systems, we can also design our systems to avoid high stress areas. We may not eliminate stress, that is part of life, but we can manage stress to prevent the strain taking people beyond their yield points.

To motivate people, for all its complexity, all we have to do is to remove the barriers and manage the stress factors, the circle of management intervention in Fig. 4.3. We can then provide the positive motivators that liberate the full potential of people to make their maximum contribution. In making this contribution, they will also gain self-fulfilment. In the succeeding chapters we build up more understanding of the nature of the firm and business and, having established the necessary understandings and context, we return to the management of people in Chapter Eleven.

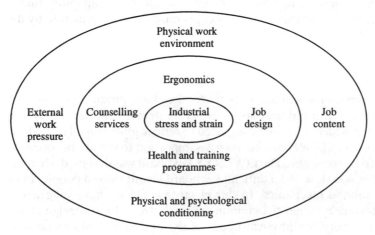

**Figure 4.3** Circle of management intervention

## REVIEW

In this chapter, the essential factor of business has been considered; customers, colleagues, subordinates and senior managers are all people and it is essential to remember that people are more complex than machines. Two theories of motivation were considered: Maslow's 'Hierarchy of Needs' and Herzberg's concepts of 'Hygiene Factors' and motivators. Personality is an important factor in our relationships with others and, using a framework developed by Isabel Briggs Myers, we noted that people could be considered under 16 personality types. This idea of personality and behaviour in teams was developed by Belbin into his structure of eight team roles.

People have capabilities and these develop with time. It was noted that if we had people reporting to people of equal or lesser capacity that stress might result. Stress could also result if people were given work that was either too demanding or too far below their capabilities. Job design and the correct organizational structure are required to minimize this problem. Physical stress can result from the poor design of the work environment. People are not able to leave their personal problems outside work and sources of personal stress, such as divorce, will be reflected into the work performance.

## KEY CONCEPTS AND TECHNIQUES

**Capacity**   People do not have the same capabilities, people's personal capacity grows with age and affects how they relate to others.

**Ergonomics**   If the physical layout of work stations etc. is not correct, people will suffer strain. Ergonomics is the science of ensuring that products and work situations are designed to best fit the people who have to use the product or work in a production line.

**Herzberg**   Theory by which some issues, such as pay, are hygiene factors and not positive motivators, but others, such as recognition, may be positive motivators.

**Hierarchy of needs**   Maslow's Hierarchy of needs: physiological, safety and security, belonging, esteem and self-actualization. Lower needs must be met before higher needs can be addressed.

**Motivation**   Motivation is the collection of feelings and manners by which an individual selects personal behaviour to attain personal goals and by which the person may select these personal goals.

**Personality**   The make-up of a person which will affect a person's perception of their work and their role and relationships with others.

## QUESTIONS

1. Mark Henderson is a 25 year old design engineer with four years' R and D experience. He has been made redundant and has applied for a job in a manufacturing company as an operator on a production line. As the production engineer for this department, would you see any problems with recruiting Mark Henderson?

2. As the works manager of a medium-sized engineering company, you have been

instructed to start an employee suggestion scheme with incentives. In the context of Herzberg theory, what incentives might you consider for good suggestions?

3. Consider yourself in the role of senior design engineer. You are to have a discussion with an able young design engineer who has been with your department for six months. He has just completed his first report which appears to have a possible invention for the company. There have been redundancies in another department in the company but you know that your group will be unaffected. In the context of Maslow's theory, what issues might you cover in your review discussion with this engineer? A key purpose of the meeting is to improve still further the motivation of this individual.

4. Consider the last lecture you attended. How could the physical layout of the facilities be improved?

5. You have been asked to assemble a project team of six to eight people to commission a new production unit. There are a large number of potential candidates in the company of varying ages and experience. What considerations would you take into account when assembling the group?

6. As the manager of a production unit, you have a problem with a member of production staff. This person has been with the company for eight years and, up until a few months ago, their performance was very good. However, in the last few months, absenteeism and late arrival has increased and even the work performance has deteriorated. The personnel department have asked you to interview the individual. What would you do before the interview, what would be the objectives in the interview, how would you go about this?

## FURTHER READING

Belbin, R. Meredith (1981) *Management Teams: Why they Succeed or Fail*, Heinemann.
Herzberg, F. (1966) *Work and the Nature of man*, Staples.
Hunt, L.J. (1986) *Managing People at Work: A Manager's Guide to Behaviour in Organisations*, 2nd edition, McGraw-Hill.
Jacques, E. (1970) *Equitable Payment*, Heinemann Educational Books.
Maslow, A. (1954) *Motivation and Personality*, Harper and Row.
Myers, I. Briggs and P.B. Myers (1989) *Gifts Differing*, Consulting Psychologists Press, Palo Alto.
Peter, L.J. and R. Hull (1969) *The Peter Principle*, Souvenir Press, London.

# MARKETING AND SALES

## 5.1 WHAT IS MARKETING?

*Marketing is the Management process which identifies, anticipates and supplies customer requirements efficiently and profitably.*
(UK Chartered Institute of Marketing definition)

*Marketing is the process of planning and executing the conception, pricing, promotion and distribution of ideas, goods and services to create exchanges that satisfy individual and organizational objectives.*
(American Marketing Association definition)

Marketing focuses the firm's attention towards the needs, wants, and benefits of the market place. It is concerned with satisfying the genuine needs and wants of specifically defined target markets by creating products or services that satisfy customer requirements. It involves, analysis, planning and control. The distinguishing feature of a marketing-orientated organization is the way in which it strives to provide customer satisfaction as a way of achieving its own business objectives. Marketing is dynamic and operational, requiring action as well as planning. It is both an important functional area of management and an overall business philosophy which recognizes that the identification, satisfaction and retention of customers is the key to prosperity. Marketing is concerned with supplying requirements profitably and therefore the marketing manager must also be concerned with the logistics of production and distribution operations.

Table 5.1 shows the various orientations of companies. The danger for the scientist, engineer or technologist is that they can love the product, but in business one must love the customer. The danger for the accountancy-dominated company is that it will become production or sales driven. This orientation can be seductive as it appears to pay off, but this is only in the short term, as the longer term relationships with the customer are sacrificed for short run profits. The danger with the traditional marketing-orientated company is that often the marketing staff do not have technical backgrounds. Thus, in many markets they do not understand the real properties of the product or understand the realities of production and design which affect pricing strategies through their effects on costs. For products with a substantive technical content, the best decisions can only be made by people who understand both the technologies and the marketing needs.

Figure 5.1 shows the structure of marketing. Marketing is seen as part of the primary value chain (Chapter Two). The control levers, the power-tools of marketing, are called

**Table 5.1**  Types of company

| Type of company | Attitude |
| --- | --- |
| Product driven | 'So it costs £1000; it is the best quality in the world.' 'If it is good enough, they will come to us and buy.' |
| Production driven | 'It will sell, no other firm can make it cheaper.' 'We will flood the market.' |
| Sales driven | 'If they will not buy, we will just get out there and sell it hard.' 'If you push hard enough it will sell.' |
| Marketing led | 'Profits come from customer satisfaction.' 'Customer is king.' |

the 'marketing mix', the 4Ps of marketing: Product, Price, Promotion (Marketing Communication), and Place (Distribution). To this is added the three additional Ps of the service extension to the marketing mix: People, Physical evidence, and Process. This mix, the 7Ps, is the engine of marketing, the power which needs adjusting and gearing to the various market conditions.

The market consists of the firm's customers, consumers and users. However, there are other key players in the market place, such as distributors and agents (the so-called 'channel intermediaries'), the communication channels (media, press, radio, TV etc.) and last, but by no means least, the firm's competitors. The competitive environment should not only include the firm's direct industry competitors but, using Porter's model of five competitive forces, the power of buyers and suppliers, and also the threats of new entrants and of substitute products. In Chapter Two, the analysis of competitive forces was covered in detail with the business environment (Political, Economic, Social and Technical—PEST). In this chapter, we develop the use of these business tools in the formulation of marketing plans.

Marketing is just like driving a car, the marketing mix is the engine and transmission. On the road, there is much activity to be observed, so with competition and the PEST environment. The marketing information system is the driver and all these external signals have to be collected, analysed, converted to useful information and decisions made and implemented.

To assist in the analysis of these signals, to understand what plans have to be constructed and what decisions have to be made there are a number of marketing concepts and theories, the marketing tools (segmentation, product life cycle, communication models etc.). The first is that of benefit.

## 5.2 BENEFITS

Benefit is one of the most powerful concepts of marketing. People do not buy products or services, they buy benefits. When considering marketing to a group of people, it is much more powerful to think of the product in terms of the benefits the customer needs and wants. When someone buys a packet of soap powder they do not buy it because they want soap powder. They require the benefit which comes from the use of soap powder. The first

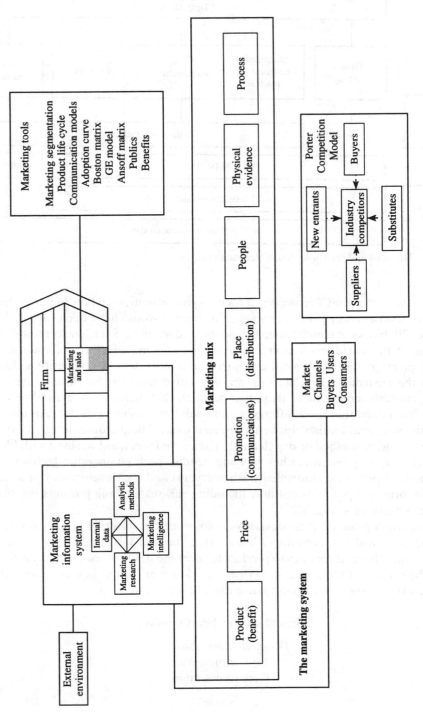

**Figure 5.1**    The marketing system

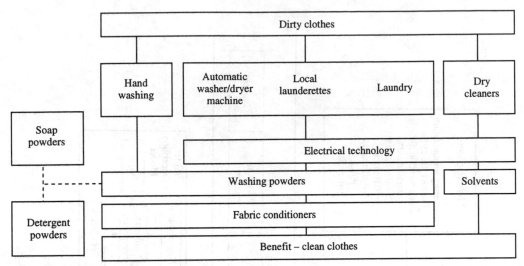

**Figure 5.2** Benefits and technologies in cleaning clothes

reaction to this is 'So what?' However, it focuses your attention on how to better meet the demands of the customer. Fifty years ago, this benefit would have been supplied by the purchase of 2lb blocks of laundry soap for use in hand washing. Such blocks are still used in large areas of the world, such as central Africa. For a manufacturer of soap powders, detergent powders based on synthetic surfactants represent a competitive threat by supplying the customer's benefits with an alternative product. So close is the average customer's benefit perception of these two products that many non-technical people will not even understand there is a difference, and will buy washing powder. An alternative way the customer could satisfy this benefit need is to send their clothes to a laundry where the clothes could be washed or dry cleaned. The move from hand washing with blocks of low quality soap to present clothes washing needed both engineering technology (the development of processor controlled washer/dryers) and the development of a range of advanced fabric care products not only including various washing powders but bleaches and fabric conditioners, Fig. 5.2.

In marketing a product, it is necessary to consider the differing benefit needs of the buyer, the user and the consumer. Very often the word customer is used with the implication that the customer buys a product to consume it. Of course, in many cases this is true, we buy a can of Coke and then drink it. However, in the general case, different people may be involved. We do not buy a can of cat food to eat it.

### Benefit sets for heart monitor

*Hospital Administration*
Low capital cost
Easy to maintain

*Nurse*
Easy to use
Light weight

*Patient*
Reliable
Comfortable

Benefits are not just physical but also involve feelings and psychological issues to the customer. Needs and wants are different. We need to drink to live and we can drink water to do this, so why do we drink tea and coffee? I need to drink and I want a cappuccino.

**Benefits for drinks**

*Water*
Satisfies thirst

*'Perrier Water'*
Satisfies thirst
Association with 'smart' lifestyle
Healthy
Taste
Carbonated
No chlorine

*Coke*
Satisfies thirst
Association with 'vibrant' lifestyle
Taste
Carbonated

*Champagne*
Satisfies thirst
Association with 'opulent' lifestyle
Taste
Sparkling
Sense of celebration
Sense of romance
Intoxicating

## 5.3 MARKET SEGMENTATION

The concepts of segmentation are common in the physical sciences. Numbers are integer, rational, irrational and unreal or complex $(a + ib)$. The chemical elements may be classified in a number of ways by their groups (lithium, sodium potassium, etc.) or by their nature, (metals and non-metals) or by their physical state (gas: argon; liquid: bromine, mercury; solid: carbon, gold).

Like the elements, all customers are not the same, markets are not homogeneous. Certain sections of a market differ from other sections. Markets are said to be segmented. Table 5.2 illustrates the situation with people who drink beer. In marketing beer, we might be interested to know if women and men differ in their drinking patterns. We might think there is a difference between young beer drinkers and old beer drinkers (for example, in consumption of heavy beers, such as stout, and lighter beers, such as lagers). We might be

**Table 5.2** Segmentation of beer drinkers

| Segment characteristics | | | | Segment number |
|---|---|---|---|---|
| **Men** | | | | |
| | *Light drinkers* | | | |
| | | *Young* | | |
| | | | Pub drinkers | 1 |
| | | | Home drinkers | 2 |
| | | *Old* | | |
| | | | Pub drinkers | 3 |
| | | | Home drinkers | 4 |
| | *Heavy drinkers* | | | |
| | | *Young* | | |
| | | | Pub drinkers | 5 |
| | | | Home drinkers | 6 |
| | | *Old* | | |
| | | | Pub drinkers | 7 |
| | | | Home drinkers | 8 |
| **Women** | | | | |
| | *Light drinkers* | | | |
| | | *Young* | | |
| | | | Pub drinkers | 9 |
| | | | Home drinkers | 10 |
| | | *Old* | | |
| | | | Pub drinkers | 11 |
| | | | Home drinkers | 12 |
| | *Heavy drinkers* | | | |
| | | *Young* | | |
| | | | Pub drinkers | 13 |
| | | | Home drinkers | 14 |
| | | *Old* | | |
| | | | Pub drinkers | 15 |
| | | | Home drinkers | 16 |

interested in who drinks frequently and those who drink little. In terms of advertising, we might want to know who drinks in pubs and who drinks at home, as we would want to run differing advertisements for the two groups. We now have a whole structure of 16 sub-segments. Why is this important? The type of advertising that will appeal to young male drinkers may well not be of interest to older male drinkers. Older drinkers may have a taste for different beers and, in fact, tend to drink heavier beers. The time and place of drinking will also differ between older and younger drinkers. So a major brewing company will brew distinctive beers for the two groups, the advertising media and message being separately targeted for the two market segments. These two groups will tend to drink in their own types of surroundings and so the distribution for the two groups will also have to be independently evaluated. For each segment that can be identified it will be necessary to construct the appropriate tailored marketing mix.

There are any number of possible segmentation variables, with beer a few possibilities have been considered (for example, segment 9: Women, light drinkers, young, drinking in pubs). So what segmentation variables should be considered in a given marketing situation? For segmentation to be meaningful, four conditions need to be met:

1. Customers in the segment should be as alike as possible.
2. Customers within the group should be different to customers outside the group.
3. It must be possible to reach the group in an effective way. We might be interested in contacting all people with their birthday on the 25th July. However, how would you reach these people without wasting 99.7 per cent of your effort on people who have their birthdays on the other dates? A feature of database use in the marketing area its application to target specific small groups by such techniques as direct mail. This area has been well developed by the marketing consultancies and the specialist trade magazines and it is possible to highly target segments in industrial and commercial markets. The availability of such lists has made it possible to target small but valuable markets that would have been impossible by conventional marketing. Little by little, the term Data Base Marketing is being used to describe this process.
4. The number of customers in the group must be valuable enough to make the construction of a specific marketing approach profitable. If we were publishing a new book on fibre optics, we might consider that translation into Japanese was profitable but possibly that Welsh was not. Again, technology has made this issue more approachable. With database marketing it was possible to identify small, valuable, market segments. This is, of course, very little use unless it is possible to tailor the products. Very specific benefit needs can be satisfied with modifications to very standard products. The average personal computer can be made very specific for particular requirements, with specialist software. It would not be profitable to make specific computers for organic chemists. However, with a few specialist packages their needs can be met. The required numbers to make this strategy profitable may not be high if the customer's benefit valuation is large enough and the costs of tailoring feasible.

**Possible segmentation variables**
**for people**
Country
Nationality
Language
Race
Sex
Age
Religion
Income
Occupation
Type of housing

Social class
Usage
Height
Weight
Education

**Possible segmentation variables for
industrial markets**
Size of company
Technology
Raw materials used
Location

Why segment markets? Let us consider the UK definition, 'Marketing is the management process which identifies, anticipates and supplies customer requirements efficiently and profitably'. At one level, the world of consumers is not the same: requirements in terms of needs, wants, benefits and ability to buy will differ. Thus, the firm may wish to offer different products to satisfy differing wants. Segmentation may not be restricted to the product related needs but also to distribution. One group of consumers may wish to buy in one way and another in a different way, so customers may be segmented on their choice of place of purchase. Segmentation may not only be restricted to purchase place but also to communications. For example, if we wish to sell personal computers to professional users, we might need to run special communications programmes to reach doctors and engineers (both may have a need for the same statistics package but read differing specialist magazines). It is therefore effective and efficient to segment the market so one may in turn efficiently and effectively target one's products and marketing plans.

## 5.4 PUBLICS AND DECISION-MAKING UNITS

The term 'public', introduced in Chapter Two, is used for any specific group who may have a beneficial or adverse effect on the firm. Earlier, we discussed the differing needs of buyers, users and consumers. There are other groups that could have a considerable effect on the firm's ability to market effectively. A car manufacturer will have many hundreds of distributors and garages who buy their cars and spares. In launching a new model, the car company will need to keep these people well informed and may well also want to give special incentives for the distributors to stock up early for the launch campaign. Firms who have traded shares on the stock exchange may be very concerned with the financial institutions. The owners of the company, the shareholders, are very concerned with the market valuation of their shares. When such a company is raising new capital it may well use all the skills of marketing communications to ensure that the firm has got its message across to the people that will determine the firm's market valuation. Consumer, conservation, environmental and even religious pressure groups may also have to be informed and persuaded.

In a simple purchase, for example, a Mars bar, a single person selects the product, pays for it and then consumes it, all in the space of five minutes. However, more complex influences can affect the purchase process. In the purchase of a child's bike, one parent may be concerned with how safe it is, another with how much it will cost, and the child with the style. The larger and more complex the purchase, the more likely several people will be influenced by the final decision. This is even more important in industrial sales. The secret of industrial selling is to know the target company well and know who are the influencers and the various considerations they might have. In industrial marketing, the nature of the buy is another indication of the likely number of people who may be involved in the decision. In a company that has 23 computer terminals of a given type, very few people may be involved when they need an additional one terminal (simple re-buy). If a new software package and a colour printer is needed, however, more people may be involved (the so-called modified re-buy). If the company is to install a new mainframe, with a new operating system with a Local Area Network (LAN), then many people will be involved in influencing the decision (complete new purchase).

## DECISION-MAKING UNIT
## DIESEL COMPANY CAR

*Managing Director*
'Green' company, so would be a demonstration of commitment to conservation to have a 'diesel only' car policy.

*Finance Director*
We have own diesel pump and storage for the transport fleet, fuel costs will be lower, there may be less abuse of the fuel card for petrol for the second family car. Maintenance costs will be lower and resale value will be higher.

*Fleet Manager*
Will I have any trouble with maintenance?

*Driver*
How noisy will it be? Will it smell? What will the acceleration be? What is the image?

*Partner*
Can I get the dogs in? How safe is it?

## 5.5 PRODUCT LIFE CYCLE

In Chapter Two, the preliminary introduction to product life cycle showed that products have periods of introduction, of growth, of maturity and decline. This life scale may be short for some fashion product (World Cup sweat shirt) or a very long period (railway steam engine). The product life cycle is different to the benefit life cycle. New products may enter the market providing the benefit in a new way and the old product may decline. This process in shown in Fig. 5.3. The needs for marketing and development are different at the various stages of the product life cycle.

In the introduction stage, the main consideration may be to inform people of the nature and availability of the new product. Later, the policy will change as competition grows and the new focus will be to persuade customers that the firm's product is more desirable than other market entry offerings. Pricing and distribution policy will also change during the

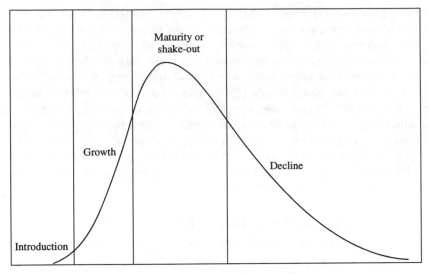

**Figure 5.3**   Product life cycle

development of the product through its life cycle; each stage of the product life cycle requiring a new combination of marketing mix optimization.

The cash needs are an important consideration. A firm introducing a new range of computer terminals will have cash flows, as shown in Fig. 5.4. The initial production will be on a modest scale, as the launch stock is made and the initial modest demand is satisfied. The production costs will be high as the full economy of scale will have not been achieved at this early stage. There is an additional effect known as the 'learning curve effect'; at the early stages of production the staff will not be experienced. They will make errors and there may be minor problems in the production systems. As the management and operational staff gain more experience, they become more efficient and the costs of production per unit will fall. The impact of learning curve effects in production operations is covered in Chapter Six.

As the rate of production increases, more stocks of components are required. The terminals will take time to build, as components are made up into sub-units such as memory boards. These will take time to assemble to finished units which will require time to test. After testing, the terminals will have to be packed and it may be some time before they are shipped to customers. The customers will usually have one month's credit after they are invoiced. The total cash demands of this process are considerable and in the introduction and growth phase large amounts of this money, called working capital, will be required. A key objective of production operations (Chapter Six) is to reduce this expensive demand for capital to a minimum.

At the maturity stage, production is no longer increasing and so there will be no demand for additional working capital. During the decline, the production levels will fall and there will be less need for working capital, stocks can be reduced and cash released to finance other projects. There is a potential trap, however, if the marketing is very bad and there is no demand for the old product at all, the stocks may have to be scrapped with a very heavy loss. Considerable coordination between marketing and production operations is needed

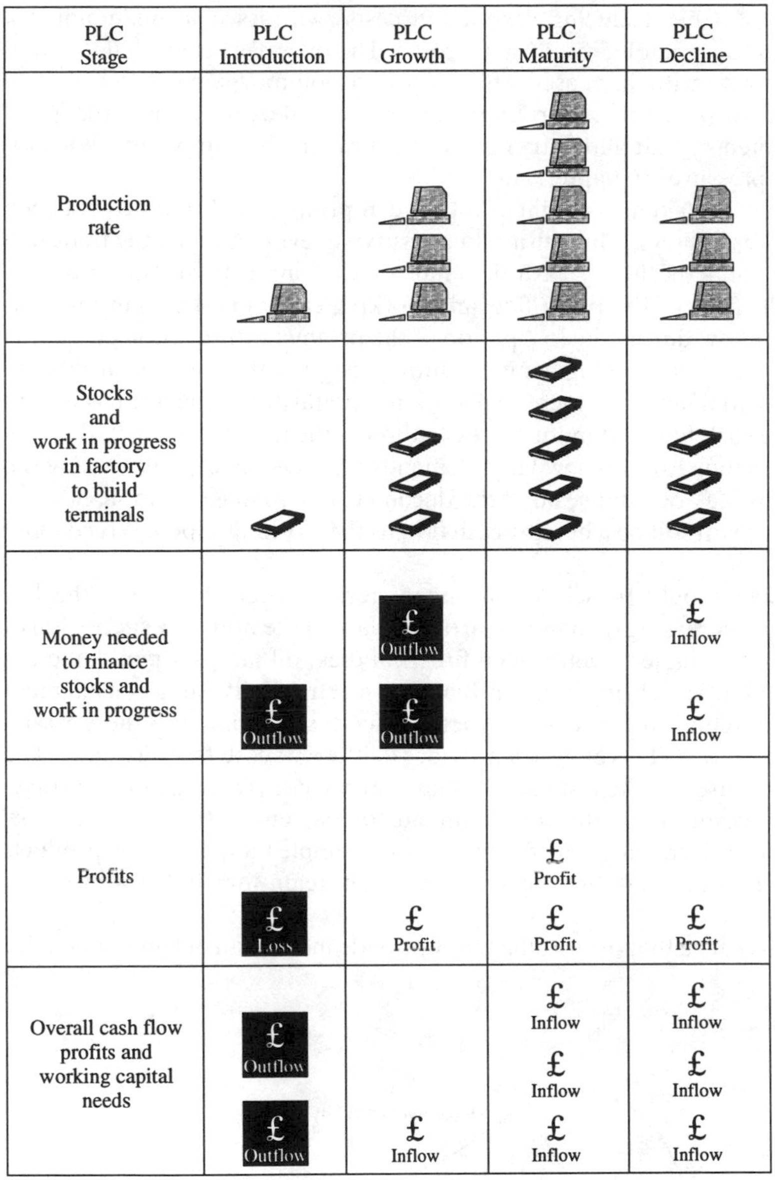

| PLC Stage | PLC Introduction | PLC Growth | PLC Maturity | PLC Decline |
|---|---|---|---|---|
| Production rate | | | | |
| Stocks and work in progress in factory to build terminals | | | | |
| Money needed to finance stocks and work in progress | £ Outflow | £ Outflow, £ Outflow | | £ Inflow, £ Inflow |
| Profits | £ Loss | £ Profit | £ Profit, £ Profit | £ Profit |
| Overall cash flow profits and working capital needs | £ Outflow, £ Outflow | £ Inflow | £ Inflow, £ Inflow, £ Inflow | £ Inflow, £ Inflow, £ Inflow |

**Figure 5.4**  Cash flows during product life cycle stages

to ensure that the necessary forecasts are used for future demands and reflected into appropriate production schedules and stock levels.

Profits in the introduction stage are often negative, with high production and marketing communication costs. There will often be high costs in setting up distribution through agents and the field service staff will need training. In the growth phase good profits should be made. As competition enters, although the volume may still grow in the early maturity stage, the competition will start to reduce the acceptable price to customers. Efficient production operations, further reducing production costs, will assist in maintaining a competitive position and acceptable, if reduced, profits. The overall effect is that the total profits may well level off, with increased efficiency and volume being matched with increasing price competition from other firms. During the decline period the price competitions may be intense. Exit and entry costs of the firm and its competitors will also shape the competitive pressures (Chapter Two).

In business, care must be taken to distinguish between profit (the difference between sales and costs) and the cash flows. Many firms do not survive, even though they trade at a profit. The problem is that the heavy cash demands of working capital can be underestimated. The overall effect of the profit flow and working capital is shown in Fig. 5.4. There will be a large outflow during the loss period of the product introduction due to the need for considerable sums of working capital. During the growth phase, if profits are good, it may be possible to finance the increased working capital out of the profits and still leave a modest positive cash flow. At maturity, even though the profits are level, the cash flow is much stronger as there are no new large demands for working capital. During the decline phase the profits may be falling, but if the decline is well managed (no stock write off and scrapping), there will still be a healthy cash flow as the working capital is recovered to finance new projects.

The product life cycle should be viewed in benefit terms. There has, over the last thousand years, been an increasing demand for artificial light in the home. A succession of products has provided this single benefit: open fires, candles, oil lamps, open flame gas lights, rare earth gas mantle lighting, carbon filament electric light, tungsten filament electric light, gas filled lights. In this case the benefit need is growing and there would appear to be no decline in this. Travel by sea provides a different case (see Fig. 5.5). The overall benefit need increased in the last century and continued increasing until air travel made a major impact, resulting in the total demand for passenger travel by sea now declining. Within this overall envelope of benefit demand a simple model of three products can be considered to have operated, first travel by sail, then steam ship and now by motor ships.

It is also necessary to realize that one product may provide more than one major benefit.

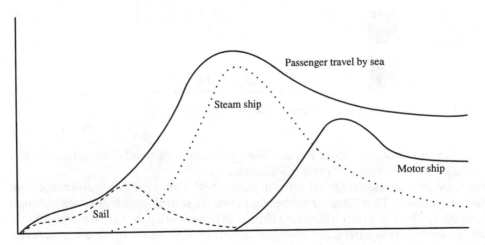

**Figure 5.5**  Benefit life cycle

A particular type of plastic did not have a very exciting mature product life cycle position. The compact disk was invented and provided an entirely new market for this material.

Although the basic concept of product life cycle is simple, the application requires considerable skill to judge the growth rates, ultimate market ceilings for various market segments and benefit needs. The competition between differing products for a given benefit need and the use of a single product to satisfy more than one benefit need ensures that the insight and skills of the engineer in marketing are fully utilized.

## 5.6 MARKETING MIX

This is the power-tool kit for the firm to manage its performance in the market place. It is essential to understand that no element of this marketing mix stands alone. Every element interacts with each other element. Considerable skill and understanding is required to maximize marketing and business performance.

This process is no different to that of maximizing the current through a simple inductive, capacitance, resistive circuit with varying frequency. Change any single element (frequency, capacity, inductance) and the others need to be adjusted for maximum outcome, maximum current at constant voltage.

Table 5.3 shows the marketing mix in more detail than Fig. 5.2. When most people are asked 'What is marketing?', they will first think of advertising. However, this is but one element of the communications mix. Possibly the single most important element of the mix is product. Regrettably, this is most often the least understood element by professional marketing people with no technical background. Much marketing was developed in the Fast Moving Consumer Goods (FMCG) markets. Often in this area little real product differentiation is possible and the differences between products can be so small as not to be perceptible to most people (two out of three people are really not able to taste the difference between Pepsi and Coke). In this area much effort is devoted to giving the customer other reasons to buy the product.

In the markets where scientists, engineers and technologists are most employed there are usually real differences in the product. A key lack of optimization has been the inability of the technically illiterate marketing person to understand the product; the reflection of the problem being the lack of marketing skills given to scientists, engineers, and technologists. It is not too difficult for the technical person to understand marketing, it is much more difficult for the marketing person to understand the technology as they often lack the mathematical and related basic knowledge and understanding that is necessary. For success it is vital that the technologist understands the marketing, as well as the technical issues, or ventures will fail and the technologist is out of job, not for a technical failure but a marketing failure.

### 5.6.1 Product marketing mix ('P' = Product)

Most standard text books will list such considerations as brand, packaging, quality, options, sizes, service, warranty, features, style, colour, flavour, odour, product mix width, product line depth and benefits. In this text, we will adopt a slightly more structured approach, given in Table 5.4.

Earlier in the chapter the concept of benefit was examined. In marketing it is not only necessary to have an idea of the benefits required and sought by a target group but also the

**Table 5.3**   The general marketing mix

1. *Product*
   - Benefit attributes
     - Intangible benefits
     - Tangible benefits
   - Feature attributes
   - Signal attributes
   - Product
     - Range
     - Depth
   - Packaging
2. *(Place) Distribution*
   - Distribution cover
   - Channel members
   - Physical distribution
     - Transport
     - Service
       - Inventory
       - Service cover
   - Nature of outlets
3. *(Promotion) Marketing communications*
   - Sales promotion
   - Advertising
     - Narrowcast
     - Broadcast
     - Publicity
   - Sales
     - Sales systems
     - Personal selling
   - Public relations
   - Packaging
4. *Price*
   - Allowances and discounts
   - Pricing gap
     - Costs
       - Fixed
       - Variable
     - Customer valuation
5. *People (service extension)*
   - Training
   - Customers
     - Customer involvement
     - Other customers
   - Appearance
   - Behaviour
6. *Process (service extension)*
   - Policy and procedure
   - Automation
   - Customer involvement
7. *Physical evidence*
   - Environment
   - Tangible clues
   - Facilitating goods

**Table 5.4** Framework of attribute analysis

Benefit attributes
  Intangible benefits
  Tangible benefits
Feature attributes
Signal attributes
Product
  Range
  Depth
Packaging

**Table 5.5** Partial schematic product line width and depth for Hewlett Packard

|  | Product line width | |
|---|---|---|
|  | *Measurement* | *Software* |
| *Product* | Spectrum analysers | Office systems |
| *Line* | Oscilloscopes | Science systems |
| *Depth* | Spectrophotometers | Computer aided design |

valuation put on these benefits. A common problem is to over-engineer the product in areas where there is little benefit valuation (for example, stainless steel bolts when plated would be acceptable and much cheaper) and not attend to areas where there may be high valuation (such as quality of design and finish of the case).

The value of a single product may be enhanced by the availability of related products. In consumer retailing an outlet may offer a small range in some depth (for example, specialist coffee and tea shop). This can be contrasted with, say, Tesco with a vast range in both width and depth. In technical areas the same concepts apply with both the very specialist software house with a select number of products and the full width and depth supplier such as Hewlett Packard, Table 5.5.

Attribute analysis (Table. 5.6) can enable more insight into the positioning of the product. A product can be considered as a bundle of attributes, which can be considered under the headings: intangible benefits attributes, tangible benefits attributes, feature attributes and signal attributes.

Table 5.7 shows some specific possible attributes for a performance car. The analysis of a product in this way can enable the product to be positioned in the market amongst the competitive products, this positioning being from a marketing, customer-orientated view. The identification of benefit gaps and subsequent positioning of products is a critical part of the innovative new product development process.

The structure of analysis depends on understanding the role of features which provide tangible benefits, which in turn impart the intangible benefits. In the marketing process the order is reversed to work back from the customer's desired intangible and tangible benefit

**Table 5.6**  Some detailed attribute analysis elements for a product

**Benefit attributes**
*Intangible benefits*
Feeling of increased sexual appeal, security, sense of belonging, excitement, sense of beauty, etc.
*Tangible benefits*
Transport, cleanliness, warmth, sound (music), communication, safety, satisfy thirst, satisfy hunger, light, speed, storage, protection etc.

**Feature attributes**
Size, quality, service, materials, texture, taste, odour, colour, sound, power, strength, concentration etc.

**Signal attributes**
Perfume, flavour, material (such as gold), style and design, colour, sound.

**Product**
*Range*
Number of different product lines.
*Depth*
Depth within each product line.

**Packaging**
Packing is included as it is so important but it can contribute to any of the attributes: intangible by branding, tangible such as ease of dispensing, features such as re-cyclable, signal by aesthetic design and product depth with single use packs, bulk packs, refill packs etc.

**Table 5.7**  Possible attribute analysis for a performance car

**Benefit attributes**
*Intangible benefits*
Excitement, feeling of sexual dominance, sense of belonging to an exclusive set or group, freedom, security etc.
*Tangible benefits*
Transport, speed, safety.

**Feature attributes**
Aerodynamic design, performance engine, low profile tyres, high acceleration etc.

**Signal attributes**
Trim, sporty paint (2 tone, stripes), styling, alloy wheels, sound, etc.

set to the other elements. It is useful to examine each element of this process in some detail:

**Benefits**   These are the benefits to the consumer from ownership, consumption or use of a product or service.

**Intangible**   The most important things in life are not tangible; love, compassion, security, freedom, self-confidence, empowerment are all important to people, but they cannot be measured with a signal analyser or a volt meter: 'we have 12.7 volts of security'. In the case of the young male executive, a key feature of company car ownership may be the feeling of self-importance. A car phone can give the feeling of empowerment to an executive in the sense that he is always in contact and does not have long periods out of contact and hence out of control. To a young female executive travelling alone it may also give a sense of security.

**Tangible**   They are physical benefits the user gains from the ownership or use of the product or service. In the case of the washing machine this will include, tangible, such as clean clothes, or intangible, such as the feeling of well-being from wearing clean clothes. In the case of car ownership, the tangible benefits may include transport, speed and safety.

**Features**   These are the things that the product is: all elements of product manufacture, composition, source and nature of ingredients, manufacturing processes, quality etc. With the executive car, this will include the power of the engine, the number of gears, in-car entertainment, electric windows. The sense of security will come from safety features such as anti-locking brakes.

**Signal attributes**   These are the properties or attributes of the product which convey the message that it has other attributes that the buyer or consumer considers desirable. In consumer products, perfume is often used as a signal attribute. When a room is cleaned, people know it is clean because it smells clean and fresh. This is an important and often neglected issue. In home entertainment one may be able to buy a low cost system for £200 or pay £500 for a better quality system. However, much of the additional features may well be in extra and more powerful chips. The basic product to look at is a black box. To signal the extra benefits the designer may put in lots of flashing lights, 5 channel graphic equalizer with LED outputs. Design style for appearance is important in all products but has a special and critical role where many of the functional features may not be apparent by simple inspection.

This process is very creative and can only be done for technical products, including products such as consumer electronics, by engineers who also have empathy (for the user's benefit needs) and the ability to translate these into the *right* features. This is the complete reverse of what happens in many poorly considered product launches where features are built in and the strategy is to hard sell to the consumers, without consideration as to whether these features *actually* address the target market's actual benefit need set. Traditional marketing staff are not good at this, as they often lack the creative inventive capability and are almost always deficient in the detailed technology which it is necessary to know to determine what features might be cost effectively included in a product or service. The need for benefits varies with groups of consumers and benefits are one way to

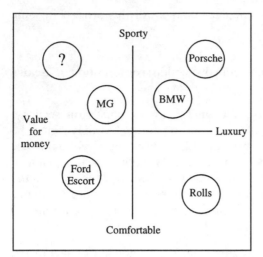

**Figure 5.6**   Schematic product map for cars

segment a market. To investigate the structure of a market in these terms it is often useful to produce a product map. Figure 5.6 shows a product map for cars. It is then possible to spot possible gaps in the market and investigate if there might be a market opportunity. In this case the need for a sporty, value for money, car is indicated.

A simple problem, which has as yet not been solved, is the perfect light source for domestic use. This problem is not trivial. Normal filament lights are about 98 per cent inefficient. A quick calculation shows that even if the efficiency of the source could be increased to just 50 per cent, the effect would be to reduce electricity demand in the UK by a few power stations. The benefit to the environment (global carbon dioxide induced warming, acid rain potential) would be considerable. Attempts have been made by manufacturers to miniaturize fluorescent fittings, but the early 90s' generation of such lights have not found acceptance with consumers. They may need existing light units to be adapted, other products are too big and/or heavy. To research a product area by attribute analysis first demands that an effective segmentation for the market has been completed. In the case of light bulbs, the benefit set for external lights may be different to those used inside the home.

**Attribute analysis for domestic light source**

**Market focus**

**Market segment: bedroom light**

This might appear to be quite a specific market segment but, even within this area, there is detailed structure segmentation within this broad segmentation. The needs of the young child's bedroom are different to the single female living alone, the married couple and the elderly. They will have some common benefit needs, but the relative importance may be different and some groups may not have certain benefit needs at all.

**Intangible benefits**    Cosiness, security and romanticism are all benefit needs by the above groups taken as a whole.

**Tangible benefits**    Electrical safety, long life, easy to fit, low cost of total ownership (cost of purchase and cost of electricity used during the bulb's life). Appropriate light intensity (note: standard dimmers will not work with fluorescent light fittings), colour, and steady flicker free light (note: the 50Hz flicker in some domestic fluorescent fittings can be disturbing in certain circumstances).

**Features**    Fit all standard domestic fittings without adaptors (both bayonet and screw fittings), long life (10 000 hours) and efficiency (70 per cent) with new technology. For security needs an indication of need to replace some reasonable time before failure of the bulb. Variable light intensity. Attractive shape, small/big sizes as required. Remote on/off control, variable colour.

The above might be a wish list. The structure of the analysis is to prompt features which might be attractive to consumers and then to challenge your engineering skills to find inventive solutions to these benefit needs. This is the divergent or creative way to use this tool. The tool is also of use in the evaluation of a product. If the ideal bulb had been invented for industrial use, the above scheme could then be used to measure how the industrial product might meet the benefit needs of the new consumer group. In industrial external lighting, yellow sodium lighting is fully acceptable and efficient but the yellow colour of this light source makes it unsuitable for domestic use.

The benefit needs identified in the above examples will have differing valuations. The young single woman will have a high benefit valuation on the security elements when compared with other user groups. In the marketing mix price, costs and benefit valuation are critical.

### 5.6.2  Price—marketing mix ('P' = Price)

The pricing mix is shown in Table 5.8. There are three key issues to consider before setting the pricing strategy:

1.  What are our cost structures? What is the minimum acceptable profitability? How does this translate into a minimum bound selling price?
2.  What is the sensitivity of our customers to selling prices? What is the upper bound of the customer's benefit valuation of the product? In the discussion of attribute analysis we discovered that differing user groups will often have differing benefit valuations.

**Table 5.8**    The pricing mix

---

          **Price**
Allowances and discounts
Pricing gap
     Costs
         Fixed
         Variable
     Customer valuation
Trade terms

---

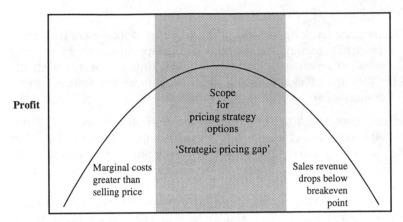

**Figure 5.7**   Strategic pricing gap

3. What are the firm's objectives:

> Maximum revenue?
> Maximum profit in the next year?
> Maximum profit over the product life cycle?
> Maximum market share?

It is not possible to maximize all these objects at the same time, since they conflict to some extent. If the wish is to increase market share this might well have to be at the expense of short run profit. However, this may yield the larger overall profit over several years.

The lower bound of the selling price is set by the level of minimum profitability. This is determined by the firm's cost structures. This issue is covered in more detail in Chapter Nine. As the price increases above this level, sales may drop a little, but profits increase. At the point of maximum short term profitability, the increasing unit profitability is just matched by the loss of sales volume. Profitability then drops to a point where the fixed costs are not covered. The region between these extremes is the region of scope for pricing strategy. One decision might be to price in the lower price region, if the objective is to capture market share. If maximum short run profitability is required then the need is to price in the middle of the region. The 'strategic pricing gap' is shown in Fig. 5.7. A complication in this analysis is the costing to use. If only the costs of production are covered, then the product may still be sold at a loss given heavy costs, such as marketing launch expenses, which do not vary directly with the number of units sold. Fixed and variable costs are covered in more depth in Chapter Nine.

This process of setting the bounds may appear to be simple. The difficulty is in estimating the customer's reactions to price changes. The rate of change of sales with increasing price is known as the elasticity of demand, Fig. 5.8. This topic is covered at length by economists. However, they do not have too much to contribute, as this curve in the real business situation is only partially governed by rational customer behaviour. It would not appear possible that sales could increase with price. However, if designer clothes and perfume are sold at too low a price, then the product is not seen as exclusive (a

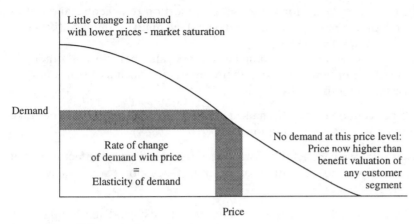

**Figure 5.8**   Effect of price on market demand

cheap product is not exclusive) and sales may fall. Rational decision behaviour would suggest that the difference between £9.90 to £9.95 and £9.95 and £10.00 would be the same. However, £10.00 is expensive, less than £10.00 (£9.99) is not. Such psychological factors can distort the curve from that predicted by economic considerations. Another cause of distortion of the curve is where some substitute product becomes cost attractive to customers. If switching costs are low then customers will buy the new better deal. Often, it may take time and money for customers to switch. If petrol was to cost 100 per cent more than Diesel it would not be possible overnight for motorists to change. In the longer term, however, as they replaced their cars, they could.

A recent development is customer awareness of the advantage of costing the *total cost of ownership* over the life of the product. Thus, a new car purchaser may investigate fuel economy, the cost of services, spares, re-sale value on disposal and insurance before selection of a new car. A computer purchaser may want to know the costs of items such as disks, software, and maintenance contracts before placing an order.

If the customer places a high valuation on the benefits then, of course, a higher price is accepted. Customer lack of knowledge can make customers less concerned about price, they may not be able to make quality comparisons or they may be unaware of substitutes. The growth of consumer journals (such as, 'Which') has done much to reduce this with consumer customers.

The list price is only one consideration. Many customers expect discounts for prompt payment (such as 2.5 per cent off for payment in 30 days). Other common areas where discounts may be given are: large orders (5 per cent off for orders in excess of 100 units, provision of a service (distributors who provide service will get lower prices than normal outlets), time discounts (resource levelling type activities, out of season holidays etc.) trade in allowances, and the most visual type in FMCG sector, promotional pricing (range of price incentives, 'Sales promotion' means that they are short term; 10 per cent off, 10 per cent extra free, free one year warranty, 0 per cent finance are all variations).

In segmenting the market, it was noted that differing segments might have differing benefit needs. Even where the benefit need is the same, however, the benefit valuation may not be the same. In fact, benefit valuation is one way to segment a market. Student and Senior Citizen Railcards are examples. Other types of differential pricing include physical form (large crystals of sugar for coffee snobs), location (city centre and out of town pricing), time (telephone pricing during the day and evening), and image (branded goods cost more—Coke versus Tesco Cola).

The scope for pricing strategy is vast. If some consumers value benefits and others do not, then make them add on options and price them separately (such as a sun roof on a car). Below some pricing methods are given:

**Mark up pricing**   25 per cent on costs. Often used in retail shops. Problem does not take into account competition or customer valuation.

**Target return pricing**   25 per cent ROI before tax. Often used in manufacturing but problems in cost allocation and allocation of capital. Does not take into account competition or customer valuation.

**Perceived value pricing**   Based on customer valuation, needs good marketing. Use minimum ROI concept as a cut off if valuation is such that business is not attractive (do not enter or get out).

**Going rate pricing**   Check with the competition. Not good marketing, always seek to see if competition may be better met with other elements of the marketing mix. You may have to compete on price but better quality, distribution or promotion may be preferable options. Price is not the only element of the marketing competition strategy.

**Psychological pricing and charm pricing**   £4.99 is less than £5.00!; charm pricing is the reverse. It can't be high fashion unless it costs £250 (perfumes, clothes, etc.).

**Remember effect of pricing on other parties and competition**   Your pricing is part of an interacting system so try to take account of potential responses. Price cuts to get volume may only give you a price war and a loss for all (typical high exit situation). Too high a price may well attract new competition into a 'soft' attractive market area.

All the above policies and methods need judgements on customer valuation and the firm's costs (the bounds of the Strategic Pricing Gap). In industrial markets, only engineers etc. may have the judgements needed for these inputs. This issue is critical to the implementation of the pricing strategy. The objective may be to gain market share by pricing on a very competitive basis to gain market share quickly (penetration pricing). However, if the benefit valuation of the customer is lower than the price set from the minimum acceptable margin on production costs, then the strategy collapses. This is a problem that many firms encounter when they enter a new and unknown market, for example, in exporting for the first time. If it is considered that there are several segments with differing valuations, then one possible strategy is to enter the market at the highest benefit valuation, a market skimming strategy. Once the highest level is saturated, the strategy is to lower the price to bring in the next highest level of segmented benefit valuation; this is a sequential skimming strategy. This strategy will often maximize the profits over the total product life cycle. Its danger is to attract competition in at the high profit levels. It is a very effective strategy when the firm is protected by patent and initial costs may be high as the firm experiences the learning curve effect. Of course, the danger with penetration pricing is that the competition may respond with corresponding price cuts, the resulting situation being low profits for all, with no competitive advantage for the firm.

In Table 5.8 two other aspects of pricing are shown; allowances and discounts and trade terms. For some products, such as cars, it is necessary to give a trade-in allowance (part exchange) for the old car. As part of the pricing strategy a loss may be made on the trade-in (the old car may be sold at a loss), but the loss is fully recovered and a profit made on the sale price of the new car. This factor is built into the price structure of the new car. If a major company is to buy 50 cars for its field representatives it will expect to get a volume discount. Many shops will offer a student discount to attract student business. In export business, the trade terms will often involve extended periods for payment and this increases the pressures on the firm's working capital. Even in the domestic market, customers may pay 'cash in hand' or pay by credit card. Many industrial sales will be made on the terms of '30 days from invoice'. To encourage prompt payment some industrial companies will invoice on the basis of '30 days or 2 per cent discount for payment in 10 days'. Industrial customers may demand more complex terms, such as stage payments during a long contract or require lease arrangements for large capital goods. Related to these terms are other parts of the sales agreement that may affect the actual cost of ownership for the customer, such as extended warranty with free on site repairs.

---

## PRICING MIX

### Advanced laser photocopier for the smaller office

**Costs**  The non-variable costs will include the design, development and initial marketing launch costs. The variable costs will include those of materials, components, packaging and distribution.

**Benefit valuation**  Every small office would like the high technology advantages of laser printing but what is the actual benefit valuation that these customers will put on such a product? If it is not higher than our total costs we do not have a potential new product in marketing terms.

**Allowances and discounts**  The small firm may well have an existing photocopier and a part exchange arrangement may be needed to encourage the customer to migrate to the newer advanced technology. A large chain of estate agents may have need for such machines at a number of their small branches and would expect a volume discount.

**Trade terms**  For many small firms the capital cost of the new machine may be too much for them to accept simple 30 day cash terms. It would be necessary to consider having alternative terms, such as lease or hire purchase.

---

### 5.6.3 Promotion—marketing ('P' = Communication)

Promotion as one of the 'Ps' of marketing is often confused with sales promotion, one of the elements of the communications mix. It is better to think of marketing communications rather than promotion.

The basic elements of the marketing communications mix are given in Table 5.9. Before getting into the glitz of advertising, one should consider the normal approach to management problems: first consider the mission and objectives. These business objectives will have some specific marketing objectives which will require marketing communications strategies and objectives for their attainment. How is this process achieved? How

**Table 5.9** Marketing mix promotion—marketing communication

| **Marketing communications** |
| --- |
| Sales promotion |
| Advertising |
| Narrowcast |
| Broadcast |
| Publicity |
| Sales |
| Sales systems |
| Personal selling |
| Packaging |
| Public relations |

do you form the firm's marketing communications objectives? The firm needs answers to some questions.

### 5.6.4 Marketing communications—objectives

**Why?** 'Because we did it last year' is very often the case. Some valid reasons are: to convey information, to alter perceptions and attitudes, to create desires, establish connections, to direct actions, to demonstrate, to generate enquiries, to provide reassurance, to remind or to give reasons for buying. These questions should have quantitative and time limited answers where appropriate: for example, 'generate fifty new sales enquiries in the first three months of the launch programme'.

**Who?** Earlier, in Chapter Two, we noted the need to communicate with publics (the various different groups of importance to the firm: customers, distributors etc.). Within any specific public, and/or organization within the public, there will also be a specific need to communicate with people with different interests. In the purchase of a new instrument, the engineer will want to know the performance and the accountants will want to know how much it will save and what leasing arrangements might be possible.

**Some additional concepts**   There are a number of models for the communication–action process. Use the model which appears most appropriate to your situation. A model for consumer purchase is given in Table 5.10 and for industrial marketing in Table 5.11.

All of these models have a common basis. We have to take people through three broad stages: *Cognitive*, *Affective* and then *Behaviour*.

In the case of the industrial situation, and where we consider the innovation adoption model, we have to take people through the stages: awareness, interest, evaluation, trial, adoption, and post purchase feelings. We can consider this for the purchase of a laser printer:

*Awareness*   Let people know laser printers exist and that we make them.

**Table 5.10**  Model for consumer marketing communications stages

| Stage | Activity |
| --- | --- |
| Unawareness | Advertising and image building to make consumers aware of the product and/or brand's existence. |
| Awareness | Advertising, demonstrations, sampling and other promotions to give the consumer understanding of the functional performance of the product and how to use. Show and tell type of advertising. |
| Comprehension | Advertising and promotion to build image, desire for the product and intention to purchase. Lifestyle association, personality endorsement and slice of life type of advertising. |
| Conviction | Reminder advertisements, posters close to shops, good point of sale material, good packaging. |
| Action | Good product performance, signal attributes to communicate and reinforce the brand image. |
| Post purchase feelings Repurchase | Reminder advertising sustaining the brand image. |

**Table 5.11**  Model for industrial marketing communications stages

| Stage | Activity |
| --- | --- |
| Unawareness | Advertising, promotion, exhibitions, direct mail, personal selling to make industrial customers aware of the product. |
| Interest | Presentations, personal selling to move simple awareness to outright interest. |
| Evaluation | Formal proposals, field trials, benchmark tests, personal selling and presentations to a wider range of customer's decision making unit. |
| Trial | Good product performance, signal attributes to communicate and reinforce the benefit message, personal selling and presentations with final tailored contract to close the sale. |
| Adoption | Critical time for long term relationship, good service, personal selling to ensure all is in order and make top up and extension sales. |
| Post purchase experience Repurchase | Reminder advertising sustaining the brand image. |

*Interest*  What will a laser printer do, what benefit will it give me?
*Evaluation*  How does that compare with other laser printers, how does that compare with my present printers?
*Trial*  Let me see what it will do in my situation.
*Adoption*  Let us buy one.

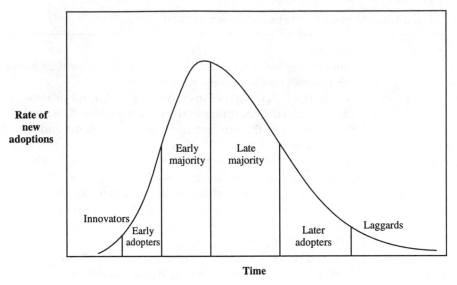

Rate of
new
adoptions

Innovators

Early
adopters

Early
majority

Late
majority

Later
adopters

Laggards

Time

**Figure 5.9**   The adoption of innovations model

*Post purchase feelings*   What do you mean, I should have ordered 2 Mb of extra memory for graphics!*?

In marketing communications the PLC concept is of use. The adoption of the innovations model concept (Fig. 5.9) tells us that the nature of buyers changes through the PLC. For a new product the innovators are key. How does this work? In the analytical instrument field an electronics company may have *red* site customers. These are forward-looking customers, looking for innovations to solve their problems (in the analytical instrument field this would include analytical research laboratories in universities and research associations). These customers develop the detailed analytical applications (sample preparation procedures etc.) exploiting the new potential of the invention and then publishing these advances in analytical methods (as opposed to instrument technology developments alone) in the academic and trade press. The early adopters then move in to use their work.

How does a company use this model and its prediction of customer response? Instrument companies have special *user groups* where these customers meet together with the instrument company staff. Very deep professional contacts are developed to ensure that these people know all about the new developments. Instrument companies use these groups as part of their total customer orientated development process. You may well make no money from these people (the profits are taken up with the special support costs). Why do they do it? A laboratory manager with no specific knowledge of a trace metal analysis needs to purchase a high sensitivity plasma emission spectrophotometer for the measurement of a whole range of trace metals in food products. Such managers know the trick, they know a man who does know all about plasma emission spectrophotometers: one of this group of innovators in the adoption curve.

This brings us to the two stage model of communication. One possible model is not to communicate directly with the target group, but rather target the opinion leaders (often the innovators) and then let them finish the communications task.

**What?**    The copy platform will be decided on the basis of the objective you wish to obtain on the specific group of people. Make the innovators aware of the new technology, say.

**Where?**    Advertising is a complex area. Leave the detail to the specialists. However, there are some key concepts so that you will run the show and not the agency! Advertising has to be effective and efficient. Let us consider what is effective communications. It is simply reaching 100 per cent of your target public with the expected level of impact (hence the need for good creative copy in consumer advertising). What is efficient communications? We need to reduce 'noise'. Good communications programme design starts from the customer's view and value set (not the firm's).

Now we come to the concepts of cover. How do we reach all our targets? We do not wish to waste our effort and money on communications to people outside the target public but we need good cover, so the effective and efficient channel and/or media is one where we hit the target, do not cover outside the target and also have the required impact.

This is why personal selling is the key communication process for high cost industrial goods. It has very accurate targeting, with a very specific message (tailored to each member of the buying unit or decision making unit in that specific target organization). Personal selling, unlike advertising, is interactive and two way.

**How?**    The creative platform, the particular way to get the message over, humour, a show and tell story for a new consumer product are both typical examples. Get the agency to do this for you in advertising. In personal selling where many engineers may be involved for industrial products, say an instrument demo, the sales engineer has to decide what is the most effective way to convince the specific customer of the benefits of your particular product.

**How much?**    How much should be spent on marketing communication each year? Try to do a zero budget exercise each year. What do we need to do, what do we need to do it? Other approaches, such as a percentage of sales or what the competition do, are not decisions, but substitutes for decisions. The basis should be to decide what the task is and then provide the resource to match the required objectives.

**Implementation, response and feedback**    The normal elements of the management control process: set objectives that can be measured, measure the actual performance against these objectives (deviation from set point) and then effect control actions to bring the business back onto the desired path. If the firm decides to run a stand at a trade show, how many people did the firm establish contact with? How many real new sales leads did the firm establish? Many organizations get into the position, 'What shall we do this year'? . . . 'Well, we always go there every year'. It is essential to ask the question: Why?

**A strategic note**    There are types of strategies one can operate. Focus on the consumer and *pull* the products through the line. The alternative is to promote into the agents and get each link in the distribution chain to promote down the chain, the so-called *push strategy*. For many consumer goods a Push–Pull strategy is adopted. TV advertising to the general public (pull) and strong personal selling to the major distributors (Tesco, Asda, Comet etc.), the push element of the strategy.

Having considered some of the broader issues, it is now appropriate to consider the various detailed elements of the promotions–marketing communications mix.

### 5.6.5 Marketing communications mix—advertising

Advertising is the marketing activity which is frequently confused with the complete activity of marketing. There are four elements in the process, the advertisers, the agencies, the media and the target publics, Fig. 5.10. Earlier, we discussed communication objectives, advertising is one of the mechanisms of meeting those objectives.

**The advertisers**  The great bed-rock of advertising from the 50s through to the 70s were the manufacturers of Fast Moving Consumer Goods (FMCG – soaps, toothpaste, foods etc.). In the 70s, a trend developed that accelerated in the 80s for other major advertisers to appear. The major retail chains started to produce and promote their own identity (for example, Tesco, Sainsbury, Asda), reflecting the concentration of power in these organizations. The major services also have become major advertisers, in the USA, AT&T, and in the UK, BT, have become major media advertising spenders. Again, in the service sector, financial services (banks and building societies) have become important. At first, some of this may appear remote to scientists, engineers and technologists. However, it is they that create the new products: microwave meals, automatic telling machines at banks, laser check-outs and associated electronic data interchange etc.

**The agencies**  The function of the agency is to advise the client advertiser in the formulation of appropriate objectives within the advertiser's overall business plan and marketing strategy. The agency then has the specialist capabilities to conduct the research, write the copy, buy the media, produce the films etc. Agencies range from the international full service agency that can mount a multimedia campaign on a global basis,

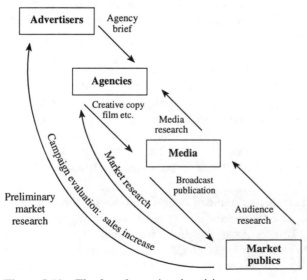

**Figure 5.10**  The four forces in advertising

through national agencies to specialist agencies who concentrate on very specific skills, such as film production or media buying.

**The media**    In reaching publics it is useful to divide the media into two groups, *broadcast media* which reach many (sometimes most) people, and *narrow cast* media that reach rather fewer people in overall numbers, but form a high proportion of some specialist interest group (such as bi-monthly journal of the Institution of Electrical Engineers). A simplified structure of media is given in Table 5.12.

*Broadcast media*    Radio, television, the national, daily, weekly and monthly press are all key broadcast media. TV has the power of colour, sound and presence in the home and rightly is a key channel. However, there is no lasting presence and colour magazines can

**Table 5.12**    A simple structure of advertising media

**Broadcast media**
*Papers*
  National
    Daily
    Weekly
  Local
    Daily
    Weekly
*Magazines*
  Weekly
  Monthly
*Radio*
  National
  Local
*TV*
  National
  Local
*Cinema*
*Posters*
*Electronic*

**Narrow cast media**
*Specialist magazines*
  Weekly
  Monthly
*Mail*
  Post
  Fax and electronic
*Audio Tape*
*Videotape*
*Posters in special location*
*Telephone*

provide an alternative or a reminder as part of a coordinated campaign. Posters can be a good reminder as people travel to the point of purchase (look at the posters on the major routes to hypermarkets).

In the UK, the national daily press has a cover that is not matched in many other countries. In international marketing it is important to understand the local characteristics of the media, which can be different to the UK, hence the value in the use of agencies that have the required specialized knowledge.

*Narrow cast media*   This is an area of great concern to industrial and commercial (as opposed to consumer) marketing. Here one may be interested in reaching say 50 000 medical practicioners, 10 000 analytical chemists or 25 000 electronic engineers. The *Sun* does not represent an effective mechanism in either cover (not all electronic engineers read the *Sun*) or efficient channel (for every target engineer one may also reach 1000 other readers that the advertiser is not interested in).

So, there is a vast range of specialist media, from *Navy News* to *Chemistry in Britain*, for almost all possible interest groups. Specialist database mailing lists can make it possible to target analytical chemists working in the health service and private hospitals, for example.

**Publicity**   Publicity can be defined as *free* advertising. That is to say, media cover that has not had to be paid for. Publicity does cost money, the preparation of press releases etc. does require resources. Editorial cover for a new technical development can be very useful additional communication. Features on radio and television on current affairs programmes can also provide exposure that might either not be possible by any other communication mechanism or vastly expensive.

Exhibitions can conveniently be covered under this heading, as publicity opportunities are frequently one of the major reasons for mounting such an event at a trade show. Trade exhibitions can be the largest single media in some industrial marketing budgets and great care needs to be taken when deciding if this is the most appropriate way to spend such large sums of money. A modest stand for a week at an international exhibition can easily cost £50 000 in total expenses (stand, agency costs, printing of literature, staff time, travel and hotel expenses etc.). Attendance at an exhibition should form part of a coordinated marketing communications strategy, not just an annual date to be covered.

**Sales promotion**   Sales promotion is the specific shorter term elements in the strategic marketing plan. Typical in the FMCG sector will be money off coupons or special offers. Competitions can be used not only for consumer goods but for industrial goods. Sponsorship can be another way of bringing the product to the target public's attention. Critical in the consumer goods area can be Point of Sale (POS) material, with eye catching displays and presentation of products from food to consumer electronics.

**Packaging**   Packaging is included because, in many areas, the product has to sell off the shelf and attractive packaging is an essential part of the marketing communications mix in this context.

**Public relations**   Public relations skills can be useful for events (opening of a new laboratory or factory) or in the professional presentation of a firm's position to specialist small publics. Given the often small number of key people in specialist industrial publics

**Table 5.13**   Stages in personal selling process

1. Research to identify targets and assemble information.
2. Broad strategy developed.
3. Relationship building, listening!
4. Presentation: show and tell.
5. Meeting objections.
6. Closing the sale.
7. After sale follow up.

and the need for firms to establish good close working relationships, the rise of the hospitality industry at major sporting and other events is not a major surprise.

**Personal selling**   This is a much neglected area of marketing as it is of little application in the marketing of FMCG goods, but it is of vast importance in the selling of major industrial products. Major commercial purchases, such as a new communications system, are more complicated than the consumer decision to purchase a bar of chocolate. Personal selling allows the firm to present its product in the most appropriate way to the target account. A number of stages can be identified, as shown in Table 5.13.

The first and critical step is the pre-call research, from internal (past visit reports etc.) and external (press, on line computer services, annual reports etc.) sources. The key issue is to build up a picture of the pattern of benefit needs and benefit valuations in the target organization. The objective is to formulate a package, a proposition whereby the firm's products can be offered in the most attractive way to meet the target customer's needs. To further identify these benefit needs and valuations and to identify the members of the Decision Making Unit (DMU), the sales person (often, for technical products, a sales engineer or applications scientist) must establish the personal relationships to allow the communication that will be necessary.

Having identified the customer's needs, the salesperson must then formulate the offer that appears most appropriate and present it. At this stage will come one of the most sensitive stages of the interaction, the handling of 'objections' (such as 'the training requirements look very high'). Here it is necessary to come forward with positive, honest, responses to the issues and then to close the sale.

This is not the end of personal selling; in the long term it is the beginning of an extended relationship between the two organizations, the establishment of true value chain links. So follow-up on delivery, installation problems, training, service or supplies of consumables are all important, as the foundation for future major sales.

**Sales systems**   In many organizations, the selling–buying process is an on-going process, say between the supplier of components and a computer manufacturer. The salesperson will make sales calls to maintain relationships and develop new business opportunities. Recent developments in manufacturing technologies and systems, such as Just In Time (JIT), require very effective and intimate communications between the customer and the firm. In the traditional company this can be represented by the well-trained sales correspondent who will accept and progress new orders and keep customers informed on a day-by-day basis. However, with increasing efficiency and speed of response demanded, there is an increasing move to Electronic Data Interchange (EDI). Here the customer's Materials Resource Planning (MRP) system will directly communicate the requirements to the supplier's order intake computer system, in effect, the process of order intake having now become a real-time communication system between the two value chains.

---

## COMMUNICATIONS MIX

### High technology laser printers
### for the smaller office

**Sales promotion**   Free stock of toner and paper for the first three months of introduction.

**Advertising**
**Broadcast**   Will be very limited for this type of product, just possible for a large company to have some limited daily press advertising or TV around the *Money Programme*. The most probable decision in this case might be to do no broadcast advertising.

**Narrow cast**   This will be the key advertising media with advertisements in the highly focused magazines read by the people who run small offices, so publications aimed at solicitors, accountants, estate agents might be selected.

In this type of market a focused mailshot might also be an option if there is economic access to good mailing lists. A common problem is that unless great care is taken to keep such lists up to date they quickly become of little value with many misdirected mailings. Response rates are often very low and, in a case such as this, may be down to around 1–2 per cent.

**Publicity**   The firm would hold some launch event, possibly to link with an exhibition such as 'Office World'. At this time, the company might loan equipment to specialist people to test drive to get reports in office magazines read by office mangers. This in itself may generate new sales leads but the re-prints can be used to give additional weight in personal selling. There are other options for publicity such as sponsoring some event or donating equipment to a charity.

### SALES

**Sales systems**   This is the normal customer orders, customer gets goods, customer is invoiced and customer pays cycle. There should be no special requirements in this case.

**Personal selling**   This might be the most important technique. If the firm has a wide network of sales staff and/or agents they could be specially trained on the advantages of the new machine, and then go out into the field with demonstration machines. An alternative adopted by some companies is to maintain a few demonstration centres where customers can come in for demonstrations and later for master operator training.

In personal selling an important element is that the salesperson sets out to solve the customer's problems, so sales engineers need to have some understanding of the nature of the customer's operations and needs in order to be effective.

For major customers, where a sale might represent a fair number of machines to a network of small offices, a major sales presentation and demonstration at the customer's head office or in the company sales centre would be appropriate.

**Public relations**   Not likely to be of great importance in this area. It would be key if the company had a major safety problem (say with defective laser components) and had to have a general recall on the product. Public relations and press briefings would be important to limit the damage and keep the public informed.

### 5.6.6 Marketing mix—('P' = Place = Distribution)

Distribution is about *channels* and *physical distribution*. It is about making the product or service available to the customer in the right way, in the right place and at the right time in an effective and efficient manner. Table 5.14 gives an overview of the framework.

### 5.7 MARKETING DISTRIBUTION CHANNEL MEMBERS

Figure 5.11 shows the role of marketing channels in the specific case of a manufacturer of car batteries. Although the ultimate user is the car driver, there are different ways in which the driver can come into possession of a battery. For the presence of a channel member in the distribution system, the channel link must add value by performing some function or service.

**Table 5.14**   The marketing mix place
(distribution) structure

**(Place) Distribution**
Distribution cover
Channel members
Physical distribution
Transport
Service
Inventory
Service cover
Nature of outlets

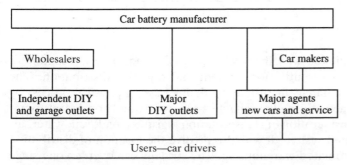

**Figure 5.11**   Some channel links in car batteries

### 5.7.1 Nature of channel outlets

Why have retailers? It is physically possible for a food company to have a baked bean shop, but most consumers want an assortment of goods. So, the retailer performs two added value functions; he breaks bulk and also provides a full assortment of the goods desired by the customer. This function may be performed in two stages. The manufacturer may send a container load to the wholesaler, who will break into individual cases which the retailer will break into individual packs for the consumer customer. Both will be providing the added value service of breaking bulk and holding a wider goods assortment than that provided by a single manufacturer.

Some large retail chains have integrated backwards (Chapter Thirteen considers strategic integration options, backwards, forwards and horizontal integration). The mail order company is another variation where the point of purchase is not at the end of the distribution system. A specialist manufacturer can use this form of distribution to supply direct to a modest and scattered market.

At the most simple level two key issues are involved in deciding the nature of the outlet:

- Image (up market, down market, lifestyle etc.).
- Added value service.

The added value service may often link to product life cycle. In the earlier stages, more added value customer service may be required. It is essential that the additional costs and margin demanded by the channel intermediary provides the customer with a perceived added value benefit. It is the customer's valuation, not the firm's, which is the more important.

---

### Micro-groove records

In the 60s Hi-Fi was new (stereo records were only obtainable from specialist outlets or to order!). A company called Imhof had a Hi-Fi sales room, a whole floor was devoted to listening rooms and a small army of sales people who were able to advise. When the student grant was £350, a good record deck, amplifier and speakers was about £600 (with valves!) and a good quality tape deck was £500. Now you can buy a better system from a discount warehouse for £300, but with much less service, as at this stage of the product life cycle customers no longer require it, and, more importantly, are not prepared to pay for a service which is of no great value to them now.

---

### 5.7.2 Physical distribution

In industrial marketing this is linked with the sales function. Good, timely reception of orders, and their processing, is essential for efficient and effective distribution. The process of physical distribution management may be defined as the physical process by which the product or service is actually made available when, where and how the customer needs it. Much of this is the consideration of transportation logistics (road, rail, water, air etc.). However, in the integrated system, it will also involve the location of distribution centres and the logistics of automated warehousing. The strategy can even go one stage further, to a decision as to the size and location of manufacturing facilities. 'How many, where?' 'One big factory for all Europe, with economy of scale in manufacture but high distribution costs, perhaps, or shall we have a number of smaller factories with higher manufacturing costs and lower distribution and service costs?' New technologies in information can change economics, to move information (money, music, words, computer programs, pictures etc.) you only need a few electrons or photons. Consider the number of services that can be fed down one optical link.

In the service industries, there are still distribution issues. 'What type of network provision do we need (telecommunications, water, gas electricity)?' 'For what hours of the day do we need to provide the service? Office hours only or 24 hours a day?'

The elements of the marketing mix interact. A problem that is common in service industries is the uneven demand for service. The telephone network is at full capacity in the day and almost unused in the middle of the night. A common feature in service marketing and distribution is to price so as to encourage use when the service is lightly used and to market skim (charge higher prices) when the service is most in demand. This may well be a more effective strategy than just providing a network for full demand which is under-used for 80 per cent of the time.

A critical area is service levels, Figs 5.12 and 5.13. This is an area of classical operations research with issues such as economic lot size and inventory levels to be considered.

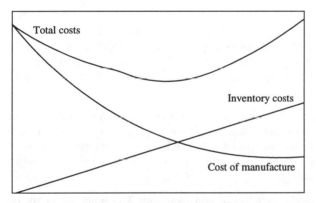

**Figure 5.12**    Cost of supply as a function of 'set up' and storage costs

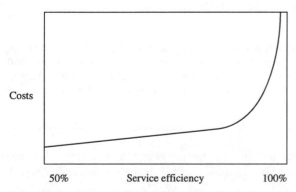

**Figure 5.13**    Increasing cost of service, classical model

However, with EDI and JIT, new attitudes have been necessary in regard to the classical model, which has underlying assumptions of set-up times and costs etc. Linear programming can assist with minimizing transport costs. Mathematical modelling, such as queuing theory can all assist. These mathematical approaches are considered in more detail in Chapter Six.

A strategic marketing issue is the extent of cover: geographic (UK or Europe etc.?), location (city centre or out of town?), time (24 hours a day? This question is often important for services; for example, the rapid acceptance of automatic telling machines, 24 hours a day money) or possibly segmentation type issues (upmarket areas and/or downmarket areas?).

---

## DISTRIBUTION ISSUES

### New range of microwave ovens

**Channel members**   For the large outlets such as the electricity boards the firm could supply direct to the retail outlets. For the smaller independent retailers there would be a need to supply via wholesalers.

**Nature of outlets**   High street and local electrical retail outlets, department stores. With many units fitted, there would also be a need to distribute through fitted kitchen contractors. With the DIY market in this area, the large DIY supercentres might also be a possibility. With the food preparation use, food outlets such as frozen food centres or major food supercentres would also be attractive.

**Physical distribution transport**   For the large volumes needed for such consumer goods, and the modest margins and the high transport costs, good fleet management and appropriate selection of distribution centres would be essential. Given the special skills needed to run a transport fleet some firms prefer to concentrate on their core business (electronics) and contract out the distribution specialist.

**Service inventory**   For consumer goods this is a major consideration. Too much cover means that very high storage and working capital costs will be involved. Consumers in this area are not likely to wait weeks and so if you have stock out situations it is likely to involve lost sales. Accurate sales forecasts will be essential with stock building for peak demand times, such as Christmas.

**Service cover**   With the above range of outlets, good physical cover of the UK should be possible. Field service cover: with such units now very reliable there is a problem in that although not many units will fail, they will still need service. The cost of scattered service would be very high. Again, a major electronics company might decide to appoint local service agents to avoid heavy costs and fragmentation of management effort.

---

The engineer has an increasing role to play in the provision of services. Financial services are an information rich, technology intensive, sector of the service industries.

## DISTRIBUTION ISSUES IN SERVICE INDUSTRIES

### Personal banking
### (Focus on cash withdrawing)

**Channel members**    Most banks and building societies provide the majority of their service to their customers direct. However, for extra cover, other channel members may be used. For the holiday traveller, travel agents, hotels and foreign banks may in effect act as agents. In terms of Electronic Funds Transfer and home banking, the telecommunications network providers may also be considered as channel members. Without their involvement it is not possible to provide the service.

**Nature of outlets**    High street, local small branches, special outpost branches with limited personal services in shopping supercentres, large places of work and on-campus branches for students.

**Transport**    In this case the term should not be taken too literally. We need to consider the quality of the network links needed for Electronic Funds Transfer. In just the same way as the manufacturer will discuss different options for its transport fleet, the bank will decide which network provider to contract and what type of network contracts it needs, private lines, open lines etc. A key feature of this network use is that high security is required, a few electrons now mean large fund transfers. This is a lot easier than running into a bank with a shotgun. The bank needs to guard against electronic criminals.

**Cover**    Banks had a lot of adverse press when they reduced opening hours many years ago and the term 'bankers' hours' is sometimes used by people in the manufacturing and process industries as a term of abuse to describe operations that provide poor access hours for service. To get round this and reduce costs in normal working hours banks have installed large networks of Automatic Telling Machines (ATMs) which enable customers to collect cash and complete a range of other transactions twenty-four hours a day. Home banking via the public networks is another form of 24 hour service provision. Other than this, banks are located for reasonable access to the provision of more complex financial services where personal contact is required (mortgage finance, foreign exchange etc.).

## 5.8 SERVICE EXTENSION TO MARKETING MIX

Services are considered to have some special properties when compared to marketing products: intangibility, inseparability, perishability, no ownership to buyer and diverse at the point of provision. There are few products which do not have some element of service. Even the simple act of shopping in a supermarket represents the use of a buying service. Products such as computers and cars need to be serviced. On the converse side, most services have products associated with them. Holidays require products such as aircraft and food. The focus on benefits shows us that some benefits (clean clothes) can be obtained by personal use of products (washing machines) or by the use of a service (a laundry). Table 5.15 gives an overview of the special elements of service. Table 5.16 gives an overview of the service additions to the classical 4Ps of the product marketing mix (Product, Price, Promotion (marketing communication), and place (distribution)).

**Table 5.15**   Special elements of a service—medical examination

| | |
|---|---|
| Intangibility | Patient not able to judge quality, patient takes no ownership, i.e. no product. |
| Inseparability | Not much can happen unless we have both patient and doctor available at the same time and place. |
| Perishability | One can store baked beans but not medical examinations. So peak demand is a problem. |
| Ownership | The patient has no ownership of a product at the end. |
| Variability | Quality will depend on the ability of the doctor, his state of alertness and even a degree of cooperation from the patient. |

**Table 5.16**   Service additions to the marketing mix

**Service extended mix**

*People*
  Training
  Customers
    Customer involvement
    Other customers
  Appearance
  Behaviour
*Process*
  Procedure and policy
  Automation
  Customer involvement
*Physical evidence*
  Environment
  Tangible clues
  Facilitating goods

**Service elements of word processing**

The product itself is a black box with very little to distinguish it from another make of black box. Service marketing can assist us to present our black box as more acceptable.

- Software, is this a product or a service?
- Software support and help lines are a pure service
- Digital communications for electronic mail
- Hardware maintenance
- User training

**Table 5.17** Service marketing mix element—people

| People |
| --- |
| Training |
| Customers |
|     Customer involvement |
|     Other customers |
| Appearance |
| Behaviour |

### 5.8.1 People

Table 5.17 shows the elements of the people mix in the service extension to the marketing mix. Training is important. How well trained are the company staff, not only in the direct knowledge of their specific job but the context? In our word processing example, the service engineer may call to fix a hardware printer problem which may not be a hardware problem, but a lack of understanding by the new users of the network software defaults. What will be more appreciated by the customer, 'Call the software support, there is no printer problem' or ten minutes showing the new users how to resolve the problem? To do the latter, the engineer not only has to be trained on the hardware (expected) and the software (some progression), but in the customer's business (essential to understand their problem). There has to be a marketing input to the firm's training strategy and programme.

In the early days of the word-processor, these could be sold by companies who had made computers and understood the technical needs well, or by companies who had been in office technology. These latter companies often did better than their products might have given one to expect. The computer company service engineer would turn up as if he was to work in the computer machine room, not the managing director's office. The companies familiar with the executive office market ensured that their engineer arrived in suits with the company tie and not a tool box but a briefcase (which happened to have tools in it).

Many words have been used to express the power and need for appropriate behaviour. The key element is to show the customer you care about their problems. The comment that a smile means so much and costs so little is very true. Successful, marketing-orientated, companies put customer care as their first and last priority. It is in each of these personal contacts that this customer care is communicated. These people–people interactions have been called 'moments of truth'. Positive behaviour reinforces the relationships, poor front line service will send the customer to the competition.

What do customers have to do with the service? In many areas of service other customers and their involvement is part of the process, who wants to go on holiday to a hotel with no other guests? Who wants to join a sports club to use the gym on their own? The type of customers and their involvement with other customers can be an important part of the benefit set perceived by the customer.

### 5.8.2 Physical evidence

Table 5.18 shows the elements of physical evidence. It can be difficult for the customer to evaluate the quality of the service (this can just as well apply to a complex computer

**Table 5.18**  Service marketing mix element—
physical evidence

**Physical Evidence**
Environment
Tangible clues
Facilitating goods

system) and so the customer may have to rely on signal attributes and clues to indicate the quality of the service. In service areas, such as hotels and restaurants, the need for a good environment is clear. However, good marketing-orientated companies have taken to making high quality provisions in service areas for car maintenance reception or training facilities for computer software. To the customer the message is clear, if they can take care of this they must be able to take care of my car or my computer problems. Often the customer does not have the ability to evaluate the purchased service and is looking for other clues to establish a view by indirect means.

Tangible clues are other little signals that a quality service has been provided. For a word processing course it might be a well designed quality certificate of completion or, for a major software course, a framed picture of the graduation group. For computer or car service, it may be a well designed service report sheet filled in by a named service person. All these little items cue the customer to the quality of the service, which the customer may have no way to estimate by direct observation.

Facilitating goods are the items that the customer needs to use the service. There is much to commend the view that computer companies should regard the supply of consumables (disks, tapes) and manuals in the same way. Such goods can be a source of revenue and stimulate further use of the service, for example, the provision of advanced telephones for purchase by domestic users by a national telecommunications network owner. Sale of the equipment is one source of new revenue. With portable handsets the ability to take or make calls where convenient will also increase the use of the service. The quality of such goods also provides an indicator of the quality of the service.

**Table 5.19**  Service marketing mix element—
process

**Process**
Procedure and policy
Automation
Customer involvement

### 5.8.3 Process

Table 5.19 gives the outline for the element process. Is the process simple and user friendly or slow and time-consuming, like completing a tax form? Does the front line contact have delegated authority to make decisions (a policy issue)? With many services, automation has become acceptable to customers. The explosive growth of advanced telling machines in banks and building societies demonstrates the acceptability of this type of automation. If a person has just completed a meal in a five star hotel and wants a coffee, the comment 'The machine is over in the corner' will not be acceptable but the same person may be very happy to use a coffee machine at 3 a.m. in the airport. It is important to determine what process will be acceptable to the customer and which will not. One of the most critical areas is customer involvement. The issue of involvement in services such as sports clubs has been discussed. These concepts go further, into areas such as medical care, the view being that in public health care you are told what is appropriate for you, but in private health care you are much more involved in the decision making process, with a more interactive discussion about possibilities, options and benefits. Such involvement in these issues has a high customer benefit valuation. Computer companies know this process well and use it in such events as user group conventions and the like.

## 5.9 MARKETING INFORMATION SYSTEM (MKIS)

*A Marketing Information System is a continuing and interacting structure of people, equipment, and procedures to gather, sort, analyse, evaluate, and distribute pertinent, timely, and accurate information for use by marketing decision-makers to improve their marketing, planning, implementation and control.*
Kotler

There is a distinction between *data* (raw facts) and *information* (data transformed by selection, relationships, analysis, statistical exploration, models, graphical presentation etc.) for management use.

The normal complaint of managers is 'too much data and not enough information'. Note also that information is often only of value if it is also timely. In science and engineering terms this is a feed-forward and a feedback system. Throughout this book, we have compared certain aspects of business with the skills of driving a car. The MkIS system is very much the driver, receiving information back on past corrective actions, noting changing road conditions and at the same time monitoring the condition of the car, fuel level, RPM, temperature etc.

The manager is often faced with derived information. A particular problem is the 'accountants syndrome'. This is irrelevant accuracy. For sales management, do we need to know that the sales figures last month were £2 156 743.81? Is the 81 pence useful?! There is a trade-off between accuracy, cost and time. Ensure that an appropriate balance is maintained for your specific management needs. One is not interested in whether there are 4.635 litres of fuel in the tank, what the driver needs to know is 'Do I need to fill up?' and 'Where is the nearest petrol station?'

For many[1] organizations the least important part of the MkIS system is *Primary Marketing Research*, the area often given most space in traditional marketing text books.

---

[1]   *This is an effect arising from the fact that much formal marketing was developed in the FMCG (Fast Moving Consumer Goods sector). Industrial Marketing is not so well developed. Moreover, many (even current) books do not adequately emphasize the effect of multivariant analysis, EDI (Electronic Data Interchange) and Point of Sale Computers (laser read outs).*

The plain fact of life is that it is expensive and often inaccurate, so it is only to be used when the **objectives** are clear and there is no other way to get the information. I am not stating that it is not of value, rather that its use should be highly selective for appropriate specific purposes (such as new market entry). What is critical is that the firm should have a good idea of the customer's view of its product in the market place. Primary research is a powerful but often expensive way to investigate this.

Information (note: data only becomes information through the MkIS) is a *key* competitive resource. *To manage the future is to manage information.* In the same way that organizations neglected their human potential in the 70s and 80s, they also neglected the potential competitive advantage of good information management. A computer and a database does not give you an MkIS system, just a large paper bill! Creative insight is required to understand what information is needed to assist in the generation of competitive advantage. A formal model view of MkIS is given in Fig. 5.14.

### 5.9.1 Internal reports system

Two critical cycles can be systematically analysed to provide good information, the *Sales Cycle:* sales order, supply product, collect money, and the *Manufacture Cycle:* order raw materials, manufacture and deliver. There are many other key internal sources of data for MkIS conversion to management information, however, for example, customer satisfaction from field engineers' service reports (why not also get them to report on any competitor's equipment they observe in customer premises?). Customer complaints can be a useful input; do specific types of service faults occur in a particular industry because of a particular type of use not originally envisaged by the design team? Such information can be a fertile ground for product improvement and new product development.

The new product development cycle is a further sensitive check of the efficiency of the MkIS system. This is the cycle from the identification of the possibility of a new marketing opportunity to the establishment of a new stable product. This cycle is different to the sales order cycle and the manufacturing cycle, in that new information sources and requirements will be essential to take the firm into new and initially unknown areas.

The use of the value chain is helpful in this process and, as is shown below, there is a requirement to integrate the commercial data (sales figures) with technical data (for example, reports on potential manufacturing improvements).

### 5.9.2 Key problem area

One of the most difficult areas in the internal reports system is often accurate costing data, referred to earlier. Frequently the accounts system will be based on standard rates (set for the year) and the budgeted plant loading and product mix. This is not an attack on accountants (even if it looks like it!). It must be appreciated that there are as many types of accountants as there are engineers and, just as you would not use an electrical engineer to design a chemical reactor, the firm should not expect a taxation expert to provide management financial information. When a costing is needed the first question should be 'For what purpose, and in what context?' Management accountants are very aware of the domain of applicability of the book costing—'kept for the annual accounts'.

In many situations, it may be necessary to run two parallel systems, the book system for the accounts (very often kept to some specific form for taxation and audit purposes, that

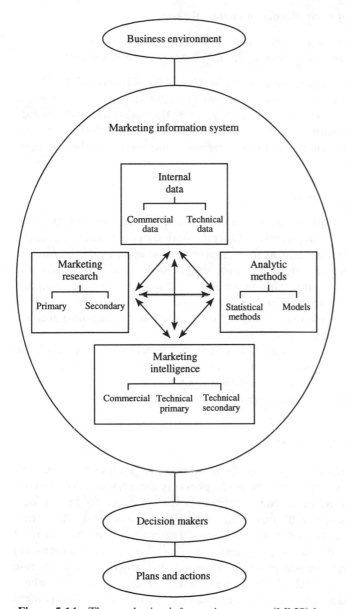

**Figure 5.14**   The marketing information system (MkIS) in a technical company

may not fit the ever changing needs for the management of the company) and a related system for management decisions. The key business skill is to assure yourself that the information is derived from the appropriate data, by the appropriate analysis, for the decision at hand. To use a computer analogy: to use information without understanding is like using software on an inappropriate operating system. You may get sudden unexpected program terminations (crashes). In business that may mean liquidation!

### Costs of early closure of chemical plant

*In a major chemical company it can be necessary from time to time to close a plant before the full time period of depreciation. What is the cost of closure?*

There will be a profit loss as the undepreciated capital sum has to be written off. This has no **cash** flow effects on the company (unless there is borrowing on the security of the asset) as depreciation is a non-cash expense and is a paper exercise by the accountants to allocate capital expenses over the conventional period for the operation of the plant, involving transfers between accounts within the company but no flow of money across the company boundary.

*These two extreme cases have occurred in practice.*

The chemical plant consisted of exotic materials for chemical resistance and performance (silver, nickel, platinum and palladium catalysts). Over the period of the plant's operation, the metal market valuation of the content of these materials had increased many times. This meant that the scrap value (for metal content) was considerably higher than the original construction costs and, with no redundancy costs, the net effect to the company was a positive cash contribution. This required a financial analysis by an engineer with an understanding of financial management as it was not obvious from the standard accountancy data, which was not collected for this purpose.

The chemical plant required the use of a toxic, but stable, intermediate stored in an underground tank which had an undiscovered fracture. Site clean-up was expensive and was a sizeable proportion of the original construction costs. The decommissioning of nuclear power stations represents a similar problem.

## 5.10  MARKETING INTELLIGENCE SYSTEM

How you keep in touch with what is happening? General reading, such as the *Financial Times*, or specifically directed reading (specific trade press) is the first level of activity. Informal search is often used in industrial conditions. If you want to buy a new photocopier, you ask your business friends which ones they have and what their experience has been. Sales representatives like to know competitors' activity with their key accounts. It is surprising what you can gain from a quick scan (and a good memory) when signing the 'Visitors' Book' in reception on a sales visit! However, a deliberate effort, usually following a pre-established plan, procedure, or methodology, to secure specific information or information relating to a specific issue is often required. Instrument and car manufacturers will buy competitors' products and take them apart to evaluate how they have been constructed and what their strengths and weaknesses are in comparison with the firm's own products.

## 5.11  MARKETING RESEARCH

Marketing research should be used for defined objectives and with established uses: *'We will enter the market if the marketing research indicates more than a million potential users in the defined market area.'*

### 5.11.1 Types of marketing research

This area is covered in extensive and excellent detail in most standard text books on marketing. This detail of cover is not repeated here (see references at the end of this chapter) but the essentials are given. The process should be regarded as the engineer, scientist or technologist in management being in the position of the architect for a new building. Some understanding of plumbing is essential for the design of the building, but the actual installation of the wash room can be left to the plumbers. With marketing research, the technical manager needs to understand the broad principles to define what needs to be done and leave the market researcher to do the detailed plumbing of structuring a survey questionnaire or the devising of a quota sampling plan. The overall process is shown in Fig. 5.15.

**Primary**  Primary marketing research is original research work, which is often expensive. Two distinctly different types of research can be undertaken. *Quantitative research* is used to answer simple questions, such as how many people buy CDs and the nature of the outlets where they purchase them. These questions can establish important issues such as market shares and people's actions. This area tends to be confined to questions of fact; 'Do you prefer product A, or product B?'

A new level of understanding may be required to determine the motivational issues of why people prefer or use one product rather than another? In the discussion of product

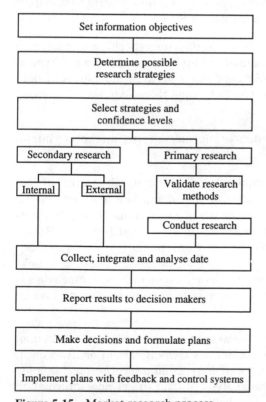

**Figure 5.15**  Market research process

attributes, it was noted that products had intangible benefits. These can be very important motivators for purchase, or not. In the UK as much money is spent on what may be called snack food as main meals. Such snacks are often not taken because people are hungry, but because they are bored or seeking comfort etc. Brands may have personalities and the M&S person is different to a Next person, who in turn will be different to a Laura Ashley person.

Many rational scientists, technologists and engineers may well be uncomfortable at this stage as these elements do not involve rational issues. However, consider that it is your partner's birthday and you decide to eat out. Do you do this just because you will be hungry or for motivations which may be described as sense of occasion, excitement, romance? Evening eating out has more to do with social and psychological motivational issues than the simple need to collect a few calories, which could be obtained from a bag of chips.

In quantitative primary research 90 per cent confidence levels are often about as much as can be expected at reasonable cost. This is not easy to accept when the engineer may have designed a 'lock on circuit' for a FM radio with an accuracy of $\pm 1$ Hz in 100 MHz. In motivational research, the situation is even more diffuse, but how do you measure important things such as love and security? With difficulty, and not to 1 part in $10^6$. Many of the motivational concepts, such as Maslow, apply as much in the area of marketing as to motivation in the context of human resource management (Chapters Four and Eleven).

If the differing types of parameters are remembered, the sampling plans and statistics in market research have much in common with those in statistical quality control (for example, preference tests follow a binomial distribution. This is no different in statistical terms to the sampling plans for lot defectives (see Chapter Six).

**Secondary**   Secondary research is the analysis of existing data for a specific purpose (often for a different need, so take care about the domain of validity). In marketing a new type of car alarm we might want to know about the growth and shape of car ownership. We would want to know how many new cars are registered and who buys them. All this information will be available in published sources.

**Internal**   Specific analysis of the internal systems (internal reports, marketing intelligence) for some new specific need.

**External**   Much valuable information can be obtained from systematic abstraction of data from published sources. This will often include syndicated market research reports published by commercial marketing organizations or trade associations. Vast collections of such data are available from libraries (Department of Trade and Industry, British Institute of Management, Packaging Research Association, are just a few examples). Electronic databases are a major development. These can be online telephone data links into public, institutional or commercial computer databases and increasingly, much data is now becoming available on CD ROM. Electronic search skills are now vital to the modern marketing person.

**Analytical marketing systems**   The analytical systems are the new frontiers of marketing. The convergence of statistical techniques (developments in multivariant analysis etc.), data collection (laser check-outs), information technology, communications technology, and analytical models gives new powers in the analysis of data to get new information insights. Demand for products as diverse as electricity and ice-cream can be correlated with the temperature. Specific models can be built and validated. This latter process is important as things can change. In the UK at present, summer temperatures may mean lower electrical power use, while in the USA, there is a much more extensive use of air-conditioning, high day temperatures are associated with very high electrical power demands.

The result can be multi-factor sales forecasting systems etc. The detection of relationships is a critical element of the analytical process; simple graphical presentation can often be of great value (easy with database and graphics packages). When the analysis is over a number of years, care should be taken to eliminate or accommodate the effects of inflation: sales per employee has grown by 7 per cent is not good news if inflation is 10 per cent!

Care must be taken to understand the limits of the validity domain for the information and, just as importantly, understand the time element and the lags and distortion that may be implicit in some control signals (for those with backgrounds in control theory, the specific operating characteristics of the feedback or feed forward systems).

There are dangers in simple sales forecasting based on time series analysis of the sales figures (Fig. 5.16). Here the downturn in activity is masked by the buffer (distortion) effect of the build-up of the back orders. In real life the situation is even worse:

- When materials are short, people duplicate orders (often with second and third supply sources), in the hope of getting part orders in an allocation situation. The up side of the order cycle may be greater than the real demand.
- When the back orders build up then customer service has broken down. If the firm's competitors have not got the same problems, there may then be an even greater loss of business.
- Optimal stock control produces a magnification effect. The above are factors which, even if difficult, are within the control of management. However, consider the above

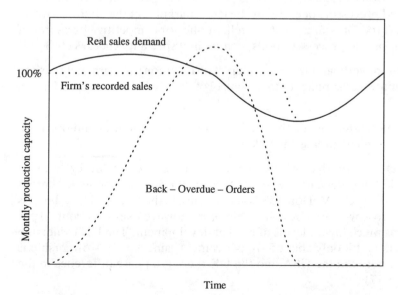

**Figure 5.16**  Danger of time series analysis on firm's sales figures alone

case with regard to the manufacture of cars. A supplier of advanced electronic ignition systems has additional problems. At the crash point, the firm will have not only the lower level of consumer car purchase activity reflected but the reduction in working buffer stock of the car manufacturer, thus increasing (magnifying) the real drop in demand from say 10 per cent to 20–30 per cent. It is quite possible that you might go an entire period without an order. Remember Porter 5 forces of competitive pressures, buyer power! Defined as their control over your business.

The defence is diversification and a key way of spreading the risk is to go international and operate in more than one market. Given the international dimensions of information, communications, food, and chemical technology, this dimension is important for scientists, engineers and technologists.

## 5.12  INTERNATIONAL TRADE AND THE INDIVIDUAL FIRM

A definition of international marketing is *'to market goods or services in more than one country.'*

### 5.12.1  Why go international? Why export?

International trade is complicated and has risks. A firm should enter this area with a specific understanding of its objectives. Some industries such as telecommunications are by their very nature international. Again, this section does not seek to provide an expert cover of the detail of the complex issues but the principles that will affect the scientist, engineer or technologist working in global markets, often needing to travel to present company products to export markets or train export customers in product use or applications. The internationalization of trade has the implication that even the small firm, operating only in its own domestic market, must take account of global market pressures. Many UK farms and food processors operate for the local market, but the effects of world trends affect them with direct pressures, such as milk quotas, or competitive pressures of imported foods (from apples to processed foods, continental speciality cheeses etc.).

**Integration**   Horizontal, or vertical (take ownership of distribution), the firm may wish to own the sources of raw materials supplies or take control of the marketing of its products in overseas markets.

**Spread risk**   A single market may make the firm vulnerable to economic conditions. To trade in a number of economies spreads the risk.

**Exploit product life cycle**   A product which may be at the end of its life cycle in an advanced domestic market may get a new lease of life in an alternative economy. There is an international product life cycle. McDonald's is very mature in the UK and USA, but it is the chic place to eat in Moscow. The UK ownership of microwave ovens is about 40 per cent, while, the USA has much higher levels of market development. The UK ownership of automatic dishwashers is still only about 5–10 per cent. Again, the USA ownership is very much higher. Even between the USA and the UK there is a phase difference in the product life cycle (Fig. 5.17).

**Domestic market too small**   To get full economy of scale, a single market may not be large

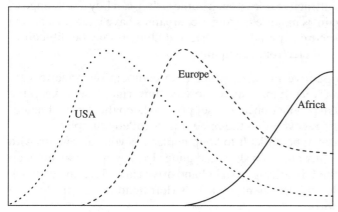

**Figure 5.17**    International product life cycle

enough. A UK commercial aircraft would make no sense, as it has to be considered in a global market (such as European Airbus).

**Different valuations**    A domestic product which is middle of the road may be chic in a foreign market and command a premium price (UK tea in the USA is an example). Imported cars can have a cult status. Very often these are small, but premium, niche markets.

**Market pull**    There may be a demand that no local supplier wishes to meet as it is too small, but that may be attractive as a premium, but marginal, market. You can buy UK national newspapers in Paris or New York, at about £2.00 a copy.

**Manufacturing advantage**    The firm's costs of manufacture may give it a price competitive advantage. Many electronic products are made in the Pacific rim area. The product life cycle is mirrored by a cycle of competitive advantage (for example, the structural decline of ship building in Europe).

**Tax**    For a firm operating in a highly taxed local market it may make sense to export, take the profits off-shore and develop the firm outside the high tax area.

**Import**    In an underdeveloped economy with exchange problems there may be a very valuable market for imported luxury goods, but only if you can gain access to the hard currency. So, a firm in that type of situation may be most motivated by gaining the hard currency rights. Counter trade (barter deals etc.) often involves high technical content, with the need for Western technologists to work with the less developed economy to effect technology transfer.

**Patent position**    A European patent can give world (if appropriate filings are made) protection for twenty years. Thus there is pressure to exploit the total market before the firm has lost its protection.

**Copyright**    This applies to computer programs, books, designer products and art (music, films, posters etc.). The firm or copyright-owner may wish to maximize the return on its creative investment and has a protected position. This issue is of critical interest (remember Porter evaluation of competitor analysis) for consumer electronics companies.

The new DAT system will not be attractive to customers unless they can buy a full range of music. This may not be easy to gain as major electronics companies have been purchasing record and music companies to secure copyright of music and films. It may be difficult to gain a copyright licence from a rival electronic company.

**Marginal production**    In a competitive market, rather than compete on price to gain market share (in the domestic market), it may make more commercial sense to keep the domestic price up and sell marginal production at a lesser price to keep the factory loaded. Taken to the limits, the cost is not recovered in the price, this is called 'dumping'.

In the EC, with free trade, this can be difficult to keep in place as you can end up with parallel exports. A UK agent can buy and then ship, and under EC law, you may not stop him. The interesting example is the UK pricing of right hand drive cars. Here an 'artificial' price difference between the UK and continental markets (left hand drive) produced a trade in 'personal' (parallel) imports.

### 5.12.2  International trade barriers

Table 5.20 gives a structured overview of the barriers to international trade. This should be thought of in the standard PEST (Political, Economic, Social, Technical) analysis context. These are the additional elements of a PEST analysis that need to considered for working on an international basis. Each of these elements is considered, with their implications for each element of the International Marketing Mix—the 4 Ps (Price, Promotion (Marketing Communications) and Place (Distribution)). Remember the additional 3 Ps which made up the 7 Ps of the extended Service Marketing Mix (Product, Price, Promotion (Marketing Communications), Place (Distribution) + People, Process and Physical Evidence).

### 5.12.3  Indirect barriers

**Class**    England is not the only country where class is considered important (even if you take the view that it should not be!). Marketing and business is a pragmatic profession, and in international marketing it is essential to take the world as it is. It may then be possible to change it for the better. One needs to be careful about class. This marketing segmentation variable is different (but has a weak correlation) to earnings segmentation. The A, B, $C_1$, $C_2$ and D refer to occupations *not* earnings. So a manual worker on shift with overtime may earn £20 000 a year and be categorized as a $C_2$; the country clergyman with a Doctorate in Divinity may earn £12 000 but be an A in social class. These issues transfer in differing ways into other countries, such as India with the caste system (occasional reports have appeared on high caste student unrest over the issue of positive discrimination for low caste Indians in government appointments). These considerations can affect the appropriate positioning of the product and also the marketing communications mix (influencing both channels and acceptable messages). It is necessary to be sensitive to these issues in all elements of the marketing mix.

**Climate**    This appears to be simple, but due account must be taken of its effect. This may just be reflected in the basic demand for products or require the modification of the product.

The international manager visiting Finland in winter may find a rack of electric cables

**Table 5.20**   Barriers to international trade

**Barriers to international trade**
*Indirect*
    Class
    Climate
    Corruption
    Culture
    Currency
    Demographics
    Development
    Distance
    Infrastructure
    Language
    Manners
    Race
    Religion
    Time
    Trade Terms
*Direct*
    Tariffs
        Import tariffs
        Quotas
        Subsidies
    Non-tariff
        Government
            Seizure
    Embargo
    Sanctions
    Currency (restrictions)
    Surcharge (import)
    Deposits (import)
    Restrictions
*Law*
    Health
    Safety
    Labelling
    Packing
    Standards
    Technical
    Liability
    Ownership
    Law (conflict)

behind a hotel reception desk. The effect of a night temperature of $-30°C$ on car oil is dramatic. The car parks are fitted with electric points to each bay. Before breakfast a car heater is connected, after breakfast the engine is warm enough to start. In tropical countries, the same car model will not be fitted with an electric engine heater but with air-conditioning.

**Corruption**   An emotive word! For example, in many countries small bribes are essential to get documentation cleared. Before one gets too moral, just consider the UK: A person arrives at a station with four large cases on the last train at 2 a.m., and gets a taxi on arrival. The driver takes the cases into the hotel, in the expectation that he will be tipped, which the average business person will do. Is this a bribe? This is a difficult and diffuse area and most major corporations give their staff firm guide-lines in the company business ethics handbook.

**Culture**   Culture is a diffuse but powerful concept, which in some ways involves a convergence of a number of elements of the indirect barriers. Culture can refer to the way people live, act and their value systems. In Muslim countries the position of women is very traditional, while, in Scandinavian countries one will find a high proportion of very professional female senior managers (many more than one would meet in the UK at present). Culture affects almost everything we do, from the large to the small. In the average provincial city, most of the town is dead by midnight. In Spain, Madrid will be at its most alive, with many people eating out.

**Currency**   Strange to relate, not all countries pay in pounds, so there is the additional complexity of conversion and risk. This problem can be managed with forward cover of currency needs, for example.

**Demographics**   Demographics refers to a whole range of population characteristics. As a simple example, the expectation of life in the UK is in the upper 70s, this may fall to the mid 40s in underdeveloped countries. There may be subtle differences within a given country. The total UK population demographics is different to that of Afro and Caribbean communities, which have many more young people than the majority population. You can make other simple errors, for example 'the USA is English speaking'. Some 10 per cent of the USA do not have English as their first language, the second most dominant language being Spanish.

**Development**   Not all countries are so developed as the UK. Take reading for example. Some 95 per cent have a reasonable standard of reading in the UK, while this figure may be well under 50 per cent in some underdeveloped countries. This is just one example of many potential problems. In the area of microelectronics, the quality of local power supplies may be a particular problem.

**Distance**   It is obvious that you may have to ship goods a long way, but there is a second dimension to this point. We have a problem in the UK, in that we live in a densely populated island. It takes almost as long to fly from New York to the USA West Coast as it does to fly from London to New York. Not only are export markets distant, but they often have much greater distances between their centres of population.

**Infrastructure**   Telephones, telex, fax, roads, power etc. Just ask for the local Fax office in Siberia; no problem, it's 1000 miles up the road in Moscow! For technical products, the lack of vital infrastructure support, such as clean power supplies, service centres or spares and supplies (computer disks etc.) may be a major consideration in entering a new market.

**Language**   Strangely enough, instructions need to be in the export country language[s]. This issue of multiple languages is more common than may be expected: in Europe, for Belgium you need French and German. In Canada, it is a legal necessity to have French and English. Export and safety documentation may have to be in the language[s] of the country of origin, the language[s] of the destination and of all the countries that the consignment has to pass through. This is a significant problem in the shipping of hazardous materials such as chemicals.

Care needs to be taken with short hand. To a UK Chemist, the CIA means the Chemical Industry Association, but it has a very different meaning to people in the USA! This may apply to professions too, for example, to business students PLC means product life cycle, but to an engineer it means programmable logic computer.

**Manners**   Social norms are different in different countries, and one needs to be sensitive to them.

**Race**   Again, it is necessary to be sensitive to the demographic race mix in the destination country. It may affect the product. In the case of perfumes and cosmetics a whole range of applications formulations are needed for the differing skin colours and hair types (dark skinned women need different cosmetics to light skinned women).

**Religion**   This may have effects varying from differing national holidays to much more specific effects and prohibitions, as in the case of alcohol within Muslim countries.

Demonstrating an understanding of these issues can build international marketing relationships; UK buyers will get many Christmas cards from non-Christian countries. Why not send New Year cards to your Jewish customers? It shows you understand and respect their special needs, as just one example.

**Time**   The two points apply as with distance: Jacksonville, Florida is four hours behind GMT and the USA West Coast is another four hours behind this. There are five time zones in the USA. One has to stay late at the office if it is necessary to ring the West Coast of the USA. Apart from the obvious effects, this wide time zoning can have subtle effects, how can you have a national evening news programme in the USA with a five hour time spread?

**Trade terms**   The total of shipment, and documentation procedures means that thirty days net for the domestic market most often will be three months for export to distant locations. This has implications on risk (exchange risk and risk in extended shipment) and simple cash flow. There can be other complications in international trade terms with the involvement of Letters of Credit (bank documents giving security of payment from an unknown customer) and other issues.

### 5.12.4 Direct barriers

**Tariffs**

Note the effect of Customs Unions such as the EC. Thus you may import into or make in one EC country and then export to the whole area without any additional duty.

**Import tariffs**   These exist for two main reasons:

- As with any tax, to get money for the government.
- As a form of trade protection (i.e. make imports expensive to protect the domestic industry).

As with any tax system these rules can be complex. Two specific mechanisms are in use:

- *Specific*: duty per unit of measure; £1/Kg etc.
- *By value*: 10 per cent of the import value.

   On odd occasions both may be applied at once, which is referred to as Compound Duty.

The rules for duty changed a few years ago, when the USA joined the world community from the Brussels System to the Harmonized System. This scheme works rather like the library reference number system. The basis of classification involves the product type and the end use. This has given some complications. In the chemical industry, most steroids are in one classification unless they are of the specific chemical types used in the manufacture of contraceptives, then they appear in that classification.

   Rates of duty can vary between classifications. This can involve creative marketing in the export of the right product to minimize duty (that is, shipment of kits for final local assembly may greatly reduce the duty profile). There is not one rate of duty for each HS number. There can be any number of rates, say between EC, EFTA (European Free Trade Association), Commonwealth Preference, Underdeveloped Country, Standard etc. Since duty can be 100 per cent or more, this aspect needs careful examination to ensure that the company can be competitive in a given market.

**Quotas**   This is another form of trade protection, where the Government sets a fixed quantity of particular product that may be imported/exported (possibly to or from a given country).

**Subsidies**   These need to be considered carefully, as they can make the domestic product in your target market below your cost price. In reverse, they may enable people to compete in your own domestic market at an artificial cost advantage. International trade even affects the non-exporter.

**Direct—non-tariff: Government actions**

1. *Seizure*   One of the problems is that in the event of change in political climate all assets of a given country in the host nation may be appropriated. The Gulf War started for the UK with the seizure of a British Airways jet.

2. *Embargo*   The total restriction on trade in certain items, often now products made from natural sources involving endangered species as well as items of a military potential.

(This can include common chemicals which could be used to make illegal poison gas weapons.)

3. *Sanctions*    The restriction of the export or import of all goods (or selected goods) to or from a given nation in support of political objectives. There is much written in the press about UN sanctions but care needs to be taken not only to look at this from the UK perspective, but on a global basis. The Arab boycott of companies who export to Israel can cause a whole raft of problems for European firms with USA connections, for example.

4. *Currency*    Many countries do not have enough currency for all their import demands. There are a range of options. Most often currency is allocated to essential goods (food, medicine, arms etc.), only restricted amounts being available for luxury goods. However, because of the artificial restriction, there is often a large unsatisfied local demand, so margins may be high. There may be reasons to persist to get limited allocations and then make a substantial profit.

The advantage can be enhanced by getting the maximum added value in, perhaps by shipping perfume into the restricted market in bulk, filling in the local market with less expensive labour and within the trade wall. This leverage can be maximized with the use of local solvents, if these are of sufficient quality.

There is the case where there is no hard money but there is still a demand. Then there is a whole new game of countertrade where no money changes hands (or that is the net effect).

5. *Surcharge*    The whole structure of international tariffs is governed by a complex of International Trade agreements (you will read about the GATT discussions in the national press). What can a country do to stay within the rules when it has a short term balance of trade problem? They may apply a 20 per cent temporary surcharge on imports of non-essential goods for six months. This should not attract any trade war action.

6. *Deposits*    A person who wants to import goods has to deposit the value of the goods with the Central Bank at the time he places the contract. The deposit is not recovered until the goods are received and paid for. This has dramatic effects on the importer's need for working capital and can, in effect, represent a very substantial duty on imports.

7. *Restrictions*    There are a vast range of restrictions. These are often enforced by the necessity of having import and/or export licences for certain goods. Typical areas would be works of art, items of historical significance, items of military use (not only arms but the materials to make chemical weapons etc.).

**Direct—non-tariff**
The complex area. With all governments stating that they are committed to Free Trade (*except when it is not to their domestic advantage*) how do they restrict trade? With non-tariff barriers. In addition, the complexity of the issues can cause problems even where there is no desire to restrict trade. For example:

1. *Health*    No two countries have the same hygiene regulations. This can cause problems with certification and procedures, a significant problem area for food products. This can also affect sales of products such as seeds and animals.

2. *Safety*    This can be a complex technical area. All nations have safety requirements, such as for electrical equipment. This is a good thing. So how come the problem? Well, the

UK regulations will now be in metric terms, USA will be in what we would call imperial measurements (ours in cms, theirs in inches, for example). There may be differing colour codes for safety.

3. *Labelling*    There is a vast amount of detailed and differing legislation on what needs to be on a pack. In the USA there must be full formula disclosure on products (a very impressive list on cosmetics). Health warnings on tobacco products is another area.

A difficult sphere is *claims*. In the food industry, claims of 100 per cent natural and no added antioxidant or no additives may be considered important. There is no single definition of what natural means. This also may require creative formulation. You wish to sell a drink claiming 'with no additives', yet it needs an antioxidant. What to do? Easy, add vitamin C. It is a good antioxidant. However, you claim 'with added vitamin C'. Such creativity may be acceptable in one country but not another. In many countries the country of origin must be shown on imported goods.

4. *Packing*    Related, of course, to labelling. There may be restrictions on certain types of packing and in the food industry, again this is a rich area of problems. Why does butter etc. come in standard packs? Because it is not legal to sell a 157gm pack of butter in the UK. There are legal restrictions on the sizes of certain products that can be offered for consumer sale. This also relates to safety. Certain pharmaceutical products must be sold in child proof packs. The precise nature of the regulations will vary from country to country.

The physical needs for more robust packaging to protect the product in prolonged transit and storage must not be neglected. Complex and precise international regulations apply to the packing of dangerous materials, such as solvents and chemicals, for international trade. UK approved, tested and certified packaging must be used. The detail is set out by organizations such as IATA.

---

A supplier of a complex electronic product was very careful with export packaging and had a 100 per cent inspected product. In a new market area a major crisis occurred when products arrived with a 75 per cent failure rate with no apparent reason.

Detailed investigation showed that this was the first time that the company had exported to a very cold ($-30°C$) country. The plastic foam anti-vibration packaging became solid at such temperatures and the sensitive product was shaken to destruction in road transport.

---

5. *Standards*    Life for those who work in an American multinational can be difficult, it can be laborious to file anything! Europe works to A3, A4 etc. The USA does not. The USA size for A4 is shorter and wider and this is why there have to be all those options on desk top publishing systems! Just one small example of a very complex and often a very technical problem area.

6. *Technical*    Related to standards. There can be any amount of complex technical restrictions or definitions of product or performance. This can relate to areas such as radio emissions from electronic or electrical equipment. In the USA consumer goods work on 120V 60Hz, in the UK 240V, 50Hz is the supply standard. Almost any element can need consideration, in the manufacture of soft drinks the quality of the water can be a major consideration.

7. *Liability*   The law on product liability is different in differing countries. The producer or the importer may be liable. Of critical importance is the emergence of strict liability. It does not matter if every care was taken and if the product was made to the state of the art. If a person suffers damage they may claim. Again, the sum they may gain may be much greater in some countries (such as the USA) than in others (UK). The practical implication is the need to effect liability insurance. The premium (and hence your product costs) will reflect the risk.

8. *Ownership*   You may wish to set up a marketing subsidiary. In some countries this may not be possible without a majority local holding in the operation.

9. *Conflict of laws*   The transactions in international business may be subject to the laws of a number of nations. This can give rise to conflict of laws. A UK firm may be in the operating division of a USA company and have a contract with a third country. The USA may decide to put a trade embargo on that country but the UK may not. In UK law, the firm may have an obligation to complete the contract. However, your parent company in the USA may be held guilty of sanctions breaking and the company's American chief executive officer may end up in jail. The whole area of UK and European Free Trade Law and USA anti-trust law may well apply to a single action in the EC. The law relating to patents and intellectual property in the international area is most complex.

A specific problem for the new exporter is the foreign laws that may apply to agency agreements. These may be attractive as a low entry method into a market. In the longer term, the local laws may strongly favour the local agent when the firm needs to terminate the agreement as business expands and the firm needs to set up its own local marketing company.

10. *Environmental*   There are differing regulations and social attitudes to environmental issues. These can apply through the law (emission regulations on cars, catalytic after-burners) or through social views on environmental issues (no consumer acceptance for products thought to be damaging or to have been made through damaging processes). The latter is now a critical product acceptance issue in the European markets, with markets such as Germany well in advance of the UK on such matters.

## 5.13 INTERNATIONAL MARKETING MIX AND OPTIONS FOR INTERNATIONAL TRADE

The possible variations in the implications of the many trade barriers, which vary for each defined national market, and the detailed issues of segmentation and marketing mix give a vast number of possible issues. As always, some will be critical and many will be irrelevant. Within the EC, tariff barriers are not an issue, in exporting luxury goods to developing countries they may make the operation impossible. The approach is not complicated but demands skill and experience. For any given marketing situation, the firm must determine the elements of the trade barriers that are applicable to its situation and adjust the elements of the marketing mix in an effective way. The foundation is market research on the overseas markets from secondary sources (Department of Trade and Industry, Embassies, Industry Trade Associations etc.) and personal visits to the market by the firm's own staff.

If the firm decides that any given market is attractive there are various ways of

**Table 5.21**   Options for international business

**Mechanisms of market entry for international business**

*Manufacture abroad in market*
Firm's own production
    Assembly plant
    Full manufacturing plant
Joint ventures with other organizations
    Licensing
    Franchising
    Industrial co-operation agreement
    Contract manufacture
    Management contract
    Assembly plant
    Full manufacturing joint venture

*Manufacture in third country within Customs Union (EC etc.)*
*Domestic production*
    Indirect export
    Export house
    Trading company
    Customer's UK buying office
    Joint exporting 'Piggy back'
*Direct export*
    Sales direct to customer
    Trading company
    Agent
    Distributor
    Branch sales office
    Marketing subsidiary

penetrating the market, from UK manufacture and direct export to the customer to licensing the product to a domestic manufacturer. These options are given in Table 5.21.

## 5.14 MARKETING STRATEGY AND PLANNING

Marketing planning is an essential part of corporate planning and these are considered jointly in more detail in Chapter Thirteen. The overall process is concerned with the evaluation of the firm (internal environment analysis) in the context of the general business situation (external analysis). This explosive and divergent process is refocused by the process of the SWOT (Strengths, Weaknesses, Opportunities and Threats) analysis. The SWOT analysis must include issues of production logistics as well as the marketing mix elements. A great amount of insight into the business situation should have been gained and many potential opportunities opened up. In the process of strategy generation and selection a number of marketing tools can assist. At this stage we shall consider three, the Ansoff matrix, the Boston matrix and the General Electric matrix.

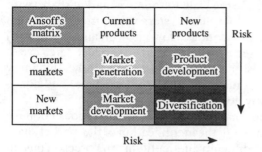

**Figure 5.18**    Ansoff's matrix

## 5.14.1 Ansoff matrix

The Ansoff matrix (Fig. 5.18) allows a systematic exploration of potential market growth opportunities by classification in a simple two by two matrix. Intensive growth involves the company working in established technologies and markets. In principle, this involves the least risk. However, the problem is often that this option may be saturated or worked out and new activities need to be considered.

The next least risky option is to change only one variable at a time and stay with one element the firm does understand well. So new product development (for existing markets) or new market development (for existing products) should represent modest areas of risk. The systematic exploration of this situation (such as by attribute analysis) can generate many new business ideas. Even so, this still may not yield an appropriate strategy option, and the firm will have to consider the possibilities of new products for new markets, a diversification market. Given that the firm will have limited knowledge of these new areas, this option area has the maximum risk. With the increasing risk comes the need for additional marketing research and market testing of the product.

## 5.14.2 Boston matrix

The Boston matrix (Fig. 5.19) allows products to be classified according to the relative market share held by the company (compared to its largest competitor) and the market

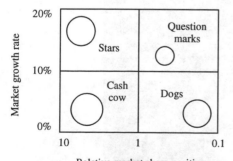

**Figure 5.19**    Boston matrix.
*Reprinted with permission from Hedley, B.,* Long Range Planning, *1977, Pergamon Press, Ltd.*

growth rate. This gives a four cell matrix (note the log scale for relative market share) with the cells called: question marks (high growth, low share), stars (high growth and high share), cash cows (high share, low growth) and dogs (low growth and low share) (B. Hedley, 1977). This classification is seen to match the product life cycle, introduction—question mark (cash hungry, loss making); star—growth (still cash hungry for working capital, but profitable); cash cow—maturity (the profit machine) and dog—decline (possibly modest profits but on the way down).

This is a good, robust, simple, model but for many business situations it does not have the required flexibility. There may be problems with the identification of the market share and market growth rates, the reflection of the difficulty of identifying the precise stage in the product life cycle. The basis of the model is that only two parameters are needed to evaluate market potential. This may be true in some cases but not in all. To consider and present more strategic issues the General Electric type matrix may be used.

### 5.14.3 General Electric matrix

The General Electric Multifactor matrix (Fig. 5.20) consists of two axes, market attractiveness (high, medium and low) and competitive position (strong, average and weak). The size of the market is marked by the area of the circle, the market share is indicated by the segment. The direction and speed of expected change is shown by the arrows. The flexibility of the model comes from the ability to select the elements that are critical for the given market situation and weight the factors. Thus two disadvantages of the Boston matrix are overcome, more than two variables can be weighted into the decision and issues other than market share and growth can be considered if relevant. The matrix scales and positions of the products are set by determining the importance of the elements (such as

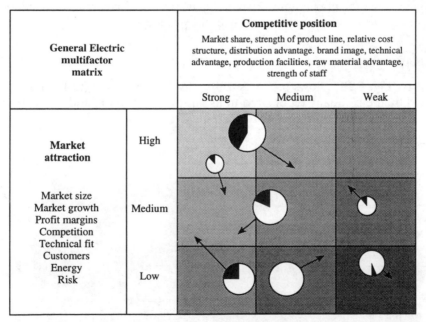

**Figure 5.20**   The General Electric multifactor matrix

market share) in the specific case and multiplying by the perceived position. This yields a weighting for the given factor in the specific case. The overall position is obtained by summing these weighting scores over the total range of factors considered for each axis.

## 5.15 MARKETING PLANS AND IMPLEMENTATION

Marketing plans are part of the overall business plan and in this context considered further in Chapter Thirteen. On the basis of the considerations in this chapter, we can derive the framework of market planning and control shown in Table 5.22. The specific areas for marketing management consideration are market segmentation, customer benefit identification, market size and market share estimation and evaluating of competitive forces in the market place. The specific areas of marketing action will be the research and information needs for the policy considerations (research and the on-going MkIS systems). The communications plan and action programme will be a very active area. Other elements of the marketing mix, such as 'P = Product' will involve the total resources of the company (for example, research for a new technology product or modification of a product for an export market). Distribution may be a simple marketing decision, from the selection of an agent for a limited export market to a major company decision involving all the necessary aspects (logistics, technology development, finance) to establish a major manufacturing presence in a major market (for example, Japanese activities in establishing a substantive European manufacturing base).

**Table 5.22**   Market planning and control

---

Determine relevant market segmentation

Identify characteristics of potential segments

Evaluate segment attractiveness and firm's competitive position

Select target market segments

Set objectives and strategies for each selected segment
(market share, growth, etc.)

Develop full marketing mix for each selected segment
*product, price, promotion, place, people, physical evidence, process*

Implement marketing plans with feedback and control
(Has market share objective been reached etc.?)

---

## REVIEW

Marketing holds a central place in the business as profits flow from customers, and marketing is the activity in the profitable linkage of customers to the business. Marketing takes an external focus on the premise that long term profitability flows from customer satisfaction. Consideration of products in terms of benefits and attributes provides the customer view insight so necessary to successful business. To further understand customers and their behaviour, market segmentation and identification of publics and decision making units is essential. Just in the same way as the behaviour of people depends on their age, so the characteristics and needs of products will vary with their position in the product life cycle.

The power tools of marketing are the elements of the marketing mix, the 4Ps of the product marketing mix (Product, Price, Promotion (Communication), and Place (Distribution)) and the additional 3 Ps of the Service Extended marketing mix (People, Physical Evidence and Process). Product was considered in terms of customer benefits and attribute analysis. The limits of price variation are set by the pricing gap, the gap between the minimum acceptable price based on costs of marketing and production and the benefit valuations of the various market segments. Promotion, marketing communications, was viewed as a sub-mix of techniques (advertising, publicity, sales promotion, public relations, personal selling, sales system) to take customers from unawareness of the firm's products through trial to regular and consistent purchase.

To sell products they need to be made available where, when and how customers require them. Physical distribution involves not only the issues of transportation but inventory and service management. In the process of making products available to customers, the position and added value of channel intermediaries and the appropriate nature of outlets have to be determined.

Service marketing is important to scientists, engineers and technologists and has the differences from product marketing of intangibility, inseparability, perishability, ownership and variability at the point of provision. However, products such as computers have large service elements. People are important as they are perceived to be very much part of the product. Given the intangibility of service, physical evidence can provide signals and reassurance to the customer of the service. The nature of the process must be considered in the context of the service provision, what is acceptable in one circumstance may well not be tolerated in another.

All this management action requires information, the management of information is the management of the future. To collect the data and convert it to timely information requires a formal system, the Marketing Information Management System (MkIS). The internal systems provide much essential data. New data can be obtained from market research, primary research involving the expensive collection of new data. The less expensive correlation of internal and external information collected for other purposes is secondary. The conversion of all this data to information often involves the use of advanced statistical techniques and models. In all information collection and analysis the limits of accuracy and underlying assumptions need to be considered or results will be extended beyond their applicability.

In the science and engineering business areas, international trade is essential as there is a global market, telecommunications being one example. Clear objectives must be set for international operations for a firm. The additional dimensions of trans-national trading can be effectively considered in the framework of the international trade barriers. The indirect barriers of class, climate, corruption, culture, currency, development, demographics, distance, infrastructure, language, manners, race, religion, time and trade terms can require any part of the international marketing mix to be adjusted. The direct trade barriers, tariffs and government action, also require adjustments to the marketing mix. The total consideration of all the barriers will make some markets more attractive than others. Moreover, market entry strategies (direct export or local manufacture) will also be influenced by the trade barriers.

The whole complex of segmentation, marketing mix and international dimensions opens up a complicated area of decision analysis. The Ansoff matrix allows the systematic exploration of options and the estimation of risk. The Boston matrix with consideration of the product life cycle allows more detailed analysis of a range of products as a group. However, its limitation to market share and market growth can be too narrowing and the General Electric multifactor matrix allows a much more flexible analysis of the situation with consideration and weighting of all appropriate variables.

## KEY CONCEPTS AND TECHNIQUES

**Advertising**   Paid for media time.

**Ansoff matrix**   A $2 \times 2$ matrix for the classification of expansion plans and the estimation of risk.

**Attributes**   The things that a product is, its make-up, the benefits (tangible and intangible) and the signal attributes which cue customers to other attributes.

**Benefits**   The things that customers gain from the ownership, consumption or use of goods or services. They can be tangible or intangible.

**Boston matrix**   A simple classification of a mix of products on the basis of market growth and market share.

**Decision making unit**   The group of people who may be involved in the purchase of an item, the buyer may well not be the decider.

**Elasticity of demand**   The reaction of customers to price changes.

**G E multifactor matrix**   A flexible classification of a mix of products on the basis of the estimation and weighting of all relevant factors into two dimensions of competitive advantage and market attractiveness.

**Marketing mix**   The power tools of marketing, the 4Ps of product marketing (Product, Price, Promotion (marketing communication), and Place (distribution)) and its extension to the service elements (People, Physical Evidence and Process).

**Market segmentation**   The division of a large, heterogeneous, market area into more homogeneous sections to allow more effective marketing.

**Media**   Any place for the communication of a message.

**MkIS**   The Marketing Information System.

**Narrow cast media**   Media which reaches a small group of people with some specific interest.

**Physical evidence**   The things that indicate to people the quality of a service that would be intangible without such indicators.

**Primary research**   The collection of new marketing data, expensive.

**Product life cycle**   The process of introduction, growth, maturity and decay in the life of a product.

**Publicity**   Media cover that is not directly paid for by the firm.

**Publics**   Any group which the firm may wish to communicate with, the group extends beyond customers and users to agents etc.

**Secondary research**   The collection and correlation of existing data, not so expensive as primary research.

**Trade barriers**   The direct (tariffs, laws etc.) and indirect barriers (class, language) which complicate the process of providing goods or services in more than one country.

---

# CASE STUDY I—PRODUCT

**Tavy Communication and Navigation**   Andrew Foster graduated in engineering two years ago and gained a job with a small specialist Ministry of Defence contractor involved in the manufacture, installation and contract service for specialist satellite navigation and communication equipment (both satellite and conventional). One of the reasons that Andrew came to Plymouth to study was the availability and quality of the sailing. With the peace dividend, the existing contract with one year to run is unlikely to be renewed. In the vacations, Andrew had worked at a local consumer electronics company and had learned about the techniques of low cost consumer product manufacture. With all this knowledge and experience Andrew considers that there is an opportunity for Tavy Communication and Navigation to enter the market for communication and navigation equipment for private boats (power and sailing yachts).

Many such boat owners know little about electronics and thus require systems that are not too complicated to operate. Many owners do not live near their boats but travel down for long weekends and holidays. A number of accidents have occurred with such people not checking their battery power supplies, resulting in failure of the equipment at critical times such as fog conditions. Boat owners put a high benefit valuation on this activity. People who enjoy this activity tend also to come from high income groups.

Communication and location equipment is important, not only for safety but also to gain a competitive advantage. Accurate location in adverse conditions allows a competitor to keep to the favourable routes to gain maximum advantage of tides and local wind patterns.

Over the last twenty years, enormous developments have been made in communication and navigation systems (M.E. Barnard, 1992). These developments have had much the same effect in this area as has been seen with computers over this time scale. Such advanced systems were only economic to the major shipping lines and, of course, the military, for whom the satellite location system was put in orbit.

Andrew has made a considerable impact in Tavy Communication and Navigation and the owner and Managing Director Ms Nicola Figes has asked Andrew to draft a brief report on the idea to discuss at a meeting of the senior management team.

Your assignment is to draft out this report. At this stage it is agreed that the report should cover: external environment analysis and proposed marketing mix.

---

# CASE STUDY II—SERVICE

**Cornwall Communications**   Peter Spencer is 23 and graduated with a degree in Communications Engineering and then completed an MBA. He joined Cornwall Communications Consultants Ltd in January 1991. This company does not make communications equipment but advises clients on their total communications needs and will supervise installation by subcontractors where appropriate. The company also offers training courses where appropriate for client company staff. He was recruited for this well paid job on the combination of his business skills and excellent technical knowledge of digital communications technology. His first small assignment was to give Peter a chance to fully understand client consultancy before taking on his first major contract as project leader.

**The project**    Cornwall Communications have been retained by a cooperative of some general practitioners. They have decided as a group to put in a cooperative communications centre to be based in a new, group practice, health centre to be built next year. The communication centre will have to take all normal calls for appointments etc. but also act as the out of hours communication centre for all doctors in the group. This will include emergency calls for home visits which have to be directed to the appropriate duty doctor on call at that time. The group of doctors in this scheme intend to sell this service to other doctors, either in a one person practice or to other group practices. The managing director has suggested that Peter draws up a report to him using marketing techniques.

In the role of Peter Spencer prepare this preliminary report. You have been asked to prepare the report under two headings: External Environment Analysis and Proposed Marketing Mix for the Service (service extended mix).

## QUESTIONS

1. Make a list of the people who you feel might be involved in the decision to buy an advanced private telephone exchange for a medium sized factory. What do you think their concerns will be? How important do you think their influence will be? If you were the engineer selling such a system, how would you plan to make such a sale?

2. Sketch the individual product life cycles that you consider might be applicable for the following benefits. Also sketch in the benefit envelope around these individual products.
   (a)  Artificial light in the home.
   (b)  Personal recording of information (writing) devices.
   (c)  Products for information transmission over distances.

3. You are the senior design engineer for a consumer electronics company. Your university course in engineering also included a module on marketing for engineers. Your company have decided to license technology to launch a small range of digital audio tape equipment into the UK market.

   Using the framework of the conventional marketing mix (the 4Ps) outline, in report format, the marketing mix issues that this company needs to consider for a successful launch in the UK.

4. You are the new product development manager for a company that makes conventional electric light bulbs (filament) for the domestic market. The company is completing a strategic review to decide its policy direction for the next five years. Complete a Porter's 5 Forces model for competition analysis, from the point of view of such a manufacturer.

5. A senior engineer at director level in a company, such as IBM, is faced with the problem that some areas of the business need to be developed and others areas scaled down or even closed. Portfolio analysis assists the strategic engineering manager in this decision making process.

The Boston matrix is one approach to portfolio analysis. How does the Boston matrix relate to the product life cycle model and what are the deficiencies in the Boston matrix as a tool for portfolio analysis.

The General Electric matrix attempts to avoid the problems of the Boston matrix by focusing on market attractiveness and competitive position. Briefly outline what the difference is between these two parameters.

6. A student project in health psychology has uncovered a need, at present unmet, for a London laboratory conducting medical (AIDS, pregnancy) tests on a personal call-in basis from people not wishing to consult in a formal hospital setting. Using the service 7Ps, what would be your analysis of the marketing mix needs for this service?

7. In the marketing of complex electronic systems involving software the service elements of the marketing mix are important. You are the senior engineer in a company that supplies total package systems to the financial industry (banks etc.). You provide a total service of hardware configuration, hardware installation, communication systems, software implementation and customer staff training. Business in this sector is good and you have recruited some new graduate engineers to supervise the implementation of major projects in customer locations throughout Europe.

Customer training not only takes place at customer locations but key customer personnel also attend a one week residential session at the company's training centre.

As part of the new graduate engineer induction programme you have decided to have a training session with these new engineers on the implications of the three service elements of the marketing mix as they apply to the above situation. What issues would you cover and why?

8. An innovative company with good marketing will be able to generate more business opportunities than it can exploit. It is necessary to evaluate the range of business options (the so-called portfolio) and select the most advantageous to the company, taking into account both the long term and present needs of the company.

Your company manufactures just three major products and the marketing department has come up with the following summary analysis.

(a) *Conventional floppy disk drives*  You have a relative market share of 30 per cent in a market that is now increasing at 5 per cent a year. This is a fragmented market with many suppliers.

(b) *CD ROM disk drives*  You have a relative market share of 150 per cent in a market that is increasing at 15 per cent a year. The marketing department think that there are only about six to ten competitors and that our company is the market leader.

(c) *A new Read/Write Optical Disk System*  This is an innovative product and our company has only one direct competitor who has about 70 per cent of the market. You consider that the market will increase at 20 per cent a year.

**Note**  *Relative market share is your company's market share divided by the largest competitor's market share.*

Sketch out a Boston matrix analysis of the above situation. What are the limitations of the Boston matrix? Brief notes only are required.

9. A medium sized company makes special products (bio-technology type machinery

and electronic controls and systems) for the cheese manufacturing industry. What type of marketing information system might be appropriate for such a company?

10. A medium sized electronics company makes special security and associated products. It has produced a new and very accurate breathalyser for alcohol in blood determinations. However, although very successful in the UK, the market size is rather limited. What countries might represent suitable export targets, what information would be needed, how could it be collected? For one selected market, what modifications might be needed to the UK marketing mix?

## FURTHER READING

Ansoff, I.H. (1957) *Strategies for Diversification*, McGraw-Hill.

Barnard, M.E. (March 1992) 'The Global Positioning System', *IEE Review* Volume 38, Number 3.

Cowell, D. (1989) *The Marketing of Services*, Heinemann.

Hedley, B. (1977) *Long Range Planning*, Pergamon Press.

Kotler, P. (1991) *Marketing Management, Analysis, Planning, Implementation and Control*, 7th Edition, Prentice-Hall International.

Lancaster, G. and L. Massingham (1993) *Marketing Management*, McGraw-Hill.

Lucey, T. (1989) *Operation Research topics: Quantitative Techniques*, 3rd Edition.

McDonald, M. (1990) *Marketing Plans, How to Prepare them, How to use them*, 2nd Edition, Heinemann.

Moore, W.L. (1993) *Product Planning and Management, Designing and Delivering Value*, McGraw-Hill.

Sowter, C. (March 1993) 'Marketing is too important to be left to the Marketing Department', *IEE News*.

# SIX

# OPERATIONS

## 6.1 WHAT IS OPERATIONS?

*'Operations' is the management activity concerned with the efficient and effective planning, development, commissioning, operation and control of the productive and/or service resources and activities of an organization in order to satisfy the legitimate expectations of relevant stakeholders.*

The subject of operations is proactive. It is not just about talking, it is about the management of the largest resources of most organizations, both in manufacturing and service. The concepts and techniques are just as applicable to manufacturing, the provision of medical care in a hospital, a retail shop or telecommunications services.

In our consideration of competitive advantage, it was noted that key advantages can be realized through cost, service and quality advantages. Being at the heart of the organization, operations touches every aspect of the firm, every aspect of the value chain. Efficient operations is the key to the achievement of these competitive advantages.

It is not enough to do things well, to be efficient. To succeed in business, we must also do the right things. Operations is not only about how to make things, but to be holistic and create the appropriate product, that which customers need, want, and value, with quality built in, whether designed for manufacture or for service provision. Operations, therefore, has as much an input to new product or service design as does marketing. Operations management is involved in the selection of the manufacturing technology and the productive capacity design (for example, factory layout for manufacturing or network design for electrical power distribution). Operations is about the implementation of these plans, the project management to build the factory or to install the new fibre optic network for an ISDN (Integrated Signal Digital Network) telecommunications system. Having created these productive resources with a strategic orientation, operations is about the day-to-day operation of the facilities, how much to make, when to make, with what specific schedules, through which units. In the electrical supply service, it involves decisions as to which units of power generation to run and which specific elements of the grid will supply the power need.

The last section of the above definition has become of increasing impact over the last decade. No longer is it acceptable to regard people as simple productive units. Modern operations does not consider it good enough to take account of the legitimate human expectations as some regrettable need, but rather to expect that the well-designed operations system is adaptive, with every person in the system contributing to its management (in the full sense of exercising discretionary control). Operations is the management area where the organization's environmental mission has to be implemented, with products designed and manufactured for appropriate concern for the environment and the eco-system.

In modern society, the most appropriate point to begin to consider a management subject is to start with the most important, the source of all profits, the customer. Our starting point for the consideration of operations will be market-driven quality.

## 6.2  QUALITY

*'Quality' refers to fitness for the intended purpose of customers and users, subject to the legitimate expectations of other relevant publics.*

This is a much more powerful and demanding definition than that used in the past, which was conformance to specifications, when the culture was to ensure quality by a rigorous application of standards, with frequent inspection from a separate quality control function. It is a marketing-orientated definition, as it involves the organization defining who its customers, users and publics are and then determining the legitimate quality expectations for each of the user groups. It places the quality responsibility on the provider rather than on the buyer. In the past, it was up to the buyer to consider the specification and determine whether this met their buyer needs. The quality publics for even a simple product are more extensive than just the buyer and user.

**Quality publics for desk top publishing software such as PageMaker**

1. Buyer
2. Technicians
3. Network manager
4. User
   (a) Author
   (b) Printer needing camera ready copy
   (c) Readers of the final publication
5. Linked software houses
   (a) Windows (for PageMaker)
   (b) PostScript software for printers
   (c) Other packages such as word-processing, spreadsheets and graphics for ease of export/import
   (d) Operating system
   (e) Network software
6. Computer manufacturers
7. Printer manufacturers

Once the quality publics have been identified then the second phase of the quality expectations analysis can be completed with the legitimate, realistic, quality expectations of each public considered. In Chapter Five, the technique of attribute analysis was introduced. The quality audit provides another source of amplified detail to feed into the full attribute analysis.

## Quality expectations

### New user (author)

1. Windows user friendly
2. Import facilities
3. Many scalable fonts
4. WYSIWYG (What You See Is What You Get)
5. Spell Checker (for all Windows Packages)
6. Full range of printing options such as:
    (a) Headers and footers
    (b) Indexing and Table of Contents functions
    (c) Page numbering
    (d) Outline sets
7. Good display of imported graphics
8. Rapid screen display, easy zoom in and out
9. Rapid printing
10. Good manual, good help features on screen, easy to configure etc.

The quality definition used in this text is in harmony with the many variations given by organizations implementing MDQ (Market Driven Quality) with a framework of TQM (Total Quality Management). In such an organization, part of the corporate mission statement will be an explicit formulation of quality values expected and, further from this, the normal hierarchy of quality aims and objectives which will affect each and every individual in the organization's value chain. The need to involve all members of the value chain extends the Total Quality Management scope outside the organization to bring in other value chain links, such as suppliers and distributors. By this definition, there cannot be a Total Quality Management department. However, there are certain key quality activities as in the audit of suppliers, presentation of specifications that need to be conducted by quality specialists and, in a TQM company, there will be a Quality Assurance Department. This group will take the lead in the formulation and coordination of TQM, and will be responsible for the effective recording and conduct of quality audits, both internal and external to the firm. Typical aspects will be the drawing up of specifications, provision and coordination of quality training, submission of quality documentation to external organizations and operational control of quality control. This increased awareness that quality rests not just on specifications but also the quality of the management systems, has led to the development of two of the most important British quality standards British Standard BS5750 (Quality Management and Systems) and BS7550 (Environmental Management and Systems). These are reflected internationally with International Standards Organization ISO9000 (quality) and ISO11000 (environment). The documents lay down the elements that an organization must have to be considered to be of BS5750 standard (for example, an explicit quality mission and quality manual) and provides a framework of independent assessors to audit the company. Thus a TQM company that chooses to BS5750 register may use this in its documentation to demonstrate its commitment to quality and the standard of its quality systems. Customers may well consider it less necessary to complete supplier quality audits from a BS5750 supplier on the basis that an effective audit has been completed and is reviewed within the BS5750 quality standard.

Within the framework of TQM and Quality Assurance there is Quality Control, the day-to-day specific activity of sampling and testing of products, conformance to specifications. Increasingly, it is possible to devolve this day-to-day work further down the line with 100 per cent inspection with automated test procedures. Such automated techniques not only apply to the manufacture of products but also to the provision of services. In a telecommunications system, for example, equipment can be installed to monitor line quality and service levels.

Many quality experts say that 'quality comes free', but all the above activities clearly involve the organization in the investment of significant management time and capital expenditure to ensure quality, so how can quality be free? One element is a statement of philosophy which it is not possible to prove in each specific instance but, when industry profitabilities are compared, those companies with the best long run profitability tend to be those with the best standards of environmental concern and of quality and safety. With such substantial sums invested, some approach to estimating the cost of quality is needed. The cost of the quality, staff and training etc., can be readily estimated. What is needed is a framework to estimate the cost of poor quality, sometimes called PONC (Price of Non-Conformance). In the manufacturing environment there are direct costs, such as cost of wasted materials, increased production costs of rework, and increased inventory costs while products are rectified. Failure to have the highest quality systems may mean increased product liability insurance costs (in the limit refusal of insurance). In the field, additional costs will involve field service or return of the faulty product, defect rectification and greatest of all, loss of customer satisfaction. The systematic estimation of non-conformity costs allows an informed management appraisal of the balance of costs and financial risks.

The traditional approach to quality control takes an oversimplistic view of the quality situation (Fig. 6.1) where the cost function is seen as a step function, a quantum well within finite barriers. Products are either acceptable or unacceptable. This is clearly not the case, and Taguchi has advanced the obvious concern that the true cost of divergence from

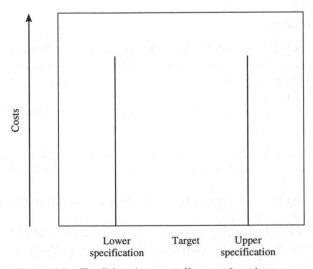

**Figure 6.1** Traditional step quality cost function

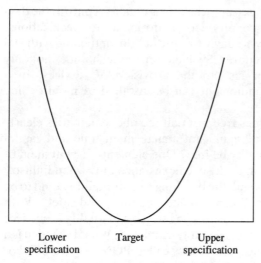

Lower              Target           Upper
specification                        specification

**Figure 6.2**  Taguchi parabolic type quality cost function

optimum is more a parabolic curve (Fig. 6.2). Small deviations from the ideal are of very modest significance but large ones are not. The key to effective and efficient manufacture is to operate with manufacturing and measurement techniques which allow statistical control of the process within the flat region of the parabolic curve.

Later in this chapter 'Just In Time' (JIT) production operations will be considered. Here the need is for zero defects, with no inspection of those incoming materials which will be delivered direct to the production line. In these conditions, the cost of any non-conformity (non-usable units) will be the shutdown of service or production line. Zero defects TQM can be said to be based on three axioms:

1.  There must be an assignable cause of rejects
2.  That prevention is better than cure
3.  You have to measure in order to control

The success of the TQM movement is that these axioms have been carried through such devices as quality circles to understanding, commitment, operation and ownership by all; the statement that every worker is a quality inspector is not a slogan in a TQM organization, it is a simple statement of fact.

A quality control system is no different to any other control system. There are certain generic desirable characteristics:

1.  The measurement system should be sensitive to meaningful changes. In technical terms, the standard deviation of the measurement system should be well within the changes it is required to detect.
2.  The response time of the measurement system should be short when compared to the time scales of the system it is desired to control.
3.  When deviation is detected, control can be quickly and effectively applied before the system deviates outside of control limits (that is, defective products are produced).

In QC sampling we have the burglar alarm problem. We need a system that is 100 per cent effective when there is an attempt to entry but has a zero risk of activation when there is no attempt at entry. As we realize every time we shop at the local superstore, the car alarm problem has not been solved; with so many false alarms sounding, that little interest is shown on activation. The situation of the burglar alarm activation where there is no entry is called the alpha error problem; a deviation from standard is signalled when there is no change or a good batch of product is rejected when it is acceptable. (This error is sometimes referred to as the producer's risk.) The reverse, beta error, is where there is an attempt at forced entry where there is no signal. In production the beta error is where there is a deviation in the conditions or the batch is substandard, but there is no detection. (This is often referred to as the buyer's risk.) The perfect situation is only possible with 100 per cent sampling. Of course, this is becoming much more possible, with automated and non-destructive methods of product test. Before considering control charts, we shall briefly consider the operating characteristic of a simple sampling plan. Consider a lot of resistors which are to be sampled and tested where a defect rate of 10 per cent is considered to be accepted, that is, 10 per cent maximum AQL (Acceptance Quality Level). If we sample only one resistor, we have very little information, but if we sample all resistors we have complete information. If test procedures are expensive, involving laboratory resources and, with some tests, the destruction of the test sample, the key issue is just how many samples do we have to take and test to obtain an acceptable level of certainty on the quality of the batch. This is a simple binomial distribution problem. Figure 6.3 shows the probabilities of finding a given number of defectives for a sample size of 20 (binomial

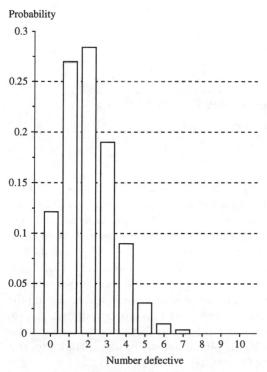

**Figure 6.3**   Binomial sampling distribution

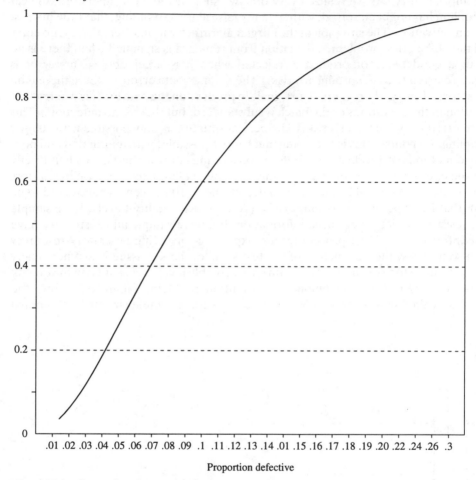

Probability of rejection

Proportion defective

**Figure 6.4**    Operating characteristic curve

probability, defective proportions 10 per cent). Figure 6.4 shows this translated to the operating characteristic curve, the probability that we will detect a defective batch for sample size 20 and varying lot defective proportions. From this it can be seen that there is a significant chance (about 0.1) that a batch with only 5 per cent defective would be rejected (producer's risk). The curve also shows that when the defective level is 15 per cent there is a significant chance (0.2) that the batch would still be accepted (customer's risk). In a typical sampling plan, we might agree a 95 per cent level of confidence and we need a procedure which will indicate the number of samples to be selected and tested. Given the number of test samples required and the small number of defectives required in production, the limits can be calculated by the use of the Poisson distribution. Under these conditions, it is an acceptable approximation to the binomial distribution. (Tables for this are given in standard texts for sampling plans (BS 6001)).

There are a number of practical problems in this type of sampling plan. The underlying statistical theory assumes that samples must be drawn in a random fashion (not just from the top of the box) and that the population is infinite. In practice, if the lot size under investigation is 10 to 20 times the number of test samples indicated, this requirement is satisfied to all practical intents. Such sampling plans can be also constructed for parameters which may be measured (such as resistance) rather than the simple pass or fail situation considered in the simple binomial distribution. Apart from the statistical issues, there are practical production problems in this mode of quality control testing. During the whole of the production of this batch of products, there might have been production drift and if this had been detected then very few defectives would have been produced. While this testing is in process, either the production unit is stopped or could be producing yet more defective products. Higher levels of quality are now demanded, six sigma programmes being common, where the acceptable defect rate is one defect in a million and, in effect, zero defects are the requirement. Fortunately, new methods of test and automation have allowed online testing of all components or products on an online production situation. To prevent the production of defectives the test procedure and the manufacturing process should have standard deviations several times more sensitive than the rejection limit to be considered.

With these conditions it is possible to run the process under statistical quality control conditions. One simple and powerful tool for this is the use of Cu-Sum charts. The use of Cu-Sum charts will be exemplified by the consideration of a production line producing resistors, where the specification calls for a product of 1000 ohms ± 1 ohm. The standard deviation of the test procedure and manufacturing process has been found to be 0.2 ohms. The figures given below represent the production of the product on the desired limit followed by a deviation of process average by one standard deviation. To plot the Cu-Sum chart we subtract the target value (or the long run average for an historical analysis) from each of the observations and then sum the differences, hence the name cumulative sum (Cu-Sum). This is shown in Table 6.1 and is plotted schematically in Fig. 6.5. If the manufacturing process is under statistical control then the line may go up and down a little, but overall will remain horizontal. If the process has drifted (one standard deviation down, in our case) then the line will start to rise or fall with the slope of the line indicating the deviation of the process in terms of standard deviations.

The first question we address is what scale we should use for the vertical scale, and decide that a vertical scale of about two standard deviations for each sequential test is acceptable. We now have an intuitive control chart. If the line is horizontal, the process is on target, a rising line indicates a deviation above the limit, a descending line a deviation below the limit. What is now required is a method of bringing some statistical rigour to allow us to set the levels of type alpha (false alarm) and beta (missed alarm). This is done by the construction of the V mask shown in Fig. 6.5.

The V mask is calculated and printed onto clear plastic, the cross piece is placed on the last observation and a signal is given when the line just touches the V mask. Such a control chart can be used by process operatives and does not require detailed knowledge of the underlying statistics. To obtain maximum sensitivity to rapid changes and the ability to pick up small long term changes, the end of the V is replaced with a parabolic section. This is called the semi-parabolic V mask, as shown in Fig. 6.5. The calculation for the V mask is shown in Table 6.2. A key parameter is the number of observations needed to produce a given signal for a given shift, expressed in terms of standard deviations. This is shown in Table 6.3 with a comparison with the traditional Shewhart chart. In a Shewhart chart,

**Table 6.1** Cu-Sum of resistance measurements

| Observation | Resistance | Deviation | Cu-Sum |
|---|---|---|---|
| 1 | 999.9476 | −0.0524 | −0.0524 |
| 2 | 1000.047 | 0.0466 | −0.0058 |
| 3 | 999.9048 | −0.0952 | −0.1010 |
| 4 | 1000.1600 | 0.1600 | 0.0590 |
| 5 | 1000.0720 | 0.7180 | 0.1308 |
| 6 | 1000.006 | 0.0056 | 0.1364 |
| 7 | 999.8762 | −0.1238 | 0.0126 |
| 8 | 999.9844 | −0.01558 | −0.00298 |
| 9 | 999.9462 | −0.05380 | −0.05678 |
| 10 | 1000.425 | 0.4246 | 0.36782 |
| 11 | 999.9316 | −0.0684 | 0.29942 |
| 12 | 999.8788 | −0.1212 | 0.17822 |
| 13 | 999.6814 | −0.3186 | −0.14038 |
| 14 | 1000.1440 | 0.1442 | 0.00382 |
| 15 | 999.8402 | −0.1598 | −0.15598 |
| 16 | 999.7682 | −0.2318 | −0.38778 |
| 17 | 999.4894 | −0.5106 | −0.89838 |
| 18 | 999.8918 | −0.1082 | −1.00658 |
| 19 | 999.7122 | −0.2878 | −1.29438 |
| 20 | 999.6652 | −0.3348 | −1.62918 |

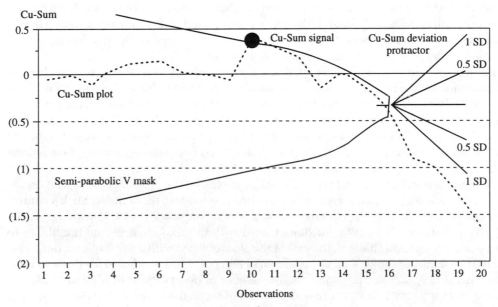

**Figure 6.5** Cu-Sum chart for resistance example

**Table 6.2**   Data for construction of a semi-parabolic Cu-Sum mask

| Distance from datum (sample intervals) i | Half width of mask at i (units of SD) |
|:---:|:---:|
| 0 | 1.25 |
| 1 | 3.10 |
| 2 | 4.65 |
| 3 | 5.90 |
| 4 | 6.85 |
| 5 | 7.50 |
| 6 | 8.00 |
| 7 | 8.50 |
| 8 | 9.00 |
| 9 | 9.50 |
| 10 | 10.00 |
| 15 | 12.50 |
| 20 | 15.00 |

Sample intervals 0–5:   $y = 1.25 + 2i - 0.15i^2$
Sample intervals 6–20:   $y = 5 + 0.05i$

(Reproduced from British Standard 5703 with permission.)

**Table 6.3**   Comparison of semi-parabolic V mask with Shewhart charts

| Shift in average from target (units SD) | Semi-parabolic V Mask | Action line only | Shewhart chart Warning and action lines |
|:---:|:---:|:---:|:---:|
| 0.00 | 470 | 1000 | 640 |
| 0.25 | 113 | 443 | 256 |
| 0.50 | 35 | 208 | 126 |
| 0.75 | 16.5 | 104 | 52 |
| 1.00 | 10 | 55 | 26 |
| 1.50 | 5.3 | 18 | 8.9 |
| 2.0 | 3.4 | 7.3 | 4.2 |
| 2.5 | 2.3 | 3.6 | 2.5 |
| 3.0 | 1.74 | 2.2 | 1.75 |
| 4 | 1.21 | 1.20 | 1.20 |

(Reproduced from British Standard 5703 with permission.)

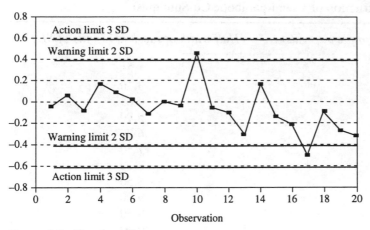

**Figure 6.6**  Shewhart chart

observations are plotted in terms of standard deviations. It can be seen that the Cu-Sum procedure is more efficient than Shewhart charts and quality control tests are now based on Cu-Sums in BS5703. Figure 6.6 shows the Shewhart chart for the resistance data.

The semi-parabolic type of mask represents an effective compromise which will pick up large changes with small average run lengths (ARL, the average number of observations that a given statistical design with a given operating characteristic will require to detect a given shift in the process) without too many false alarms (type beta errors). The advantages of Cu-Sum charts are that they can be run by inexperienced staff with only modest training, yet allow the use of advanced statistical control theory.

Visual methods are excellent in communicating and in the identification of problems. A particular problem exists in many products with difficulties, for example, surface defects to the final finish or scratches in the finish of a floppy disk. The simple recording of defects as 'scratches' etc. may conceal useful information. The use of a simple measles diagram, Fig. 6.7, where the nature and location of faults are indicated, can often give insight as to where the major problem is.

A common feature of defects is that 80 per cent are caused by 20 per cent of the possible causes, the Pareto curve shown in Fig. 6.8. Thus, it is most often found that most defects in quality assurance will be caused by a small number of all the possible snags. This rule applies not only to quality but to most situations in management. Eighty per cent of the work days lost through illness will come from 20 per cent of the staff, 80 per cent of the sales of the company will come from 20 per cent of the customers. In inventory management, 80 per cent of the inventory value will be accounted for by 20 per cent of the parts. This is not a law, but a commonly observed feature. To construct a Pareto curve for raw material stocks, products should be ranked in order of ascending stock value and then the cumulative value of stock plotted against the number of materials. The value of the approach is to concentrate management attention and action on the 20 per cent of potential decisions that will have major effects on the productivity of the company.

The 'fishbone' or Ishikawa diagram allows the simple but powerful identification of influences on a quality problem and investigation of possible causes. Figure 6.9 shows a

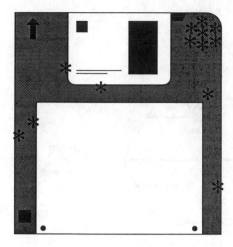

✳  Surface defect

**Figure 6.7**    Measles diagram for surface defects on a floppy disk

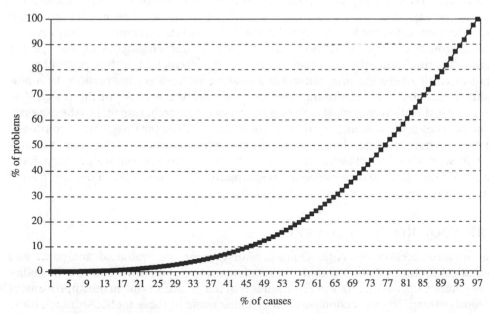

**Figure 6.8**    Pareto curve

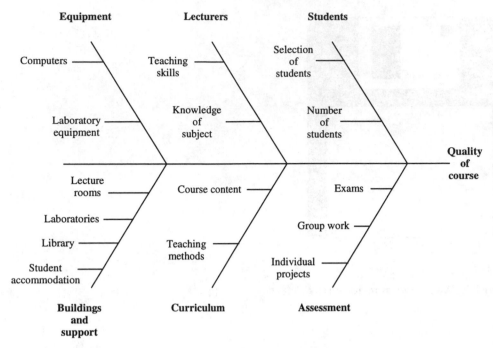

**Figure 6.9** Ishikawa or 'Fishbone' diagram for the quality of a course

'fishbone' diagram for the quality of a university course. Again, the value of the technique is not only the power of diagnosis and creative insight, but also of communication.

The axiom of Total Quality Management is that the whole company, from the managing director to the newest employee, identify with the quality mission and have received the appropriate training to enable them to make a real and discretionary input to the provision of total customer quality satisfaction. In other words, for employees to manage the 'moments of truth' with the customer. Every single interaction with a customer is a moment of truth where the firm can make a positive or negative impression. In a new computer installation, the marketing does not end with the winning of the order. The delivery and installation staff must continue the service, remembering that to the majority of the employees in the customer's premises their image will be the image of the company. When the customer hits a new bug in the program and telephones to ask for help, is there a prompt answer? Can the call be directed to somebody who can sort out the problem in the minimum of time? Each and every contact is an opportunity to reinforce or damage a good corporate image and supplier–customer relationship.

## 6.3 THE TOOL KIT AND CONCEPTS

In the previous section on Total Quality Management, the value of analytical and mathematical tools was demonstrated. There are many areas of business where the ability of the engineer to use mathematical techniques is of the greatest value in the improvement of decision making. In this section we shall examine some of these tools. Although these are presented in the context of operations, these tools can be of equal value in other areas of management. Forecasting is not only important in operations, but also in marketing. The use of linear programming is not only of value in determining the optimum production mix for a factory, but can be used to determine the optimum use of a limited advertising budget in marketing.

## 6.3.1  Forecasting and estimation

It is not the purpose of a text of this length to present in detail the mathematical theory which underlies these topics; leading references are given at the end of this chapter to selected readings, where the detailed mathematical treatment can be examined. Here, emphasis is given to the common pitfalls of simple mechanical application of statistical techniques. In most cases, excellent statistical packages exist, allowing the non-statistician to do much analysis, but some understanding of the areas of applicability are needed or major errors can be made.

If we could forecast which horse will win the 2.30 p.m. tomorrow with 100 per cent certainty, then we would no longer need to work. In almost any activity, we wish to make some estimates of the future. In the supply of electricity, the prediction of the future is most important, as electricity must be generated at the time of demand because if we do not have enough generation capacity, voltages will drop with brown outs. If we have overestimated, power-stations will be on stand-by at vast expense. Estimates are required for different time scales. The example below gives some factors. (A full analysis would require a both PEST and Porter analysis.)

---

### Some needs and factors in electricity supply forecasting long term (years)

**Needs**  To ensure the provision of capacity in the future where it may take ten years from first decision to full commissioning of a nuclear power plant and to make appropriate modifications to the national grid.

**Factors**  Technologies, the more efficient use of electricity might reduce demand. Social trends, the use of more labour-saving devices, such as combined washing machines and tumble dryers, automatic dishwashing machines will increase the demand for electricity.

### Medium term (monthly)

**Needs**  The engineering managers need to schedule planned maintenance for both the grid and power generation capacity. This has to be done at times when the demand is expected to be low.

**Factors**  Level of commercial activity (less during holiday season), seasonal factors. Higher domestic energy use in the winter in the UK (note that with the extensive use of air-conditioning in the USA the summer months represent another time of peak demand in that market).

### Short term (day)

**Need**  The managing engineer needs to decide what generation capacity will be needed next day to schedule which plants must be available. It is not possible to start up a coal power station in 10 minutes.

**Factors**   Day of the week, bank holidays, major strikes, weather.

### Micro (hours and minutes)

**Need**   To bring in or stand down the marginal capacity as demand fluctuates.

**Factors**   Time of the day (less energy used at 03.00 a.m. than at 3.00 p.m.), when the big film ends (everyone turns on the light in the kitchen and puts on the electric kettle for a coffee).

---

The time series analysis of this type of problem involves elements of trends, seasonality, and shorter time cycles, as well as random elements. Before the examination of a number techniques for forecasting, these three golden rules should be noted:

1. Always graph the series to be forecast, if possible together with the errors of the forecast. The preferred technique is Cu-Sum, discussed in the earlier section.
2. Never rely solely on objective statistical forecasting if other reliable information is available and can be used.
3. The master rule of all operational research, mathematical modelling and statistics. Keep your methods simple unless it can be shown that some more sophisticated method could give significantly better forecasts.

The reader is referred to the reading list at the end of this chapter for detailed statistical treatment. Under any statistical method, simulation or mathematical approach there is some model of the system. With this model comes a set of assumptions, such as independence of error distributions, which if violated render the approach invalid.

**Statistical independence of errors**   In the collection of sales or production figures, it may be assumed that the variations around the trend are random. In the production situation, units may often be produced in lots. If a lot is nearing completion it may not be counted in that day's figures, but with very little effort will be completed in the next period. Thus, a poor day may well be matched with a succeeding good day and there will be some correlation in the errors. In sales or production, a month is often taken as a convenient reporting period. Clearly, however, there are differing numbers of working days in different months (number of weekends, bank holidays, etc.). Thus in looking for any trends, figures should be adjusted for any confounding influences which could obscure the real trend and the structure it is desired to identify. In the long running financial analysis, it is essential to ensure that the effects of inflation are properly treated.

### 6.3.2 Regression

The simplest form of regression is where a linear relationship is assumed of the form:

$$y = a + bx$$

and any observation may be expressed as

$$y = a + bx + e$$

Where $a$ is a constant, $b$ is the slope of the fitted regression line and where $e$ is the random error of the process and its measurement.

**Table 6.4** Regression analysis

| Length in metres | Resistance in ohms |
|---|---|
| 1 | 2.322 |
| 2 | 4.76 |
| 3 | 6.167 |
| 4 | 4.456 |
| 5 | 5.483 |
| 6 | 6.559 |
| 7 | 6.992 |
| 8 | 6.955 |
| 9 | 9.771 |
| 10 | 11.125 |

Using any of the many spreadsheet or statistical programs, or even scientific calculators, the calculation is simple. It should be noted that the engineer needs to determine which are the dependent and independent variables. Table 6.4 gives data for two variables, the resistance and the length of a wire, where the test procedure is not very accurate. The data is plotted with the regression line shown in Fig. 6.10. The 95 per cent confidence interval (we are 95 per cent certain that the true line is between the upper and lower curves based on the number of observations we have) for resistance as the dependent variable and the length of the independent variable are also shown. For the details of such calculations, reference should be made to the reading list at the end of the chapter or the reference manual of the specific computer package used for the calculation. The greater the number of points, the better our estimate of the true regression line. When we come to use the regression line as a predictive estimate and seek to estimate the

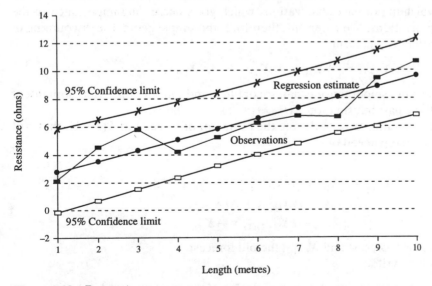

**Figure 6.10** Regression

resistance of a wire from its length, the error of this single estimate may not be reduced below the underlying error of the test procedure. Increasing the number of observations increases the precision of the estimate to this limit. If we require improvement in the accuracy of our estimate we have to improve the accuracy (reduce the variance) of the test procedure.

For the example given, there appears to a good reason for the selection of a starting linear relationship. By suitable transformation, higher order (power functions) or other functions, such as exponential, may be fitted. In time series analysis, the regression may provide a short run prediction where the growth rate approximates to a linear rate over a limited range. Unless there is some good physical reason to believe there is a linear relationship between two variables, it is most dangerous to extrapolate the linear prediction much out of the range of direct observation. Certainly, it is not wise to use a linear regression equation to predict sales far into the future. Where there is more than one effect, such as temperature and length in the resistance of a wire, the techniques of multiple regression may be used.

### 6.3.3 Exponential weighted moving average (EWMA)

Historically, one of the earliest methods was to smooth the original series by simple averaging.

$$X_{(t+1)} = [X_{(t)} + X_{(t-1)} + X_{(t-2)} \ldots + X_{(t-7)}]/8$$

Where:

$X_{(t+1)}$ is the next future observation that it is desired to predict and $X_{(t)}$ is the last observation, $X_{(t-1)}$ the next to last etc.

One may note that each of the past eight observations have equal weights (1/8) which conflicts somewhat with our intuitive feeling that the observation further into the past should bear less relevance to the future than the more immediate past observations. Thus, we look for a weighting of past observations which gives decreasing importance to the more remote observations. We entertain, therefore, the simple geometric discounting of the past observations of the form

$$X_{(t+1)} = [AX_{(t)} + ArX_{(t-1)} + Ar^2X_{(t-2)} \ldots$$

where $0 < r < 1$), as our smoothing mechanism or filter, and consider this as an estimator of $X(t + 1)$ with all the past information $X(t), X(t - 1) \ldots$ to hand.

We shall use the notation $X_{t(1)}$ to denote the estimator or forecast of $X(t + 1)$, that is of the observation one step ahead of $t$.
Thus:

$$X_{t(1)} = AX_{(t)} + ArX_{(t-1)} + Ar^2X_{(t-2)} + \ldots$$
$$X_{(t-1)(1)} = AX_{(t-1)} + ArX_{(t-2)} \ldots$$
$$X_{t(1)} - rX_{(t-1)(1)} = AX_{(t)}$$

where $X_{t(1)}$ is the new forecast and $X_{t-1(t)}$ the old forecast.
We may therefore write:

new forecast $= r$(old forecast) + some fraction of the most recent observation.

Now, since any forecast of a base level ($k$) should reproduce that level, we should have:

$$A + Ar + Ar^2 + \ldots = 1$$

i.e.
$$A/(1 - r) = 1 \text{ or } r = 1 - A$$

Hence:

$$X_{t(1)} = (1 - A)X_{(t-1)(1)} + AX_{(t)}$$

i.e. the new forecast is a weighted interpolation between the old forecast and the current observation.

The full forecasting formula is:

$$X_{t(1)} = AX_{(t)} = A(1 - A)X_{(t-1)} + A(1 - A)^2 X_{(t-2)} + \ldots$$

and for obvious reasons is called an Exponentially Weighted Moving Average Forecast (an EWMA Forecast).

The EWMA model is of use where one suspects there should be a level demand for product, but one wants to be able to detect if there should be a step change in this level of demand for any reason. Figure 6.11 shows a step function and the way in which a simple moving average and an EWMA forecast would track this step change. It should be noted that the EWMA is more sensitive to picking up the step change as it gives more weight to the recent observations. However, in the previous section, regression was discussed where it was suspected that there was a trend in the data. Figure 6.12 shows the same EWMA and weighted moving average tracking a trend. Here it is noted that the model will never give a good estimate as the model will always track at a lower level. These methods are not effective when a trend is suspected in the data.

### 6.3.4  Extensions to the EWMA model (Holt-Winters)

Many parameters we may wish to estimate may not only have a trend and error but also some systematic periodic component, for example, the replacement sales of car batteries increases in the early winter. The Holt-Winters model allows the estimation of all three components, the base level, the trend component and the seasonality superimposed on the trend and base level. Figure 6.13 shows trend with seasonal data superimposed.

To take account of trends and seasonality in series, we allow for these to undergo changes through time in structuring the model, depending on whether we suspect the best fit is an additive component or a multiplicative, as follows:

*Additive model*

$$M(t) = a(X(t) - S(t - n)) + (1 - a)(M(t - 1) + T(t - 1))$$
$$T(t) = b(M(t) - M(t - 1)) + (1 - b)T(t - 1)$$
$$S(t) = c(X(t) - M(t)) + (1 - c)S(t - n)$$
$$X(t + 1) = M(t) + T(t) + S(t - n + 1)$$
$$X_t(1) = M(t) + 1T(t) + S(t - n + 1), 1 = 1, 2, \ldots n$$

$$n = \text{a seasonal number e.g. } 12$$

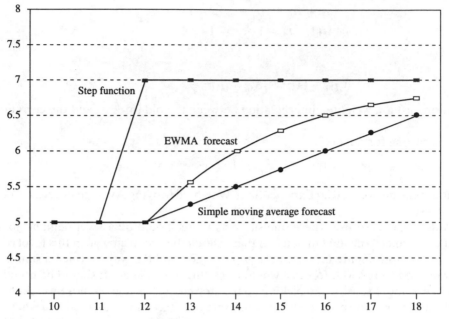

**Figure 6.11**   EWMA for a step function

*Multiplicative method*

$$M(t) = aX(t)/S(t - n) + (1 - a)(M(t - 1) + T(t - 1)$$
$$T(t) = (1 - b)(M(t) - M(t - 1)) + (1 - b)T(t - 1)$$
$$S(t) = c(X(t)/M(t)) + (1 - c)S(t - n)$$
$$X_t(1) = (M(t) + 1T(t)) \cdot S(t - n + 1)$$

Commonly used values are 0.2, 0.2 and 0.6 for *a*, *b*, and *c* respectively.

Box and Jenkins (1970) produced a general class of models for time series analysis of which those we have mentioned can be shown to be special cases. However, the latter have been shown to be very useful as automatic methods in practice because of their simplicity. The Box and Jenkins models, whilst allowing more flexibility and choice, are nevertheless more difficult to estimate but, once estimated, are as straightforward to use in forecasting as the others.

### 6.3.5  Optimum stock and quality control

The simplest system is to consider a deterministic model where components are ordered at fixed periods in fixed quantities against a steady demand. This is shown in Fig. 6.14.

Total Annual Cost

=

Annual Purchase Cost + Annual Ordering Cost + Annual Holding Cost

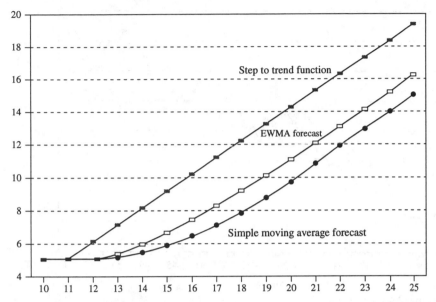

**Figure 6.12**    EWMA for a trend

This can be put in equation form:

$$TC = DC + S(D/Q) + H(Q/2)$$

$TC$ =  Total annual cost of purchase, ordering and holding
$D$   =  The total annual demand
$C$   =  Unit cost
$S$   =  Cost of ordering (purchase decision)
$S$   =  Set-up cost for line change (production)
$Q$   =  Quantity to be ordered or manufactured
           Called Economic Order Quantity (EOQ) for optimum value
$H$   =  Cost of holding
$R$   =  Reorder level
$L$   =  Lead time (placement of order free for production use) to purchase

By the normal techniques of differential calculus it can be shown that the Economic Order Quantity (EOQ) is given by the equation:

$$EOQ = (2DS/H)^{1/2}$$

Consider the example of an electronics firm purchasing a specific type of disk drive:
$D$ =  1000 units
$C$ =  £5
$S$  =  £200 an order
$H$ =  25 per cent of stock value a year

The cost curves are given in Fig. 6.15 and by the application of the formula the Economic Order Quantity can be seen to be:

$$EOQ = (2*1000*200/(0.25*5))^{1/2} = 566$$

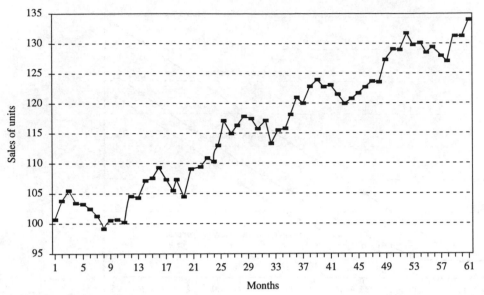

**Figure 6.13**   Seasonal data with trend

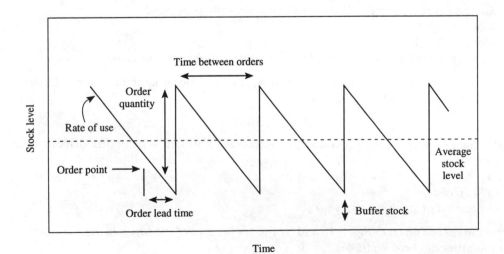

**Figure 6.14**   Simple stock cycle

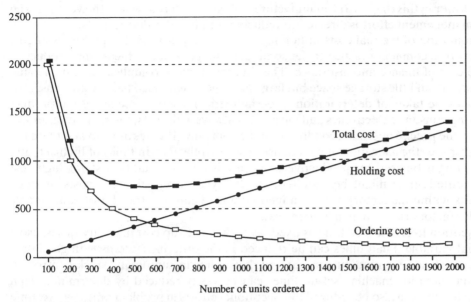

**Figure 6.15**   Cost of stock holding and ordering

There are many deficiencies in this simple model, demands are rarely certain and susceptible to random changes. It may be more convenient not to order fixed quantities, but rather order at fixed periods. There are many variations to this, which are covered in major texts on stock control. In this short section we shall concentrate on the problems with the assumptions in these models and the key managerial issues.

Given a mix of products, there is a high premium on standardization. The stock holding equation indicates that if the demand for a unit increases by a factor of four the optimum stock will increase by a factor of only two. The demands for products tend to be subject to some random demands. If assemblies can be used on several products then the total, proportional, estimate of the error should be less, giving more security for a set level of stock cover.

The price for a unit may not be a simple calculation involving break points for volumes and, in most cases, there may be differing prices from differing suppliers. For security reasons, the firm may wish to buy from more than one source, even where there is a modest price premium to be paid. In certain circumstances, the company may have the option to manufacture a sub-assembly or contract out by purchase.

There are problems in the estimation of ordering or set-up costs. In Chapter Nine, Finance, this issue is considered in more detail. However, consider this simple case for the reorder situation. The firm employs an order clerk who is paid £200 a week and places 50 orders a week. The temptation is to say that the cost of an order is £4, but does it cost the company another £4 to place the 51st order? There are two issues; the first is the problem of more or less arbitrary allocation of costs which will greatly affect the position of EOQ. Moreover, the blind use of the equation assumes that the key managerial issue to be addressed is the EOQ. Clearly, the set-up time or the cost of ordering is also a managerial variable. Later in this chapter JIT manufacture will be considered, where the view is taken that the management effort is directed to reducing set-up and ordering costs.

The estimation of the real costs of holding are also subject to all the problems of cost allocation. It is common practice to set some percentage of the value of the product to cover the cost of finance and insurance. The situation is more complicated, a high value product may need little storage space but large packages might need half a warehouse. No account may be taken of deterioration (food industries) or obsolescence of the product (fast moving consumer electronics and music). As always with costs, the real expenses will depend on the precise operating conditions of the company. If times are bad and there is a lot of free space, the allocation of warehouse costs is irrelevant. In times of high activity, the space might be used for productive units (a missed opportunity cost) or high cost external rented space might be required. In this type of equation the costs of stock movements within the factory are often ignored and, again, the transfer of components around the factory can be a high hidden cost.

The equation takes the lead time as fixed, as with the set-up cost in reality this is also a managerial variable. Lead times can be reduced in the ordering systems with good data exchange, such as laser read-outs in supermarkets, allowing automatic stock control. In the internal situation machine set-up times can be vastly reduced by determined team effort. Such times can also be reduced by exceptional efforts in problem times by overtime working or express delivery orders.

As always with mathematical models, great care must be taken with the assumptions or, even with great mathematical skill, less than optimum solutions may be taken. Such techniques are an aid to managerial decision making, not a substitute for it.

The same types of issues apply to quality inspection.

$$\text{Total Annual Quality Cost}$$
$$=$$
$$\text{Inspection and Testing Cost} + \text{Internal Failure Costs}$$
$$+ \text{External Failure Costs}$$

This theoretical curve follows the same form as for economic order quantities. The same problems exist with difficulty in the estimation of the costs. Online testing can greatly reduce the costs of testing. All too often, internal failure costs are underestimated and the disruption of production schedules is a massive hidden cost. Likewise, the marketing costs of external failure are impossible to estimate but are considerable.

### 6.3.6 Queues

Briefly, a queue develops when people or things require a service facility and the rate of service cannot cope with the rate of requirement. Given such a situation in practice, the problems facing the manager or analyst are often to determine the properties of queue length at any time, the average waiting time per customer, and to study whether improvements are possible through changing the service rate or the queue discipline.

Queues are classified in the literature by $X/Y/Z$, where $X$, $Y$, and $Z$ refer to the type of stochastic input (arrivals), stochastic output (service), and the number of servers respectively. The simplest type of situation is the $M/M/1$ queue, that is, random input, random output and one server only. This is the most easily studied queue mathematically and very often constitutes a benchmark relative to more complex queuing situations. We shall study this simple queue in a little more detail later but first some common situations.

Clearly, queues are natural phenomena; they arise spontaneously depending on a suitable environment, and evolve. They can be useful and harmless, for example, in hospital appointments systems, or dangerous and costly, such as when aircraft are waiting to land in bad weather at a congested airport. In business, a queue of finished products in store can give customers an off-the-shelf service, but if too many are held then it becomes costly in terms of tied-up capital, deterioration, etc.

We remarked earlier that a queue forms when the servicing rate is comparable with the arrival rate. If it is much greater, then a queue of any size is unlikely to form. However, if it is smaller than the arrival rate then the queue grows and never stops growing, leading to an unstable situation. The ratio (arrival rate)/(service rate) is known as the traffic intensity and we shall consider this to lie between zero and unity, in which case the system will give rise to a stable queue.

If we attempt to improve the service to meet every demand immediately it is required, then we will, in general, have periods of time when the service facilities are idle. This could be costly, if a high investment is involved. The analysis then aims to compromise, according to some criterion. Very often this is done by minimizing some cost function, but this is not always the case, for example when human life or the natural environment is concerned. Figure 6.16 shows how the costs of operating a system may appear.

At slow service rates, queues build up and so does the cost of waiting. For an oil tanker, such delays could be exceedingly expensive. If the service rate is increased then, almost certainly, this requires expenditure, but the waiting times decrease from which we should make a saving. We need to find the service rate which minimizes the total cost of operating the system.

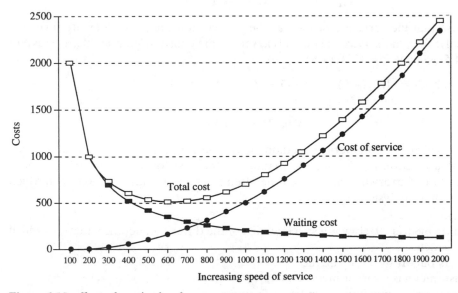

**Figure 6.16**   Cost of service levels

**The simple queue ($M/M/1$)—a practical example**   Suppose by inspection or from specification we can write down the average arrival times ($1/a$) and the average service time ($1/b$) in our system. These are the only two numerical values necessary to evaluate the behaviour of the system, under the discipline of first-come first-served. Suppose these two statistics turn out to be 5.4 and 4.5 minutes respectively, then $T$ (where $T = a/b$), the traffic intensity, is 0.833, a fairly high figure. The average queue size from theory is ($t/(1 - T)$), giving a value of 5 for our example, while the average waiting time for a customer is equal to the:

$$\text{(average service time)}/(1 - T)$$
$$\text{or 27 minutes in this example.}$$

The percentage of time the server is busy is 100T per cent or 83.3 per cent. The probability of the server being idle or equivalently the probability of an arrival not having to wait is ($1 - T$ or 0.16).

   If the rate of arrivals increases so that the average inter-arrival time decreases to 5 minutes, not 5.4 as before, then the mean waiting time becomes $4.5/(1 - 0.9)$ of 45 minutes, a rather steep increase. The graph of mean waiting time against $T$ 9 shows clearly why this occurs. The figure of 0.8 appears to be a warning limit above which serious congestion will occur.

### Economics of a queuing system

Mean service time        4.5 minutes
Service costs            £12 per hour
Mean arrival time         5.4 minutes
Waiting costs           £3 an hour/a person

Total hourly cost = 12 + 3(average waiting time).(average number of arrivals)

$$= 12 = 3.(27/60).(60/5.4) = £27$$

Now suppose that the service cost rises as the service times fall (i.e. they are inversely proportional), then the service cost equals $k/s$ for some constant $k$. Since this cost is £12 when $s = 4.5$ we have $k = (12).(4.5)$.

Total cost an hour = $(12).(4.5)/s + 3(s/(1 - T).1/60).60/5.4$
$$= 54/s + 3s/(54 - s)$$

*Note $T = s/5.4$*

Using either calculus or numerical methods it can be found that the value of $s$ which minimizes this function is 3.5 minutes. Estimating the costs of queuing is by no means always easy, but arbitrary managerial scoring often gives enough information upon which to carry out some analysis.

**Other queuing models**   Below is a specimen list of the differing queuing situations which can arise in practice.
1. Customers put off by a long queue
2. Each customer has a server made available if required
3. Queue with only a maximum numbers of servers

4. Limited queue size, such as doctor's waiting room
5. Machine maintenance
6. Queues in series or networks

**Simulation**   By far the most common situation in practice is the queuing system for which the mathematics has not been worked out or is too difficult. Here, the only resource is to actually create a numerical history of the system and observe its character. Clearly, there will have to be many repeated runs carried out before any statistical precision can be achieved in the result for the queue size, waiting times, etc. Computers and special programming languages make this chore much simpler to carry out than it was a few years ago. A simple simulation example follows:

*Simulation example* $(D/M/1)$   The arrivals are supposed to occur after alternate intervals of 5 and 15 units. The service is random with an average service time of 8 units. Thus $(1/a = 10)$ and $1/b = 8$ giving $T = a/b = \cdot 8$ which should normally give rise to fairly long queues. We shall compare the results of simulating this model with the $M/M/1$ queue.

The first task is to sample for service times from the exponential distribution using random numbers. Since for an exponential distribution the cumulative distribution is $1 - e^{-bs}$, in order to obtain a sample time we choose a random number $(RN)$, either from tables, calculator or computer and solve:

$$RN = 1 - e^{bs}$$
$$-\ln(1 - RN) = bs$$
$$s = -\ln(1 - RN)/b$$

This has been carried out for thirty such arrivals and the queue development tabulated as shown overleaf.

One can see immediately the advantage in having fixed intervals for the arrivals. The queue size and the waiting time are both considerably reduced, even though the average arrival and service rates are identical in both of the two models studied.

## 6.4 LINEAR PROGRAMMING

Linear programming is a method of optimization, either of maximization or minimization. We shall consider a very simple case with the 'graphical' solution first and then discuss the extension to the real world with the 'simplex' computer programmes and the real life approximations and adjustments required.

Take a factory making two products, a '386' computer and a '286' computer. These are made through three production stages; CPU assembly, disk drive assembly and final assembly. Final assembly takes two hours' production time for both models. The '386' model has an advanced disk drive system that is state of the art. However, it takes three hours' assembly time. The '286' model has a simple disk drive that only takes one hour of assembly time. The advanced '386' CPU has been 'designed for manufacture' and takes only one hour of assembly time. The '286' CPU has not been designed for manufacture to such an extent and takes two hours of assembly time. So assembly time in hours is:

## Simulation of a D/M/1 queue

| Arrival | Time of arrival | Time service starts | Service time | Time service ends | Server waiting time | Arrival waiting time |
|---|---|---|---|---|---|---|
| 1 | 5 | 5 | 16 | 21 | 5 | 0 |
| 2 | 20 | 21 | 5 | 26 | 0 | 1 |
| 3 | 25 | 26 | 10 | 36 | 0 | 1 |
| 4 | 40 | 40 | 2 | 42 | 4 | 0 |
| 5 | 45 | 45 | 5 | 50 | 3 | 0 |
| 6 | 60 | 60 | 10 | 70 | 10 | 0 |
| 7 | 65 | 70 | 16 | 86 | 0 | 5 |
| 8 | 80 | 86 | 3 | 89 | 0 | 6 |
| 9 | 85 | 89 | 5 | 94 | 0 | 4 |
| 10 | 100 | 100 | 20 | 120 | 6 | 0 |
| 11 | 105 | 120 | 1 | 121 | 0 | 15 |
| 12 | 120 | 121 | 7 | 128 | 0 | 1 |
| 13 | 125 | 128 | 4 | 132 | 0 | 3 |
| 14 | 140 | 140 | 2 | 142 | 8 | 0 |
| 15 | 145 | 145 | 6 | 151 | 3 | 0 |
| 16 | 160 | 160 | 3 | 163 | 9 | 0 |
| 17 | 165 | 165 | 19 | 184 | 2 | 0 |
| 18 | 180 | 184 | 5 | 189 | 0 | 4 |
| 19 | 185 | 189 | 9 | 198 | 0 | 4 |
| 20 | 200 | 200 | 15 | 215 | 2 | 0 |
| 21 | 205 | 215 | 8 | 223 | 0 | 10 |
| 22 | 220 | 223 | 12 | 235 | 0 | 3 |
| 23 | 225 | 235 | 6 | 241 | 0 | 10 |
| 24 | 240 | 241 | 12 | 253 | 0 | 1 |
| 25 | 245 | 253 | 7 | 260 | 0 | 8 |
| 26 | 260 | 260 | 15 | 275 | 0 | 0 |
| 27 | 265 | 275 | 3 | 278 | 0 | 10 |
| 28 | 280 | 280 | 3 | 283 | 2 | 0 |
| 29 | 285 | 285 | 18 | 303 | 2 | 0 |
| 30 | 300 | 300 | 4 | 307 | 0 | 3 |

- *Disk drives:* '286' 1 hour; '386' 3 hours
- *CPU assembly:* '286' 2 hours; '386' 1 hour
- *Final assembly:* '286' 2 hours; '386' 2 hours

There are only a restricted number of production hours in the next production period. The available hours in the next period are:

- *Disk drives:* 750 hours
- *CPU assembly:* 600 hours
- *Final assembly:* 700 hours

There is a larger profit on the '386' than on the '286': '286' profit contribution of £1000, '386' profit contribution of £1500. There are no sales limitations. The practical problem

### Tabulation of queue properties

|  | M/M/1 | D/M/1 |
|---|---|---|
| Probability of Customer waiting: $T$ | 0.8 | $17/30 = 0.57$ |
| Mean Number in system: $T/(1 - T)$ | 4 | 1.5 |
| Mean Queue Size (including $Q = 0$) $T^2/(1 - T)$ | 3.2 | 0.47 |
| Mean Queue Size ($Q = 0$): $1/(1 - T)$ | 5 | 1 |
| Mean Time in System: $1/b (1 - T)$ | 40 | 11.3 |
| Mean time in Queue: $T/b (1 - T)$ | 32 | 4.6 |

$$T = 0.8; \quad a = 0.1; \quad b = 0.125$$

we have is what is the production plan for '386' and '286' computers that will maximize our profits within the above constraints? Throughout this discussion refer to the Fig. 6.17.

**Final Assembly**    If we make no '386' computers we can make 350 '286' computers. If we make no '286' computers we can make 350 '386' computers. We can, of course, make any linear combination between these extremes. Formulated in mathematical terms in hours where: '386' = number of 386 computers made, and '286' = number of 286 computers made:

$$['386' \times 2] + ['286' \times 2] = \text{or} <700$$

Thus we can make any number of computers on the line or in the region below the line. Any combination of computers above the line is in the infeasible region.

**Disk drive assembly**    If we make 100 '386' computers we can make 450 '286' computers. If we make no '286' computers we can make 250 '386' computers. We can, of course, make any linear combination between these extremes. Formulated in mathematical terms in hours:

$$['386' \times 3] + ['286' \times 1] = \text{or} <750$$

Thus we can make any number of computers on the line or in the region below the line. Any combination of computers above the line is in the infeasible region.

**CPU assembly**    If we make no '386' computers, we can make 300 '286' computers. If we make 150 '286' computers, we can make 300 '386' computers. We can, of course, make any linear combination. Formulated in mathematical terms in hours:

$$['386' \times 1] + ['286' \times 2] = \text{or} <600$$

Thus we can make any number of computers on the line or in the region below the line. Any combination of computers above the line is in the infeasible region.

*Total feasible region:* If we take all these constraints at once we end up with the feasible region shown in the Fig. 6.17. By the graphical methods given over the page or by mathematical solution of the simultaneous linear equations, we can determine the

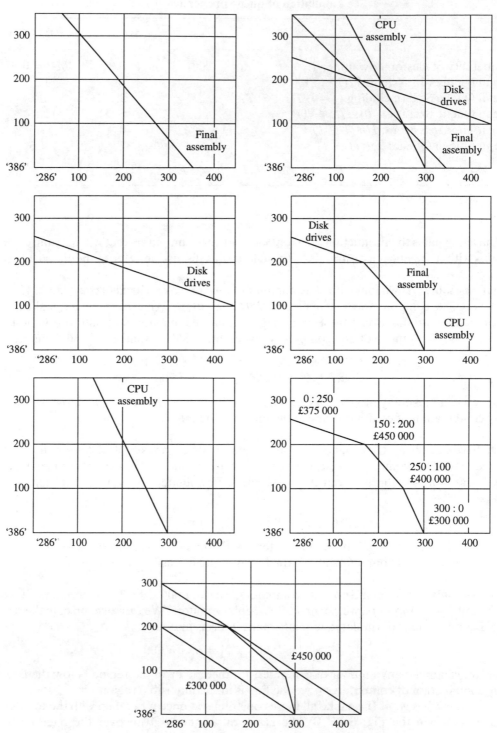

**Figure 6.17**   Linear programming: feasible regions

production volumes at the vertices of the feasible region. Moreover, we can calculate the profit for each 'production mix' or 'sales mix'. These are:

| '286' | '386' | £'000 |
|-------|-------|-------|
| 0 | 0 | 0 |
| 0 | 250 | 375 |
| 150 | 200 | 450 |
| 250 | 100 | 400 |
| 300 | 0 | 300 |

From this we can see that the maximum profit of these five points is £450 000. Is this the maximum profit? We can calculate a line of equal profit, say £300 000 and £400 000. You will note that these are a set of parallel lines. If we continue to move (by increasing the profit) the line of equal profit until it just touches the feasible region, we see that we end up with the £450 000 line just touching the feasible region at the point:

| '286' | '386' | £'000 |
|-------|-------|-------|
| 150 | 200 | 450 |

### 6.4.1  The real case

For real-life complexity, a linear programming simplex computer program may be used. The constraints are set up as a set of linear inequalities, as in our simple example. However, many more constraints may have to be considered. Apart from greater complexity in the production constraints, there may be materials availability constraints, sales constraints etc. There may also be buffer stock to be taken into account between one production period and another. However, the problem can be formulated.

The next stage is to set up the 'objective' function that it is desired to maximize (say profits) or minimize (say, costs). In our case it could be:

$$\text{Maximize [sales revenue]} - \text{[costs]}$$

The linear programming simplex program starts off at one solution (say 0,0) and searches for a better solution, tests if there are any better solutions and, if there are, searches for one. When it can no longer find a better solution, one has reached the optimum solution. Detailed information is given in the references at the end of the chapter. The operating manual for the specific computer program used should be consulted. For simple problems, many spreadsheet programs have linear programming included as an option.

### 6.4.2  Problems with linear programming

Often the functions in real life are not linear. The normal device used is to break the curve up into a number of shorter linear regions as an approximation, and so production costs may be broken down to normal and overtime. The elasticity of demand will in most cases suggest that the sales price will vary with the sales volume. This may require introducing several pseudo models '386'a, '386'b, '386'c, to represent to an approximation of the price : volume breaks.

In a multinational chemical company producing aroma chemicals, the model representing the production of aroma chemicals in the USA (Jacksonville) and the UK (Widnes) involved some 300 products which could be made through a whole range of 300 production units. Raw materials could be made in the USA, intermediates and finished products could be made at either the USA or the UK site, moved between sites or even purchased on the open market if required. The matrix of variables was some $400 \times 400$ representing a notional 160 000 data points. The nature of the problem, in fact, meant that many data points were 'zero' (some products could only be made on a given type of unit).

However, some 16 000 data points had to be maintained. Not a simple management job. These included such items as availability (and prices) of raw materials, intermediates and finished products, and current operating efficiencies of all units (could vary with conditions such as the quality of raw material feed). The whole balance could be changed by a large \$/£ move! Any linear programming package requires the maintenance of a large data file on period-by-period basis. Failure to do this will mean that with great care you will produce a sub-optimal production program!

Many of the figures entered are estimates. The simplex program will produce the optimum solution to, say, four decimal places (note another limitation, what does 0.4189 of a computer mean? Integer programming is even more complex). Just as with DCF analysis, the solution is to perform a sensitivity analysis on at least the key variables where you have some considerable uncertainty. You can then see the sensitivity of the optimum solution to the key input data. This can need lots of computer time and has only become possible with the great reduction in computing costs.

In our simple case, we are profit-limited by disk drive production, but we could contract out or buy. One value of this type of model is to help to decide such situations. However, the model needs to be told of the possibility! The model can also produce a cash flow analysis for a capital investment to remove a production constraint. Another common problem is the phasing of the sales mix. Is this really fixed or are some customers prepared to wait or accept a phased delivery? This is a slightly different case to that of the accuracy of a given cell. These problems regularly involve the setting up of additional constraints (in fact, most often more expensive flexibilities, which are of use if they increase the profit function enough, in a maximization problem).

In our discussion of Cu-Sums, we found that the concept was easy to communicate. This is not so with linear programming. The model is a complex nest of linear algebra and matrix calculations. This can be very difficult to communicate to staff without an advanced knowledge of mathematics. An even bigger danger is the use of a 'black box' computer model with a user friendly data entry system, which can give some people the idea they understand the model when all they have is a black box. Do build these models with care and understanding. Failure can result in non-optimum solutions and loss of acceptance of a model which could be of great value.

The uses of linear programming are as follows:

*Production planning*   As above, to maximize the sales mix or to minimize the cost of production.

*Distribution planning* (so-called transportation model)   A typical problem is the number of service centres and sizes to minimize overheads, running costs and travel costs.

*Inventory planning*   Classic problem is the make or buy.

*Stock cutting*   Given, say, sheet metal of a set dimension, find the most effective cutting pattern to minimize waste.

*Product composition*    A classical problem in the chemical industry. In the manufacture of fertilizer of a given nitrogen, phosphorus and potassium content, there were varying blend materials of differing NPK analysis. The problem was to find the minimum cost blending programme for the next period.

*Scheduling*    Another classic problem is finding the optimum programme for taking a number of products through a number of sequential processes, each with their own capacities and characteristics.

## 6.5  EXPERIMENTAL DESIGN

The sampling plan problem covered earlier is one example of the use of structured experimental designs. The need for these runs through all of operations, research, development and even marketing, where market research costs can be just as high as in development. A key experiment is the simple comparison. Consider the example where it is thought that a given type of resin will improve the breakdown voltage of a particular type of capacitor and laboratory trials are conducted. Two test rigs are available and at first sight it would appear that all one needs to do is to make two batches for testing, standard resin on Rig 1 and the new resin on Rig 2. Table 6.5 shows the results that might be obtained if there was a small bias in two rigs of one standard deviation and the rig was tested using a single test batch of resin to check for bias. Moreover, due to the rise in temperature of the laboratory over the working day, there is a systematic drift upwards of five standard deviations. Using the standard formula (T. Lucey, 1989) for the estimation of the significance of two means we obtain a result that is inconclusive.

Standard error of the difference in averages is:

$$S_{(\text{Rig A average}-\text{Rig B Average})} = [(s_a)^2/n_a + (s_b)^2/n_b]^{0.5} = 0.595$$

Given the large sample, the normal rather than the '*t*' distribution can be assumed.

$$z = (\text{Rig B average} - \text{Rig A Average})/S_{(\text{Rig B average}-\text{Rig A Average})} = 1.599$$

This result is not significant. However, if we use paired comparisons (comparing results obtained at the same time of day) then we have:

$$z = \text{Difference Average}/[S_{(\text{difference})}/(n)^{0.5}] = 4.390$$

This is highly significant.

If we were to prepare compared samples of new and old on the same test rig, we would eliminate the problem of systematic bias between the two rigs, but if we always kept to the same order we would still have some systematic bias in the results from the temperature drift effect. However, if we were to ensure that the design was balanced, testing new resin and old resin first alternately, the effect of the drift during the day would be reduced. Using this paired comparison test, more significant results can be obtained.

It is outside the scope of this text, but by the use of a more structured design (factorial design) with analysis of variance it is possible to estimate the difference in the performance of the resins, the bias in the test rigs, the effect of morning and afternoon testing and what the true standard error of the test procedure is.

**Table 6.5**   Tests results for two rigs A and B

|  | Rig A Kv | Rig B Kv | Difference Kv |
|---|---|---|---|
| 1 | 49.277 | 49.506 | 0.229 |
| 2 | 49.565 | 49.127 | −0.438 |
| 3 | 48.190 | 49.865 | 1.675 |
| 4 | 50.265 | 50.930 | 0.665 |
| 5 | 49.296 | 49.505 | 0.209 |
| 6 | 49.094 | 50.462 | 1.368 |
| 7 | 49.806 | 49.589 | −0.217 |
| 8 | 49.402 | 50.052 | 0.650 |
| 9 | 48.670 | 51.777 | 3.107 |
| 10 | 50.428 | 50.247 | −0.181 |
| 11 | 51.638 | 52.822 | 1.183 |
| 12 | 52.844 | 52.658 | −0.186 |
| 13 | 52.715 | 54.564 | 1.849 |
| 14 | 51.323 | 53.455 | 2.132 |
| 15 | 53.186 | 54.198 | 1.012 |
| 16 | 52.778 | 54.055 | 1.276 |
| 17 | 53.275 | 54.127 | 0.852 |
| 18 | 51.703 | 55.925 | 4.222 |
| 19 | 53.145 | 53.292 | 0.147 |
| 20 | 52.733 | 52.391 | −0.344 |
| 21 | 51.700 | 52.525 | 0.825 |
| 22 | 53.473 | 53.762 | 0.289 |
| 23 | 52.008 | 53.989 | 1.981 |
| 24 | 54.975 | 54.035 | −0.940 |
| 25 | 56.209 | 55.744 | −0.465 |
| 26 | 52.258 | 54.001 | 1.743 |
| 27 | 55.505 | 55.304 | −0.201 |
| 28 | 54.569 | 56.055 | 1.486 |
| 29 | 53.863 | 56.127 | 2.291 |
| 30 | 55.595 | 57.925 | 2.330 |
| S | 2.222 | 2.385 | 1.187 |
| Average | 51.982 | 52.934 | 0.952 |

Such systematic sources of error are possible in even the simplest experiments in the research, production or marketing situation. The experienced engineer considers the potential sources of such confounding errors and selects the appropriate experimental design with the maximum efficiency (minimum number of tests) to test the proposition. Typical sources of systematic error are machine and operator differences. Day-to-day variations can occur caused by small variations in voltage, temperature, humidity etc. When it is not possible to use one lot of components or test material, systematic bias in the properties should always be suspected. In the absence of any specific information, test orders should be randomized to at least minimize the effects of any possible trend bias.

## 6.6 PRODUCT AND PROCESS DESIGN

In the earlier discussion of attribute analysis, we found that the needs of customer groups can be built into the features of the product. This is only half the job, as this is of no interest to the customer if the product is so expensive to build that the costs exceed the benefit valuation or the prices offered by competitive products. Concurrent design is essential to design not only for use but for manufacture and distribution (100 per cent at the factory must still be 100 per cent quality on arrival with the user).

The basic principle is to keep the product as simple as possible, the best part is the one that has been designed out. A nut and bolt may be replaced with a self-tapping screw. More and more functions can be built into a single chip, involving fewer and fewer sub-assemblies. Computer Aided Design can greatly speed up the design process and allow the comparison of various alternative designs. The systematic examination of the contribution of a component to costs and performance is sometimes known as value engineering. Production requirements need to be considered at every stage, the design process must not be based on the 'over the wall' strategy: 'We have designed it, now you work out how to manufacture it.'

In Chapter Ten, the technique of critical path analysis is presented. This technique for project planning can also be applied to the assembly and manufacture of a product or the provision of a service. The schedule of operations and materials can be determined and the timings for operations measured or estimated from previous experience with similar operations. This in-depth analysis not only helps in the determination of the work schedules but also in the calculation of production costs.

The process technology and plant layout needs to be determined and managed. In some cases this may largely be set by the nature of the product and production technology; the production of commodity chemicals or iron and steel requires highly specialized plant operating continuously 24 hours a day, 365 days a year. The manufacturer of electronic systems could opt for highly automated lines with robots. This option would be appropriate for high volume consumer type products where high capacity utilization and only restricted flexibility is required. In the manufacture of science instruments, with runs often less than 100, less automated methods of production with increased flexibility and shorter set-up times on product changeovers would be better. In the engineering industry, numerically controlled and computer-aided manufacture can provide considerable flexibility, with automatic selection of tools and the production of a range of components from a single work station without extensive set-up times between different components.

Much of the early work in the area of operations was concentrated on the maximum efficiency in the operation of facilities in the mechanical industries, perhaps the optimum layout of lathes and milling machines. Of increasing importance in this day and age is the application of the powerful concepts and techniques to service industries. This is vividly exemplified in the area of eating out, where many different strategies can be observed at close quarters. McDonald's represents the ultimate in predetermined automation, where all operations have been value engineered to provide predetermined products to exact quality specifications. An alternative approach is to allow the customer to do much of the work themselves (the salad bar or carvery seen in many pub restaurants), the loss of portion control being off-set by reduced staff costs and greater customer satisfaction in terms of customer involvement. At the other end of the spectrum is the five star 'a la carte' restaurant with total customer flexibility and individual assembly and delivery of the product with total flexibility.

Similar considerations apply to the supply of services in telecommunications. International Direct Dialling and memory re-call telephones have empowered the consumer to undertake the initiative in the process with no manual support, as automatic routing and switching will route the call through the most cost effective network path available. There is still, however, the need for personal service in areas such as emergency calls.

Several types of configurations are possible. In the product layout (assembly or production line) the sequence of operations needed to manufacture a given product are placed in order and the product to be manufactured travels down the line with each operation conducted in succession. Such a layout is appropriate to the production of volume consumer goods such as washing machines. In the job shop or function layout, operations are grouped by the technology or the type of equipment used. This type of layout may be found in universities where laboratories, lecture theatres, language laboratories or computer facilities are grouped into units and students move between the facilities as the demands of their courses dictate. This type of configuration gives considerable flexibility, but at the cost of much waiting and moving time between the differing resource or technology centres.

In group technology layouts, a number of differing units are grouped to allow the manufacture or the provision of service using a number of differing technologies. The precise optimum layout will depend on the conditions at any given time. Layouts should not be regarded as fixed, but as another managerial variable to be changed as conditions demand. Under certain conditions, such as mature product life cycle, the need may be for maximum production volume with minimum cost, with flexibility not being the major priority. The traditional production line may well be the best solution. Where a range of new products are to be introduced, flexibility may well be the major requirement and group technology may allow rapid changes in production mix to meet the demands of an uncertain marketing environment. In circumstances where the production is of largely one off or very small volumes of a wide range of products, the job shop layout may give the desired total flexibility, often, however, at the cost of much movement of products and corresponding higher inventory costs.

A key issue in production layouts is to balance the facility. In an ideal situation, all units will be fully loaded, in practice this is not possible. The optimal layout is one which minimizes the idle time. Taking the most simple case of a linear production line, the required cycle time is the available production time divided by the number of units required. The unit operations can be timed and shorter tasks may be grouped. A major problem is when one task has a cycle time which is greater than the desired cycle time for the line. This is similar to the problem we encountered in critical path analysis; we have a rate limiting step and production efficiency depends on the reduction of this cycle time by some device. The two obvious solutions are to redesign the product to simplify the operation or to improve the efficiency of the operation. Another option is to see if part of the operation can be completed either before or after the rate limiting step. The least desirable solution would be to run the line for the extra time.

Computer-aided manufacture can assist in the management of this complexity. Complex products, such as aircraft, cars and computers, can be exploded back in stages to sub-assemblies right back to raw metal. Projected demands can then be converted into production demands and schedules and evaluated against actual capacity capabilities. Discrepancies in the capabilities can be resolved by re-balancing the schedule (possibly delaying the production of certain units) or involving make or buy decisions.

In a book of this length it is not possible to detail the full complexity of facility layout and scheduling, so the type of day-to-day scheduling problem faced by a university reprographics department is a simple example. There are a mixture of photocopiers and printing machines. In this case, 'finishing' may mean binding and/or punching the finished booklets, so the production controller of such a department is faced with a complex situation of high loads and work scheduling between units. The department may be limited by the machinery (operators always available for a machine) or by the staff (operators may move between units), which is the more usual situation. This is a complex problem and no simple computer algorithm exists which will always provide an optimum solution. This depends, of course, on how one defines the optimum solution. This could be defined as the minimum number of late orders or minimizing the work in progress. The most usual type of order in such a facility is the photocopying of lecture notes with collation stapling, all done on a single advanced copier. Differing rules might be used to schedule the work flow, orders could be progressed in the order that they were received or they could be progressed in the order of the due date. A particular rule is to run those jobs with the shortest processing time first and, in many cases, this rule will provide a better solution than the first two rules.

To ensure the maximum use of production time the traditional solution was to use buffer stocks so that if a unit failed, down stream operations could be fed from the buffer stock. Modern thinking takes the view that this is too costly in terms of working capital and assumes that problems will occur and are not preventable. 'Just In Time' (JIT) takes the view that problems are capable of management (prevention) and that all this great weight of stock does is hide the problems that should really be addressed. As the fat inventory is stripped away, the real problems surface and management can concentrate on maximizing efficiency. This requires a definition of what the measure of efficiency is. Prior to JIT philosophy, if 1000 parts a month were required, the production unit was run to produce the 1000 units in one run. Under JIT conditions, only that number required for the next period (day's) production would be produced. When optimal stock theory was considered the set-up time was taken as fixed. Under JIT conditions, management effort is devoted to increasing flexibility and reducing set-up or change-over times so that more flexible production becomes possible. When 500 units of two types are required, less stock is needed if a steady mix of units is produced, rather than a long run of one, then the other, unit which would require much more stock to cover the day-to-day mix of orders. Clearly, as discussed in the section on quality management, first time quality is essential because any quality problem will bring the assembly process to a stop. The whole philosophy of JIT precludes the re-work of the product down the line or off-line rectification cells.

Traditional methods of production management and stock control depended on stock estimates at certain times (end of day, end of week). The management of a JIT production facility is more about the management of flow. Given that there is no room (in a literal sense for buffer extensive buffer stock) for large amounts of work in progress, then only flow has to be managed. Under JIT philosophy, as much of the control as possible is delegated and devolved to the production staff. Kanban systems are one specific type of approach to this. This is a paperless and computerless system. The basic principal is a Kanban pull system; the demand for production is controlled by the down stream production demand. In our simple computer example, disk drives would not be produced until the final assembly line demanded it. When a Kanban container is empty, it is returned to the sub-assembly unit for further manufacture of the disk drive units. It is not possible to over-produce disk drives, as there is simply not the room in the Kanban temporary storage area for anything but the minimum buffer stock. The value of this system is that the production process is under visual control, either a Kanban container is full or empty. This is in complete contrast to the movement of stocks to an unseen store where operators have no idea of the stock situation. The production system is adaptive and under operator control. The concept is extended to the supply of purchased parts where delivery of parts is in Kanban containers, direct to the line, without any incoming quality control.

To control an operation effectively, materials resource planning is necessary (MRP). The first core computer database is the full detailed specification of each and every unit, sub-unit and component, broken down by level. To take a simple example, a computer assembly would detail the final assembly schedule (CPU unit, disk drive unit, power supply etc.) and then down to the lower level for each sub-assembly (CPU mother board, list of chips etc.). The production capacity and production times for the production of units will be held and the sales and marketing department will produce a sales schedule of products. The MRP system will then break this down to a production schedule, level by level, which will specify both the plant time and the components and raw materials required. In real life, the first run may well produce a schedule that is not feasible and discussion will have take place to adjust the demands and/or production schedule to produce a plan that can be operated. Flexibilities may be to delay an order where the time is not critical to a customer, to work overtime or to purchase a sub-assembly rather than make. With thousands of products and many product configurations, MRP systems become complex.

The MRP computer system will contain a file, called the bill of materials, which explodes the components and materials, level by level. Care needs to be taken that this is complete and up to date with the latest design modifications as even a small missing part may prevent the manufacture of a product. Clearly, the system needs to know what is in stock and an inventory records file is required. Again, it is essential that this is accurate and updated. Care has to be taken that odd events, such as damage or loss of materials, are quickly reflected in the file. The demand has to be set by careful consideration of the projected sales demand in the planning period and any adjustments to the finished buffer stock. From this the master schedule of the output of the production can be set. The parts explosion through the bill of materials will reflect this back into the full detailed materials to be purchased and the parts to be manufactured. The final element is capacity planning. One must not only ensure that the materials are available but also that the production capacity of the right type is available at the right times. In most cases this will not be so on the first pass. This is the value of the MRP system, to be able to identify potential problems. Once areas of difficulty are identified, alternative courses of action can be considered and their consequences tested on the MRP system. It must be remembered that the MRP system is much more than a smart computer system. Unless there is total commitment from the whole company then it will not work. The system must be fed accurate data in real time or else the MRP system is managing some shadow factory, not the real factory, and crisis management will reign.

## REVIEW

Operations is about being efficient and effective, it is necessary to do the right things and to do them well. Thus, our starting point was market driven quality; how we ensure that the results of the production process truly provide customer satisfaction. The first stage of this was to identify all the quality publics and then to determine their quality expectations. BS 5750 provides a formal framework for the management of this quality process and the process of implementation, Total Quality Management (TQM). The starting point for the efficient management of quality was that there must be assignable causes of defects, that prevention is better than rectification and that you have to be able to measure to be able to control. Control systems are subject to two errors, false alarms and no alarms when there is a problem, alpha (produce risk) and beta (buyer risk) errors. Statistical quality control allows the quality assurance engineer to build sampling plans to specific operating characteristics, to ensure that the control system meets the management requirements for acceptable levels of alpha and beta errors. Increasingly, with online testing, it is possible to run production process with control systems which can detect deviations before defectives are produced. Cu-Sum techniques provide an effective and efficient method for the rapid identification of deviations from targets, being simple to use, yet with full statistical control of the Alpha and Beta errors with the design of the V mask.

Not all quality problems can be solved by these techniques and the 'measles' diagram, Pareto (80:20) rule, and the 'fishbone' diagram are additional tools complementary to the highly statistical designs. The starting and finishing point of all quality systems is the motivation and commitment of the entire work force with a clear quality mission statement. Thus, though we discuss the analytic tools here, all the issues of human resource management are critical to the implementation and support of these techniques. Information is only of use if it is accurate and people take action on it. The secret to success in quality is ownership of quality by all the firm's staff, suppliers and agents.

In operations, marketing and quality assurance there is a need to forecast the future. PEST analysis can help us detect the changes in the environment but, given a series of past data, a number of statistical techniques may be of help, if applied with care. Regression allows us to fit a line to a set of data and is of special value when we have reason to suspect some real physical model connecting the dependent and independent variable. If we suspect that we have a stable system but wish to check if it may have shifted its level then the moving average techniques (simple and exponential) allow us to track this situation. Many business situations have both trend and seasonal components, the Holt-Winters technique provides a robust model to investigate this type of data.

Inventory costs are high and an essential management concern is to control the cost of working capital contained in inventory. The simple economic order quantity model allows an approach to this situation. Although the deterministic model may be adapted in many ways, interest is increasingly being focused on alternatives, such as Just In Time manufacture. Here, management attention is focused on reducing the set-up times and eliminating inventory by manufacturing or purchasing only when the materials or components are needed. Many situations involve the provision of a service from resources with variable rates of arrival and of service times; queuing theory enables us to investigate the economics of such situations. Management is about the allocation of scarce resources to maximize profits or minimize costs. Where the situation is too complex for intuitive methods, linear programming provides a mathematical tool for optimization.

Operations is about managing a dynamic environment and about the management of change and the adoption of new manufacturing methods or the use of alternative materials. Often the environments in which the changes are to be effected are subject to other sources of variation. The use of statistical experimental designs allows the estimation of these other influences and the isolation of the effect under consideration, which could be overlooked if the other sources of noise are not eliminated.

Operations is about the effective use of the production facilities and various layouts and technologies may have to be considered to ensure that production processes are not out of balance, with some units overloaded and other links in the production chain having ideal time. Linked to this are schemes of linking operations without heavy buffer stock with Just In Time manufacture and Kanban type systems. Materials Resource Planning (MRP) systems allow the development of a proposed master production schedule into the full detail of the procurement of all materials and parts and the manufacturing schedule for final products and sub-assemblies. Again JIT, Kanban and MRP systems require total staff commitment and the techniques and understanding of human resource management is critical to the effective implementation. Such systems are more than just computer programs.

## KEY CONCEPTS AND TECHNIQUES

**Alpha error**   The risk in a statistical sampling plan that the producer will produce a 'good' lot of product yet reject it.

**Average run length**   ARL: the average number of observations that a given statistical design with a given operating characteristic will require to detect a given shift in the process.

**Beta error**   The risk in a statistical sampling plan that the customer will get a 'reject' batch.

**BS5750**   The British Standard for Total Quality systems for both design and manufacture.

**Buyer's risk**   The risk in a statistical sampling plan that the customer will get a 'reject' batch.

**Cu-Sum**   A statistical method for the detection of variations in a process for statistical control, the cumulative sum of differences are plotted, on target a level line, above target the line rises, below target the line drops. The statistical operating characteristics are determined by the calculation of the V Mask.

**EOQ**   Economic Order Quantity: in traditional models of stock control the optimum amount of product to order or make given the usage conditions, the lead times, set up (or ordering costs) and the cost of holding stock. Challenged by JIT philosophy, where management effort is directed at reducing set-up times and costs and elimination of stock costs.

**EWMA**   Exponentially Weighted Moving Average: a statistical technique for forecasting which gives more weight to recent observations, useful for detection of a change of one stable state to another; not recommended for trends where regression should be used.

**Fishbone diagram**   A simple, powerful tool, for investigating and communicating influences on a problem and potential assignable causes of trouble.

**Holt-Winters**   A statistical technique for forecasting time series where trends and seasonality is suspected.

**Just In Time**   JIT manufacture is the management philosophy and activity where buffer stocks are eliminated and components or materials are manufactured or brought in just when manufacture is required, TQM and zero defects are essential as manufacture is done without any further inspection.

**Kanban**    A particular type of work layout and control which uses visual control and minimizes stock holding.

**Linear programming**    A technique for the optimization of a situation, such as production value, against constraints, such as machine and materials availability.

**Market driven quality**    MDQ is the name given to the philosophy and approach to quality where the starting and ending point is a marketing orientated view of total quality satisfaction, ultimately to 'surprise and delight' the customer in all those quality 'moments of truth'.

**Measles diagram**    Where defects are attributes (surface defects etc.), rather than quantitative, the superimposing of the location of the defect occurrence on a parts drawing can often indicate a specific problem area, a pictorial Pareto chart.

**MRP**    Materials Resource Planning: used to describe systems that control inventory or a production and inventory system or, most powerfully, a manufacturing resource planning system.

**PONC**    Price Of Non-Conformance: an approach to the measurement of the regret costs of poor quality management.

**Producer's risk**    The risk in a statistical sampling plan that the producer will produce a 'good' lot of product yet reject it.

**Operating characteristic**    The curve for a statistical sampling plan that gives the buyers and producers risk for given levels of actual defectives in the lot.

**Operations**    The management activity concerned with the efficient and effective planning, development, commissioning, operation and control of the productive and/or service resources and activities of an organization in order to satisfy the legitimate expectations of relevant stakeholders.

**Pareto analysis (80/20)**    In many situations 80 per cent of the problems are caused by 20 per cent of possible causes, 80 per cent of the sales come from 20 per cent of the customers and 80 per cent of the stock value is in 20 per cent of the items. The suggestion is that management should concentrate on the 20 per cent that count.

**Quality**    The fitness for the purpose of customers and users, subject to the legitimate expectations of other relevant publics.

**Quality assurance**    The total set of management activities covering all the company's operations from design to field service and from order intake to customer use involving all the company's staff and agents.

**Quality control**    An activity within quality assurance involved with the formulation of specifications and ensuring conformance to those specifications at all points of the operations, from vendor assessment to installation and/or customer service provision.

**Shewhart chart**    Old style statistical control chart, now largely replaced by Cu-Sum charts.

**Total quality management**    TQM is the label given to the management philosophy and activity when top management build quality missions, aims and objectives into the firm's core strategy statement.

## CASE STUDY

'Operations' applies to service situations as well as manufacture. In fact, as we noted in Chapter 5, the provision of services is more demanding as it is not possible to store a service. At an expanding university it was decided to refurbish the refectory and to improve the standard of service and extend the selection of meals and drinks. In the old refectory a single coffee machine (type A) was installed to provide fresh coffee in two forms, black or white. The mean arrival time for customers during the mid-morning was 30 seconds and the mean time for customers to serve themselves with coffee was 22 seconds. How long on average did a customer have to queue for coffee?

As part of the refurbishment, it was decided to improve the service by the installation of a new coffee machine (type B) which not only makes standard coffee, but also high roast continental, expresso and cappuccino. It was found that the mean time for customers to serve themselves increased by three seconds, as some customers took some time to decide which coffee they wanted. Moreover, the university was expanding and the mean arrival time for customers dropped to 28 seconds. How long, under the new conditions, did customers have to queue for coffee? Do you consider this acceptable?

Seventy per cent of customers did not want special coffee and were not very happy with the increased waiting time. Their mean time for coffee machine use had not changed. Further analysis showed that customers using the type B machine for special coffee spent 31 seconds making their selection and serving themselves. Clearly, some additional facility is needed. What would you do? The university numbers are planned to increase at 20 per cent compound per year. For how many years would your new facility provide an acceptable service?

The study of operations is best completed with the physical inspection of actual resources and operations. Consider a refectory at your university or an external fast food restaurant of your own selection. If the number of customers was projected to increase by 30 per cent and the facility was due for full refurbishment, what layout would you adopt to provide improved service with maximum use of staff resources? Decide how you would install a computer stock control system for your menu to link with the pay point analysis of meals consumed.

---

## QUESTIONS

1. A quality control inspection system for a particular product requires that ten items be drawn from the lot and tested. Using the binomial distribution, what are the chances that at least one or more defective items will be found in this sample if the proportion defective in the entire batch is 10 per cent?

   **Note:**

   If                        $p$ = Probability an event will happen
   $q$ = Probability an event will not happen
   $q = (1 - p)$

   The probability that a given event will happen $a$ times and fail to happen $b$ times in $n$ trials:

   Where                     $n = (a + b)$
   $p = (n! p^a q^b)/a! b!$

   What assumptions are there in such a simple sampling plan? Briefly indicate the advantages in moving from a batch sampling plan to 100 per cent inspection with in-line test equipment.

2. Your company manufactures two computers, a 286 and a 386. You are the product manager for the computer range. You wish to optimize the profitability of your product line. You have the following information on production and marketing constraints. The production of the advanced mother board for the new 386 computer will be limited to 1000 a month for this year until the new production line is built next year. There is a long term contract with one more year to run which requires the company to produce a minimum of 400 286 computers a month for this year. There is a production limit on disk drives used in both machines of 3000 units a month. The 286 computer has a single unit, the 386 computer uses two units in each 386 computer. The assembly time for the computers is the same and there is a limit of assembling 2250 computers a month. You have estimated the profit contribution per unit from the 286 computer to be £1250 and the profit contribution per unit from the 386 computer to be £1000.

Using the graphical method of solution for a linear programming problem, what is the optimum number of 286 and 386 computers to manufacture each month?

To arrive at the above solution it was necessary to have an estimate of the profit contribution for each type of unit. What are the problems in estimating profit contribution?

3. You are the production manager for a company that makes fire protection equipment for life critical applications. Your company has full BS5750 certification.

You have installed a new production line for a new range of domestic fire detectors. You have built in online test equipment and the operators will have to use Cu-Sum techniques to check deviations from set points, well before the manufacturing operation is outside quality control specifications (that is, the standard deviation of the manufacturing and test procedure is well within the manufacturing specification limits). Through TQM and online statistical control you intend to move to full zero defect production.

New operators have been selected for this production line. They will have one week of induction and training. You are to explain the use of Cu-Sum charts to these operators. How would you do this? What key points would you make? You have decided to use as an example the test of a sub-unit that should have a resistance of 100 000 ohms. The standard deviation of the manufacturing and test procedure is 200 ohms. The acceptance limits for this component is 99 000 to 101 000 ohms ($\pm$1000 ohms). What other points on TQM would you make to these new operators and why? Brief notes only are required.

4. Your company manufactures and installs private branch telephone exchanges for medium-sized organizations. The company supplies equipment and services but is not a network operator itself. In this situation, who are the 'quality publics' (specific groups with their own quality concerns)? Identification only is required, no detailed discussion is necessary for this section.

For *two* of the above quality publics you have distinguished, identify *three* issues of system benefits *or* system quality that might concern them? How would you take account of these in the design and installation of the system?

5. An engineer is checking the resistance of a device at various temperatures. It is thought that the resistance will be a linear function of temperature. The results obtained were:

| °C | Resistance ohms |
|----|------|
| 10 | 111.017 |
| 20 | 112.044 |
| 30 | 113.120 |
| 40 | 113.553 |
| 50 | 117.606 |
| 60 | 116.332 |
| 70 | 117.686 |
| 80 | 116.516 |
| 90 | 119.332 |
| 100 | 120.686 |

Using regression analysis, what is the effect of a 1°C temperature rise on the resistance of the device? What is your estimate of the device's resistance at 55°C and 0°C? Which of these two estimates is more reliable?

6. An engineer is installing a control system on a pressure system which is subject to random fluctuations. However, it is suspected that when other systems cut out, the base pressure may change. The following results were obtained one evening. Plot the simple and exponential weighted moving average for the data. You may assume that the starting long run average is 43 psi.

| Time minutes | Pressure psi | Time minutes | Pressure psi |
|------|------|------|------|
| 0 | 43.102 | 11 | 46.456 |
| 1 | 43.322 | 12 | 46.483 |
| 2 | 44.760 | 13 | 46.559 |
| 3 | 45.167 | 14 | 45.992 |
| 4 | 42.456 | 15 | 44.955 |
| 5 | 42.483 | 16 | 47.322 |
| 6 | 42.559 | 17 | 48.760 |
| 7 | 41.992 | 18 | 49.167 |
| 8 | 40.995 | 19 | 46.456 |
| 9 | 42.771 | 20 | 46.483 |
| 10 | 43.125 | 21 | 45.734 |

7. A new test rig has been built to check the concentration of salt in a food factory. The rig has been run for 40 batches over the weekend. The project engineer has been given the following results which appear to be less consistent than was expected. The test run should have been completed with one consistent batch of salt solution used at the start of the process. However, the engineer suspects that more than one batch of brine was in fact used. Plot a historical Cu-Sum for this data. How many batches of brine were used over the weekend? Once this effect has been eliminated, what is the approximate standard deviation of the results from the test rig?

| Batch | g/litre | Batch | g/litre |
|-------|---------|-------|---------|
| 1 | 165.322 | 21 | 166.322 |
| 2 | 165.760 | 22 | 167.760 |
| 3 | 165.167 | 23 | 168.167 |
| 4 | 164.456 | 24 | 165.456 |
| 5 | 164.483 | 25 | 165.483 |
| 6 | 164.559 | 26 | 163.559 |
| 7 | 163.992 | 27 | 162.992 |
| 8 | 162.955 | 28 | 161.955 |
| 9 | 164.771 | 29 | 163.771 |
| 10 | 165.125 | 30 | 164.125 |
| 11 | 165.456 | 31 | 163.456 |
| 12 | 165.483 | 32 | 163.483 |
| 13 | 165.559 | 33 | 163.559 |
| 14 | 164.992 | 34 | 162.992 |
| 15 | 163.955 | 35 | 161.955 |
| 16 | 166.322 | 36 | 164.332 |
| 17 | 167.760 | 37 | 165.760 |
| 18 | 168.167 | 38 | 166.167 |
| 19 | 165.456 | 39 | 163.456 |
| 20 | 165.483 | 40 | 163.483 |

## FURTHER READING

Box, G.E.P. *et al.* (1978) *Statistics for Experimenters: An Introduction to Design, Data Analysis and Model Building*, John Wiley. (See Part 1 Comparing Two Treatments, Part 2 Comparing More than Two Treatments.)

BS 5703, *Guide to Data analysis and quality control using Cu-Sum techniques*, BSI. (See Parts 1, 2, 3, and 4.)

BS 5750, *The British Standard for Total Quality systems for both design and manufacture*, BSI.

BS 6001 (1972) *Specification for Sampling Procedures and Tables for Inspection by Attributes*.

BS 7750, *The British Standard for Environmental Management, complements BS 5750*, BSI.

Chae, R.B. and N.J. Aquilano (1992) *Production and Operations Management: A Life Cycle Approach*, 6th Edition.

Davies, O.L. and L. Goldsmith (1972) *Statistical Methods in Research and Production with Special Reference to the Chemical Industry*, 4th Edition.

Krajewski, L.J. and L.P. Ritzman (1987) *Operations Management, Strategy and Analysis*, Addison Wesley. (See Appendix C, Linear Programming.)

Lucey, T. (1989) *Quantitative Techniques*, 3rd Edition, DP Publications.

Roy, R. (1990) *A Primer on the Taguchi Method*. Van Nostrand Reinhold.

Schroeder, R.G. (1989) *Operations Management: Decision Making in the Operations Function*, 3rd Edition, McGraw-Hill.

Stebbing, L. (1990) *Quality Management in the Service Industry* Ellis Horwood.

# SEVEN
# PROCUREMENT

## 7.1 THE NATURE OF PURCHASING

In this brief chapter, the issue of Procurement (Purchasing) is considered. The term 'Procurement' is used as it is most often used in management literature. In the same way as 'Total Quality Management' is a broader and more demanding definition of quality than 'Quality Control' Procurement means more than just the administration of purchasing. The term involves the total procurement management of the input resources of the firm, because for any sale there must be a purchase. In Chapter Five, the nature of the decision making unit was considered within the scenario of the firm selling to another organization. In this chapter we consider the issue from the standpoint of the company making the purchases.

**Table 7.1**  Mix of purchases for a typical firm

*Capital purchases*
   Production plant, computers, etc.

*Support purchases*
   Travel
   Telephones
   Financial services
   Security services
   Office purchases
   etc.

*Production Purchases*
   Raw materials
   Components
   Packaging
   Utilities
        water, heat, power, etc.
   Direct maintenance materials
        Spare parts for plant, etc.
   etc.

Table 7.1 shows the make-up of the cost structure for a typical manufacturing company. Though there may be large variations in the overall make-up, a key feature is that a surprising amount of money is involved in the provision of goods and services other than those involved in the manufacturing process.

## 7.2 TYPES OF PURCHASING DECISIONS

The influence of the purchasing function in the decision making process will vary with the nature of the purchase. One way of considering purchases is to divide them into three groups:

- New purchases
- Modified re-purchases
- Simple re-purchases

In the packaging of liquid flavours, glass is an ideal package as it is totally impervious both to the migration of the flavour constituents out of the pack, and oxygen diffusing through the pack, oxidizing the flavour. However, glass has the disadvantage that it is heavy and fragile and so glass containers need to be protected by wood or heavyweight fibre outer boxes. Moreover, glass is not considered acceptable in food factories, as the only way to keep broken glass out of food is not to allow glass in the manufacturing areas. Simple plastic containers, such as low density polythene, are not effective, allowing loss of the flavour and diffusion of air through the pack to degrade the flavour. Advances in the engineering of bottle manufacturing equipment with microprocessor controls have allowed the manufacture of multi-layer plastic packs, which have increased performance over simple plastic containers. This is the classic new purchase situation, with the procurement manager searching for sources of supply of the new technology packs, and the research and quality assurance departments evaluating the performance and the marketing department researching the reaction of customers to the new packages. Production would need to consider what adaptation of the filling lines would be needed. The procurement manager would also need to evaluate sources of supply for the lighter outer boxes that would be possible, given the less fragile nature of the packs. The cost accountants would be involved in estimating the cost reductions possible (such as lower transport costs), against the capital costs of the modifications to the filling line. The new purchase decision can thus be complex, with a whole team required to make all the required inputs.

Later, if it was decided that a new size pack was required, a much less complex process of consultation is needed, the technical performance of the new package having been established and only simple modifications to the filling line etc. being required. In terms of the re-buy situation, orders for day-to-day production needs will be on a simple, semi-automatic basis, with the purchasing manager negotiating appropriate price reductions as delivery sizes increase. This ability to negotiate the best deal for the firm is a key skill for the purchasing manager.

Table 7.2 shows the complexity and number of people involved in a purchasing decision. The purchasing DMU will also be affected by the nature of the goods or services purchased. Thus the purchase of advanced test equipment will be under the control of the R and D or test laboratories and the procurement function will act as a contract administrator. Such specialist purchases are not restricted to the technical area and the

**Table 7.2**   Complexity and number of people involved in purchase decision

| |
|---|
| Degree of newness in product |
| Technical specialisms needed in purchase decision |
| Size of purchase decision |
| Size of effect of wrong purchase on firm |
| Number of people directly affected by purchase decision |

marketing department will decide which creative consultants it wants to use for the design of new publicity material.

For many firms working in the international area with extensive marketing and field support needs, travel and transport can be a major expense. The skill of the procurement manager can effect very considerable savings by the negotiation of specific contracts for fleet rental or the arrangement of corporate discounts for hotel accommodation etc.

The size of the purchase decision will affect the role of the purchasing manager. The purchase of a new automated production line will be a major strategic expansion. The purchasing manager will be one member of the multi-disciplinary team reporting to the main board, the ultimate decision to proceed or not to proceed being a board level decision.

In analysing the competitive pressures on a company, the power of suppliers was identified as a key issue. The procurement manager has the responsibility of playing a major role in the management of this. In the sourcing of raw materials or components, the purchasing manager will be searching for second and third sources of supply. This is not only essential in order to strengthen the firm's position in purchasing contract negotiations, but is vital in ensuring security for the firm. Should there be a strike, fire or some other major problem with a supplier, then the firm has established links ensuring a continuity of supply for vital components or raw materials.

### 7.2.1  Special procurement markets

Very special markets can exist for products as diverse as oil, metals, coffee etc. In such commodity markets, the firm needs buyers with an intimate understanding of the market, coupled with the ability to react quickly to ensure supply and best prices. The purchasing manager has the same problem as the marketing manager in that the purchase of raw materials or components may be in the currency of the country of origin. Currency movements may not only affect the sales of the company products in overseas markets but may also affect the company costs.

### 7.2.2  Strategic role of procurement in firm's strategy

Given the complexity of this area, the procurement function has a vital role in the MkIS system. In Chapter Five, the strategic pricing gap was introduced—the difference between the customer valuation and the firm's costs of providing the goods or services.

In evaluating the sales budget a year in advance, good market insight into the costs of the components and raw materials is essential. In industries with a high commodity type content (such as gold) the MkIS system must be very responsive (that is, have a very short up-date time). If this is not so, then when prices are increasing it would be possible for the sales department to accept an order which makes a profit on the costs of the materials that were purchased in the past, but that will not cover the cost of the new stocks required for future production. In real terms, the sale will have been made at a loss. It is thus essential in costing for future business that the procurement department's best estimates for the future cost of materials are used, not the historical actual costs.

In the new product development process, the procurement manager will have to search out sources of supply for materials which the firm has never purchased before. While the technical staff are evaluating the quality of the various potential sources of supply, the procurement manager will have to investigate the stability of new suppliers. The incorporation of a specialist component from a supplier who then goes out of business could well provide the firm with a major crisis. The administration of the contracts will need attention to the fine print of the supply contracts to ensure the maximum protection of the firm's position in the event of problems. Given the move to JIT manufacture and immediate ordering from the firm's Materials Resource Planning computer system, using direct transmission with Electronic Data Interchange (EDI), the procurement manager is a pivot person in an interface value chain link which involves the whole company (remember the front end of the MRP system is being driven by the marketing and sales estimate of the future sales volume and sales mix as well as current inventory levels and production activity). Market Driven Quality (MDQ) and TQM programmes will also involve the procurement manager in audits of suppliers' quality capabilities. With JIT manufacture, there will be no inspection of incoming components, with zero defects on incoming supplies assumed. Any supplier quality failure will result in major product disruption.

## REVIEW

For every sale there must be a purchase. For most organizations the cost of procurement is a large percentage of the total annual costs of the business. These costs are not only associated with the cost of purchasing the materials and services required for the direct production or provision of the firm's services, but also for capital purchases and infrastructure purchase for items such as office supplies.

The number of people involved and the complexity and length of the purchase decision will be affected by the strategic nature of the purchase, the technical complexity, the newness of the purchase and the number of people directly affected by the purchase decision. In many industries special markets exist for raw materials, and procurement managers with detailed and expert knowledge of these markets are needed by firms seeking to compete effectively.

Procurement is in as critical a value chain link position as marketing. Marketing manages the expectations of the firm with its customer publics. Procurement manages the relationships with the suppliers without which the firm could not produce the goods or services to satisfy its customers.

## KEY CONCEPTS AND TECHNIQUES

**Capital purchase**   Purchase of large items, such as machinery, which will depreciate over some considerable period. Spares and service are often important issues.

**Commodity markets**   Many products, such as fuel, food and metals, must be bought in free markets where there may be large changes in price over short periods of time.

**Modified repurchase**   The purchase of new models of existing products, such as the addition of a new model to the firm's car fleet.

**New purchase**   A purchase which is new to the company, the purchase of products or services the company has not required before. The most risky type of purchase.

**Simple repurchase**   The day-to-day purchase of items of a well-known nature to the organization.

## CASE STUDY

Joan Farmer has just completed her degree in mechanical engineering, which contained a substantial element of business studies. Her father owns a small chain of fifteen petrol stations in the area around her home town. The business has been built up on a site-by-site basis over 20 years and each station is run by a manager who participates in a profit-sharing scheme. The existing contract for fuel expires in six months. Moreover, the major fuel company wishes to divest itself of four local fuel stations to concentrate on its major inner-city sites. The bank have indicated that they will be prepared to finance the expansion but want a full business plan. Joan has been asked to prepare this plan by her father.

The stations do not engage in major accident repairs, but do MOT and minor repair work for all makes of cars, people in the area liking the local service rather than a long journey into the city centre main dealers. The chain does not get involved in buying or selling cars. To maximize profits, managers have opened up shops, which sell a mixture of goods depending on the local manager's judgement (local managers at the moment make their own supply arrangements): items stocked (not in all locations) include souvenirs, maps, books, local tourist guides, confectionery, tobacco, papers, flowers, vegetables, convenience foods, fast food (using microwave ovens), sandwiches, hot and cold drinks, as well as the range of motor accessories. The area is in a tourist location and the appearance of the sites is important. There is at present no uniform brand image and the bank has indicated that additional funds could be available for the refurbishing of the existing outlets over two years to strengthen the marketing image.

Joan has completed their strategic plan and the marketing aspects. The latter, with the emphasis on the extended service marketing mix (Chapter Five) places an importance on achieving a uniform image and quality. Joan is now completing the implementation section of her business plan and has to consider the procurement issues. What procurement issues should Joan consider? What arrangements should Joan make for the implementation of these plans? How should these plans link with the marketing plans and the MkIS systems?

The outline marketing plan is for the shops to have a uniform image and range of stock (quality and range) and for the garages to have a uniform brand image with staff dressed in smart uniforms and overalls. Each location in turn will need some minor building work to extend the shop areas and each shop will have to be fitted out.

## QUESTIONS

1. What would be the range of goods and services the procurement manager of a major hotel chain would have to consider?

2. As the manager of a research facility, you need to purchase a new advanced and expensive measurement instrument. You have a short list of possible instruments from various suppliers. What issues would you consider in your purchase decision?

3. As the procurement manager, you are to visit a major supplier of critical components for your advanced systems to review next year's purchase contract. What issues would you wish to investigate? Who else in the organization would you need to involve and consult before your visit? Why would you need to consult these people?

## FURTHER READING

Baily, P. (1991) *Purchasing Systems and Records*, 3rd Edition, Gower in association with the Institute of Purchasing and Supply.

Dobler, D.W. *et al.* (1990) *Purchasing and Materials Management*, 5th Edition, McGraw-Hill.

Heinritz, S.F. *et al.* (1986) *Purchasing Principles and Applications*, 7th Edition, Prentice-Hall.

Stevens, J. and J. Grant (1975) *The Purchasing/Marketing Interface*, Associates Business Programmes.

# EIGHT

# FIRM INFRASTRUCTURE

In the firm's value chain, the primary and support activities take place within the infrastructure that the owners and senior managers have constructed for the organization. The firm's infrastructure is the foundation upon which all other strategies rest.

An engineer, faced with a problem of how to provide transport across a river, has a range of options which would include a ferry, a tunnel or a bridge. Even when they have decided that a bridge would be the most appropriate solution, further options are open for construction (suspension, arch) and for a given type of structure there may be further alternatives, such as concrete, stone or brick. The most appropriate solution will be influenced by the demands, current technologies and cost considerations. Similar alternatives exist for the firm's infrastructure.

There is a danger in considering a business simply under headings such as finance (accountancy) and organizational structure (human relations). Within the business these elements are integrated into one single entity. A practical example of this is that a critical activity for all business operations is to construct an annual financial plan. How this plan is constructed and the division of responsibilities for the plan's formulation and implementation will be determined not only by the accountancy conventions, but also by the organizational structure, marketing orientation, production technologies, vertical integration etc. (Topics such as organizational structure, role relationships, job descriptions and succession plans are covered in further depth in Chapter Eleven.) The purpose of this section is to provide an integrated overview of how these aspects of the firm build up into the firm's infrastructure. Having gained an insight into the context and linkages in these issues it is then possible to develop our understanding of each element in depth, but not 'lose sight of the wood for the trees'.

## 8.1 FINANCIAL STRUCTURE

A computer company will be faced with the need to deliver computers, provide field service, provide transport for its staff (for example, field training staff). The company could opt to own its fleet of vehicles and provide its own in-house maintenance facilities (Fig. 8.1). This decision has considerable implications on the financial structure. The company has a considerable amount of its money invested in the transport fleet, more money invested in the vehicle maintenance facilities and staff costs in the fleet operation.

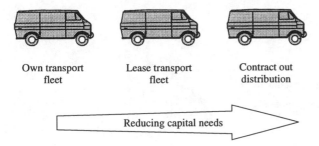

Own transport
fleet

Lease transport
fleet

Contract out
distribution

Reducing capital needs

**Figure 8.1**   Differing financial structures for transport fleet

In order to restructure this financial demand, the company could select not to own its vehicles but to long-term lease the vehicles. This would have a significant impact on the capital needs, as the capital costs would become a revenue cost. Care should be taken that such contracts are long term and long-term leases (obligation to pay rental charges for some years) are often considered jointly with the assets which the company owns. The company could go further to reduce its operational activity in this area. In many companies, even though the vehicles run with the company logo on, they are neither owned nor operated by the company. The service is contracted on an on-going basis with a specialist distribution company. This enables the computer company to focus its energy and finances into the business it understands, computers. It reduces the need for capital outside the core business, and in operations it avoids the dilution of management energy into areas outside the organization's distinctive skills.

In the above simple example, it can be seen that even within a single business element, strategic operating decisions affect the capital structure and size and nature of the revenue expenses. Two companies providing integrated computer solutions to the banks could have two very different strategies and financial structures (Fig. 8.2). A major company might build the computers, write all the software, including the operating systems, and deliver and maintain the hardware with their own resources. The financial structure of this company would have large capital needs (manufacturing facilities, working capital for computers in course of manufacture and delivery etc.) and a large staff. Another company operating in this area, providing—as far as the customer is concerned—the same benefits and service, might buy the computers from a major company with the appropriate operating systems for direct delivery to the customer's site. The company would load the specialist software, configure the system and train the customer's staff. This alternative has vastly different financial structure implications. The company has, in relative terms, almost no physical assets. Its real asset is the intellectual (software development) and marketing skills of a relatively small, but highly professional, group of staff.

The financial structure implications of a given policy are an important issue in the process of strategy selection, indeed in extreme situations it may be the driving force to select a given strategy. The general tendency is for operations to concentrate capital, management skills and energy into the core business and out-source (contract, hire etc.) other activities, such as transport, catering, payroll, security etc. The above discussion has focused on what the company should own and do for itself. Another aspect of the financial structure is the framework of capital for a given business.

Just as different materials may be used to build a bridge, there are options for the

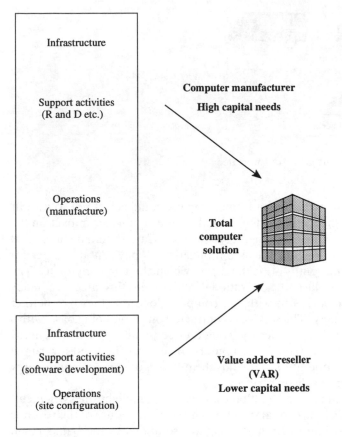

**Figure 8.2**    Schematic capital structure for VAR and computer manufacturer

financial structure of the company. For a simple business, such as that of a technical author, the capital requirements may be low and the business is financed by the single owner. If the owner needs a larger computer, a bank loan could be obtained; most loans are secured on some business asset, such as the computer purchased. How such issues affect the company is considered in more detail in Chapter Nine. A very simple schematic diagram of the capital structure of a company is given in Fig. 8.3.

In a larger company, many people may own the company through the mechanism of share ownership. In the financial structure of a company, there are other sources of money. Suppliers will not be paid immediately (typical terms and conditions are thirty days for payment) and this represents, in effect, a source of money for the company. This is, of course, balanced by the money owed to the company by its customers, which represents a drain of capital to be financed. The company can borrow money from the banks on a simple overdraft. If the company has a good reputation it may be able to attract individuals and organizations with loan stock, offering the investor a fixed period and rate of return, the company having the benefit of more secure financial planning with the term of the loan and its cost fixed. The overall financial structure of a company thus involves money from the owners, suppliers, customers (most often negative, a cash need) and sources of long term and short term loans (both secured against some asset and unsecured).

| Owner's capital | |
| --- | --- |
| Long term loans unsecured | Long term loans secured |
| Short term loans unsecured | Short term loans secured |
| Money owed to suppliers Less money owed by customers | |

**Figure 8.3**   Simple structure capital for a company

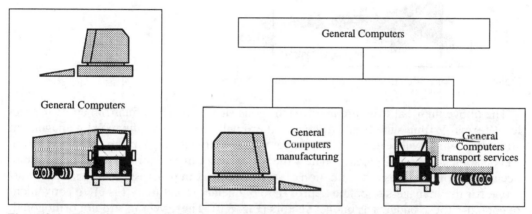

**Figure 8.4**   Two operational and financial structures for General Computers

A large company may wish to divide its operations into separate financial units (organizational structure and financial structure are linked). Earlier in the chapter, we considered two options for a computer company faced with the need to deliver computers, to own its own transport fleet or to contract. However, the managers of this company might decide that the delivery of complex electronic, high value equipment demanded special skills and special transport and that the company had built up valuable, distinctive skills in this area. An alternative for this computer company would be to set up the computer delivery operation as a separate but wholly-owned operation (Fig. 8.4). The new computer delivery company would, of course, provide the company delivery needs on a contract basis. This wholly-owned, but independent, company could then provide delivery services for other manufacturers or removal services for companies relocating and needing to move computer systems. This financial structure provides for the profit accountability of this aspect of the company's total operations and the computer manufacturing sector is not burdened with non-core business complications. Moreover, the independent financial structure allows for effective, financially accountable, development and diversification of the transport business.

Two companies may wish to cooperate in any given area, such as an expansion into some new product area or distribution into an export area. It may then be appropriate to create a financial structure for this new venture which has an independence from both partners. A convenient device is for the new operation to be established as an independent company with appropriate percentage ownership from the new venture partners. This may often be the case for very large projects such as military or civil aircraft, Fig. 8.5.

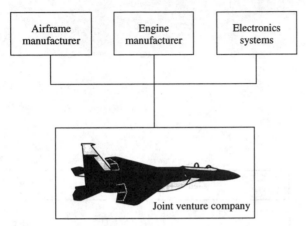

**Figure 8.5**  Formation of joint venture for a large project

The above financial structure involves the construction of a new financial entity in strict legal terms. Within such legal structures, there will need to be a financial management structure, which will be set up to best meet the operational needs of the company. There will be some legal requirements on how the formal accounts are formulated (for example, declaration of capital assets, valuation of stock and work in progress), but this allows vast scope for the managers to define appropriate budgetary structures. It is often convenient to consider these budgets as budget vectors (Fig. 8.6). These vectors are not orthogonal, but interact and thus the marketing function will provide a forecasted sales budget for the next financial year, which will be broken into customers and a product mix (numbers and types of systems to be purchased). The production (operations) function will then project this into a production cost budget and the procurement (buying) function will project this into a raw materials budget. It can be seen that the budgetary structure provides a firm framework of interlocking forecasts and estimates. This financial structure not only provides a framework for building up an overview of the cash flows and profit but also provides the context for financial and managerial accountability of individual managers.

## 8.2 PHYSICAL STRUCTURE

To conduct an operation, facilities are required both for manufacture or provision of the service (for example, a telephone exchange) and to make the product or service available to the customers (such as the telephone network). To manage the organization offices, information (computer database systems, etc.) and communication systems (Electronic Data Interchange (EDI), telephone systems, meeting rooms etc) are required.

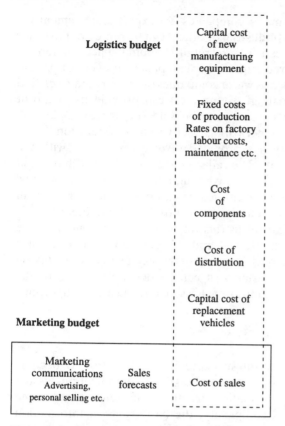

**Figure 8.6**  Simple structure relationship between marketing and logistics budget

The company management have to decide their own options for this physical structure. In general, the more modern and flexible the firm's buildings and facilities, the more efficient its operations are likely to be. There are 'trade-off' issues for the managers in considering the physical structure. Should the manufacturing, R and D, administrative and marketing aspects be contained in the same site? Should the firm have just one or two major sites or should it operate from a larger number of smaller sites reducing the distribution costs?

The quality of the physical surroundings and equipment (lighting, noise, air-conditioning, etc.) affects the efficiency and well-being of people. The layout of an office will affect the sense of community and communication flows within the office. A remote production site with a central administration centre may well provide the company with apparent operational efficiency, but possibly with hidden costs in terms of creating a 'them' and 'us' culture.

The creation of a separate R and D centre can have similar problems, in that the dedicated R and D centre can be located close to a major university, be provided with lavish central resources in terms of technical instruments and test facilities, yet be considered an ivory tower, with people out of touch with the real problems of sales and production.

The physical structure and land assets of the company should be regarded as a resource capable of diversified exploitation. Many major companies use expert management for their office space and sites. Marginal space (industrial or office) can be rented out to other organizations. A city centre office block can feature retail shopping space for rent at ground level. Conference rooms can be hired out to other companies or even for private functions, such as weddings. Operations such as water companies or forestry may well find that tourism, leisure and activity use (boating, fishing etc.) can provide major profit contributions. Even marginal production capacity can be sold off, for example, toll manufacture of chemicals or sale of marginal network capacity to other operations.

The provision of new network capacity has provided diverse operations with the opportunity to exploit their physical structure. The railways and canal owners have land rights between the major centres of population and have found that cooperation with new optic communications networks has provided additional profit opportunities. Even wall space can provide a source of advertising revenue for city centre travel providers.

The provision of an appropriate physical infrastructure is not only essential to the effective conduct of the core business, but its effective and efficient management can also provide an attractive source of additional profits. To prevent this asset exploitation taking senior managers' attention from the core business, it can be desirable to regard the physical infrastructure management of the organization as a separate business in appropriate areas.

## 8.3 INFORMATION STRUCTURE

The hidden danger in considering information structure is to allow this to become perceived as an Information Technology (computers and digital communications) issue. IT should be considered as an element of information structure management, not as the information structure. For all the detailed complexity, the basic rules of information structure and management are simple:

1. *The IT or computer manager is not the information manager*   The IT manager provides a resource of critical competitive advantage to the company. Information has to be collected by people (field sales representatives and production operators etc., who are outside the managerial control of the IT manager) and although providing the technology, the IT manager does not manage the information. To consider the IT manager as the information manager is to consider the laboratory technician as being responsible for the practical content of a degree course. Without skilled input, the desired objectives will not be achieved. The responsibility for the total policy on information must be a strategic, top management, decision.

2. *Capture of the information should be as close to the source of the information as possible*   When the input of information becomes detached from the understanding, two problems occur: Firstly, there is loss of understanding and secondly, errors that are obvious are keyed in as the information is in numerical form and physical understanding is lost.

---

In an order booking system a key operator made an error in the unit of measure and keyed 1000 tons rather than the normal order of 1000 kg. As the entry was devolved from the front line sales staff, the error was not corrected. When received by production, the Production Engineer realized the problem and the correct order of 1000 kg was dispatched. However, again the key entry was devolved from the source of the information and the order entry system accepted a simple key entry of 'order dispatched' without correction. The automated invoicing system was in perfect order and invoiced the customer for 1000 tons, a sum in excess of £1 000 000. At least the profit figures for that month looked good!

Related to this is that remote keying results in a loss of ownership of the information. Errors are made, but operators are not concerned in a real sense as they are not part of the team but part of some human slave system to the computer. The 1980s computer manager had a statistical solution: just get two operators to key the information. In Chapter Eleven, we will consider the motivational issues of job design. In the above example, a much better solution in efficiency and personal satisfaction would be to bring the data entry as close as possible to the customer with the sales staff. With laptop computers it is much more effective for field sales staff to enter orders on their calls during the day, the orders can be down loaded by modem from the hotel overnight and the latest information on stock availability and prices can be sent in return.

3. *Where possible the capture of information should involve the minimum number of people keying in information, that is, the maximum of direct data input*    There is no human satisfaction in keying in information that can be collected by machine. To do this is to convert a human into a machine with the consequent devaluation of the person. Major retailers have long realized that laser reading of bar codes is more accurate and provides less operator stress. If an error should occur, the bar code contains a check digit at the end which will pick any single error in the laser reading process.

4. *GIGO (Garbage In: Garbage Out)*    Non-computer users find that the computer is a convenient screen for their errors. If a figure is entered in error, then the output will also be in error. Given that commercial information is often used in many ways, then a simple error in an order entry will not only throw out the sales budget but also the Materials Resource Planning system (MRP).

5. *The long term storage of data must be a specific responsibility*    No sooner is data entered into a system (computer or manual) than it starts to decay. In commercial mailing lists it is estimated that within two years there will be 30 per cent error rate if the list is not maintained (people move jobs, change names when they marry, etc.). When it is decided to hold information on some aspect of the company, it must be the responsibility of a named individual (departmental role) to ensure that the data is fully maintained, changes are tracked and then updated. However, in some cases, great care must be taken not to overwrite the old data. In the development of a product, the specifications etc. should be updated as soon as changes and improvements are made. As a new specification is written and recorded, the old specification should be archived, not erased or overwritten. Then a customer who has an enquiry at some time in the future can be advised in the knowledge of the state of development of the product at the time it was sold.

In the areas of tax, commercial transactions and quality assurance it may be a legal requirement to maintain formal records for audit purposes for a defined period of time, often of the order of seven years (or as advised by the company legal department). It is often necessary to move such old, but necessary, archived records to remote storage or convert to alternative media (such as microfilm) and, again, named responsibility is essential for the accuracy of this process.

6. *The more powerful the IT system the more damage when (note: not if) it crashes*    In a modern company, the loss of the IT system and data may well involve the destruction of the company. A critical activity is to back up the data onto a separate physical system. A typical procedure will be to have a mechanism of overnight archive back-up and a duplication of transactions between back up so that in the event of failure, it should be possible to restore the system to the state it was in just before the failure. It should be remembered that the disaster plan must take account of the total destruction of the computer (fire or explosion) and that archive copies should be held on another site. Major companies will subscribe to a computer disaster service which will provide a twenty-four hour replacement computer ready to load the archive data and get the company up and running in one or two days.

7. *Only one master database must be allowed for each set of information*    In many organizations, data will be used by a number of different functions. In a chemical company, a product description will feature in the MRP system, the quality assurance system, the marketing system etc. When a computer system is first implemented all these databases will be loaded with the same information. As the business evolves, product descriptions may be amended. If a master database is not used, then the time of amendment may differ between data applications or, even worse, some systems may become fossilized and deviate from the real state. To avoid this problem, one database should be regarded as the master and other users should draw their information from this.

8. *Information should be freely available to those who need and are authorized to use it*    A key issue is the provision of rapid access to authorized users. Complicated log-in procedures or slow response times can greatly reduce the perceived quality of an information system.

9. *Information should be inaccessable to those who do not need or are not authorized to use it*    For reasons of commercial sensitivity, other users should not be allowed access. Password protection with PIN (Personal Identification Number) is only of limited efficiency (even when subject to changes at reasonable intervals). Additional checks, such as limiting access hours and a transaction security log, provide additional levels of security.

10. *Data is not information*    Given the complexity and ease of data storage, the problem for managers is having too much data and not enough information. Data becomes information when it is presented in an appropriate format, in an accurate and timely fashion. For complex, fast moving databases (such as order entry systems), this may involve the presentation of information in a graphical format and/or providing exception reports; a sales manager may only be concerned with orders where delivery may be delayed.

11. *Data is an asset*    Once data has been obtained it may, subject to any legal and ethical constraints, be used for other purposes. Professional institutions keep a record of members' special subject interests and areas of employment. Subject to the members'

agreement, such lists may be rented to companies wanting to market specialized services.

12. *Legal and ethical issues must be fully considered*   Data given in confidence should only be used for the purposes which the provider agreed. Computer data is subject to the provisions of the Data Protection Act and must be used within the provisions of the law and for the purposes specified. Critical areas are information on employees' personal affairs and credit information on customers.

13. *The value of information can be subject to exponential time decay*   A critical use of information systems is to provide the mechanism of feedback and control for the company. As in physical systems, if the time between an event and its feedback to the control system is too long, the control loop becomes inefficient. When this happens in a large IT system there is often a huge hidden expense, where the system is maintained but the real managerial control takes place through a set of informal systems, taking up vast amounts of time and costs.

---

In the 80s, within a company with a ten day order cycle, it took three days to up-date a stock record on the mainframe. The mainframe database was used for invoicing customers etc. However, any sales manager who wanted to know the state of an order would ring up the production office where a card index was the real management system for production.

---

## 8.4 ORGANIZATIONAL STRUCTURE

Organizational structure is often considered as a human resource issue, as the most obvious statement of structure is the company organogram, with its set of job descriptions and role relationship definitions. However, organizational structure affects the total infrastructure, such as information management and financial structure, served markets, production technologies, degree of integration etc. The organizational structure of a company is a strategic management decision to align the firm's total resources, skills and energies to gain the maximum competitive advantage.

The most simple structure is to group the firm's capabilities into certain resource or functional areas and an outline of a possible structure is given in Fig. 8.7. Accounts and

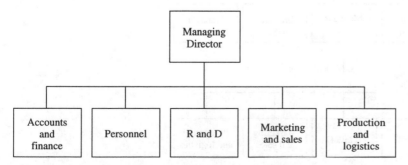

**Figure 8.7**   Simple functional organizational structure

finance will keep the books, check credit status of customers and arrange banking and capital requirements within the context of the policy determined by the managing director. The personnel department will keep track of employees' welfare, effect the mechanics of hiring and firing, coordinate staff development programmes, administer safety, administer the payroll, conduct industrial relations negotiations etc. R and D and the technical group will develop the new products and technologies, as well as manage quality assurance. Marketing and sales will research markets to determine the new market needs, communicate the company products to its customer groups and provide the day-to-day sales drive and order entry to maintain market position. The production group will be responsible for materials (raw materials and components in and finished products out), manufacture the product and deliver it to the customers. This is only one possible arrangement, any given firm may well have considerable variation around this simple division of responsibility.

There are hidden problems in coordination, as the formal lines of responsibility are augmented by lines of cross-functional relationships. Marketing must coordinate with production (production of next month's sales demand) and R and D (development of new market driven products).

When the company grows into diversified markets, either with different products or by geographical expansion into other countries, such a simple structure will not accommodate the size and diversity of the operation. Some modification is necessary as the complexity and weight of information and range of decisions will defeat the simple structure. A common response to this is the regionalized structure, where certain administrative functions are held at the corporate head office and the functional structure is replicated in each of the major market areas (Fig. 8.8).

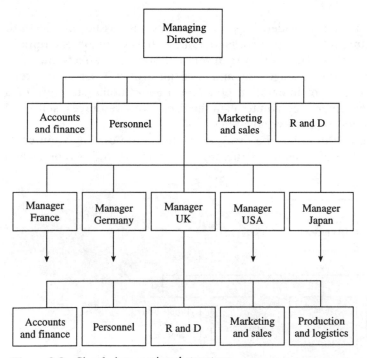

**Figure 8.8**  Simple international structure

Some functions will be retained at the headquarters. The accounts, finance and legal groups will coordinate the overall financial management (international currency cover, investments, capital, major capital borrowings etc.), consolidate the divisional accounts for total management of the company and provide legal financial reports, such as the annual accounts, to the owners (shareholders). Such a function will also provide expert legal services to the divisions, for example, the registration of trademarks, filing of patents and major contract legal advice etc. The headquarters personnel function may well be small, providing central coordination of training programmes and ensuring consistency in issues such as industrial relations and appraisal and job evaluation schemes. The central marketing function may well provide major resources for advertising, implement corporate image communications programmes and ensure that individual divisional programmes keep within the corporate style. This group may have special technical experts, such as statisticians for time series analysis or for the analysis of market research results. A central R and D function may well be considered necessary to look at long term projects, such as new materials development or total new technologies. For the detailed day-to-day operation in each of the major geographical areas there will be some simple functional structure.

This type of organizational structure would be ideal if the company only segmented its business in one set of market variables. However, a company working in a number of countries and in a number of product areas, requires a more complex infrastructure to manage the complexity of the business. Here, either at an informal level or in an explicit way, a matrix structure is required. A simple possible structure is shown in Fig. 8.9 for a company working in a number of countries, in a number of market areas. A company in this position would be concerned that its financial performance and effectiveness was right in each of the countries. In addition, such a company would also want to view each of its international market areas (such as science instruments) as a business and take a view in this dimension. This international business would need coordination, thus there would be people in each specific country responsible for the national marketing and sales of the product range.

Even this structure does not represent the full complexity of many modern industries. A company may use components (such as microchips) in all of its products and may well have to consider a global manufacturing structure. Major research activities, into the area of materials technology, for example, will again affect the whole of the company's competitive advantage and will require corporate direction. Such a company may trade with other major multinationals who might buy across the entire product range (for example, a major chemical company, such as ICI, would have a need for all the products shown in Fig. 8.9). To ensure an appropriate focus and coordination of effort on such an important customer, an account manager might be appointed.

The matrix structure is not highly favoured as it can make individual accountability difficult and managers in the matrix have a difficult task in the balancing of the demands of two bosses. Often the compromise is to appoint product managers and account managers, whose responsibility is to manage a cross-functional response to maximize the competitive response in the firm's selected market areas.

The above account is simplified in order to illustrate some of the key issues that need to be considered in the determination of a company structure. As market conditions, company size and technologies change, so too must the organizational structure, to better meet the competitive demands of the current situation.

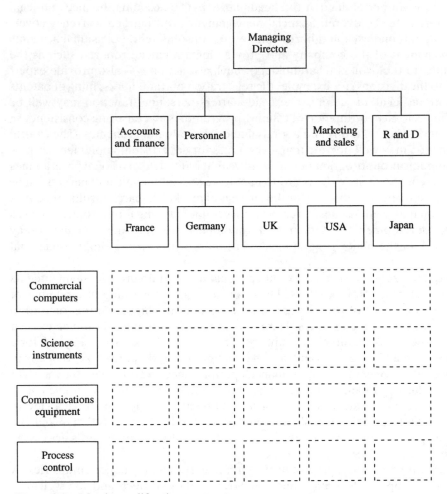

**Figure 8.9**   Matrix modification to structure

## 8.5  DEMOGRAPHIC STRUCTURE

More often than not, a company does not come into existence in some 'big bang' with the ideal structure, human and physical resources. Again, this topic is most often considered within the context of human resource management (Chapter 11), where skill succession is a critical issue. There is not only a demographic structure to the skills and age of the company's people. The same issues also apply to the company sites and productive capacities. There will be a mixture of new and ageing plants using differing states of technology.

## 8.6  CULTURAL STRUCTURE

Quite clearly, the multitude of decisions that face the firm's people every day may not be resolved by continual referral to senior management or to massive corporate policy manuals. The company mission, its structure of doing things, has to be an internalized part of people's working life. To be successful, a firm needs a culture where people have an intuitive ability to know what is expected of them in a given situation; they know 'where they are coming from' and hence what they have to do.

A major multinational is faced with problems when its culture may be seen to be at variance with local culture in overseas divisions. The transfer of people around the organization through international secondments is often used to ensure the acceptable and effective diffusion of the corporate culture. Major culture conflict will occur when firms merge or are taken over. Cultural structure has to be managed just as much as the physical resources of the company. A culture that succeeded in one decade, technology or industry may not succeed in the changed circumstances.

Every firm has a corporate formula. Fig. 8.10 shows the structure of this. The formula is determined by the number of input variables or influences. The characteristics of the formula are reflected in various ways in the organization; for example, the customs, procedures and symbols. In part, the formal expression will be the company mission statement.

In Chapter 2 the influences of firms' publics were discussed. The *values of society* will be reflected in the values within the company. Particular changes have occurred in attitudes to equal employment opportunity (sex, colour, religion, social class etc.) and environmental issues. Not only will these values be reflected directly into the company, but they may well be magnified and structured by the *external stakeholders*. Financial publics may not wish to invest in an organization which is not perceived to have sound environmental policies. A problem commonly occurs when a firm's competitive technology takes it into new *served markets* with a different culture. Microprocessor technology developed for

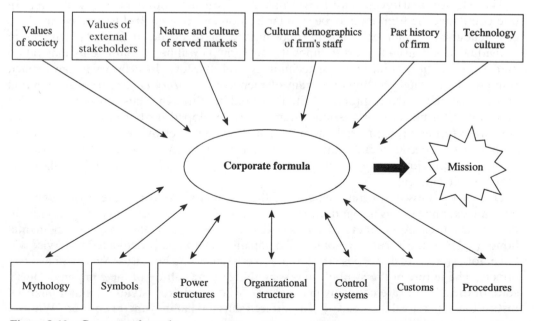

**Figure 8.10** Corporate formula

science instruments and computers is the basis of domestic computer games systems. The firms that developed the microprocessor had the technical capability to construct such systems, but not the marketing empathy with this type of market to conceive such products in the first place or the understanding of how to market them once developed.

In Chapter Four, it was noted that people have different personalities and that personality is one factor in career selection. This is reinforced by the training and career development structures that various people receive. *The cultural demographics of the firm's staff* are important. In particular, the culture of the top management pervades the process and the nature in which policy is arrived at and then implemented. A company with many of its top management having technical backgrounds may see the competitive advantage grounded in innovation and state of the art products. A company in broadly the same market place, but run by senior managers with a marketing background, may see competitive advantage founded on saturation advertising and distribution cover.

*The past history of the firm* will not only affect the nature of the existing structure (for example, geography of served markets), but also the public perception of the company, the corporate image. In the financial services sector, many services are provided by both the building societies and by the clearing banks. Given the cooperative and membership structure history of the building societies, they are have corporate images of being more 'friendly' than traditional banks.

*Technology* not only changes the way in which business is done or makes new ventures possible, it also creates new cultures. Rapid air travel and instant ISDN (Integrated Signal Digital Networks) have created a new way to run multinational companies with a far greater degree of control than was possible 20 years ago. This has created the culture of the 'jet set' geocentric executive and engineer. The introduction of computer technology into the newspaper industry not only changed the economics but also the culture of the industry.

These factors and forces shape the formula that a firm develops to meet any situation. In one company, the formula may be standardization and cost control to give competitive cost leadership. Another company may have a more devolved formula, with more individual scope given to staff to innovate. Its formula will be to compete by innovation and to be at the leading edge of technology and markets. In a firm with an explicit framework of strategy formulation many elements of the *corporate formula* will be shared and proclaimed to the full range of the firm's publics through a mission statement. The nature and formulation of mission statements is developed further in Chapter 14. The corporate formula is expressed and maintained by a number of mechanisms. These are both formal (procedures and control systems) and informal (mythology and customs). The informal expressions are of as much significance to the maintenance of the formula as the more visible elements.

One of the most powerful elements of the formula is the corporate *mythology*. An extreme example of this is found with the armed services where accounts of battles fought before any present members of the services were born form the basis of 'regimental honour'. The same is true of commercial companies. A company dedicated to service will have 'folk stories' of deliveries effected in force 10 gales and blizzards. *Symbols* have two effects. The nature of the symbols tells something of the culture of the company. Thus a state of the art software company may have very informal dress styles. A major financial institution may regard the wearing of a coloured shirt too flamboyant for comfort. Within a company there will be symbols of status and power. The size of the office, the provision of a reserved parking space, the assignment of an unnecessary secretary, a private fax line and the quality of the office furniture are all indications of status. The company car has a special place as it not only displays the symbol to other staff but the world at large.

Power structures can be complex. In the fast growing company controlled by an entrepreneur owner, the structure can be centred on a single person who exercises absolute power. In a stable company, the power may follow the lines of the classical organization structure. However, in more technical companies the power may follow the expert knowledge. Power is not always fully indicated by the position of a person in the organizational structure; for example, a person with long service may be a confidant of members of the board and have considerable influence. The managing director's secretary or personal assistant does not appear to have executive power, but no sane manager will antagonize this person, who may well be able to limit access to the person in power.

*Organizational structure* is a reflection of the corporate formula. In a bureaucratic company, there will be a firm structure of responsibilities and coordination may have to be effected through meetings of the most senior managers, with problems being referred up and solutions handed down. Such a process is slow and puts a heavy demand on senior managers and so is only effective in stable technical and market conditions. The first indications of flexibility are when dotted line responsibilities occur across the organizational structure, indicating that people have the right to work across their strict organizational boundaries. More flexible companies may have fewer layers of management, with greater devolution of responsibilities to first line managers. This may also include the flexibilities and uncertainties of matrix type management structures described earlier.

The nature of control systems can differ. In a formal company or government departments the control may be very precise and a senior management signature may even be required to buy the office paper clips. This is tight direct control, but it is achieved at the expense of flexibility and the sense of control is more often imaginary than real. With so many decisions to make, the senior manager can spend time signing many documents without any real time to read them, let alone exercise any real judgement. In more devolved companies, the power will be delegated in large bundles and a manager may thus be delegated authority to manage a department within an agreed budget. The day-to-day decisions as to how the budget and resources should be deployed are the responsibility of the first line manager. The manager's accountability is to provide the agreed level of performance within the total of assigned resources.

*Customs* form an important part of the corporate formula and culture. In some organizations people who have worked together for many years may still address each other as Mr or Ms. In more open companies, however, the senior executive may well be addressed by first name by all members of staff. There may be a single staff restaurant but 'staff' and 'workers' by common consent may well not associate at the same tables. In more open companies, there will be a genuine sense of single status; we are all employees of the organization. Another sensitive indicator of the customs and culture of the company is association of company staff in their leisure time.

*Procedures* are the final way the corporate formula is expressed. It should not be thought that procedures are in themselves an irritation. A procedure is set up so that when a frequently met situation is encountered there is a simple formula to be applied with the minimum of management effort. The problem is that within an autocratic and bureaucratic company, when a condition is experienced that is not precisely covered, paralysis results as there is not a procedure.

## 8.7 EXTERNAL STRUCTURE

Companies exist in an environment. In Chapter Two, a structure of publics was considered. To enjoy long term competitive advantage, a firm must manage its relationships—value linkages—with its key publics. To do this the firm must have an external structure. A computer with the fastest CPU in the world is of little use unless it has a good printer interface. EDI is the corporate equivalent, with companies placing orders direct without manual intervention. TQM and JIT (Just In Time) require extensive links between the firm and its suppliers. A culture of partnership is needed, rather than an arm's length negotiation just to get products at the lowest price, the emphasis now being placed on the greatest long term value for the partnership.

To participate in the regulatory environment, firms will group into industry associations, such as the CIA (Chemical Industries Association) or research associations (such as the Food Research Association).

## 8.8 QUALITY STRUCTURE—TOTAL QUALITY MANAGEMENT

In TQM, the definition of quality will be 'comformance to requirements'. This is a much more demanding definition than the simple 'conformance to specification'. Conformance to requirements means fulfilling customer requirements and expectations. This is a marketing-orientated definition, requiring that the firm has both the sensitivity and sufficient two-way communication with its customers to understand their needs, wants and expectations. It is not possible to achieve this by inspecting quality in with a simple process of quality control inspection and measurement. Every member of the organization must be a quality inspector. Each function must regard its value chain partners as customers. Quality is not inspected, it is built in and designed, starting with the customer expectations. The achievement of BS5750 and ISO9000 registration is but one step on the path to TQM.

Given the diversity of products and services, there is no single prescription for effective quality structure and management. To evaluate whether the company structures are appropriate, it is necessary to audit three cycles, the new product development cycle, the manufacturing delivery cycle (manufacture and service systems audit) and the order invoicing cycle (sales system audit).

In the new product development cycle, the first stage is to ensure that the marketing and communications are such that the firm has an accurate perception of the customer's needs and quality perceptions. In particular, the company must have a good understanding of what value means to the customer, remembering that value will involve total cost of ownership to the customer (direct cost, service costs and running costs, such as energy etc.). The environmental audit will evaluate the total life cycle impact of the product; the environmental impact of the manufacture, use of the product and ultimate disposal or recycling of the product. The design process will not only ensure performance to the customer's requirements, but also provide designed-in component quality and simplicity, together with methods of construction that allow easy error-free manufacture (such as reduction of component count and manufacturing complexity with the design of application specific integrated circuits).

The manufacturing cycle is the traditional area of quality assurance audits: the evaluation of sources of supply (only sourcing from BS5750/ISO9000 suppliers), appropriate storage of materials on delivery, the efficiency and zero defect manufacture of the product or provision of the service, the appropriate storage, delivery and installation of the product. Care must be take with such concerns as packaging, a 100 per cent pass rate at the factory is not what is required; 100 per cent quality on delivery is.

Errors can arise from the company order system. Often, customers do not know what they need to order, they only know what they want the product to do. Many computer users will not know the difference between a parallel and a serial interface board to the printer. They just want the computer to print. The order system must be sensitive enough to understand the customer's needs and, when necessary, translate and interpret them accurately into the appropriate specific service or product configuration. The system must not only capture this information but also ensure that it is accurately and quickly distributed to the manufacturing or operating areas that will be responsible for the provision of the product or service. A key source of customer dissatisfaction is poor delivery information. If there should be unexpected delays, the sales system must be alerted so the customer can be kept informed. Needless to say, the customer must receive an accurate and complete invoice. The systems must be flexible to the customer's needs, a component may well have one part code number in the supplier's system and another in the customer's systems and the invoice and documentation must provide the flexibility to quote both. A particular test of the efficiency of the sales systems is in export orders, some 30 per cent of export orders being delayed as a result of errors in the complex documentation required.

## REVIEW

No firm will survive without a secure *financial structure*. Different strategies may involve the company in the ownership of most of its resources but, at the other extreme, a company may exist by contracting most of its activities and simply concentrate on the distinctive skills and competitive advantage in the market. The effective conduct of the operations will depend on the appropriate *physical structure* with the provision of appropriate facilities for the conduct of the business and supply of its goods and services.

To manage a business the firm's management must manage information. Information and its flows have a structure. The firm's *information structure* is more than just the provision of computer systems, it also involves the ownership of data. Computer systems collect data, often collected by people (direct data capture is not always possible) to be analysed, collated and distributed for other people in the organization to use for the effective conduct of the firm's activities. Thus, the firm's information structure is about databases and network architecture, but it is also about people.

The firm's *organizational structure* is shaped not only by the culture and the human resource management policies, but also by the geography of the company's businesses, the firm's technologies, its served markets and its financial structure. Structures may be highly centralized, hierarchically, or devolved with wide delegation of authority. Companies evolve over time and have to live with their history. The *demographic structure* of the company involves the mix of facilities (old plant and technologies as well as state of the art), the mix of experience and skills of its staff as well as the physical demographics of its workforce (age etc.).

All of the firm's activities and its core values and mission statements are affected by the *cultural structure* of the organization. The technical history of the company and the climate of the firm's markets, as well as the values and expectations of the internal and external stakeholders will affect this mix, described as the *corporate formula*. This formula will be expressed in the corporate mission statement and maintained by symbols, the firm's mythology, control systems, customs and procedures, as well as its organizational structure.

To interface with the external world, the firm has to ensure an appropriate *external structure* to manage its links with customers, suppliers and other publics such as the regulatory authorities. The area of this activity is the quality structure for the Total Quality Management of the company.

## KEY CONCEPTS AND TECHNIQUES

**Culture structure**   The values, and corporate formula expressed in the mission and supported by customs, symbols, control systems etc.

**Demographic structure**   The age, physical and technical make-up of the firm's products and facilities. The age, skills and other characteristic make-up of the firm's staff.

**External structure**   The way the firm adapts to manage the interactions with its key external publics, including customers, distributors and suppliers in the firm's value chain.

**Financial structure**   The nature of the ownership of the company, the sources of its finances and the application of its finances to capital equipment and working capital.

**Information structure**   Information has its sources and flows through the company systems to the various users. Information is not only electronic and its use by people means that its structure and flows involves more than just information technology.

**Organizational structure**   The framework of accountabilities, role relationships and allocation of power between the people in a firm.

**Physical structure**   The capital infrastructure of the company, the mix of buildings and equipment the company needs to conduct its business, including the company information networks.

**Quality structure**   The framework of management structure, formal and informal systems, to achieve total quality management. This involves the quality links with customers, distributors and suppliers and all the members of the firm's quality publics.

## CASE STUDY

Professional institutions have to respond to the changing environment, as well as commercial firms. The Chartered Institute of Marketing operates in a fast changing environment. Below is a simplified outline of the forces on this institute. A working definition of the purpose of the institute is the preservation and advancement of the profession of marketing for the benefit of the members of the institution and society at large.

Make-up of the members: people become members of this institute through three routes: they may follow the institute's examinations from certificate to diploma and thus become full members after three years' part time study while in employment; they may take a degree in marketing and have many exemptions; they may have another degree (engineering, science, etc.) and take the diploma examinations with the graduate entry examinations. Thus the membership includes people (in addition to student members) who have directed their careers to marketing and those who have moved through professional development into senior positions and acquired significant marketing responsibilities. The members work in a variety of organizations: advertising, media, agencies, FMCG manufacturers, consumer durables, industrial organizations, service organizations (consumer and industrial), non-profit sectors (hospitals, local authorities etc.) and education. Other professional organizations (such as the Royal Society of Chemistry and Institution of Electrical Engineers) have marketing special interest groups and within marketing there are other professional associations concerned with areas such as market research and education.

The institute provides services including a library and extensive publications. The institute sets its own examinations and also approves other courses (such as degrees in marketing) where appropriate. It is also concerned with the presentation of the profession to external publics and the ethical conduct of its members. The institute is responsible to its members who, in the end, control the structure of the society through its general meetings (subject to charter requirements). The institute seeks to provide its members by activity, organization, professional interest and by region, a full package of support and activities. Its head office and training centre is situated near the M4.

What organizational structure would you consider suitable for this institute? What other structural problems would have to be considered? What political, cultural and power issues would have to be considered? If you prefer, you may substitute any other professional institution of your selection.

## QUESTIONS

1. What are the advantages and disadvantages of a firm's ownership of support services, such as a transport fleet for distribution of the firm's products?

2. Map out the information flows in a local supermarket equipped with laser check-outs. How would such a shop detect that it had been raided by a team of shop lifters?

3. What are the advantages and disadvantages of a matrix organization? In what types of situation would you expect a matrix structure?

4. Explain the differences, and the reasons for them, between the culture of a service unit (navy ship) and a university.

5. Who are the key external publics for a university? How might a university structure the management of these relationships with its external publics?

## FURTHER READING

Ansoff, H.I. and E.J. McDonnell (1990) *Implementing Strategic Management*, 2nd Edition, Prentice Hall.
Grosse, R. and D. Kujawa (1992) *International Business: Theory and Managerial Applications*, 2nd Edition, Irwin.
Jauch, L.R. and W.F. Glueck (1988) *Strategic Management and Business Policy*, McGraw-Hill.
Johnson, G. and K. Scoles (1988) *Exploring Corporate Strategy*, Prentice Hall.
Knight, K. (1978) *Management, A Cross-functional Approach to Organisation*, Gower Press.
Sadler, P. (1991) *Designing Organisations*, Mercury.
Steers, R.M. *et al.* (1985) *Managing Effective Organisations: an Introduction*, Kent Publishing.

# NINE

# FINANCE

## 9.1 WHAT IS MONEY?

Money may be considered as the *energy* of business. It is a measure of wealth and a mechanism of exchange. If an engineering company takes metal bars and converts them to screws it is adding value, creating wealth. The value of the final product is greater than the cost of the raw materials and the conversion costs (energy, labour etc.). This increase in wealth, this added value, is the profit of the business.

In such a business we need to compare the value of bars, part-made screws, screws, the value of the equipment and premises. To do this we need some common unit, just as when we are comparing energy. The firm could select to value all its items in terms of a 'standard screw' (just like a non-standard energy measure such as the BTU), but this would not have much meaning outside of the firm. Therefore, all the wealth, value addition and transactions of the company are measured in terms of money. This gives a common unit of financial energy, just as we can compare the energy of different systems in terms of a unit such as the joule.

The company needs to enter into exchanges. People such as carpenters need the screws, but the firm does not want to be paid in terms of furniture. Money provides a common unit of exchange which enables the ready transfer (exchange) of wealth between people or organizations. Money has no real value in itself, it is merely an acceptable representation of wealth. A screw does not have a fixed value, if imported screws are available much cheaper then the value (money that can be obtained) for the firm's screws will be reduced. Money is an artificial concept, it rests on the trust that people have that other people will be prepared to accept it for goods or services. There is not too much value in a Confederate dollar.

The above discussion is necessary as, unlike the conversion of electrical energy into mechanical or heat energy, where the conversion factors are constant and known to a fair number of decimal points, there is a far greater element of subjective judgement in the estimation of the value of a stock of screws. Later in this chapter we will discuss taxation and accountancy rules. These may appear to give precise conversion factors. However, these exist for legal rules where certain conventions and consistency are required for such purposes as ensuring the payment of appropriate amounts of duty and tax. However, in the real day-to-day management of the business, the difficulty and lack of precision in attaching money values to goods and equipment must be remembered.

## 9.2 ACCOUNTANCY AND FINANCIAL MANAGEMENT

There are as many types of accountants as there are of engineers. A mechanical engineer has a very different skill profile to an electronic engineer. So it is with those labelled 'accountants'.

## TYPES OF ACCOUNTANCY ROLES
## FOR A MANUFACTURING OR SERVICE FIRM

| Types of accountant | Predominant focus |
| --- | --- |
| Tax accountant | To ensure that tax laws are obeyed and to seek within these tax laws to minimize the firm's liability to pay tax by efficient tax planning. |
| Cost accountant | Very often found working for a production manager, the role is to estimate the costs of production of the firm's goods and services. Given the wide range of machines, people and resources used as inputs and the diverse range of outputs, this can be a complex and demanding role. Poor costing can kill a profitable product or allow the sale of product or service below its 'real' cost at a loss. |
| Treasury accountant | Very often found at corporate headquarters of large companies. Works very closely with the tax accountants and the company Legal Department. Concerned with financial structure of the company, how to secure large sums of money for investment, how to make geocentric provisions to minimize currency risks, investment of firm's money reserves pending use in the conduct of the business. Will often work with the business analyst in the assessment of take over evaluations that involve both technical/market evaluations and financial structure type implications. |
| Auditor (internal) | Accountants who check that no persons are taking the company money (stealing). They are also charged with ensuring uniform accountancy practices, such as stock valuation. Essentially concerned with the accurate recording of past events. |
| Management accountant | Often in business this role may have a differing names such as business analyst, or may be a role linked to a broader management responsibility such as new business development manager, whose role is to assess the new directions the company should move in, business to move out of, new business and new venture the company should enter. This role is often not filled by a career accountancy specialist, as it involves a great amount of marketing, operation and technical knowledge of the firm's business and markets. This role is most often filled by an engineer or the like who has either gained a second formal qualification in accountancy or received appropriate skills though continuing professional development and the firm's own training programmes. |

In this book we shall concentrate on the needs of financial management, the area where the engineer will be most involved in the first decade of his or her working life. Enough outline will be given to understand the broader scope of the career accountant. Leading references are given at the end of the chapter for students that need more depth and detail.

## 9.3 THE BALANCE SHEET

In mechanics, there is the theory that to every action there is an equal and opposite reaction. Take, for example, energy. It is not possible to destroy energy, only to convert it from one form, such as electrical energy, to heat energy. Accountancy has its own law of action and reaction, the principle of double entry. If a company spends £100 on raw materials, its cash account at the bank is reduced but its working assets (raw materials for production) are increased by £100.

$$\text{SUM Assets} = \text{SUM Liabilities}$$

Assets are the things (expressed in money terms) a company owns such as the buildings, equipment, stock etc. Liabilities are the amounts of money the firm owes, including to the owners of the company and to people from whom the firm has purchased goods or services but not paid (the firm's creditors). Expenses are the amounts of money that the company has to pay for goods or services, such as materials for production. Revenues are the sums of money that the company receives from the sale of its products.

The situation is best considered with a practical example. If B. Clark, a Chartered Engineer, sets up his own business to make special electronic contacts for specific applications with a special machine, using gold to provide the best quality, his business might look something like that below.

### OUTLINE OF GOLD CONNECTIONS

B. Clark rents a small enterprise unit which comes with basic insurance, services etc. for £5000 a year. The business is started with £11 000 of personal money and a long-term bank loan of £9000. There is a need to purchase some general office equipment (word processor, desk etc.) and this costs £4000. The special equipment was purchased second hand for £10 000. The gold wire and other materials for the manufacture are rather expensive and the firm started up with £1000 of gold wire and other materials to assemble the contacts. During the course of the year, it is found necessary to hold stocks of certain types of the finished contacts and business is good, so additional raw materials are purchased raising the total of input material held on stock to £2000 and an additional £1000 of finished stock. Sales for the first year are quite good at £30 000. Customers are allowed one month to pay, so at any one time B. Clark is owed £2500. However, the suppliers of parts and materials, once the business has been established, also allow one month to pay; so at any one time the business owes £1000. B. Clark takes £1000 a month as pay. At this stage of the business no other staff are employed. Products are dispatched by Datapost costing £100 a month. Other odd expenses, such as supplies for the computer and telephone charges, are £200 a month. The cost of components for production is £600 a month.

The balance sheet shows the state of the firm at a given instant so we can consider the state of this company at the start of trading and one year later.

## BALANCE SHEET AT START OF YEAR'S TRADING

| FIXED ASSETS | £ | CAPITAL | £ |
|---|---|---|---|
| Office equipment | 4 000 | Personal money | 11 000 |
| Production equipment | 10 000 | Long term loan | 9 000 |
| | | | |
| CURRENT ASSETS | | CURRENT LIABILITIES | |
| Starting stock | 1 000 | Creditors | NIL |
| Debtors | | | |
| Cash | 5 000 | | |
| TOTAL | 20 000 | TOTAL | 20 000 |

## THE CASH FLOW STATEMENT FIRST YEAR OF TRADING

| REVENUE | £ | £ | £ |
|---|---|---|---|
| Sales | 30 000 | | |
| TOTAL | | 30 000 | |
| | | | |
| EXPENSES | | | |
| Opening stock | 1 000 | | |
| Purchases for production | 9 200 | | |
| (Less) Closing stock | (−)3 000 | | |
| Total materials | 7 200 | | |
| Wages | 12 000 | | |
| Rent and service charges | 5 000 | | |
| Datapost charges | 1 200 | | |
| Other expenses | 2 400 | | |
| Bank interest charges | 1 500 | | |
| TOTAL | | 29 300 | |
| PROFIT | | | 700 |

## BALANCE SHEET AT END OF YEAR'S TRADING

| FIXED ASSETS | £ | CAPITAL | £ |
|---|---|---|---|
| Office equipment | 4 000 | Personal money | 11 000 |
| Production equipment | 10 000 | Long term loan | 9 000 |
| | | Net profit | 700 |
| | | | |
| CURRENT ASSETS | | CURRENT LIABILITIES | |
| Stock | 3 000 | Creditors | 600 |
| Debtors | 2 500 | | |
| Cash | 1 800 | | |
| TOTAL | 21 300 | | 21 300 |

The first, and most obvious point, to note is that although the company has traded well, at the end of the year it has less cash than when it started! It is possible to run a profitable business, but go out of business simply because it is not possible to finance the working capital needs of the firm. In the next short section we will consider the nature of working capital and its effect on the cash flow and the firm's cash balance. This topic was briefly considered in Chapter Five in looking at the cash needs of a product during the product life cycle (PLC)

## 9.4 WORKING CAPITAL

'Gold Connections' will start up like any small business, producing a limited range of products for some defined initial market. As production and market experience is gained, new products will be produced and new markets served (See Chapter 5, Marketing, Ansoff matrix analysis). 'Gold Connections' may find that sealed units suitable for use on ships represent an attractive and profitable specialist market. Some customers who have found the products of use in normal applications might request the range be extended to also provide contacts for higher power applications. This has two implications for the production operations:

1. As the production volume increases more stock is needed to service the business (see Chapter 6).
2. As the diversity of production increases, the range of materials and components must increase (for example, different gauges of gold wire will be needed to be stocked).

Working capital in such a simple operation will consist of the raw gold wire and the components, such as housings, needed for production. (Fig. 9.1) It may take a little time for the final units to be moved down the production line (time to allow the sealing to fully cure) and for final soak testing. Once assembled, the units have to be packed and to provide good customer service, standard types may need to be held in stock. Moreover, goods take time to deliver, so it may take a week or more for orders to arrive at the customer. All this material has to be purchased and the money needs serviced.

In general, once this company is established, the suppliers will allow one month for payment for the materials (at the start of a business with no credit references, cash with order may be demanded). This will reduce the need for hard money to finance the stocks, but this is more than off-set by the need to extend the same one month credit to 'Gold Connections' customers. This customer credit represents a major drain on the money resources of a new small firm.

A diary of the second year of operation of this company might look like the one below.

---

*January*   Start of trading year with £3000 of components, gold wire, part assembled and finished contacts in stock. Stock to the value of £750 being used for goods for sale and replaced each month. One month payment terms being given by suppliers. Sales are £3000 a month and one month given for customers (debtors) to pay

*February*   No change in operations

*March*   No change in operations

*April*   New large orders for standard products, total sales up to £4000 a month. It is decided to increase stock levels (past level £3000) by 33 per cent to secure a base for the new level of activity. £1000 of stock to be replaced each month for products sold

*May*   No change in operations

*June*   No change in operations

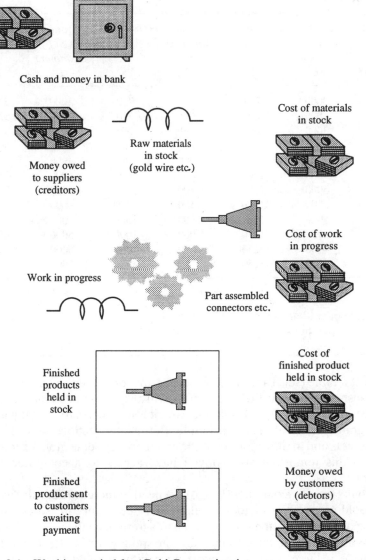

**Figure 9.1**  Working capital for 'Gold Connections'

*July*  New orders for a new range of high power contacts demanding a new range of components and heavier gauge gold wire. With new major orders worth £2000 a month, it is decided to stock a basic £1000 of materials and £500 worth of materials will have to be replaced each month for production of this unit. Again, we give one month's credit to our customers (debtors) and are given one month terms by our suppliers (creditors)

*August*  No change in operations

*September*  No change in operations

*October*  Customer for the new heavy duty contacts has not been successful in the product launch and sales for the rest of the year will be only 50 per cent of past sales. It is decided to reduce level of working stock to £500. Sales for the new heavy duty unit are now £1000 a month

**Table 9.1**   Spreadsheet

| Month | Start stock | End stock | Used in production | Total purchase | Money to pay | Money owed by customers | Total cash needed |
|---|---|---|---|---|---|---|---|
| | £ | £ | £ | £ | £ | £ | £ |
| Jan | 3000 | 3000 | 750 | 750 | 750 | 3000 | 5250 |
| Feb | 3000 | 3000 | 750 | 750 | 750 | 3000 | 5250 |
| Mar | 3000 | 3000 | 750 | 750 | 750 | 3000 | 5250 |
| April | 3000 | 4000 | 1000 | 2000 | 2000 | 4000 | 6000 |
| May | 4000 | 4000 | 1000 | 1000 | 1000 | 4000 | 7000 |
| June | 4000 | 4000 | 1000 | 1000 | 1000 | 4000 | 7000 |
| July | 4000 | 5000 | 1500 | 2500 | 2500 | 6000 | 8500 |
| Aug | 5000 | 5000 | 1500 | 1500 | 1500 | 6000 | 9500 |
| Sept | 5000 | 5000 | 1500 | 1500 | 1500 | 6000 | 9500 |
| Oct | 5000 | 4750 | 1250 | 1000 | 1000 | 5000 | 8750 |
| Nov | 4750 | 4500 | 1250 | 1000 | 1000 | 5000 | 8500 |
| Dec | 4500 | 4500 | 1250 | 1250 | 1250 | 5000 | 8250 |

*November*   No change in operations
*December*   No change in operations

We can now construct a table (see Table 9.1) of the amounts of money, such tables being referred to as spreadsheets. In real life, most firms will use a computer and a special accountancy spreadsheet program. For this simple case, it is not necessary, but if you have access to such a program you should enter this table. In the later sections we will look at more uses of spreadsheets and in the questions at the end there are some more examples to help you to develop this important skill, if you have access to a computer with a spreadsheet program.

There are a few points to note from Table 9.1. As we need to increase our sales we have step increases in 'Gold Connections' stock levels which need 'one off' stock building purchases. Of course, we also have the normal purchases to replace the materials used in production. At the same time, we have to increase the money we in effect lend to our customers, so we have a large increase in working capital to feed these new sales. However, when sales drop we have to lend less money to our customers and we can reduce our buffer stock of materials, and thus for two months we do not need to purchase any material to meet the new, lower, level of production activity for the heavy duty contacts.

This is, of course, a highly simplified example, although it does illustrate two key facts of business life: To expand sales needs large amounts of cash, so the sales may be profitable in the short term, but more money is needed by the business before the extra profits feed back into the firm. Moreover, when the business drops it can often take longer to recover the working capital than it took to feed it into the business during the expansion period.

Apart from fluctuations in the level of business activity, working capital can be affected by the cost of the materials. This is a particular problem with materials such as gold. Gold prices may increase or decrease by large amounts as investors 'get into' or 'get out of' gold

Remaining value £000s

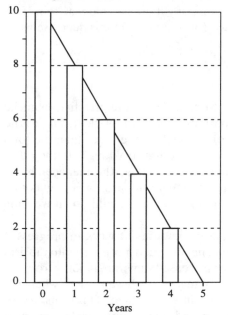

**Figure 9.2**    Depreciation for 'Gold Connections'

depending on world financial situations. This can have two effects, either increasing or decreasing the cost of the replacement stocks. Moreover, from time to time, the existing stock must be revalued and then the firm will have a stock loss or gain on stock valuation (depending on the direction of the movement). Even for a very simple business such as 'Gold Connections', considerable care is needed to manage the cash flow.

## 9.5 DEPRECIATION

In the previous section, we briefly explored the problems of stock revaluation, depending on the movements of supply markets. There is another problem of valuation. In the very simple balance sheet for 'Gold Connections', we showed that the value of the operating machine was the same for the opening and closing balance sheet. However, we know that the machine will need replacement after a number of years. It might be judged that this could be after five years. It would be wrong to take the expense of the machine into the first year's operating costs, as this would cause a large loss which would not represent the real position since the machine still has four years' productive life. Accountants have found a simple way round this problem. They depreciate (sometimes called 'write off') an appropriate fraction of the total value of the equipment each year. In this simple case, with the equipment costing £10 000 and lasting five years, it would be depreciated at the rate of £2000 a year (Fig. 9.2). Two things need to be noted: that depreciation will reduce the profit, which is correct as we have lost value (wear on the machine), but that this does not affect the external cash flows on the firm. At the start of the company we have to spend the full £10 000. In a quite literal way, we see this £10 000 of machine wear away over five years. As the value of the equipment decreases, we reduce our valuation in the balance sheet. We take this decreased valuation out of our profit. As stated in our opening section on accounts, to each and every financial action in a company there is some reaction. If we reduce our value of the equipment we have to place (or account for) this decrease as an expense, as the total value of the company has reduced.

## 9.6 CASH FLOW AND PROFIT

A Business Manager has a number of key issues to consider in the effective financial management of a firm. Hopefully, the two most important issues are now clear. There is no point in the conduct of a business where the cost of production is greater than the total value of sales. Clearly, that situation cannot be maintained for very long. On the other hand, even when profits are good and the business is expanding, the manager has a considerable problem, because although the business is generating profits, it may not be generating cash at a fast enough rate to provide the money for the additional working capital described above.

A particular problem of businesses which have large amounts of work in progress is inflation. The effect of inflation is to create a continual need to feed more cash into the firm in order to finance the extra costs of materials and the increased sums outstanding from the customers (debtors). This situation is likely to be made worse because just when the company most needs to borrow money, interest rates will also be high. This is one major reason why inflation is such an adverse, depressing and constraining factor on most businesses. There are other effects which will be discussed later, when the issue of project appraisal is considered.

When a company decides to export, apart from the expense of the additional documentation and the cost of currency fluctuation, insurance working capital needs will be inflated. In almost all cases, there will be a need to stock additional materials, even if it is only packaging printed in the language of the destination market. The product will take longer to reach the destination and the credit terms are more likely to be 90 days rather than 30 days.

Most strategies to expand the business have considerable cash flow implications, where the expense has to be taken before the expected, but not certain, additional sales and profits are gained. If 'Gold Connections' decides to increase the awareness of its products by advertising in the specialist trade journals, there will be the cost of designing the copy and the cost of buying the space. It may be many months before the return on additional sales is obtained.

If 'Gold Connections' decided to increase production, taking on a full-time person for production and employing a person to visit potential customers, there are again considerable cash flow implications. The staff have to be trained and equipment for them to do their work may have to be purchased (for example, a car for the sales representative). There will also be the costs of advertising for likely candidates and in the selection process itself (such as travel expenses for candidates).

Though depreciation will not affect the cash flow of a firm (depreciation is a non-cash expense), it will affect the profit. A large capital outlay needs to be spread over the number of years of the useful life of the equipment but the cash outflow from the firm is at the start. However, by holding the asset (plant) on the balance sheet and writing off over a number of years, a better estimate of profits is ensured.

The above discussions have focused on the cash flow and profit implications of a simple operation. When many operations are involved in the provision of many services or products, some care is needed to answer the simple question 'Is product or service $X$ profitable?' It may come as a surprise to a person new to industry when asking an accountant for a cost not to get an answer but another question 'What cost do you want?' After all the question is simple:

$$\text{Profit} = \text{Sales Revenue} - \text{Costs}$$

In the case of an analysis of the last month's performance it may be required to know the cost of production in the past period. However, if the firm is accepting a new large order for delivery in three months time, the cost that is required is an estimate of the future cost of production. In the next section, we shall consider the issue of costing and our first tool for estimating financial risk, break even analysis.

## 9.7 COSTING AND BREAK EVEN ANALYSIS

If 'Gold Connections' were to produce just one type of contact and could sell all the contacts it could produce, the analysis would be simple. The Mk 1 0.5 amp connector is made on a special machine which has an all-inclusive maintenance and insurance contract of £2000 a year. It will require a full-time operator who will have total costs (pay, insurance etc.) of £15 000 a year. Each unit takes £7 of materials and components to make, packaging and dispatch costs is another £3. The unit sells for £25. We can draw up the graph of 'fixed' costs (labour and annual machine contract costs), the 'variable' costs (the costs of materials, packaging and dispatch) can then be added to this to obtain the total costs for any given level of units produced and sold. The sales revenue will be simply the number of units sold multiplied by the selling price.

$$\text{Sales Income} = (\text{Selling Price}) \times (\text{N}^\circ. \text{ Units Sold})$$
$$\text{Costs} = (\text{Fixed Costs}) + [(\text{Variable Costs}) \times (\text{N}^\circ. \text{ Units Sold})]$$

So the break even point in terms of number of units to be sold is:

$$(\text{Fixed Costs})/(\text{Selling Price} - \text{Variable Costs}) = \text{Break Even Point}$$

In our example

$$17\,000/(25 - 10) = 1133 \text{ Units}$$

The full figures are shown in Table 9.2 and the results shown graphically in Fig. 9.3. The variable costs are added to the fixed costs to give the sum of fixed and variable costs for any given volume of production.

Below 1133 units, the total cost of production will be above the sales revenue and the firm will make a loss. Above this number of units the firm will make profits. The point at which the firm makes neither a profit or a loss is the break even point. If the firm is able to reduce its fixed costs (for example, gain a lower cost contract for the machine), lower the costs of production (such as lower cost method of delivery or reduced component costs) or increase the selling price, then the break even point will be at a reduced number of units. Of course, if any of the above figures moves in a reverse direction, then the break even point will be an increased number of units. Although very simple, this is a good way to quickly check out the risk and profitability of a project. If the profit area is small and

**Table 9.2**   Simple break even analysis for 'Gold Connections'

|  | *0 Units* | *1000 Units* | *1500 Units* | *2000 Units* |
| --- | --- | --- | --- | --- |
| Sales income | 0 | 25 000 | 37 500 | 50 000 |
| Fixed costs machine | 2 000 | 2 000 | 2 000 | 2 000 |
| Fixed costs labour | 15 000 | 15 000 | 15 000 | 15 000 |
| Total fixed costs | 17 000 | 17 000 | 17 000 | 17 000 |
| Variable cost materials | 0 | 7 000 | 10 500 | 14 000 |
| Variable packing, etc. | 0 | 3 000 | 4 500 | 6 000 |
| Total variable costs | 0 | 10 000 | 15 000 | 20 000 |
| Total income | −17 000 | −2 000 | 5 500 | 13 000 |
| Break even point units = | 1 133 | | | |
| Sales income = | 25 Unit | | | |
| Fixed cost machine = | 2 000 | | | |
| Fixed cost labour = | 15 000 | | | |
| Variable cost materials = | 7 Unit | | | |
| Variable packing, etc. = | 3 Unit | | | |

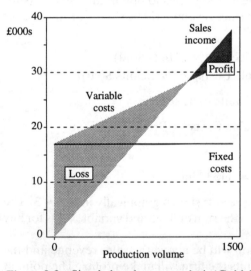

**Figure 9.3**   Simple break even analysis 'Gold Connections'

narrow, then the project is risky. If the profit area is large and thick then the project is less risky and more profitable. In evaluating the future selling price, it is very possible that some estimation error will be made. The recalculation of the break even curve with figures ±10 per cent of the best estimate is a good, yet simple, way to estimate how vulnerable a project is to changes in the figures. Such an appraisal is called a 'sensitivity analysis'. This

**Table 9.3** Simple break even analysis for 'Gold Connections' 10 per cent reduction in sales price

|  | 0 Units | 1000 Units | 1500 Units | 2000 Units |
|---|---|---|---|---|
| Sales income | 0 | 22 500 | 33 750 | 45 000 |
| Fixed costs machine | 2 000 | 2 000 | 2 000 | 2 000 |
| Fixed costs labour | 15 000 | 15 000 | 15 000 | 15 000 |
| Total fixed costs | 17 000 | 17 000 | 17 000 | 17 000 |
| Variable cost materials | 0 | 7 000 | 10 500 | 14 000 |
| Variable packing, etc. | 0 | 3 000 | 4 500 | 6 000 |
| Total variable costs | 0 | 10 000 | 15 000 | 20 000 |
| Total income | −17 000 | −4 500 | 1 750 | 8 000 |
| Break even point units = | 1 360 | | | |
| Sales income = | 22.5 Unit | | | |
| Fixed cost machine = | 2 000 | | | |
| Fixed cost labour = | 15 000 | | | |
| Variable cost materials = | 7 Unit | | | |
| Variable packing, etc. = | 3 Unit | | | |

sensitivity analysis is shown for our case in Table 9.3 for a 10 per cent decrease in selling price. The graphical situation is shown in Fig. 9.4. The area of profitability is greatly reduced and the break even point moves up to 1360 units. Table 9.4 and Fig. 9.5 show the position for the reverse situation, a 10 per cent increase in selling price. This has a very beneficial effect. The break even point is brought down to 971 and the area of profit enlarged. Business ventures with high breakeven points are risky. Expensive, capital intensive, production lines needing to be run at 75 per cent of capacity can be very dangerous in a recession. The reaction to keep the volume up in a recession is to cut the price. However, as the discussion has shown, this will sharply increase the break even point; to the extent in some cases that the break even point exceeds 100 per cent, the capacity of the plant. Thus the greatest of care should be taken in the evaluation of a project to ensure that the break even is at a reasonable level and that it is not too sensitive to errors in the estimates of sales price or sales volume. Tables 9.5 and 9.6 show the effects of the sensitivity of this project to variable costs. Figure 9.6 combines the information from Tables 9.2 to 9.6 to show the sensitivity of the break even point to sales price and sales volume. By far the greatest problem is the effect of a drop in selling price. The situation gets more complicated when more than one unit is made on a machine and more than one type of machine is needed to complete any given unit (See Chapter Six, for the discussion on Linear Programming).

This classification of costs into 'fixed' and 'variable' is useful, but care must be taken. In the above example the cost of the maintenance contract is fixed, no matter what the production level is. The same variable amount of materials is needed for each unit. This is, however, the first complication we may get in real life. If production is increased, we may well be able to get bulk discounts for the materials and so the variable cost of the materials

**Table 9.4**   Simple break even analysis for 'Gold Connections' 10 per cent increase in sales price

|  | 0 Units | 1000 Units | 1500 Units | 2000 Units |
|---|---|---|---|---|
| Sales income | 0 | 27 500 | 41 250 | 55 000 |
| Fixed costs machine | 2000 | 2000 | 2000 | 2000 |
| Fixed costs labour | 15 000 | 15 000 | 15 000 | 15 000 |
| Total fixed costs | 17 000 | 17 000 | 17 000 | 17 000 |
| Variable cost materials | 0 | 7000 | 10 500 | 14 000 |
| Variable packing, etc. | 0 | 3000 | 4500 | 6000 |
| Total variable costs | 0 | 10 000 | 15 000 | 20 000 |
| Total income | −17 000 | 500 | 9250 | 18 000 |
| Break even point units = | 971 | | | |
| Sales income = | 27.5 Unit | | | |
| Fixed cost machine = | 2000 | | | |
| Fixed cost labour = | 15 000 | | | |
| Variable cost materials = | 7 Unit | | | |
| Variable packing, etc. = | 3 Unit | | | |

is not linear, but may have break points depending on the applicable bulk discount rates. We have considered that labour is a fixed charge. If we got to the limit of production in normal working hours, then overtime working is possible. Unlike the basic working week, overtime can be varied depending on whether a demand for extra production exists. At this point, the labour cost ceases to be fixed and becomes a variable cost. We have assumed that this operator could not be assigned to another machine if demand is light. If it were possible to move the operator to other productive work then the labour cost would not be fixed at all, the machine could be used and manned only when production was required.

In a factory, other expenses can also have this semi-variable nature. The amount of energy to heat and light the factory does not much depend on the level of activity. The energy to machine the parts will depend on the production levels. Maintenance is often semi-variable. There will be annual maintenance and insurance inspections (for example, for pressure vessels) and this will not depend on the work load on the unit (just like the annual MOT on a car). Other maintenance expenses will depend on the level of use (again as with the 6000 mile service on a car). Clearly, the break even analysis is useful, but some more detailed costing methods are needed, not least of all for the simple question 'What is the minimum price at which it is acceptable to sell this unit?'

The correct costing of products or services is quite critical to the effective management of the business. Any firm will have a variety of resources to produce a diversity of products or services (the product mix). Most often, the firm will be able to sell, in total, more than it can produce. So which products should it attempt to sell more of, and of which can it accept lower sales? If the firm is production limited, it may well be possible to purchase sub-assemblies or subcontract out work. Which products should be purchased, which operations should be subcontacted and how does the cost of external sourcing compare with

£000s

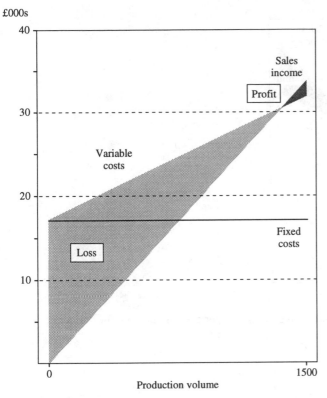

**Figure 9.4**   Break even analysis 'Gold Connections': 10 per cent decrease in selling price

the internal expenses (costs) of manufacture? These are the everyday issues that face management, right decisions ensure a profitable company, wrong decisions a lame duck. This why the good cost accountant earns his keep, just as much as the production engineer.

'Gold Connections' will make a range of Mk 1 connectors in power ratings from 0.1 to 10 amp. It is not too difficult a process to cost out the list of components and materials needed to make each unit. (See Chapter Six; part on Materials Resource Planning (MRP).) Considering only the expenses on the special machine, each type of connector will have differing lengths of assembly time, with the highest power units taking three times as long to make as the lowest power unit. To estimate the manufacturing costs (excluding the materials cost) the cost accountant will use a convenient device, the cost of a machine hour. To arrive at this figure is not a precise art. In the 60s, a process of absorption costing would be used, where even the cost of the managing director's pay would be allocated around each and every unit. This is not only futile but will almost always give you an unrealistic cost (any method of division of such costs will be on some arbitrary rule) as the strategic pricing decision is not being made on sound business judgement, but by a process little better than adding on costs if there is an 'R' in the month. The skill of the cost accountant is to determine the realistic costs of running the machine for the year. Reasonable costs would be: maintenance, depreciation (note this is a non-cash expense), energy and direct labour to run the machine (on the basis that if it does not run the labour can be moved to other operations). Unrealistic costs would be,

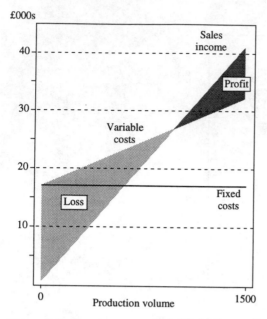

**Figure 9.5**    Break even analysis 'Gold Connections': 10 per cent increase in sales price

**Table 9.5**    Simple break even analysis for 'Gold Connections' 10 per cent increase in variable costs

|  | 0 Units | 1000 Units | 1500 Units | 2000 Units |
|---|---|---|---|---|
| Sales income | 0 | 25 000 | 37 500 | 50 000 |
| Fixed costs machine | 2000 | 2000 | 2000 | 2000 |
| Fixed costs labour | 15 000 | 15 000 | 15 000 | 15 000 |
| Total fixed costs | 17 000 | 17 000 | 17 000 | 17 000 |
| Variable cost materials | 0 | 7700 | 11 550 | 15 400 |
| Variable packing, etc. | 0 | 3300 | 4950 | 6600 |
| Total variable costs | 0 | 11 000 | 16 500 | 22 000 |
| Total income | −17 000 | −3000 | 4000 | 11 000 |
| Break even point units = | 1214 |  |  |  |
| Sales income = | 25 Unit |  |  |  |
| Fixed cost machine = | 2000 |  |  |  |
| Fixed cost labour = | 15 000 |  |  |  |
| Variable cost materials = | 7.7 Unit |  |  |  |
| Variable packing, etc. = | 3.3 Unit |  |  |  |

**Table 9.6** Simple break even analysis for 'Gold Connections' 10 per cent reduction in variable costs

|  | *0 Units* | *1000 Units* | *1500 Units* | *2000 Units* |
|---|---|---|---|---|
| Sales income | 0 | 25 000 | 37 500 | 50 000 |
| Fixed costs machine | 2000 | 2000 | 2000 | 2000 |
| Fixed costs labour | 15 000 | 15 000 | 15 000 | 15 000 |
| Total fixed costs | 17 000 | 17 000 | 17 000 | 17 000 |
| Variable cost materials | 0 | 6300 | 9450 | 12 600 |
| Variable packing, etc. | 0 | 2700 | 4050 | 5400 |
| Total variable costs | 0 | 9000 | 13 500 | 18 000 |
| Total income | −17 000 | −1000 | 7000 | 15 000 |

| Break even point units = | 1063 |
|---|---|
| Sales income = | 25 Unit |
| Fixed cost machine = | 2000 |
| Fixed cost labour = | 15 000 |
| Variable cost materials = | 6.3 Unit |
| Variable packing, etc. = | 2.7 Unit |

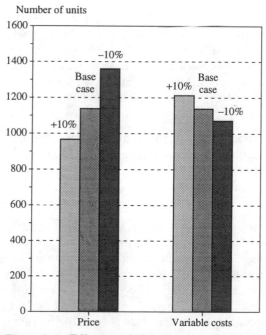

**Figure 9.6** Effective of 10 per cent sensitivity on break even point

for example, attempting to allocate the site manager's wages. On this basis the cost of production would be:

$$\text{Materials Cost} + (\text{Machine hourly rate} \times \text{hours needed per unit}) = \text{Cost}$$

Such a cost is often called a 'standard' cost. In any run, it is unlikely that this will be achieved. If the operator is very skilled the lot may be completed in less time than the 'standard' estimate. If there has been a problem with the storage of some of the materials, then it may take more time, for example to clean connections. The lot will then take longer to make than the 'standard' estimate. We shall return to this issue in budgets and variance analysis.

In many industries, such as the chemical or service industries, there is an additional complication in that one operation may produce two products with different market uses. Turpentine is produced in the manufacture of paper from wood. Turpentine can be distilled to produce two materials; alpha pinene (used as a solvent) and beta pinene (used to produce perfumes). How should the cost of the unit operation be divided between the two products? A simple and very logical answer would be to divide the total cost of the operation by the total weight of product and use a uniform cost per kilo of product obtained. The market valuation of alpha pinene (solvent use), however, is less than the market valuation of beta pinene (fragrance use), and to maximize the yield of the more valuable beta pinene, the distillation has to be run in a more intensive, slower and costlier way. Under these conditions, it may be better to allocate the production expenses having taken into account the market valuation (that is, if the market valuation of the beta is twice the alpha then the beta should be assigned twice the expenses of production per kilo relative to alpha).

A related issue is marginal production. 'Gold Connections' may receive a 'one off' export offer for a specific export contract (at a lower than normal price), for a very specific and special type of contact. The prices charged for this will not affect the market process for any of the firm's other products or customers. To decide whether to accept the order the firm needs to know the cost of producing this special lot. In simple terms three possibilities exist for the company:

1. 'Gold Connections' has spare labour and capacity (often true in times of recession).
2. 'Gold Connections' does not have spare capacity in normal time but could make the product on overtime.
3. 'Gold Connections' does not have any spare capacity.

Clearly, given the lower price, if the company is in the last state it should not accept the order. If it is in either of the first two states, what is its cost of production for the order? 'Conventional' costing may well say that the selling price is below the cost of production. This 'standard cost' will have been arrived at on the basis of direct labour costs which have been based on the assumption of a near full capacity loading. This is not the case in the present state. Whether or not the firm accepts the order, the staff will have to be paid. In this case, the company would be better off accepting the order, even though the margin is much less than for 'normal' orders.

In the case of expenses for a 'standard machine hour', certain assumptions will have been made about machine use in 'normal' hours. If the machine is to be used in additional hours, the direct cost of the additional hours needs to be considered (certain costs such as maintenance costs will be 'diluted' by the additional hours of working). Of course, in this case there will be direct labour costs as the overtime will be worked as a direct result of this order. Two points should be noted:

1. The key to determining the costs in such a case is to consider the 'difference case'. What would be the costs of the company if it accepted the order? What are the costs of the company if it did not accept the order? The difference between these two figures is the marginal cost of production for the order.
2. The acceptance of too many low price (low profit margin) orders will result in the firm not making the direct profit contributions necessary to pay the fixed overheads (such as the managing director and the accountants). Thus the 'hard nosed' accountant uses the standard costings to put pressure on sales and marketing to maintain margins and not take the easy road by lowering prices. It is essential in such situations to take a balanced view, fully understanding both the production situation of the firm and the total market and trading conditions. Too often, conflict in this area results from too narrow an understanding of the situation.

Another situation can arise when the company gets a large potential order at a higher price. This can happen when there may be a need to meet the order quickly. For example, a major firm requires rapid replacement of much of its equipment due to a fire and is prepared to pay a premium for speedy delivery. In this situation, if the firm accepts this order and is working to capacity, then the order can only be taken on the basis that other business is rejected. There will be a loss in rejecting this business. This loss is called a 'regret' cost. There are two components to 'regret' costs, the direct and indirect costs. The direct regret cost is the loss of the profit contribution of the orders that will be rejected. This is not too difficult to calculate from the discussion above. The much more difficult cost to estimate is the 'indirect regret' cost. If the order is accepted and an order is rejected from a long-established customer, the customer may well consider that this level of service is not acceptable and take not only the rejected order, but other business away. In a hard world, the firm will have to take a view of how easy this might be (see Chapter Two, Porter's 5 forces of competitive pressure). Of course, other options could be explored, such as rescheduling production or subcontracting (see Chapter Six).

The issue of marginal costing and pricing becomes of critical importance in service industries and service marketing (see Chapter Five). What is the cost of providing a telecommunications network? It is easy to say that the cost per hour is the annual cost divided by the available hours, but networks have to be designed for peak capacity and get very little use in the midnight hours. Such a simple view may under cost the peak hours expenses (where all the additional costs are encountered) and greatly over estimate the 'real' cost of the line in the early hours. Hotels and like business have this same issue, hence price reductions for 'out of season' holidays and 'happy hours' in bars.

In our discussion we have taken the view that the cost of a product is the sum of the expenses relevant to the issue under consideration. This can be formalized to some extent with a classification of levels of cost.

## LEVELS OF COST FOR AN ENGINEERING COMPANY

### (Brief outline only)

| | |
|---|---|
| **Batch** | Direct materials actually used |
| | Direct labour actually used |
| | Direct machine hours cost on actual hours used |
| **Machine** | Total cost of maintenance |
| | Total cost of provision (such as services, energy used) |
| | Total labour needed to run |
| | Insurance and like charges |
| **Department** | Total cost of all the machines for the period in question |
| | Direct support and administration costs, shop foreman, etc. |
| | Direct cost of maintenance of the building and insurance, etc. |
| **Site** | Total cost of all the individual department costs. |
| | Cost of support activities |
| |    Training |
| |    Security |
| |    Quality control |
| |    Site accounts |
| |    Site administration (site manager, etc.) |
| **SBU** | Total cost of all the individual sites |
| | Cost of support activities |
| |    Marketing and sales |
| |    Legal |
| |    Divisional (SBU) accounts |
| |    SBU chief executive officer |
| |    Planning |
| |    SBU technology development and new product and process design |
| |    Training coordination |
| **Corporation** | Total cost of all the SBUs |
| | Cost of support activities |
| |    Accountants |
| |      Internal audit |
| |      Treasurers |
| |    Reporting to shareholders |
| |    Corporate legal |
| |      Patents and intellectual property, etc. |
| |    Corporate marketing |
| |    Corporate long-range planning |
| |    Corporate R and D |

Earlier in this section the term Direct Profit Contribution (DPC) was used without a full definition. Now we have recognized the need to consider cost applicable to the decision in question and the levels of costs, we are in a position to take a considered view of direct profit contribution. Many people when looking at an apparently simple operation are surprised at the 'mark up' levels. We have noted that costs should be related only to those that are relevant at the level we are considering. However, from the understanding we now have of break even analysis, we know that if, on our targeted sales, we do not fully recover our fixed costs, we will make an overall loss and go out of business. With 'Gold Connections', the cost of a connection (direct labour, materials and component) might well be £2 for a given unit, against a selling price of £4, a 'mark up' of 100 per cent.

We can define 'mark up' as:

$$100 \times (\text{Selling Price} - \text{Direct Costs})/(\text{Direct costs}) = \text{Mark up } \%$$

for the above case

$$100 \times (£4 - £2)/£2 = 100\%$$

There is often confusion between mark up and direct profit contribution. Direct Profit Contribution can be defined as:

$$100 \times (\text{Selling Price} - \text{Direct Costs})/(\text{Selling Price})$$
$$= \text{Direct Profit Contribution } \%$$
for the above case

$$100 \times (£4 - £2)/£4 = 50\%$$

Direct profit contribution provides a powerful and flexible management tool for devolved marketing management of the marketing of the firm's product mix. A fixed mark up rule (we will reject any business that does not have a 100 per cent markup) or a pricing policy based on mark up (for example, price = costs × 2) will involve the firm in the rejection of profitable business and/or incorrect pricing (too high or too low for market conditions). The management of the product mix, knowing the overall direct profit contribution required to meet the profit targets, can adjust the individual prices in response to market conditions, in the knowledge that failure to meet the overall target will mean that the profit for effective and healthy development of the business has not been achieved.

Costing is not the mechanical application of a few mathematical rules; it is an essential aspect of the judgement of the managers of the firm. In determining targets for direct profit contribution and estimating costs, levels of sales and activity have to be estimated. This process of future cash implications of management activity is know as budgeting. We are now in a position to consider the budgeting process.

## 9.8 BUDGETS AND VARIANCE ANALYSIS

A student entering university might have some simple budget for the first term

| Income | £ | Costs | £ |
|---|---|---|---|
| Grant | 1300 | Rent | 500 |
| Part time work | 300 | Food | 400 |
| | | Drinks | 100 |
| | | Books | 200 |
| | | Travel | 200 |
| | | Reserve | 200 |
| TOTAL | 1600 | TOTAL | 1600 |

A budget is something we all have to consider in our normal day-to-day life. Unfortunately, most budgets do not work 100 per cent; a student may end up spending more or less on books and drink than planned. Care needs to be taken to consider the appropriate factors in drawing up a budget. A typical motorist will need to have a rough estimate (budget) of running costs. If a motorist took delivery of a car shortly before going on a motoring holiday in the summer, they could estimate the petrol costs on the basis of petrol used on the holiday and the miles covered. On the basis of this and an idea of the miles of domestic motoring for the rest of the year, an estimate of the monthly petrol costs can be made. However, two errors in this simple estimate are apparent: domestic motoring involves more short journeys in town where mileage is less; this effect is greatly increased with cold starting in winter. It is essential in constructing a budget to consider all the relevant factors, often involving seasonal factors.

Budgets are a simple and powerful tool of management control. If 'Gold Connections' were to consider a new Mark II connector, a budget might be drawn up.

| Cost | Budget £ | Actual £ | Variance £ |
|---|---|---|---|
| Marketing research | 1000 | 1200 | 200 |
| Design | 6000 | 5500 | −500 |
| New production tools | 2000 | 2400 | 400 |
| TOTAL | 9000 | 9100 | 100 |

In this case, the overall performance is only slightly outside the original budget and a manager who was not too well informed might consider that no action was necessary. Are the design team to be congratulated, however, in completing the design well within budget? The overrun on the tool expense might need to be investigated. It is possible that the design team 'cut corners' in the design and that this had to be corrected as the new machine tools were being made, increasing the costs.

The skilled manager will not only examine the costs against budget at the end of the project, but will examine costs against project progress with a spreadsheet. The same considerations apply to the analysis of sales variance. Table 9.7 shows a typical, very simple, sales budget for three months. The sales volume and sales price expected are budgeted allowing the calculation of the expected, budgeted sales revenue. We can record the actual levels of units and selling price per unit achieved against the budget. In the analysis of such variances the causes of the global sales deviation need to be determined. In this case we can calculate, for example in month two, that £20.50 of the sales price variance comes from the volume variance and £30.50 from the price variance. It will be noted that there is a small 'unexplained' variance caused by the interaction of the price and unit volume variances.

By referring to Fig. 9.7, the reason for the interaction effect can be seen. Sales value is the product of sales volume and selling price. Where both change there will be an interaction effect which is not accounted for by the simple variance analysis (this is the effect of both the selling price and volume variances).

**Table 9.7**  Simple sales budget for a month for 'Gold Connections'

| Month | Plan type I No | Plan selling price £ | Plan sales £ | Actual type I No | Actual selling price £ | Actual sales £ | Sales variance £ |
|---|---|---|---|---|---|---|---|
| 1 | 500 | 2 | 1000 | 450 | 1.95 | 877.5 | -122.5 |
| 2 | 600 | 2 | 1200 | 610 | 2.05 | 1250.5 | 50.5 |
| 3 | 700 | 2 | 1400 | 720 | 1.9 | 1368 | -32 |

| Month | Sales volume variance number | Actual selling price £ | Sales volume variance £ | Sales price variance £ | Actual type I No | Sales price variance £ | Calculate variance total £ | Actual sales variance £ | Interaction effect £ |
|---|---|---|---|---|---|---|---|---|---|
| 1 | -50 | 1.95 | -97.5 | -0.05 | 450 | -22.5 | -120 | -122.5 | -2.5 |
| 2 | 10 | 2.05 | 20.5 | 0.05 | 610 | 30.5 | 51 | 50.5 | -0.5 |
| 3 | 20 | 1.9 | 38 | -0.1 | 720 | -72 | -34 | -32 | 2 |

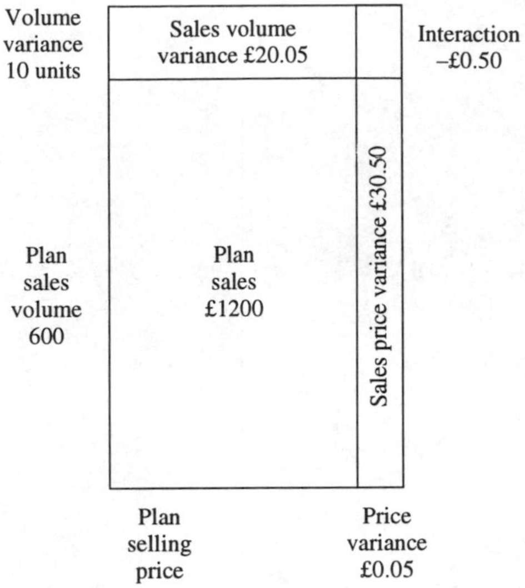

**Figure 9.7** Variance analysis for Month 2

For all the simplicity, budgeting is one of the most important and powerful tools of management and the budget plan comparison with variance analysis is one of the most important tools for the feedback and control of the company.

As with most simple powerful tools, there are hidden complexities both in the setting of the budget and its analysis. (For more detailed consideration, the reader is recommended to refer to the texts at the end of this chapter.) Even for 'Gold Connections' there are a number of problems with the estimation of the figures for a planning budget. To arrive at the sales value estimate, the firm has to analyse past sales patterns (for example, see Chapter Six, Time Series Analysis). The sales value is the product of both this and the selling price, so the manager faced with this task needs not only to estimate product by product the selling volume, but also the prices that will be obtained. This will need views to be taken about inflation, general economic activity, the reactions of competitors, etc. To obtain these sales, 'Gold Connections' will need to have an active marketing plan, with expenses for market research, marketing communications, agents' commissions and product improvements. The most common error in many budgets is to see advertising budgets set as a percentage of sales, which is, of course, absurd. If the company is up to full capacity, it may need to reduce marketing communications for a time as there is no point in attracting orders that cannot be served. This breaks the key rule of marketing, creating an expectation and failing to keep the promise. A common error as far as bookkeepers are concerned (good accountants understand the issue) is that as sales fall, it may be just the time that, despite all the cash flow problems, additional marketing communications are needed. As mentioned earlier, the panic reaction of simply cutting price will often only give a short term advantage, as the competition may follow the firm down in a price war where all firms enter a loss area. When we considered break even, a simple price reduction was seen as having a major adverse effect on the break even point.

For a budget it is not only necessary to estimate and plan the total sales effort and estimate the prices, but also to consider the phasing of the budget. Many products such as electrical power, clothes and CDs show strong seasonal trends. Such seasonal effects are not restricted to the products themselves but to the suppliers of products into those industries as they stock build for their peak periods.

At the same time as the sales budget is prepared, 'Gold Connections' needs to estimate its other cost of sales expenses, the cost of manufacture. The costs of labour for the next year have to be estimated, as do other purchased services such as electricity, heat etc. The cost of the components and the raw materials need to be estimated; these costs will depend on demand and economic conditions (great effects in markets such as gold), learning curve effects for new technology products (cost of high technology products tend to fall as they advance in the product life cycle), expected demand levels (bulk discounts), need to second source, inflation and exchange rate movements (for imported products).

This still leaves one additional complexity: in setting a selling price for a product we need to know the strategic pricing gap (customer benefit valuation less cost of production). At this stage of the budget preparation, 'Gold Connections' may well find that, given a great increase in the cost of gold, one product is budgeted to be made at a loss. Except in rare conditions, this is not acceptable and the minimum acceptable price needs to be calculated. At this higher price, there may still be some special applications for which there will be sales, but overall there will be a reduction in sales volume. The budgeting process is not a single pass process but requires several loops to arrive at a good estimate.

For production planning (see Chapter Six, MRP, etc.), the production phasing and loading on the machines needs to be estimated. Thus, in making an estimate of the machine hour costs, the production cost accountant will need to form some views on the future production efficiencies and utilizations of equipment. If the plan calls for a high seasonal demand, additional storage space may need to be rented for the large pre-seasonal demand stock build (such as chocolate companies with Easter eggs).

The central expenses also need to be estimated, such as tax (rates etc.), telecommunications, interest charges, central staff expenses (personnel, legal, etc.). This, in most companies, will involve large amounts of money and as it is not under line managers' control, considerable care needs to be taken to ensure rigorous cost control. There is no point in re-designing a product to take £0.05 a unit off its production costs if the central overheads are not also subject to similar cost management.

Who prepares this budget and on what basis is the budget prepared? In the real world this is often a political battle ground where budgets are prepared on the basis of what is acceptable to the senior management, rather than best estimates. Senior management can make this happen if they do not take great care with their actions on deviations from budgets. If a best estimate is made, there should be as much chance that this is an under-estimate as over-estimate. If the senior management punish under-performance against budget and reward performance above budget, without detailed consideration, the answer for the managers setting the budget is simple. Set one that allows some room to achieve.

If there may be political problems, there can also be other reasons why differing views are taken. The sales and procurement may take differing views on currency movements and thus arrive at budgets which are based on differing assumptions.

So who should set the budget? In many companies this is seen as a 'simple' accountancy function. The budgets will be cast in good professional style and will be calculated on a uniform set of assumptions and rules, even if they are all wrong. The accountant will be unable to make any realistic judgement about future prices, future raw materials costs or the impact of new production technology and designs in bringing down the assembly costs in production. Good accountants know the problem and try to understand the business. In high technology industries such as pharmaceuticals, chemical process, electronic, digital communications, computers etc., this is not easy. The key lies with engineers, scientists and technologists who not only understand the production technology, but the technology and structure of the markets. Apart from the issue of the technical ability of a person to make the judgements, in Chapter Four, we discussed the issue of motivation. What motivation does a production engineer have in attempting to meet an unrealistic production budget set by a person who has no idea of the realities? No matter how the budget is arrived at, it is essential if it is to be a real management control and not some paper accountancy exercise, that the people who will be responsible for meeting the budget accept that it is challenging but realistic. In short, the accountable people for the budget must accept ownership of the budget. If they have not been directly responsible for the budget, they must feel that they have had a full and realistic input to the setting of the targets.

The solution appears simple. In reality, it depends on the production engineer etc. If they have taken full account of the need to exercise their technology in a business environment, they will be in a position to set budgets with appropriate skill or know how to make the appropriate inputs. If the budget is to be prepared by a central planning accountant, of course, similar considerations apply to the setting of the marketing budget. Here it is not only necessary to understand the production technology, the technology, benefit needs and benefit valuations of the market but also the technicalities of accountancy (that is, 'This export contract is profitable, yes, but we cannot accept the working capital implications').

In the above paragraphs, we have considered who should set the budget but we have not considered the logical basis on which budgets should be set. In a pure selling, accountancy-driven company, it is easy to set the selling prices. It costs £20 to produce the unit (according to our accountancy conventions) and a 20 per cent mark up on production costs is our target, so the realistic market price is £24. This, of course, neglects the fact that a company faced with the exact trading conditions and situation could arrive at a cost that is different (since they have different accountancy conventions). In Chapter Five, we came to the conclusion that the only way that such a pricing policy could result in the correct pricing mix was by accident. Other options exist, we will price on the competitive basis that our competition is working. This at least has the merit that it takes some account of the market conditions. It does not, however, take account of the full benefit set that a customer may value, superior quality, delivery, distribution coverage or simply better marketing communications. For the successful firm, the setting of price can only be done by expert marketing considerations, by people who understand markets, benefit needs and the company ability to supply the product or service. Most often it will be a technologist who has the detailed understanding and who has also acquired the business skills.

In marketing, similar considerations apply to how the marketing budget should be constructed. One possible way is to simply follow last year's budget: 'We have six salesman, that's the personal selling budget set, and we go to three trade fairs a year.' Why should this company do this? Well, they have done it for the last ten years, so 'it must work!' Such a company may have survived ten years, but it will not survive much longer!

This is not the way to do it. The company could possibly get the market place to solve the problem for it. 'All we need to do is employ a smart financial analyst who can do a survey of what the competition spend on marketing, we will then spend the same percentage. That will get it right.' Again, such a policy, although often used, is not much better than the last year spend system. It does take some account of the market conditions and it has to be admitted that those applied last year. The issue, however, is that next year may be a different market, needing greater or lesser spends than last year. Also to be taken into account is the probability that our marketing situation is different to that of our competitors. Moreover, the marketing spend (as determined by published figures, such as balance sheets) can be distorted by accountancy conventions. In one company, a redesign of the packaging may be seen as a production expense, but in another company this expense may be regarded as a marketing expense.

It is suggested, particularly in the area of marketing, that the zero budget, objective and resource needs is the most realistic way to complete a penetrating budget analysis. In a zero budget option, the marketing manager starts with a blank sheet of paper and considers what the marketing objectives are. Realistic strategies can then be determined to see how these objectives can be achieved. Having done this, it is possible to cost this strategy in terms of an action plan. This may give a cost that is not acceptable. It may well give a cost which the firm considers it is not able to finance, in which case the company needs to consider whether its objectives are realistic. If not, it may need to re-evaluate its strategies to match its resources. Again, the key issue is, not only is there a real appraisal to assess if the resources are sufficient to meet the objectives, but that people concerned with the process are likely to be motivated. They have been involved and can see that the budget represents realistic targets. Budgets are not worth the paper they are printed on unless people are motivated to achieve them.

Given all the above problems, some firms have opted to give the budgeting process to a group of financial planners. These can often be a good mixture of technologists and accountants and in theory this should be a perfect solution. However, these people may draw up the budget, but they are not accountable for its achievement. Without the greatest interpersonal skills, they can be seen as an overpaid elite who have power (to set budgets) without responsibility (accountability to meet budget levels), but without some such central direction operational budgets could be set to differing standards on differing (often unknown) assumptions. Some operations have opted for yet another path which has much to commend it. The central group of planners is not seen as setting the budget but as expert financial advisers to assist and facilitate (collaborate in the technical interpretation of operational judgements) operational managers in the preparation of their budgets. This has the merit of providing some consistency in the standards of preparation of the budgets and ownership to achieve the targets by line managers. This is not an easy task as the financial planners can be seen as the HQ spies and again need good interpersonal skills and integrity to perform this complex and delicate task.

Earlier in this chapter, we noted that there were levels of cost, at the operation, machine, department, site, division (SBU) and group levels and thus the overall budget has to be built up through these levels. If the overall picture does not add up to an acceptable performance, the strategy has to be changed and then reflected back down through all these operational levels.

One technical issue has not been considered in the above discussions, how do we account for depreciation? In a simple analysis, the young and inexperienced accountant may suggest that it is not possible to accept a certain range of business as the costs (including the depreciation) are too high. On this basis, the plant will not run, after all, no profit will be made by running it, since the depreciation is too high. However, as we have noted before, depreciation is a non-cash expense, and we will have this expense whether the plant runs or not. The question in this situation is how much the loss will be, but the effect on cash flow and reduction of loss may well make it useful to run the unit at a paper loss. Again, we return to one of the golden rules of financial management: look at the difference case (see p. 244). If we do this, will the company, taking all issues into account, be, on the 'bottom line', better or worse off? If the answer is yes, the company should consider taking the low profit option, possibly without any celebrations. To balance this argument, two considerations need to be taken into account. The acceptance of low profit orders at low profit levels may depress market prices, attracting an unwelcome competitive response and, if the company has too much low profitability business, it will not attract enough direct profit contribution to cover its overhead expenses or earn enough return on its existing investments to finance the new investments needed for the future healthy growth of the business. Of course, critical consideration needs to be given to the cash flow implications of marginal business and the effect on breakeven points.

So far, we have considered the case of the simple company. Many major firms have a divisional structure (SBUs), each being regarded as accountable for its own profitability. This is a good principle, as people can only be held accountable for those operations over which they have control. A typical type of structure would be where a 'core' operation makes feed-stock (chemical process industry) or provides a network or like resource (for a service such as transport or telecommunications). The 'core' SBU makes its profit by selling its products on the open market and to the 'down stream' activities. The down stream SBU's add value to the base and sell onto the market. The profit of the core and the down stream units depends on the transfer value (transfer price) between the units. If the greatest care is not exercised by the senior management, much effort will be lost through internal management friction in protracted battles, with each unit attempting to gain as much paper profit from the other as possible, rather than concentrating on the market place outside the company. The situation is worse than this as if the price for the core product is too high (the core unit attempting to take too much of the profit), the down stream unit may well find itself priced out of the market, to the disadvantage of the overall benefit of the total group. Of course, the reverse is also possible. If the down stream unit receives its network or core feed-stock at an artificially low price, it is able to price its products at a very low level and still make a paper profit, but with an overall under-performance of the whole organization. In short, there is a danger the group will try to take two profits when there is not the market scope or take a half profit when there is scope for more. Groups working in this situation have attempted to come up with a single solution. Three possibilities are:

1.  Core company transfer price to be set at ROI (Return On Investment) level and to base transfer prices on the minimum transfer price to meet this criterion. The problem with this solution is that it takes no account of market conditions, thus the price may be well above or below market levels.
2.  Core company to set transfer price at some fixed percentage below market prices. The problem with this policy is that in difficult conditions it may leave the core unit trading at a loss.
3.  The so-called 'arm's length policy' where the core unit and the down stream units act as if they were independent firms and the down stream SBU is free to purchase from the core unit or any other source as suits its trading conditions. The problem with this

policy is that the core unit may not gain volume it needs and function at uneconomic levels.

The above situation assumes that the operations are trading in the same general environments. In international business operations (chemical process, pharmaceuticals, communications, electronics, etc.), the separate units may well be in differing countries and have differing tax profiles. One operation, set up as a legal company, may have had large losses in past years. Those losses may be taken against present profits in that country, so in one country tax may have to be paid on profits, in another country with the back losses no tax on profits may need to be paid. The mechanism of the transfer price allows the international company to move profits from one tax situation to another, to the great advantage of the owners. However, if great care is not taken, the long term financial direction of the firm can be determined by some device to take advantage of medium term tax planning issues.

In the previous section, we considered the issues of who should set the budget and the guidelines and principles upon which budgets should be set. Apart from the complexities of the transfer of profits, we noted the implication of depreciation on costings and the danger of under-recovery of past investments. This brings us onto the key issue for the Engineer; how to evaluate new projects to assess their profitability. In the next section we shall consider how to measure the profitability of a project, allow for risk in an investment project and how to compare the relative merits of one project against another.


## 9.9 PROJECT APPRAISAL

A simple measure of the profitability of a project is the pay back period, how long it will take to get our investment back. We might decide to buy a long life bulb as it will save us money on the electricity used. We can calculate how many months it will take us to recover our extra capital expense for the bulb in reduced revenue expense for electricity. We can do the same for a major improvement such as the installation of a heat and energy plant to provide low cost electricity and waste heat. This is a simple test and it also allows the comparison between projects to some extent, as more profitable projects have a shorter break even point. However, it does not take account of a key problem with money, money has a value depending on time.


## 9.10 TIME VALUE OF MONEY

If I am given £1000 today, I can invest it so it will be worth more than if I am given £1000 in a year's time. The precise amount will depend on the rate of interest I can gain. The value of £1 in a year's time is:

$$(100 + \text{Interest Rate})/(100)$$

Of course, if the time period were longer it would be worth more so we have a general equation for the future value of money invested for a number of years as:

$$[(100 + \text{Interest Rate})/(100)]^{\text{Number of years invested}}$$

$$\text{or}$$

$$[(100 + \text{Rate \%})/(100)]^{N}$$

When we are considering investment projects, we make an investment in a new plant or some other facility and then get a cash flow over the next few years. From the above discussion it can be seen that the sooner I get the money, the more it will be worth. The amount that it will be worth will be determined by the interest rate under consideration (the Discount Rate) and the number of years into the future I will receive the income. This present value of future money discounted by the rate of interest and the number of years into the future is called the Net Present Value (NPV) of the cash sum. This can be written as:

$$NPV = [(100)/(100 + \text{Rate per cent})]^N$$

*(Where N is the number of years in the future in which we will receive the cash sum.)*

Table 9.8 and Fig. 9.8 show the effect of interest rates and time on the future value of £1000 to be received at various years in the future. If we have a series of cash flows for years 0, 1, 2, 3, 4 and 5, we can sum all the individual NPVs of the cash flow to arrive at the total NPV for the project.

If 'Gold Connections' were to consider the addition of an advanced control unit, costing £22 000, to cut down on the amount of gold used in the contacts and expected a saving of £6000 a year in materials cost after the installation, the simple cash flow would look as shown in Table 9.9. By convention, the capital of the project is taken to take place in year 0. In such simple cash flow calculations the cash flows in later years are taken to happen at year end. This is, of course, an approximation, as the cash flows take place throughout the year. Given the likely errors in the estimates, however, this approximation is acceptable.

Application of the discount formula at rates of 10 per cent, 15 per cent and 20 per cent gives us net present values of £3228, £102, and −£2449. This effect is shown in Fig. 9.9. As the discount rate increases the present value of the later cash flows becomes of less and less

**Table 9.8**   Time value of money: Net Present Value of £1000 to be received in a number of years time

| Years | Discount rate 5% | Discount rate 10% | Discount rate 15% | Discount rate 20% | Discount rate 25% | Discount rate 30% |
|---|---|---|---|---|---|---|
| 0 | 1000 | 1000 | 1000 | 1000 | 1000 | 1000 |
| 1 | 952 | 909 | 870 | 833 | 800 | 769 |
| 2 | 907 | 826 | 756 | 694 | 640 | 592 |
| 3 | 864 | 751 | 658 | 579 | 512 | 455 |
| 4 | 823 | 683 | 572 | 482 | 410 | 350 |
| 5 | 784 | 621 | 497 | 402 | 328 | 269 |
| 6 | 746 | 564 | 432 | 335 | 262 | 207 |
| 7 | 711 | 513 | 376 | 279 | 210 | 159 |
| 8 | 677 | 467 | 327 | 233 | 168 | 123 |
| 9 | 645 | 424 | 284 | 194 | 134 | 94 |
| 10 | 614 | 386 | 247 | 162 | 107 | 73 |
|  | 5 | 10 | 15 | 20 | 25 | 30 |

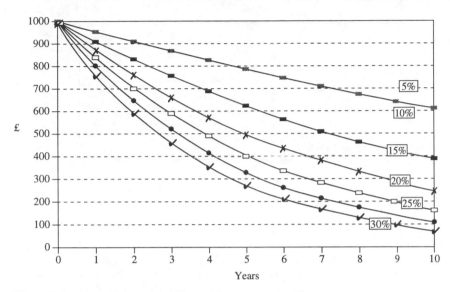

**Figure 9.8**   Time Value of £1000 received N years in future

**Table 9.9**   DCF analysis of simple project

| Cash flow element | Year 0 | Year 1 | Year 2 | Year 3 | Year 4 | Year 5 | Total NPV |
|---|---|---|---|---|---|---|---|
| Capital cost | −22 000 | | | | | 4000 | — |
| Savings | | 6000 | 6000 | 6000 | 6000 | 6000 | — |
| Total cash flow | −22 000 | 6000 | 6000 | 6000 | 6000 | 10 000 | — |
| Discount factor 20% | 1 | 0.8333 | 0.6944 | 0.5787 | 0.4823 | 0.4019 | — |
| NPV 20% | −22 000 | 5000 | 4 166.7 | 3 472.2 | 2 893.5 | 4 018.8 | −2449 |
| Discount factor 15% | 1 | 0.8696 | 0.7561 | 0.6575 | 0.5718 | 0.4972 | — |
| NPV 15% | −22 000 | 5217.4 | 4 536.9 | 3 945.1 | 3 430.5 | 4 971.8 | 101.64 |
| Discount factor 10% | 1 | 0.9091 | 0.8264 | 0.7513 | 0.683 | 0.6209 | — |
| NPV 10% | −22 000 | 5 454.5 | 4 958.7 | 4 507.9 | 4 098.1 | 6 209.2 | 3 228.4 |

Internal rate of return
15.181

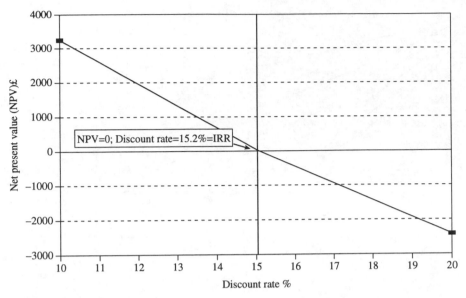

**Figure 9.9**   DCF Analysis of a simple project

value. A point is reached where the sum of all the Net Present Values for the cash flow (project NPV) just equals zero. The discount rate which yields a zero NPV is called the Internal Rate of Return (IRR) of the project. This point is shown on the graph. Spreadsheet computer programs have functions for NPV and IRR calculations and in this case the actual IRR is 15.18 per cent. In the earlier section, we discussed the pay back analysis of a project. This is shown for this project in Fig. 9.10. Two pay backs are shown, the simple pay back where the cash flows are not discounted and the discounted pay back period. In the discounted pay back calculation the value of future money is discounted at the firm's objective rate of return.

This type of simple cash flow analysis is often of use to the production engineer as this

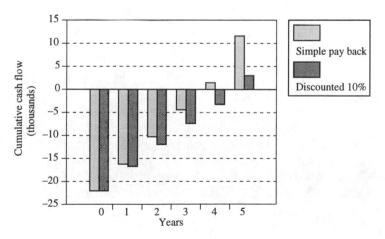

**Figure 9.10**   Pay back

person is often faced with the justification of 'Why should we make this improvement?' This type of analysis is called the 'difference case'. The engineering analyst measures the cash implications of effecting the project against the base case of doing nothing. In this case, should the company effect the improvement? This will depend on the rate of interest that the firm considers is applicable to its operating environment. A firm can invest its money without risk on deposit with a bank. Clearly, if the firm invests in a project with elements of risk, a higher rate of return is demanded to make the risk acceptable. In this case, by the standards of the 90s this project is borderline unacceptable, firms tending to look for projects showing rates of return of about 20 per cent. A simple go, no-go test is to calculate the NPV of the project at the firm's current objective rate of return for projects. If the result is a positive NPV then the project is acceptable. If the result is negative the project is unacceptable.

Many investment decisions are for the production of a new product or service. An investment is made and product is manufactured and sold. 'Gold Connections' has decided to expand capacity with a new advanced Mk III unit which will require a new production unit costing £40 000. It is considered that the life of the machine will be five years and at the end of this time its scrap value will be £5000. The marketing estimate is that it will take two years to build up to the full sales volume: 35 000, year 1; 45 000, year 2; 50 000 in years 3 to 5. It is considered that the selling price for this product will be £0.70 a unit. The Production Engineer and design department have estimated that the variable cost of production is £0.25 a unit. The fixed costs of production have been estimated as £10 000 a year. The firm operates on the basis that average debtors and creditors are 20 per cent of sales value and variable production costs, respectively. This yields the cash flow table shown in Table 9.10.

The calculation of the working capital should be examined with care. As production builds up from year 1 to year 2, only the additional working capital is required as an additional cash flow. At the end of the project, all the materials and work in progress is taken to completed units. These are sold and all outstanding debits are collected. Thus all the working capital is recovered at the end of the project.

At this stage we are in a position to calculate the project cash flow. By the application of a series of discount rates from 5 per cent to 20 per cent we can estimate that the Internal Rate of Return is just above 16 per cent (using a spreadsheet program, 16.79 per cent).

In the earlier sections of this chapter we examined the difficulty of estimating the sales, costs etc. The spreadsheet Table 9.10 represents a best estimate but with the probability of errors in projections. To evaluate the effect of errors, it is common practice to recalculate the spreadsheet with key variables changed by some convenient amount (often + and − 10 per cent). Table 9.11 shows this calculation for a −10 per cent error in sales price and Table 9.12 shows the effect of a −10 per cent error in sales volume. These calculations are shown for −10 per cent sales price and −10 per cent sales volume in Table 9.13.

As we do not have the cost of manufacture when we lose volume, but we still have the costs of production and work in progress when only the price drops, the effect of an error in selling price is more serious and causes a much greater drop in the Internal Rate of Return to 10.74 per cent. This process of examining the sensitivity of a project to individual errors in estimates is known as sensitivity analysis. This should be compared with the break even sensitivity analysis covered earlier in the chapter. An outline sensitivity analysis for this project is shown in Fig. 9.11.

One problem with this type of analysis is that it gives a range of NPVs and makes it

**Table 9.10**   New production analysis for Mk III contacts

| Cash flow element | Year 0 | Year 1 | Year 2 | Year 3 | Year 4 | Year 5 | NPV |
|---|---|---|---|---|---|---|---|
| + Capital costs | −40 000 | | | | | 5000 | — |
| Sales no. units | — | 35 000 | 45 000 | 50 000 | 50 000 | 50 000 | — |
| Selling price | — | 0.7 | 0.7 | 0.7 | 0.7 | 0.7 | — |
| + Sales value £ | — | 24 500 | 31 500 | 35 000 | 35 000 | 35 000 | — |
| Variable costs unit | — | 0.2 | 0.2 | 0.2 | 0.2 | 0.2 | — |
| − Total variable | — | 7000 | 9000 | 10 000 | 10 000 | 10 000 | — |
| − Fixed costs | — | 10 000 | 10 000 | 10 000 | 10 000 | 10 000 | — |
| − Stock | | 1400 | 400 | 200 | 0 | −2000 | |
| − Debtors | — | 4900 | 1400 | 700 | 0 | −7000 | — |
| + Creditors | — | 1750 | 500 | 250 | 0 | −2500 | — |
| Total cash flow | −40 000 | 2 950 | 11 200 | 14 350 | 15 000 | 26 500 | — |
| Discount factor 5% | | 1 | 0.9524 | 0.907 | 0.8638 | 0.8227 | 0.7835 | — |
| NPV 5% | −40 000 | 2 809.5 | 10 159 | 12 396 | 12 341 | 20 763 | 18 468 |
| Discount factor 10% | | 1 | 0.9091 | 0.8264 | 0.7513 | 0.683 | 0.6209 | — |
| NPV 10% | −40 000 | 2 681.8 | 9 256.2 | 10 781 | 10 245 | 16 454 | 9 419 |
| Discount factor 15% | | 1 | 0.8696 | 0.7561 | 0.6575 | 0.5718 | 0.4972 | — |
| NPV 15% | −40 000 | 2 565.2 | 8 468.8 | 9 435.4 | 8 576.3 | 13 175 | 2 220.9 |
| Discount factor 20% | | 1 | 0.8333 | 0.06944 | 0.5787 | 0.4823 | 0.4019 | — |
| NPV 20% | −40 000 | 2 458.3 | 7 777.8 | 8 304.4 | 7 233.8 | 10 650 | −3576 |

Internal rate of return<br>16.793

difficult to compare one project with another. Consider a simple case where only the sales volume is expected to vary. 'Gold Connections' have placed some probability estimates on the sales volumes. These are shown with the NPVs in Table 9.14. From statistics we know that the sum of all of the probabilities must be one. If we add the product of the NPV and the expectation probability of that sales volume, we end up with a single figure: the expected NPV of the project. This expected NPV takes into account risk. This calculation is shown in Fig. 9.12.

$$\text{Expected NPV} = \text{Sum [Probability} \times \text{NPV]}$$

Such an analysis is normally considered acceptable, given all the problems with precise estimates. It is, however, open to the theoretical criticism that it only considers one at a time errors in estimates (it can be extended with the application of decision trees, see p. 251) and does not allow for the estimates for the first years being better than the

**Table 9.11**   New production analysis for Mk III contacts: 10 per cent reduction in sales price

| Cash flow element | Year 0 | Year 1 | Year 2 | Year 3 | Year 4 | Year 5 | NPV |
|---|---|---|---|---|---|---|---|
| + Capital costs | −40 000 | | | | | 5000 | — |
| Sales no. units | — | 35 000 | 45 000 | 50 000 | 50 000 | 50 000 | — |
| Selling price | — | 0.63 | 0.63 | 0.63 | 0.63 | 0.63 | — |
| + Sales value £ | — | 22 050 | 28 350 | 31 500 | 31 500 | 31 500 | — |
| Variable costs unit | — | 0.2 | 0.2 | 0.2 | 0.2 | 0.2 | — |
| − Total variable | — | 7000 | 9000 | 10 000 | 10 000 | 10 000 | — |
| − Fixed costs | — | 10 000 | 10 000 | 10 000 | 10 000 | 10 000 | — |
| Stock | | 1400 | 400 | 200 | 0 | −2000 | |
| − Debtors | — | 4410 | 1260 | 630 | 0 | −6300 | — |
| + Creditors | — | 1750 | 500 | 250 | 0 | −2500 | — |
| Total cash flow | −40 000 | 990 | 8190 | 10 920 | 11 500 | 22 300 | — |
| Discount factor 5% | | 1 | 0.9524 | 0.907 | 0.8638 | 0.8227 | 0.7835 | — |
| NPV 5% | −40 000 | 942.86 | 7 428.6 | 9 433.1 | 9 461.1 | 17 473 | 4 738.2 |
| Discount factor 10% | | 1 | 0.9091 | 0.8264 | 0.7513 | 0.683 | 0.6209 | — |
| NPV 10% | −40 000 | 900 | 6 768.6 | 8 204.4 | 7 854.7 | 13 847 | −2426 |
| Discount factor 15% | | 1 | 0.8696 | 0.7561 | 0.6575 | 0.5718 | 0.4972 | — |
| NPV 15% | −40 000 | 860.87 | 6 192.8 | 7 180.1 | 6 575.2 | 11 087 | −8104 |
| Discount factor 20% | | 1 | 0.8333 | 0.6944 | 0.5787 | 0.4823 | 0.4019 | — |
| NPV 20% | −40 000 | 825 | 5 687.5 | 6 319.4 | 5 545.9 | 8 961.9 | −12 660 |

Internal rate of return
8.1704

estimates for later years. For major projects where the most extensive analysis is needed, the financial analyst will attempt to get best possible estimates of the errors of the estimations for all the factors. This can be collected into a set of error distributions for all the individual cells in the spreadsheet. By the use of random sampling of these error distributions for each of the cells and recalculating the spreadsheet many times (several hundred at least) a distribution of NPVs and IRRs can be obtained. This represents the best estimate of the probabilities of various net present values. Again, from our general knowledge of statistics, we know that the sum of the probabilities must be one and so we can calculate the expected net present value.

For some projects, this type of simple spreadsheet analysis is not appropriate, as it does not fully represent the actions management may take. The example in Fig. 9.13 shows a simple decision tree. Here management evaluates the possibility of the various outcomes

**Table 9.12**    New production analysis for Mk III contacts: 10 per cent reduction in sales volume

| Cash flow element | Year 0 | Year 1 | Year 2 | Year 3 | Year 4 | Year 5 | NPV |
|---|---|---|---|---|---|---|---|
| + Capital costs | −40 000 | | | | | 5000 | — |
| Sales no. units | — | 31 500 | 40 500 | 45 000 | 45 000 | 45 000 | — |
| Selling price | — | 0.7 | 0.7 | 0.7 | 0.7 | 0.7 | — |
| + Sales value £ | — | 22 050 | 28 350 | 31 500 | 31 500 | 31 500 | — |
| Variable costs | | | | | | | |
| unit | — | 0.2 | 0.2 | 0.2 | 0.2 | 0.2 | — |
| − Total variable | — | 6300 | 8100 | 9000 | 9000 | 9000 | — |
| − Fixed costs | — | 10 000 | 10 000 | 10 000 | 10 000 | 10 000 | — |
| Stock | | 1260 | 360 | 180 | 0 | −1800 | |
| − Debtors | — | 4410 | 1260 | 630 | 0 | −6300 | — |
| + Creditors | — | 1575 | 450 | 225 | 0 | −2250 | — |
| Total cash flow | −40 000 | 1655 | 9080 | 11 915 | 12 500 | 23 350 | — |
| Discount factor 5% | | 1 | 0.9524 | 0.907 | 0.8638 | 0.8227 | 0.7835 | — |
| NPV 5% | −40 000 | 1 576.2 | 8 235.8 | 10 293 | 10 284 | 18 295 | 8 683.8 |
| Discount factor 10% | | 1 | 0.9091 | 0.8264 | 0.7513 | 0.683 | 0.6209 | — |
| NPV 10% | −40 000 | 1 504.5 | 7 504.1 | 8 951.9 | 8 537.7 | 14 499 | 996.77 |
| Discount factor 15% | | 1 | 0.8696 | 0.7561 | 0.6575 | 0.5718 | 0.4972 | — |
| NPV 15% | −40 000 | 1 439.1 | 6 865.8 | 7 834.3 | 7 146.9 | 11 609 | −5105 |
| Discount factor 20% | | 1 | 0.8333 | 0.6944 | 0.5787 | 0.4823 | 0.4019 | — |
| NPV 20% | −40 000 | 1 379.2 | 6 305.6 | 6 895.3 | 6 028.2 | 9 383.8 | −10 008 |

Internal rate of return
10.743

and the alternative actions that may be taken. (This is not taken into account in the simple spreadsheets given above which analyse the situation where there is an error in the estimate, not different strategies given different performance levels.) Again, the concept of the expected profit allows the calculation of a single figure representing the expected profitability. In such calculations, where the time value needs to be considered, the expected NPV should be calculated, the discount figure used being the firm's current objective rate of return.

Apart from the issue of risk, the other problem that confronts the development manager (if the R and D staff are any good) is the probability that there will be more projects than the firm will have finance to support. In Chapter Five, we considered the issue of general selection from a portfolio of potential investments with the use of the GE matrix. One of

**Table 9.13**   Sensitivity analysis

| Rate | | | Price | Price | Units | Units | Both |
|---|---|---|---|---|---|---|---|
| | | Base | −10% | +10% | −10% | +10% | P + 10% |
| | | NPV | NPV | NPV | NPV | NPV | V − 10% |
| 5 | | 18 468 | 4 738 | 32 198 | 8 683 | 28 253 | 13 150 |
| 10 | | 9 419 | −2 426 | 21 264 | 996 | 17 841 | 4 811 |
| 15 | | 2 220 | −8 104 | 12 546 | −5 105 | 9 546 | −1 811 |
| 20 | | −3 576 | −12 660 | 5 508 | −10 008 | 2 856 | −7 137 |

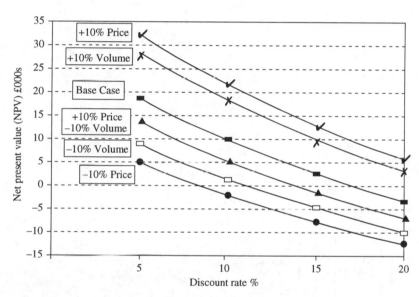

**Figure 9.11**   Sensitivity analysis for DCF

the elements in this analysis is the future profitability of the projects (a factor to be weighted into the attractiveness of the project). The NPV does not give us a single measure to compare differing projects, which will have differing starting capital needs. There are a number of measures we can use to evaluate profitabilities projects against one another:

1.  Internal rate of return (IRR)
2.  Pay back (simple or discounted)
3.  Break even analysis
4.  NPV divided by the initial investment to give a ratio
5.  Sensitivity analysis
6.  Risk analysis (Expected NPV and IRR)

**Table 9.14**    Expected NPV for sales volume

| | | | |
|---|---|---|---|
| −30 | 0.1 | −15 848 | −1 584.8 |
| −20 | 0.2 | −7 425 | −1 485 |
| −10 | 0.2 | 997 | 199.4 |
| 0 | 0.3 | 9 419 | 2 825.7 |
| 10 | 0.15 | 17 841 | 2 676.15 |
| 20 | 0.05 | 26 263 | 1 313.15 |
| | 1 | | 3 944.6 |

(Note: 10 per cent objective rate of return.)

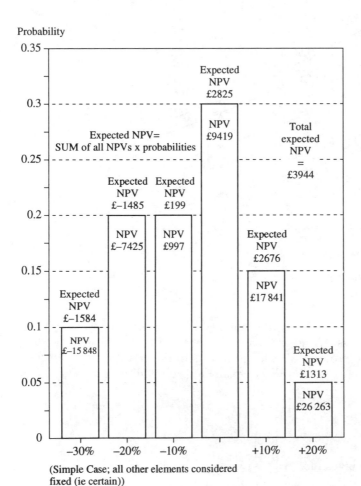

(Simple Case; all other elements considered fixed (ie certain))

**Figure 9.12**    Expected NPV for sales volume

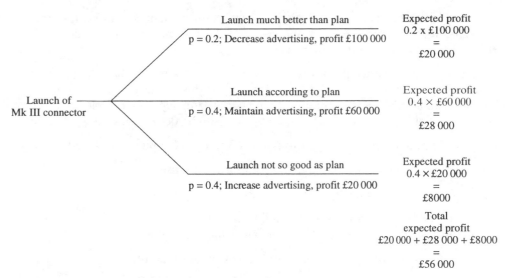

**Figure 9.13**  Simple decision tree for launch of a new product

Profitability is one very important consideration to be taken into the portfolio analysis, involving tools such as the GE matrix. However, a major corporation may well take actions which do not satisfy simple financial analysis on the five year time scale. Major corporations may accept a loss on the first five years of market entry to a new export market on the basis that pay off may take 10 or even 20 years. The final analysis has to be taken with the other elements of strategic management in decision making, it is a critical part of the management tool kit, not the only element.

NPV, pay back and ROI parameters provide a numerical indication of performance analysis. In the next section we shall consider the approaches to performance analysis in more depth. Again, it needs to be restated that break even and cash flow are issues that can never be neglected in financial appraisal.

## 9.11 PERFORMANCE ANALYSIS

A number of key issues have to be remembered in performance analysis:

1. The trends in time, as well as the absolute value, are important.
2. Differing operations will have vastly different ratios. A manufacturing operation (electronics, chemical process industry) will have a much higher capital base as opposed to a retail operation. Thus the comparisons with other operations should be with firms operating in the same type of business.
3. For differing operations the key ratios may well be different. For a manufacturer of chemicals, a key parameter may be profit per hour of a specific type of plant time. For a retail operation it may be sales and profit per square metre.
4. Even for firms in the same business, simple comparisons may be difficult. If two operations are identical except that one runs its own transport fleet and another contracts its distribution, the sales and profit per employee will favour the company that has contracted out. This does not mean of necessity that it has a 'better' operation.

Great care has to be taken in setting key indicators for managers as targets, so that in meeting them real competitive advantages are achieved, not merely political adjustments to hit poorly selected performance ratios.

There is one key performance ratio which must be used in the performance analysis of all businesses. This is the return on Capital Employed. If this is below that which the firm could obtain from a risk free investment with no work (bank deposit) then clearly the area is either not suitable for operation or something needs to be done to restore profitability.

$$\text{Return on Capital Employed} = [\text{Profit (Before Interest)}/(\text{Capital Employed})]*100$$

In comparing operations the percentage of profit on sales is useful.

$$\text{Sales Profitability} = [\text{Profit}/\text{Sales}]*100$$

Of concern to banks and investors is the liquidity of the firm. Is the firm in a position to cover its liabilities? The first test of this is known as the Current Ratio:

$$\text{Current Ratio} = \text{Current Assets}/\text{Current Liabilities}$$

The figures for this calculation can be taken from the firm's balance sheet. However, this test is not sensitive for some aspects of the business, as current assets may include plant that may be on the balance sheet at valuations that might be difficult and slow to realize. A more sensitive test of the health is the Quick Ratio.

$$\text{Quick Ratio} = \text{Quick Assets}/\text{Current Liabilities}$$

Quick assets are money assets (such as cash in the bank) and assets that can be quickly turned into money (such as debtors, money owed to the firm, finished stock).

Given the critical impact of working capital on the health of the business, the amount of resource contained in stock, debtors and creditors should be monitored:

$$\text{Stock turn} = [\text{Materials Cost of Sales}]/[\text{Raw material stocks}]$$
$$\text{Debtor ratio} = [\text{Sales}]/[\text{Debtors}]$$
$$\text{Creditors ratio} = [\text{Creditors}]/[\text{Purchases}]$$

These are general financial ratios which will be of value in the analysis of almost any firm. For each specific operation, each given market condition and/or each department, other ratios will provide sensitive measures. For a manufacturing operation, sales and profit per machine hour might be a good measure. For a retail operation, sales per square metre of floor space or sales per employee could be key ratios. In retail operations, other measures might be sales and profit per customer visit. In service operations, such as hotels, a key ratio may be occupancy rate (percentage of bedrooms occupied each night). For field service operations, sales and profit per visit, number of visits per operator might be considered suitable performance ratios. Clearly, the selection of the key performance ratios for a given operation is matter of management judgement, there is no set simple formula.

## 9.12 ACCOUNTANCY RECORDS

The engineer in business will have to supply information to the formal accountancy systems and may well be involved in information technology implementations. The accountancy records of a major company will be a complex structure and the detail is best left to the career accountant, but the basic principles are simple. Most transactions in a company will be conducted on the basis of 'double entry', that is to say, any single action such as the purchase of gold wire by 'Gold Connections' will affect not one ledger but two. (*Ledger* is an old term, still used by accounts, referring to when transactions were recorded by pen in large books, known as ledgers; in current practice this will refer to high security computer files.) 'Gold Connections' purchases £1000 of gold wire. The cash is reduced by £1000 and the stock is increased by £1000.

Apart from the formal, legal, records of the company, other files will be held in the accountancy area. Given the critical role of cash flow credit control is most important. The debtors' file will contain information on who owes, how much, for how long. The credit control department can then keep an on-going analysis of the situation. The global check is to keep track of the overall level of debtors both absolute and as a percentage of sales. The computer records will allow the detailed ranking of debtors to determine who are prompt payers and who are slow payers. When a firm that has previously paid promptly starts to slow down in payments, it may be that the firm is in trading difficulty and may become a bad debt. The firm must manage the amount of credit that it gives its customers and so another function of the credit control group will be to investigate the credit standing (bankers' references, published accounts, confidential online computer databases) of customers and agree with the marketing and sales departments the credit limits and terms for given customers. A key, day-to-day, housekeeping activity will be to check that accepted orders for a given customer will not take the customer above the agreed credit limit. A customer account that rises above a credit limit and/or starts to show an increasing time for payment is an indication for action, a visit from a sales representative to determine (with considerable tact) the reasons for the 'problem'.

As discussed earlier, the stock valuation required for the formal, legal, accountancy records may in many cases be most inappropriate for management of the company. A frequent problem is stock valuation. Accounts tend, for obvious reasons, to hold information on what has happened: how much did the last batch cost to make? Very often what management is concerned with what needs to be done in the future, and here the firm is concerned with what the next batch will cost to make. The historical cost records may not be a good indicator. There may be an announced price change for raw materials. These may be imported and the exchange rate may have moved since that last purchase. So, apart from the historical records of past performance, additional management files need to be maintained.

For the good management of the firm, the speedy capture of data is of great importance. There is no point in an efficient credit control department reducing debtors from 45 to 42 days, if the field operations take one week to notify deliveries to customers (in effect adding seven days to the credit period). Information is not only required on costing, but on what lots of material have been used for which products. Statistical analysis of field defects may show that components from one supplier are more subject to failure than from another supplier. To collect this information on a manual basis is slow, error-prone, and expensive. Increasingly, engineers are involved in ensuring that where possible there is direct data capture by such mechanisms as bar coding of components.

In the area of stocks, the information needed for accountancy and for materials resource planning overlap and common databases may be used, double keying of information is expensive and ineffective. Earlier in this chapter the link between sales and marketing and credit control was discussed. If the accountancy sales records are linked into a marketing database with such information as market segmentation, the accountancy records can form a vital part of a responsive marketing information management system. This allows a responsive and in-depth analysis of the historical performance and trends.

## 9.13 TAXATION

In a book of this nature, it is not appropriate to consider taxation in any depth, but rather to note that the implications on the management of the company are profound. The taxation situation for a firm can be completely changed with one single finance act. Given the complexity and rapidity of changes, this is an area where the services of an accountancy taxation expert may well be required. Some general comments may be made. Value added taxation requires the strictest recording of purchases and sales, including the exact tax time at which the transaction is considered to have taken place. Profits are subject to taxation. The calculation of profits for taxation may include the inclusion of non-cash elements such as depreciation. Precise rules govern the rate at which capital assets may be depreciated, these can be changed from year to year with any given finance act. The implications will depend on the precise situation of the firm. To take a simple example, it may be more tax efficient for one company to own its transport fleet and take the depreciation over the appropriate period. For another firm, it may be more appropriate for the company to contract out distribution and accept the costs as a wholly tax deductible revenue expense. Thus, when taking any operational management decision, the firm's accountants need to be involved, as there may be tax implications in the decisions. In a full discounted cash flow analysis, the rate at which the depreciation can be off-set against tax will have cash flow implications, and only an expert can advise just what these might be. Earlier in the chapter, in the discussion of transfer prices, we noted that one consideration was the profit implications and deciding where a complex company might wish to accrue its profits. Profit tax planning will be one factor in this decision process.

## REVIEW

Money provides a uniform unit to measure the performance and evaluate both the static state of the company (balance sheet) and the dynamics of a firm (cash flow). Profit represents the realizable added value of the firm's operations, the difference between sales revenue and total costs. However, a profitable firm can be forced out of business if it is unable to finance its working capital. Cash flow and break even analysis, though simple, are powerful tools and essential to ensure the financial health of the organization.

No plan, including financial plans, will work as intended. The use of budgets, implemented on a spreadsheet program, allows the measurement of performance with that planned or predicted. Using the computing power, in-depth understanding for the reasons for deviations can be revealed by variance analysis. In the analysis of investment projects the time value of money needs to be considered with discounted cash flow analysis. Sensitivity analysis, break even analysis, pay back periods and expected net present value enable some account to be taken of risk in the evaluation of projects. Use of pay back periods and internal rates of return enables the relative profitability of various projects to be compared, even where these may have differing investment sums.

The use of performance ratios can be used to track the performance of a company over time and allow comparisons of one firm with another. Care has to be exercised in this analysis, as there is no single right set of performance ratios. Accountancy records also need to be used with care if the information is to be used for management decision making, as the needs for the formal accounts may be different to the information needs for the management issue to be considered. Taxation has an important influence on a company and given the complexity and rapid changes in this area, the career taxation expert should be consulted in all but the most simple cases. Spreadsheet programs provide a flexible and powerful insight in to a wide range of company operations. With the use of database capabilities and graphics, extensive analysis can be completed.

## KEY CONCEPTS AND TECHNIQUES

**Absorption cost**    Attempt to allocate fixed costs to production by some set of accountancy rules. Basis rests on some set of rules which may be quite artificial. May have its value in formal accounts for tax purposes where it may be of advantage to be able to take certain expenses into stock valuations. Not recommended for financial decision making.

**Assets**    The items which comprise the worth of a company including fixed assets (plant and buildings), working capital (work in progress, debtors) and cash. Also includes intellectual property which is often difficult to value and may not appear in the balance sheet.

**Balance sheet**    Representation of the financial state of a company in terms of the assets and liabilities. Represents the situation at a given instant of time.

**Break even**    In business situations where there are fixed and variable expenses, it is the production volume where the total sales income just equals the total of fixed and variable expenses.

**Cash flow statement**    Representation of cash flows for a period of time.

**Creditors**    Individuals and organizations that are owed money by the firm.

**Debtors**    Individuals and organizations that owe money to the firm.

**Decision tree**    Device to allow the calculation of an expected profitability, allowing for different actions (hence costs) in the event of certain possible situations (such as sales above, on, below target). Compares with expected net present value. Sum of products of estimated probabilities and estimated profits.

**Depreciation**    Items of capital equipment have a productive life of a number of years. Depreciation is the accountancy process where only part of the value is assigned to a given production period. Depreciation affects profits but is a non-cash expense and so it does not affect cash flow and does not enter discounted cash flow calculations.

**Direct cost**    Calculation of the actual costs (direct costs) of a given operation.

**Direct profit contribution**    Sales revenue − Direct costs, often expressed as a percentage: 100*(Sales − Direct Costs)/Sales.

**Discount rate**    The interest rate used to reduce (discount) the future value of money in Discounted Cash Flow calculations.

**Expected net present value**    Used in the evaluation of risk in projects, the sum of the individual estimated net present values by their estimated probabilities (sum of probabilities must equal one).

**Expenses**   The money needed to run the business, to provide the goods or services. Includes fixed expenses such as rent, which do not vary with sales volume and variable expenses such as components, which vary directly with production volume.

**Fixed Costs**   Those costs, such as rent and insurance, that tend not to vary with the level of sales.

**Internal Rate of Return**   The discount rate that in a Discounted Cash Flow Analysis yields a Net Present Value of zero.

**Liabilities**   Financial obligations of the company, owners' capital (shares), loans, creditors, deferred tax.

**Linear programming**   Mathematical process to optimize given sales, production or distribution problems subject to various constraints and given various resources. Requires good estimates of optimization objective, variable expenses, production capacities and constraints. Needs no information on fixed costs.

**Marginal cost**   The direct cost only of the production of an increment of additional sales. Will neglect fixed expenses.

**Objective rate of return**   The minimum percentage rate of return acceptable to the firm. This rate may be changed with the firm's judgement of risk involved in the project, the larger the element of risk the higher the objective rate of return required. Minimum rate of return is set by the return the firm could get from a 100 per cent safe investment, such as a bank deposit.

**Pay back**   Simple measure of the profitability of a project. The time it takes to recover the money invested in a project. This calculation may be simple (pay back period) or discounted by the firm's objective rate of return (discounted pay back period).

**Ratio analysis**   Analysis of business situation, looking for trends or in comparison with other like operations, ratios such as ROI, stock turn, sales per employee are just three of a vast range of potentially useful ratios.

**Return on Investment: ROI**   The percentage profit (before interest) on the capital employed by the company.

**Revenue**   Money that the firm gains from its sale of goods or services in a period.

**Sensitivity analysis**   Used in budgets, break even and discounted cash flow (DCF) to estimate the effect of marginal changes (for example ±10 per cent) on individual cost or revenue element estimates (such as selling price).

**Spreadsheets**   Known in the past to be large ruled tables used to complete financial analysis, now mostly referring to computer programs which construct such tables with all the necessary financial functions (for example, internal rate of return).

**Standard cost**   In a fluctuating market or with fluctuating performance, it is often useful for analytical work to assign a uniform cost or rate (standard cost) for the period in question. Thus, in a production unit there may be standard materials costs and standard hourly machine rates, allowing the calculation of standard costs of production.

**Work in progress**   In the production of products, money will be locked in part assembled products. This is known as work in progress.

**Working capital**   The money needed to finance the day-to-day operation of the business in terms of stocks, work in progress, finished product stocks, goods in transit to customers and the difference between money owed to the firm (debtors) and money owed by the company (creditors).

**Variable expenses**  Those costs that tend to directly vary with the level of sales, such as the cost of raw materials and components.

**Variance analysis**  Analysis of deviations from a budget and/or a standard cost to determine assignable causes for the deviations from plan or standard.

## CASE STUDY

Brian Wilson has developed a new device for the measurement of the thickness and colour of surface coatings and has decided to go into business. He has secured a small industrial unit with office space. The unit does not need too much special assembly facilities, much of the advantage comes from the applications software. The rent for the industrial unit is £10 000 a year and the cost of other services (telephone, water, insurance, rates etc.) is £5000 a year. He employs one part-time secretary (£5000 a year) and has two production staff who assemble and pack the devices (£12 000 a year each). Brian pays himself £20 000 a year. The cost of the equipment for the assembly line was £20 000 and Brian has been advised to depreciate it over five years. The office equipment and the computer cost £8000 and Brian has been advised to depreciate this over three years. Components and parts to build the units cost £1000, packaging and distribution costs for the unit are £100 a unit. The marketing communications costs were £1500 for the design and printing of the brochure and an initial mailing. A monthly advertisement in the trade press costs £1000 a year. The components are made to order and Brian needs to keep good stock cover and so holds three months' production as stock and work in progress and finished goods. Brian pays his bills on a one month basis as do his customers. Brian was able to start the business with £50 000 of his own money, a personal loan of £50 000 from his mother and a £50 000 bank loan. Interest on both the bank and the personal loan is 15 per cent. The units sell for £2500 each and Brian sells 20 a month. Brian buys an initial stock of components on starting the business to cover the one month's manufacture. During the year this builds up to three months' stock as components, work in progress and finished stock.

For Brian's business draw up a balance sheet for the start of the business, a cash flow analysis for the first year's operation and a closing balance sheet for the end of the first year's trading. What is the break even volume for the production of units? What will be the working capital demands if business expands 50 per cent in the second year?

Brian finds that he can reduce the cost of components by £100 with the purchase of an additional machine costing £50 000 with a 5 year operational life and a scrap value of £10 000. Should Brian purchase this new machine?

## QUESTIONS

1. Discounted cash flow analysis takes account of the time value of money.

   **Part A**
   You have completed a full analysis of a new capital project to build a new device. The final cash flows are given below:

| Year | Cash flow £000 | |
|---|---|---|
| 0 | −1900 | Capital investment |
| 1 | 200 | |
| 2 | 500 | |
| 3 | 700 | |
| 4 | 700 | |
| 5 | 1400 | Includes scrap value of plant and recovery of working capital. |

Calculate the net present value of this cash flow at 15 per cent, 20 per cent and 25 per cent discount rates. Using a graphical method estimate the internal rate of return of this project.

**Part B**
The internal rate of return is one way to compare different investments with differing initial capital sums and differing later cash flows. What other considerations might you take into account when selecting one project from several when there are limited investment funds? Apart from the internal rates of return for the projects what other quantitative techniques could you use?

2. You are the production engineer in a company that manufactures fire detection equipment. The design engineer has come up with an innovative new domestic fire detector and you have been asked to complete a financial appraisal of the project for the managing director. You have completed a thorough analysis and have come up with the estimates given below. Design costs and modifications to the production line will cost one million pounds. At the end of the project there will be no residual value from this investment. The cash flow estimates over the life of the project are:

| Cash flow element Once production starts | Year 1 £'000 | Year 2 £'000 | Year 3 £'000 | Year 4 £'000 | Year 5 £'000 |
|---|---|---|---|---|---|
| Fixed costs | 200 | 200 | 200 | 200 | 200 |
| Marketing costs | 100 | 50 | 25 | 25 | 0 |
| Variable costs | 300 | 400 | 500 | 500 | 500 |
| Sales income | 900 | 1200 | 1500 | 1500 | 1500 |

There is a corporate policy for investment analysis that the working capital requirement for a year is taken to be 25 per cent of that year's sales income (that is on sales of one million pounds, £250 000 working capital will be required). The same policy guide-lines also state that at the end of the project all working capital will be recovered.

**Part A**
Prepare a net present value appraisal on the basis of the above information using a 20 per cent discount rate. Assume, for simplicity, that all annual cash flows occur at the end of the year to which they relate.

**Part B**

In such a discounted cash flow analysis, the estimation of costs is critical. If you were conducting the DCF analysis, in the above case, what issues would concern you regarding the collection and estimation of *cost* data?

**Part C**

Using a spreadsheet programme calculate ±5 per cent sensitivity analysis for this project.

**Part D**

The marketing department have estimated the following probabilities:

| Sales income | Probability |
|---|---|
| −20% | 0.1 |
| −10% | 0.3 |
| on target | 0.4 |
| +10% | 0.1 |
| +20% | 0.1 |

Calculate the expected NPV at 20 per cent discount rate.

**FURTHER READING**

Drury, C. (1987)  *Costing an Introduction*, Van Nostrand Reinhold.
Drury, C. (1988) *Management and Cost Accounting*, 2nd Edition.
Horngren, C.T. and Foster, G.F. (1987) *Cost Accounting, A Managerial Emphasis*, 6th Edition. Prentice-Hall.
Ward, K. (1989) *Financial Aspects of Marketing*, Heinemann.

# TEN
# TECHNOLOGY DEVELOPMENT

## 10.1 PROJECT MANAGEMENT—OVERVIEW

Projects are part of our everyday life. In industry, a project can range from a minor one of a few weeks, such as the installation of a new machine, to the major introduction of a new product extending over years, with a budget of many millions of pounds. This involves groups of people of different disciplines and different personalities. A project can be defined as the bringing together of a group of people to achieve a given defined objective, in a defined period of time and with defined resources.

In this chapter we will concentrate on the specific needs of project definition and critical path analysis, which is the analytical tool of project management. These are not the only tools required, strict budgetary control is also necessary and this is covered in Chapter Nine. The management of a project team differs little from the management of group covered in Chapter Eleven. Projects differ in that often the project leader will have less direct line authority over team members who will be drawn from their functional groups. Where major projects are concerned, which extend for some considerable period of time with a major impact on the company, it may be appropriate for the team leader to press for line responsibility by the secondment of team members for the duration of the project. Projects also differ in that a specific objective is to be attained in a defined period of time. In a competitive industrial environment, time pressures are immense. Time to market for a new product is seen as a critical advantage for market success. Late entry products mean later and less profitable cash flows. The team leader has to establish the team norms in the shortest period of time possible.

## 10.2 PROJECT DEFINITION

The first stage for a project is its definition. This is most often a senior management responsibility. The selection of the project leader will be on the basis of an understanding of the project requirements. This chapter is written from the point of view of the engineer who is required to assume project leader responsibility.

Once appointed, the project leader must define the project mission, set the aims and the specific objectives. This is the standard business planning process, not an easy task, as often senior management will have defined the project in broad, diffuse and ambiguous terms. The project leader must, after full consideration of the nature of the project, confirm these vital parameters with senior management. The project must not only be defined in terms of the outcomes (objectives), but the nature and amounts of resources required. This is more than the simple agreement of the financial budget. Key company skills may well be needed which are in short supply, resulting in regret costs well in excess of the actual budget costs to the project. The early acceptance of the commitment of the resources to the project is vital to its future success. Properly defining the project is a long way on the road towards success. The project leader then enters a period of negotiation to obtain the specific resources and people that, on first analysis, the project will require. Once the project group has been agreed, the project leader needs to implement the team building process (see Chapter Eleven).

To define the resource requirements, define the time critical elements and communicate with the team members, resource providers and senior management, some management framework is required. Critical path analysis is a powerful formal tool for quantitative analysis of the situation, subsequent management and control. It is a useful method of communicating project objectives, motivating staff and coordinating activities. The latter qualitative elements are as important as the analytical insight for the project leader.

## 10.3  CRITICAL PATH ANALYSIS

Critical path analysis is a technique for the planning and coordination of projects. Consider the case of an engineer who is in the position of product manager (responsibility for marketing as well as production coordination) for a company manufacturing printers. The USA parent company has launched a new, advanced laser printer in the USA and you have been given the responsibility to launch it in the UK. The product will be made in the UK. The objective of this chapter is to present only the basic concepts so a very simple outline will be used. The full complexities of real life projects are best carried out using any of the many excellent computer packages that are available. The amendment of a single activity can cause the complete recalculation of the path which, with several hundred activities in progress, would take several hours by hand.

An outline of the necessary operations might include (with estimates of the required times for completion):

| Label | Time Weeks | |
|---|---|---|
| | 0 | Decision to launch. |
| A | 12 | Hardware re-design for UK (new voltage, EC safety needs, etc.). |
| B | 18 | Marketing research (new font styles needed for UK, etc.). |
| C | 6 | Manufacture of prototype. |
| D | 4 | Modification of production line. |
| E | 6 | New UK font PROM. |
| F | 8 | EC safety testing in independent laboratory. |
| G | 12 | Training of the field engineers and sales engineers. |
| H | 8 | Manufacture of the launch stock. |
| I | 6 | Marketing communications programme. |
| | | Final launch. |

This set of activities can be set out in a simple network. It is not possible to start the

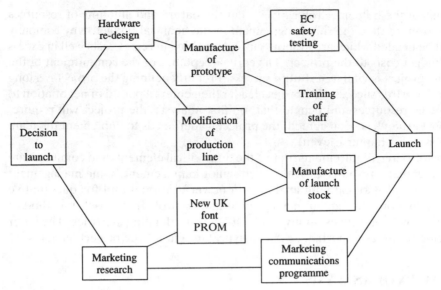

**Figure 10.1**   Network diagram for printer project

| Earliest start time | Activity label | Earliest finish time |
|---|---|---|
| Latest start time | Estimated activity time | Latest finish time |

**Figure 10.2**   Activity on node structure

modification of the production line or the manufacture of the prototype until the design work has been completed. If we lay out all these needs we might end up with a network as shown in Fig. 10.1.

There are several conventions for the construction of critical path diagrams, but we shall consider one particular form, the 'activity on node'. To implement this, we redraw the diagram with the convention shown in Fig. 10.2. We have six sections:

- activity label
- estimated activity time
- earliest start time
- latest start time
- earliest finish time
- latest finish time

We also need some working conventions:

1. Earliest start time is the earliest possible beginning time for an activity;

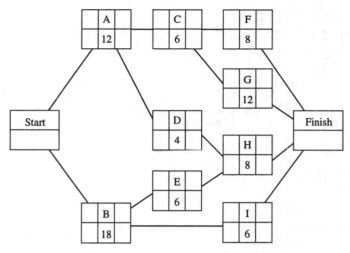

**Figure 10.3** Printer project activity on node activity times

2. The latest start time is the latest possible beginning time for an activity which will allow the project to be completed on time;
3. The earliest finish time is the earliest start time with the addition of the time for the activity;
4. The latest finish time is the latest time for all the activities to be completed and the project completed on time.

So we can construct some simple rules:

1. Earliest finish time = Earliest start time + Activity time
2. Earliest start time = Maximum of all the earliest finish times of the immediately preceding activities
3. Latest start time = Latest finish time − Activity time
4. The latest finish time = Minimum of all the latest starting times of the immediately following activities

We shall use the conventions:

- Earliest start time = EST
- Latest start time = LST
- Activity time = AT
- Earliest finish time = EFT
- Latest finish time = LFT

To calculate the earliest times, we begin at the start of the project and calculate the set of ESTs. For activities A and B these are 0. The EFTs for A and B are the EST + AT. The EST of a succeeding activity is the latest EFT of *all* the proceeding activities. For activity H there are two proceeding activities; D (EFT 16) and E (EFT 24); the EST is 24. This set of calculations is continued until we have all the EFTs to the finish of the project. This is shown for the printer project in Fig. 10.4.

We are then in a position to do the reverse calculation and, starting from the finish time, calculate the LFT. The LST is the LFT − AT. Where an activity has two later activities the

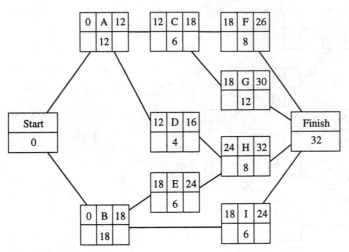

**Figure 10.4**  Printer project activity on node earliest start times

LFT, for the earlier activity, is the lower LST, for the latter activities. Activity C has two succeeding activities; F (LST 24) and G (LST 20); the LFT for Activity C is 20. The rest of the calculations are completed working back to the start of the project. This set of reverse calculations for the printer project is shown in Fig. 10.5.

We then note an odd feature. Some activities have both ESTs and LSTs. By inspection, we can note that there is a path linking such activities. This is the Critical Path. In these activities, any delay in the start time must delay the project. The first value of this type of analysis, therefore, is to enable us to focus on the critical activities, where any delay will cause problems with the project completion. This path is shown by the heavy line in Fig. 10.5.

We can now define an additional term as we can see by inspection that some activities

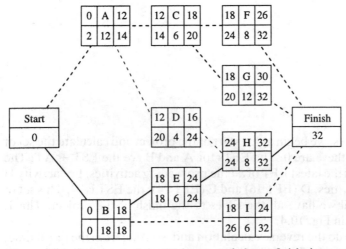

**Figure 10.5**  Printer project activity on node latest finish times

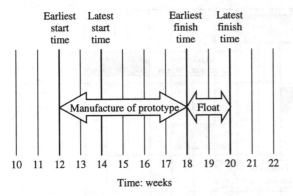

**Figure 10.6**    Float for manufacture of prototype

have 'float', that is to say, we have a time gap where we can delay or extend the activity time without the delay of the whole project.

$$\text{Float} = \text{LFT} - \text{EST} - \text{Duration time}$$

Figure 10.6 shows the float for Activity C (manufacture of prototype) for the printer project. The data in Fig. 10.5 can be summarized in spreadsheet form.

| Label | Time, weeks | Earliest start time | Earliest finish time | Latest finish time | Latest start time | Total float (LFT-EST-D) | Critical |
|-------|-------------|---------------------|----------------------|--------------------|--------------------|--------------------------|----------|
| Start | | | | | | | |
| A | 12 | 0 | 12 | 14 | 2 | 2 | no |
| B | 18 | 0 | 18 | 18 | 0 | 0 | yes |
| C | 6 | 12 | 18 | 20 | 14 | 2 | no |
| D | 4 | 12 | 16 | 24 | 20 | 8 | no |
| E | 6 | 18 | 24 | 24 | 18 | 0 | yes |
| F | 8 | 18 | 26 | 32 | 24 | 6 | no |
| G | 12 | 18 | 30 | 32 | 20 | 2 | no |
| H | 8 | 24 | 32 | 32 | 24 | 0 | yes |
| I | 6 | 18 | 24 | 32 | 26 | 8 | |
| Finish | | | | | | | |

We are then in a position to look at the implications in term of resources and to complete a bar chart as in Fig. 10.7. This bar chart indicates the sequence of activities, grouped by specific resources. By indicating the critical activities and the slack, all staff involved in the project have an overview of their contribution to the project. In particular, people can see the impact of any delay in the completion of their part of the programme on the overall completion date.

**Taking it further**    Figure 10.8 shows in schematic form the detailed resource loading for a given activity. For a design project, the time scale would be in weeks and the resource required would be the number of people needed to work on the project at that time. The

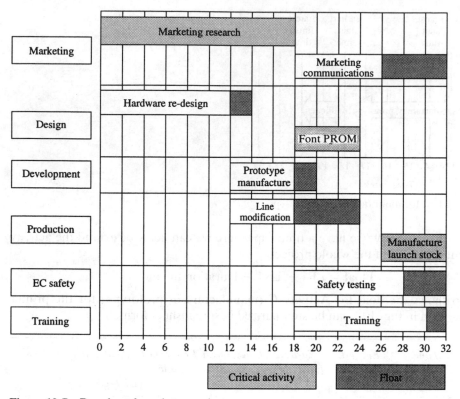

**Figure 10.7**   Bar chart for printer project

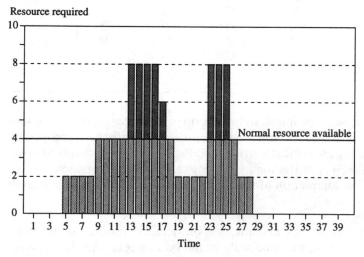

**Figure 10.8**   Projects and resource loading

situation will arise where the project demands exceed the number of people available with the required skills.

The first option the firm has is to increase the resources. The firm could use overtime working or hire temporary staff. With additional cost, the project element could be completed on time. A related option would be to re-examine the time-critical project elements and see if additional resources would enable the critical element completion to be reduced. Reducing the time of a critical element will have an impact on the total completion time of the project. The precise impact requires the recalculation of the critical path chart, but this is no problem with the available computer packages.

The second option is for the company to work within its normal resource limits (see Fig. 10.9). Work which would cause overload should be delayed and rescheduled until the resource is no longer fully loaded. When this is done, the completion time of the project element will be increased. If this is still within the float time, then there will be no impact on the overall completion time for the project. The increased time for the activity element will have an impact, on other elements, reducing their float time. To evaluate the full impact, the complete network can be recalculated. In the schematic example given, the resource levelling will cause the project time to be extended from 28 weeks to 33 weeks.

Most organizations will have a number of projects, each with their own pattern of resource demands. Figure 10.10 shows a schematic outline of the demands on a single resource where the organization has four projects in hand. The senior project manager will use the project management computer system to check which project elements are on critical path elements. To allow any drift in these elements will, of course, cause delay to the project completion dates. The non-critical project elements can be examined to evaluate which elements can be rescheduled into slack periods where there are available resources.

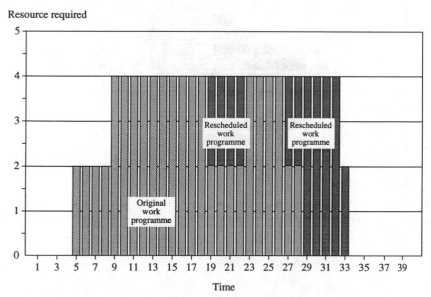

**Figure 10.9**  Projects and resource loading—resource levelling

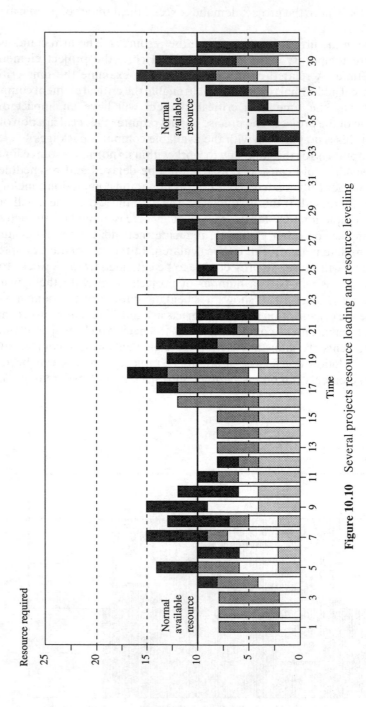

**Figure 10.10** Several projects resource loading and resource levelling

**Other values of the technique**    One key value of the technique is that it allows the identification of critical activities. Often, however, the most useful feature is its ability to communicate a sense of urgency when a diverse set of departments (often on remote sites) have to coordinate and cooperate to hit a tight deadline. This is reflected in the use of the technique as a feedback and control tool. If an activity is to last longer than the LFT, then action is necessary, either to ensure that the activity does not do this, or to crash (accelerate, at high cost) some later activity on the critical path or even to set back the completion date of the project. The technique allows the detection of the problems and the evaluation of the options.

### 10.3.1 Problems

The above discussion suggests that all that is needed to be an effective project manager is a good computer package to contain all the complexity of the above calculations. Critical path analysis is a highly effective tool, but the network is not the real world, it is only a model of the real world. In constructing this model, we are making assumptions. If these should not be true in all respects, then just as with linear programming, forecasting and materials resource planning (see Chapter Six), the model will give distorted results. In constructing the model, estimates of the activity times are required. There will be errors in these estimates and there will be random effects on completion times. In construction projects, the weather may affect certain elements of the project, some of the development outcomes may not be easy to predict or it may take more or less time to complete a section of programming or design. This is very much like the problem encountered with discounted cash flow analysis in estimating future cash flows and the same approach can be used. The project manager can take the best estimate and also estimate probability distributions for the possibility that the activity might take a longer or shorter period. Using simulation techniques, a picture can be built up of the most probable completion time for the total project, based on best estimates and error estimates.

This is only one source of possible error in the project. The critical path network is an expression of the logic structure of the project. It is possible that an error could be made in the sequencing of the project elements. Related to this is an assumption that one element of the project may not start until the previous elements have been fully completed. Often this is not the case. In the printer project, the assumption is made that the manufacture of the prototype will not be started until the design has been fully completed. In many cases, this is not true and the major points of design may be quite clear well before all the minor detail has been completed. In such a case, it may be possible to overlap some activities. Where this type of concurrent engineering is possible, the logic of the critical path diagram needs to reflect this. In the printer project, the design and prototype manufacture could be broken into two elements, preliminary work on construction taking place after completion of the preliminary design work and concurrent with the completion of the detailed design of the last few remaining components. These types of techniques have earned the name 'time compression'.

It was noted earlier that critical path networks and bar charts provided a powerful mechanism of communication. To be a motivator the charts have to provide objectives that are agreed, challenging but achievable. Thus the resource allocation is not just some technical job, but a political management issue where power is as important as logic. In

Chapter 8, the use of the matrix organizational structure to balance the needs of resource and project management were considered. Apart from the random probability factors, the activity resource element estimated needs are coloured by the psychological nature of the manager arriving at the estimate. In a company with a conservative culture and perceived high penalties for non-achievement of objectives, the logical outcome is defensive estimates for amounts of resource and time required. The continual addition of fat and hidden buffer time will create a sense of complacency and acceptance of under-achievement. In a more risk-taking environment, there will be the temptation to accept estimates that are too optimistic. When it becomes obvious that these are not reliable, the whole planning process becomes discredited.

As with any control system, the dead time of the feedback system is important. The project manager must not only set out and negotiate the critical path structure for the project, with all its resource implications, but also ensure that there is effective collection of progress data. In the printer project, the design of the new PROM is on the critical path and the activity is scheduled to take six weeks. If two weeks into this activity it is clear that eight weeks will be required, but this is not reported, the firm exists in the most dangerous of states. People think there is a control system but, if the response time is too long, only the illusion of control exists. In the practical implication of such network systems the effort in setting up the basic network is acceptable. It will assist in the costing of the project and enthusiasm exists. To keep the project on schedule, each activity needs to be monitored for slippage which will cause delay and expense overrun. Within each lengthy activity element, there needs to be review milestones for the checking of progress. If this is done, the critical path model becomes a most powerful tool for flexible, effective and efficient project management. The impact of a problem can be evaluated and decisions taken with extensive knowledge of the potential consequences, possibly some considerable time in the future. It must be remembered that a delay on the critical path may have major effects which may not be fully apparent until near the project end, that is to say, if the critical path planning tool was not being used. With care, the same mechanism to report progress for the critical path control of the project can be used for the budgetary control, providing both a financial and a time control system for the project.

Critical path techniques are useful as a tool for the management of a project, but the model structure and computer programs are an aid for managerial decisions, not a form of management by robots.

## 10.4 THE STAGES OF NEW PRODUCT DEVELOPMENT

Figure 10.11 shows the overall new product development process. New ideas have to be generated. This is not a simple process, but a very creative process that requires imagination, an expert understanding of the firm's environment and markets and an understanding of the firm's capabilities or potential capabilities. These have to be matched with the firm's markets, or potential markets, benefit needs or potential benefit needs. Some innovations will occur through the sudden burst of inspiration. The multinational company needs a flow of successful products and would not survive if this was the only source of new ideas. This is not to say that innovative companies do not look for and support inspirational ideas by any member of the staff. Successful firms encourage and reward such contributions but they also recognize that a structure of search is necessary. In

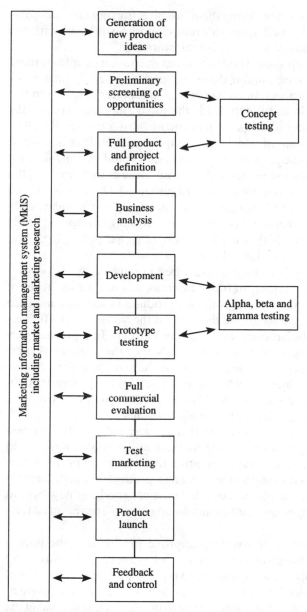

**Figure 10.11**   New product development process

a wide range of industries (electronics, pharmaceuticals, and aerospace are examples), many new products are not possible without fundamental research.
Need for MkIS

### 10.4.1  Generation of new product ideas

Ideas can and do come from individual moments of creative inspiration but overall, under the right conditions, groups are more creative and effective than individuals. One individual can build on another's ideas, often taking them in a direction not considered by the first person. The most commonly used form of creative group working, with the deliberate intention of stimulating creative thought, is brainstorming.

For a brainstorming session the group should be from about five to ten people. If there are too few people there are too few ideas, and if there are too many people then many individuals will not contribute to the process. In the latter case, it is better to split into two groups. A person introduces the topic and lightly leads the discussion and explains the group rules. The most important being to suspend judgement during the session. The group will make many suggestions, some of which may be quite wild and, at first sight, totally impractical. At this stage, no judgement on practicability should be made, as it interrupts the creative process. The session leader will write up ideas as they flow, on flip chart paper. (This is better than a board as there is a record for later.) The session should not last too long, about 30 minutes should be enough to generate some 20 or 30 ideas. Only after the creative period is over may people revisit the ideas and suggestions and apply judgement. The value of these sessions is that it allows people to get out of logic and thought tramlines and come at concepts in a lateral way.

Another way to approach creativity is to take a structured creative view. It is again critical to suspend judgement to some extent, in order to break out of a strait-jacket of thinking. Groups and individuals can consider the company products or services and then change some important parameter. What would be the effect if the service were 10 times faster? What would be the effect if the product were ten times larger? In a process very similar to brainstorming, a group can come to a view on whether there might be new benefits with the radical product concept. The analytic side is then to see if the extreme idea can be realized in some way. The objective is to arrive at a new way to provide benefit needs in a competitive way, as discussed in Chapter Three. The starting point can be a company resource (spare capacity, by-products etc.) or a market need.

In Chapter Five, the Ansoff matrix was presented as a way to classify business opportunities, whether they were for new or existing markets and involved new or old products. This device can be used as a structured creative tool. What might be a new market is as much a creative process as forming an idea for a new product. Indeed, for most organizations, the term 'new product' should be extended to cover servicing new benefit needs. Even if an existing product is to be used, a new marketing mix will be required for a different market segment.

Customer complaints can be a very useful way to improve products. Sometimes a product fails as the customer is using the product or service for a purpose that it was never intended or designed to fulfil. This opportune development represents the identification of a new benefit need, a possible potential for product extension or even a new product. Many new products are not new to the world but simply new to the firm. The firm, using the full capabilities of its marketing information system (MkIS, market research, internal systems, market intelligence and analytical systems) may create clone or near clone adaptations. Two key elements are marketing research (often secondary), to track what is happening in the market, and market intelligence. The engineer may be involved in an extensive stripping down and analysis of the construction and performance of competitor's products, purchased by the company for this very purpose.

A company may simply purchase its new products by acquiring a licence or even by the outright purchase of the company.

## 10.4.2  Screening of opportunities

For a project to be successful, there must be a market. The firm must have a competitive position and the opportunity should fit in with the firm's long term mission and objectives. If the opportunity looks highly attractive, yet does not fit in with current strategies, the company has two options: the simplest is to market the idea, design or patent for licence with an organization where there is a strategic fit; the alternative is to examine the firm's basic mission and amend. A change in mission is a change in the basic philosophy of the firm and may affect more than just the single project that has precipitated the major review.

Where the product, its manufacture or application involves a significant development of new technology, the simple question 'Can it be made to work?' needs to be asked. This requires the most skilled of broad based judgements, as this will often depend on an expert consideration of how much research or development will be needed when, given the early stage of the project, many factors may only be poorly definable.

For a product to have a market, the potential market segments have to be identified and their size and benefit valuation for the new product estimated. The benefit valuation and possible market penetration will depend on the direct and indirect competition in the segments. The firm should, even at this early stage, appraise the physical distribution. Can an established framework be used? The channel outlets and links required may be new to the company. Can they be established at reasonable cost? Parallel to this, the requirement for complementary products and goods ought to be considered. The product may need special fuel or power, maintenance materials or consumable products. The product might be a vehicle for the delivery of a benefit such as music or information. Will the firm have access to any copyright or other intellectual property that the firm or the user may require to gain the benefits of ownership?

Where a high element of innovation is involved and the benefit need is new or to be satisfied in an original way, the concept should be tested. Apart from the reduction of risk by having some specific evidence of market acceptability of the product, the early feedback of market requirements can greatly assist in the better definition of the later development stage of the project. The product need not be available, even in prototype form. Simulations, concept sketches or mock-up demonstration models may be used at relatively low cost.

An often-neglected facet of this preliminary evaluation is the consideration of the length of time and cost for the marketing communications. If the product is a simple line extension this might be modest, but in entering a new market segment, the potential costs of the promotional effort may be comparable with the product development costs. The provision of the benefit in a competitive way is a bed-rock of the product strategy. If the product is a 'new to the world' product, the benefit may be quality or even the provision of a benefit need that technology did not exist to satisfy. Often, the competitive position will be based upon a manufacturing cost advantage which may be based on raw material or component strengths, design innovation or superior production technology. It is advisable to make estimates of the break even point for the project at an early stage. Low costs may only be possible at very high volumes. For a new product these may take time to build and in a competitive world may not be achieved. The environmental product life cycle should be considered as failure to appraise possible green impact problems which may kill the

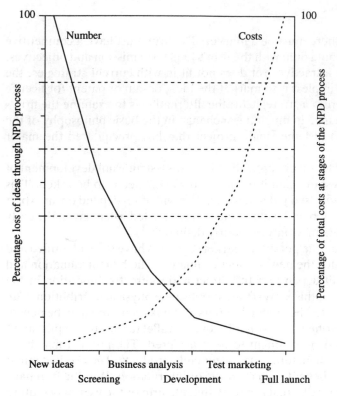

**Figure 10.12** Mortality of new projects and commercialization costs

project or introduce large costs. The final paradox in the new product appraisal process is that the maximum exit costs on the failure of the project need to be known. Only with a complete picture, is the firm able to judge whether the product may be truly viable and profitable.

It is essential that the above evaluations are completed in as much depth and insight as is practical. Figure 10.12 shows that the rate of increase in project costs is logarithmic with respect to the progression of the project. As the project progresses to the next stage the stakes, profit or cost of failure, are significantly raised. The firm that is successful in long term innovation knows that it is essential to judge the risks and reduce them where possible. The most effective way to reduce risk is to ensure that each stage of new product process is completed with care. Early errors may mean expensive redesign or even complete failure of the product.

### 10.4.3 Project definition

From the earlier discussion, it is evident that a successful product has to be designed for the target customer's use (benefit needs), manufacture and marketing (physical distribution involving such issues as packaging). The engineer managing the new product introduction has to integrate a large amount of information and then translate it, with the full involvement of the project team, into a product specification and an action plan. The

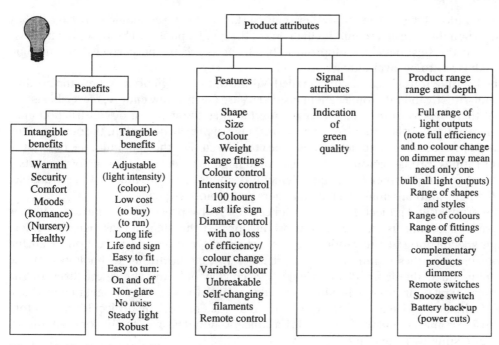

**Figure 10.13**   Product attribute analysis—electric light for bedroom

structure of critical path analysis allows for the expression and communication of the potential action plan. It enables the project engineer to consider what types and quantities of resources need to involved in the project with some idea of the timings. This detailed consideration will allow reasonable estimates of the total probable costs.

Attribute analysis, introduced in Chapter Five, provides the mechanism for expressing the customer's benefit needs into a design brief. Figure 10.13 shows a preliminary attribute analysis conducted by a tutorial group of undergraduate engineers for the ideal electric light bulb for the bedroom. The discussion between the engineering design team and the marketing specialists should first cover the intangible benefits that the customer segment may gain from the ownership or use of the product. As there may be different benefits from different groups, this process of attribute analysis needs to be considered for each major customer segment and each quality public (see Chapter Six). The design leader can then define with the marketing staff the tangible benefits required, both directly and also to support the desired intangible benefits. In a bedroom, one benefit is a sense of comfort. This requires that the light should produce no noise (a problem with some types of fluorescent lighting with a low frequency hum). The design team are provided with a full brief of the product requirements. Then and only then, can the detail of the features and nature of the product be fully considered. The design team is then faced with a creative challenge to find innovative, effective and efficient solutions and features to provide the benefit set. One feature required by customers is that the light should not burn out in an unexpected way. This group of engineers suggested that this could be solved by the use of a second, lower intensity, filament with a limited life to provide a warning, allowing time for the bulb to be changed when convenient. If features are designed in without first considering the benefit needs, there is a danger of arriving at a technology push product where features have to be sold, rather than marketed. Features should only exist if they satisfy a benefit need or a requirement of one of the quality publics. This process is not easy and often the best possible compromise has to be reached, the perfect domestic light source has yet to be invented.

The list of features becomes the detailed outline of the design brief. Where the product may not directly indicate some benefit need in its use (such as low energy, recyclable green bulb), then by styling or some other feature (such as the material of construction etc.) signal attributes can be provided. Even at this stage of project definition, the outline of the required product range and depth should be considered. For the light bulb, the number of power ratings, fittings, colours and styles would need to be defined. For many products it will be necessary to either design complementary goods or ensure that they are available. For the light bulb this might include dimmers and remote switches.

The product and project definition will need to involve procurement (purchase of new materials, components etc.) as well as production. At this stage a reasonably complete design specification of the product can be achieved, with a good indication of all the supporting activities required, such as changes in manufacturing technology. At the screening stage the depth of knowledge is such that only the sketchiest 'back of the envelope' type of financial feasibility can be done. With the wealth of insight that has been gained, the business analysis can be completed by the engineering project leader. Before this business analysis the redefined product concept should be checked by some additional concept testing with the market.

### 10.4.4 Business analysis

If the definition of the project has been done well, the preliminary cost analysis is not a difficult process. The critical path resource estimates can be translated into project expense budgets in a spreadsheet. The projected marketing expenses can also be added to the large spreadsheet. There are two difficult questions that have to be considered at the business analysis stage: the first is 'will the project be profitable'? The expenses have been calculated on the careful work done in the project definition. The second, an estimation of the future cashflow, is much more difficult. Even market research on present market acceptability, careful estimates of pricing and market sizes and shares achievable does not take account of future competitive responses. 'Porter 5 forces' analysis and consideration of the position of the new product within a general product life cycle provides qualitative information. It is not possible to make accurate forecasts. Even for major projects estimates will have to be based on sound judgement of all the issues, rather than any simple regression equation.

With the best possible estimates of the cash flows a DCF analysis of the project can be completed (see Chapter Nine). If the project shows a negative net present value on the firm's current objective discount rate, the project can be rejected or re-examined to see if the costs can be reduced. Time to market is a critical issue for two reasons. If a given amount of research and marketing effort is required, this should be done in the shortest realistic time to bring forward the cash inflow. Table 10.1 shows this effect for a simple project with £6 000 000 R and D and a simple profit cash flow of £10 000 000 over the first three years, of sales. If the development is allowed to take three years, the project is unprofitable, but if this is reduced to two years the project becomes just profitable. This is much improved if the development can be achieved in one year. There is a second effect:

**Table 10.1**   Value of concurrent engineering on time to market—DCF effect

*Cash flows slow development*

|  | 0 £'000 | 1 £'000 | 2 £'000 | 3 £'000 | 4 £'000 | 5 £'000 | Total £'000 |
|---|---|---|---|---|---|---|---|
| Development | −2000 | −2000 | −2000 |  |  |  | −6000 |
| Sales profit |  |  |  | 2000 | 4000 | 4000 | 10 000 |
| Cash flow | −2000 | −2000 | −2000 | 2000 | 4000 | 4000 | 4000 |
| 20% interest rate | 1.0000 | 0.8333 | 0.6944 | 0.5787 | 0.4823 | 0.4019 |  |
| NPV | −2000 | −1667 | −1389 | 1157 | 1929 | 1608 | −362 |

% Internal rate of return = 17

*Cash flows fast development*

|  | 0 £'000 | 1 £'000 | 2 £'000 | 3 £'000 | 4 £'000 | 5 £'000 | Total £'000 |
|---|---|---|---|---|---|---|---|
| Development | −3000 | −3000 |  |  |  |  | −6000 |
| Sales profit |  |  | 2000 | 4000 | 4000 |  | 10 000 |
| Cash flow | −3000 | −3000 | 2000 | 4000 | 4000 | 0 | 4000 |
| 20% interest rate | 1.0000 | 0.8333 | 0.6944 | 0.5787 | 0.4823 | 0.4019 |  |
| NPV | −3000 | −2500 | 1389 | 2315 | 1929 | 0 | 133 |

% Internal rate of return = 21

*Cash flows very fast development*

|  | 0 £'000 | 1 £'000 | 2 £'000 | 3 £'000 | 4 £'000 | 5 £'000 | Total £'000 |
|---|---|---|---|---|---|---|---|
| Development | −6000 |  |  |  |  |  | −6000 |
| Sales |  | 2000 | 4000 | 4000 |  |  | 10 000 |
| Sales profit | −6000 | 2000 | 4000 | 4000 | 0 | 0 | 4000 |
| 20% interest rate | 1.0000 | 0.08333 | 0.6944 | 0.5787 | 0.4823 | 0.4019 |  |
| NPV | −6000 | 1667 | 2778 | 2315 | 0 | 0 | 759 |

% Internal rate of return = 27

*Cash flows very fast development profit flows continued*

|  | 0 £'000 | 1 £'000 | 2 £'000 | 3 £'000 | 4 £'000 | 5 £'000 | Total £'000 |
|---|---|---|---|---|---|---|---|
| Development | −6000 |  |  |  |  |  | −6000 |
| Sales |  | 2000 | 4000 | 4000 |  |  | 10 000 |
| Sales profit | −6000 | 2000 | 4000 | 4000 | 4000 | 4000 | 4000 |
| 20% interest rate | 1.0000 | 0.8333 | 0.6944 | 0.5787 | 0.4823 | 0.4019 |  |
| NPV | −6000 | 1667 | 2778 | 2315 | 1929 | 1608 | 4296 |

% Internal rate of return = 46

higher profits can be expected and profit flows extended if the product is introduced during the growth, rather than maturity, stage of the product life cycle. If this effect, for the extended profitable life of the product, is included for the project shown in Table 10.1, the product becomes most profitable.

In most cases, the firm will not have a single project to evaluate but a number of projects, only some of which the company will have the resource to implement. At the stage of business analysis, it is often necessary to select a restricted number mix of best projects. The techniques of portfolio analysis (see Chapter Five) can assist in this. Projects may need to be considered in groups when technology development for one project may also be used in other products.

### 10.4.5 Development

At this stage the product development team needs to be assembled. For a major project there will be an inner core of full-time team members and an outer group of supporting links. Chapter Eleven covers the issues of team building in detail. The time and effort required for this team building can be reduced if potential team members are used in the project definition stage. The members of the team must know and understand their own roles and how those relate to the other team members. The project mission and objectives must be fully accepted by all team members as reasonable and challenging, but achievable.

The outer group of support links involves all the people who, although not involved full-time in the project, nevertheless provide vital information and/or resources. This group may extend outside the company to support suppliers, who may be required to build sub-assemblies or supply specialist components or materials. Such links may be required with any of the quality publics, including regulatory bodies, customers, manufacturers of facilitating products (such as magnetic storage media for computers) and distributors. The team must be open to the most up-to-date information on market issues and manufacturing technology. The product will have been conceived in one business situation. As the project progresses, it is essential that there is flexibility to trim the project to the precise requirements of the firm and market situation as these change. In particular, in fast moving markets, the technical and commercial activities of the firm's competitors must be taken into account.

Given the high commercial priority of a short time to market, the detailed product specification must be drawn up at the same time as the development team refine the product design and the manufacturing policy. This activity should be concurrent with the development of the marketing launch plan, with a full definition of the market segments to be attacked and the appropriate marketing mix for the task.

### 10.4.6 Prototype testing

As the hardware develops the product should be subjected to alpha, beta and gamma tests:

*Alpha test* Does the product fully work to design specification in the laboratory test environment?

*Beta test* Does the product fully work to design specification in the customer use situation: less skilled operators, poor power supplies, possible poor physical conditions (dust, heat, cold, dampness, dust, corrosion), installation problems (fit with other customer equipment, physical installation)?

*Gamma test*   The product has been designed to do the job and work in a way that the design team have gauged is what the customer needs and wants. Is this really so? A check that the product fulfils the customer's benefit need set in a way that is fully acceptable to the customer.

In the latter stages of the development this work should be conducted with products as close to production quality as possible. If the company has built up relationships with the trail blazing customers (the innovators in the adoption of innovations model) positive experience can be used to influence the early adopters and the early majority.

### 10.4.7 Commercial evaluation

Even at this late stage, when much of the technical development money is committed, the decision to market will involve additional large sums of money. In many cases, the commercialization expenses will far exceed the development costs. The production line may well have to be retooled, which is not only a direct cost but leads to additional loss of revenue while the change-over is effected. The production of the launch stock with stocking of field spares will involve large sums of money. If the product fails it may not be possible to fully recover this working capital. The marketing costs for the launch may involve large expenses in marketing communications (advertising, promotional launch events) and for innovative products additional expense will be involved in the training of the company staff and agents.

   If the preceding stages have been done properly the commercial evaluation will be a re-examination of the cash flow estimates formulated during the business analysis. As the project progresses and better information becomes available, this evaluation should be continuously updated. Full, detailed plans need to be drawn up for the production capacity, with the distribution channels fully identified. The logistics of physical distribution and field service must be fully considered. A particular problem is to ensure that complementary and facilitating goods which are to be supplied by other originations will be available. Any remaining legal or regulatory issues, such as safety approvals and validations, must have been completed or near completion. The project team and senior management can then make a conscious decision to proceed, before the final large sums of money are dedicated and the full capabilities of the organization committed to the launch.

### 10.4.8 Test marketing

For many products it may be wise to test out the full programme with a limited launch in a single region. The advantage of this strategy is that the production levels can be built up at a steady rate. In the production of an innovative product problems will occur, delaying achievement of full capacity and efficiency. This is the 'learning curve' effect. The firm has direct management control of these problems but similar effects may well apply to the providers of the facilitating products and it takes time to train field and service staff. The market positioning concepts and the marketing communications programme will have been well considered and researched but this is no substitute for direct field experience. On the basis of this limited, but full production scale experience, the detail of the full launch plan can be adjusted. The disadvantage of this strategy is that it takes time and the competition will be analysing the marketing strategy and its success with every bit as much interest as the firm itself. In the case of a 'me too' product, new to the firm but not to the market, this may give the existing competition enough time to improve production efficiency and meet the new market entry with an aggressive marketing response, for instance, increased advertising activity, promotional offers or just simply a head-to-head price war.

### 10.4.9 Product launch

The key factor is the effective, efficient and coordinated implementation of the plans developed at the full commercial evaluation stage, with the amendments needed from the experience gained during the test marketing process. The coordination must extend to suppliers of raw materials and components to production. Collaboration must be continued to ensure that there is field availability from other firms of facilitating and complementary products. The field and agents' training programmes must be linked in with the marketing communications so that, as customer response is built up, there is the field capability to service the demand.

The field problems must be well managed. An inexperienced agent may not install the equipment properly. Early production products may have lower than expected quality. A close rated component may give frequent field failures but the problem may not have been identified until a significant number of units have been installed and in use for some time. Such issues must be quickly identified and the 'new product' team must react promptly to resolve the difficulties quickly, to keep the innovative customers content and to ensure that later product and installations benefit from the lessons learnt. The use of extended beta and gamma tests can reduce the likelihood and size of such problems.

The detailed issues that need to be implemented have been covered in the discussion of the planning process in the earlier stages of the new product development process. The only certainty of this implementation is that, no matter how careful the research and the test marketing, things will not go exactly to plan. Built into the plan must be flexibility to react to the actual situation. However well the firm does its own planning, it will not be possible to predict the competitive response. This will have to be countered in a judged way as soon as the competing companies' strategies become apparent. Even success may have its own problems and if demand grows much faster than the plan, it may exceed production capacity and service levels will fall away. In this situation, the flexible response may be to reduce advertising and marketing activity until the production capacity can be brought into line with the higher than expected demand.

### 10.4.10 Feedback and control

The firm is operating in a competitive environment and it is essential that the appropriate efforts are made to impede, by legal means, the marketing intelligence activity of competitors. Members of the project team must be known to be secure, where design information flows outside the organization to suppliers or manufacturers of facilitating goods the information release may need to be covered by a secrecy agreement. It may be advisable that information is released outside the team on a 'need to know' basis, so that only the senior management and the team have the full picture. In certain situations and technologies, specific features may be built into the product to make it difficult for the competition to fully understand the product. Sections of code may be added to computer programs to make it difficult to read the detailed structure. In formulated products non-functional additives may be added to make chemical analysis of the product difficult to protect the formulation. This is often necessary because it is difficult to protect such products by patents.

The firm, in its turn, should be making every effort to gain maximum information on the competition. Competitive products should be bought on the open market and retro-engineered, taken apart to gain insight on the performance, quality and even possible methods of manufacture used. The field sales and service force should be alert to pick up information on new products in the market and customer reactions. Market intelligence is as important to a new product launch as market research. It can help management judge the capability and direction of future competitive responses, whereas market research tends to give information on the current market position.

During the launch period, the firm's marketing information management system must work to full sensitivity. What is the level of market penetration? Is the product selling in unexpected customer areas? Is the marketing positioning and marketing communication strategy working as intended? Which media and messages are more effective? Answers to these types of question enable the launch programme to be adjusted to gain maximum impact. All through the project cost control against budget has been necessary. At this stage, close analysis of plan against budget is vital. Any deviations must be identified, the causes investigated and appropriate management action taken.

## REVIEW

The successful project needs full definition with specific objectives. To control a project, it is necessary to decide what has to be done in terms of specific skills and resources. For the effective management of projects, the timing of resource needs is important. Critical path analysis provides an effective tool for the coordinating and cost control of projects. Critical path techniques require large amounts of good quality data which must be updated as the project proceeds.

The new product development process is the most complex type of project the company will encounter. The complexity arises from the need to gather information from the market on concept acceptability, market sizes and benefit valuation and competitive forces. To reduce the chance of failure, careful evaluation of the situation is necessary at each stage. This must involve customer trials on the product, with attribute analysis providing a structure to translate the customer needs into a specific engineering brief. At each stage of the process some product part will fail and the costs associated with a new product increase greatly, as commercialization is approached. The purpose of the re-evaluation process is to ensure that poor products are terminated early, before heavy development expenses are incurred, and to maximize the success of the remaining new products by the best possible planning. The planning process has to have good feedback and control systems with flexibility of response, as markets change and competitive responses are outside the firm's control, but still have to be managed. Time to market is not only important for the time value of money, higher profits can be obtained for longer if the product is introduced at the best time in the product life cycle for the firm. To reduce time to market, concurrent engineering must be used, with the manufacturing and marketing plans being developed at the same time as the product design process proceeds.

## KEY CONCEPTS AND TECHNIQUES

**Activity time: (AT)**   The time taken for a single activity in a critical path analysis.

**Alpha test**   The testing of a product in the laboratory to ensure full performance to design criteria.

**Bar chart**   Chart to show resource use against time in critical path analysis.

**Beta test**   The testing of a product in the customer situation to ensure full performance to design criteria.

**Brainstorming**   A group process used to generate new products or new solutions.

**Concurrent engineering**   The process of coordinating the production and marketing planning for a new product, concurrent with the design process rather than in sequence. Done to reduce the time to market.

**Critical path analysis**   A process of structuring a project in a network allowing the interconnection of individual activities to be seen and project completion times calculated. Used to control projects.

**Critical path**   The path through the logic network where any delay in any single activity will cause the project to be delayed.

**Earliest start time: (EST)**   The earliest time that an activity can commence in a critical path analysis.

**Earliest finish time: (EFT)**   The earliest time that an activity can be completed in a critical path analysis.

**Float**   Slack time by which an activity can drift in a critical path analysis without causing the project to be delayed. Applies to non-critical activities, the float on one activity will often affect the floats on other activities.

**Gamma test**   Evaluating, in the customer-use situation, whether the product does what the customer really requires.

**Latest finish time: (LFT)**   The latest time that an activity can finish without delaying a project in critical path analysis.

**Latest start time: (LST)**   The latest time that an activity can start without delaying a project in critical path analysis.

**Time to market**   The time taken from initial product concept to full product launch. With short product life cycles this time is critical.

## CASE STUDY

Exeter Security is a well-established company that have made locks and security devices for over 100 years. Sam Chadwick, an electronics engineer, was recruited when the company decided to diversify into fire protection equipment and Sam introduced Exeter Securities' range of smoke detectors and intruder alarms. These were first launched into the commercial market for industrial premises but, over the last five years, they have been successfully adapted and sold to the domestic market.

A particular strength of Exeter Security has been the development of electronic access systems for secure areas, such as computer rooms and development laboratories. These systems are based on a magnetic smart card that can restrict access by day, time of day or even just for a single specified period. In use, the card is programmed from a simple unit and all the user does is 'swipe' it past the security read device and entry is allowed if the card is in order. The card also has the ability to record information at this time. One company has used this to log the movement of staff in a highly sensitive secure facility. Another feature is that the cards can be reprogrammed, so that if a card is lost or an employee leaves, all cards can be reprogrammed. Encryption technology makes the breaking of the security codes almost impossible.

Last week Sam lost the keys to the house when his car was stolen. The house was broken into three days later, before Sam could get the locks changed. A few days later, a company visitor complained that her jewellery had been stolen from her hotel room as the 'pass' room key had been copied and the thief had been able to enter some 30 rooms. That evening Sam started to consider how the secure smart card could be developed for these two applications. On loss, the entry locks could be reprogrammed not to accept the old cards. Existing old cards could be updated from the control unit at no cost. New cards only cost 50 pence. Sam thought that this system could be useful in the domestic setting as the control locks could now be produced for £40, which was comparable to a high security mechanical lock. The central control unit could possibly be built into the spare slot in the domestic intruder alarm and even retro-fitted. This drop-in unit would cost only about £100 to £200 on a very quick calculation.

Sam also thought that the card could record data onto a point-of-sale computer which had a reader for credit cards. Thus, the card could be used in hotels for high security access to rooms (code numbers could be changed between visitors) and, moreover, the card could act as a charge card for telephone use, meals and bar bills. Sam discussed this with the managing director the next day and got a warm response, as the company was looking for new products. Sam was asked to draw up a new product development plan for the idea and to produce a provisional report on how the potential of these products could be estimated and the products launched.

In the role of Sam Chadwick draft out this preliminary report.

---

## QUESTIONS

1. The launch of a new product involves a number of stages which, as with all projects, need coordinating. You are the UK new product development manager of a large international company. It has been decided to launch a European version of a successful product introduced into the USA last year. You have estimated the length of time it will take to complete each stage and completed the flow chart shown below.

|   | *Weeks* |   |
|---|---------|---|
| A | 16 | Hardware redesign |
| B | 12 | Manufacture of prototype |
| C | 6 | Modification of production line |
| D | 10 | EC Safety testing |
| E | 12 | Training of field staff |
| F | 10 | Manufacture of launch stock |

Complete a critical path analysis for this project. What is the shortest time in which the project can be completed? Identify the critical path.

Briefly, in report format, comment on the problems encountered in applying critical path techniques to projects in the real business situation.

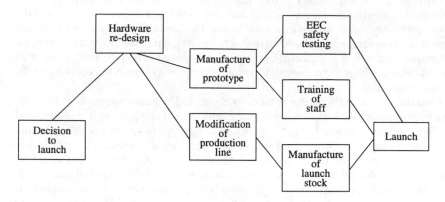

2. It is estimated that over 90 per cent of new products launched onto the market fail. You are the 'new product development' manager of a major company that manufactures communications equipment. Your design engineer is second to none in the world and has just come up with a prototype portable telephone which has greater range and more features than any on the market. Moreover, by clever circuit integration and your advanced CAD/CAM capabilities (Computer Aided Design and Computer Aided Manufacture), he thinks that it should be possible to produce this product at a price that might allow penetration of the higher end of the domestic, as well as the small business, market. You have decided to proceed with the project. In 'new product development' terms what issues must be considered to maximize the chance of a successful market introduction?

## FURTHER READING

Dussauge, P. *et al*. (1987) *Strategic Technology Management*, John Wiley.

Kotler, P. (1991) *Marketing Management; Analysis, Planning, Implementation and Control*, 7th Edition, Prentice-Hall.

Schroeder, R.G. (1989) *Operations Management*, 3rd Edition, McGraw-Hill.

CHAPTER
# **ELEVEN**
## HUMAN RESOURCES—MANAGING PEOPLE

In Chapter Four, we discussed some of the basic characteristics of people. In Chapter Five, we discussed the characteristics of customers and markets. With our basic understanding of infrastructure and operations, we should now be in a position to discuss how to begin implementing business plans. A marketing person when asked who are the most important people to a company will respond 'customers'. The human resources manager when asked what the firm's most important resource is will respond 'our people'. Both are right. Without customers, the company will not be able to sell any products or services and equally, without responsive, motivated, well-trained staff, the company will not be able to meet customer needs. In this chapter, the central role of human resource planning is discussed. There is a short digression as to how this affects the graduate engineer when applying for a job, and then we return to the management of career development. In conclusion, the formal responsibilities of personnel in areas such as health and safety, equal opportunities and industrial relations are presented.

### 11.1 THE ROLES OF THE LINE MANAGER AND THE FUNCTION OF PERSONNEL

In discussing the formulation of budgets, the problems of possibly remote central expertise and 'front line' responsibility were outlined. The responsibility for the effective management of a department or function resides with the line manager responsible for that function. The manager of a department is responsible for the career development and training of his/her staff. This specific responsibility is often called 'direct line responsibility'. The role of the personnel department is to provide the support to ensure that the line manager has the capability of fulfilling this responsibility, to ensure that appropriate resources exist (central training programmes etc.), to audit procedures and ensure uniformity of treatment (such as disciplinary procedures) and to provide certain central functions (much in the same way as a treasury and tax accountant has certain specific and important roles to play, not associated with the conduct of the actual core business). Such activities will be the central management of industrial relations, the maintenance of appropriate legal records (such as sickness, equal opportunity, etc.) and the effective provision of training to all staff, both senior management and front line operational staff.

### 11.2 HUMAN RESOURCE PLANNING—THE STRATEGIC ISSUES

The strategic management of a company requires that it examines its markets and its ability to serve these markets. To serve these markets, the company needs to maintain and

285

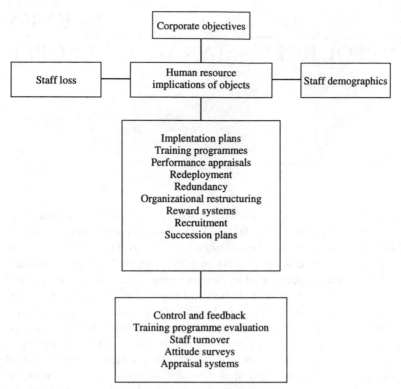

**Figure 11.1**   Strategic implications of human resources

develop its capabilities. The creative direction of a firm resides with the staff and their skills, not in the physical assets of the company. If the computer room burns down, the insurance will provide a new facility within days. The company staff will ensure that it works. If by some strange accident all the staff were to vanish, the real skills of the company would have disappeared and recovery would be impossible even if all the infrastructure were in place. To maintain and develop the company, the skill base and staff demographics need to be examined as part of the implementation strategy. The normal process of strategic management contains, the three steps:

1. Where are we?
2. Where do we want and need to be?
3. What do we need to do to get there?

In human resources terms, we can express this as shown in Fig. 11.1. The human resource objectives will be to have the right mix of people, with the right skills, for the implementation of the next period of the firm's strategic plans. Two obvious problems will stand in the way of this. The firm's existing staff demographics (skill profiles, numbers and types of people, age distributions etc.) will be unlikely to match that which will be required. Moreover, even in the steady state, company people leave the firm (retire, find other jobs etc.). The firm needs to appraise the make-up and skill profile of its existing workforce. In value chain terms, a human resources audit is required. Just like the marketing information system, this should not be a one-off exercise every time the firm hits a crisis, but rather be part of the normal control and feedback system. The firm may make some judgements about staff loss. Some types of staff loss, such as retirement, can be anticipated with confidence, but others may be more difficult. This is an issue that needs to be managed.

The action plan will include training to provide existing staff with the skills they will need for any new directions the firm intends to travel in. To decide which staff need training and just what training is necessary, individual performance appraisals will be required. Where people may not be able to acquire the new skills, they may need to be moved (redeployed) to other parts of the organization. If this is not possible, the firm may have no option but to make staff that can no longer fit the organization redundant. This is never easy, but to retain staff that cannot make a full contribution will corrode the competitive capability of the firm and, in any case, staff in such situations need to be helped to find roles that will fully exploit their skills. A forced move from the company is never easy, but is essential for the good health of all concerned in the longer term.

The changes in technology or strategy may well require new organizational structures. Organization structure was covered in Chapter Eight as, although organization structure involves human resource issues, these have to be considered in the broader context of the external (markets and technologies) strategies that the company operates and the selected strategies that the firm intends to pursue (such as level of backwards or forwards integration).

The reward system is more complex than the simple pay structure. It includes non-cash, but nevertheless valuable, rewards, such as payment in kind (company cars) and recognition. Pay itself is not a positive motivator, for long but poor reward systems which are seen to be unfair or inappropriate are powerful demotivators. The achievement of a satisfactory redundancy system (both for employees and the firm) is a necessary foundation. It is a hygiene factor in Herzberg theory (see Chapter 4).

The firm may not recruit for the more demanding jobs, but promote people who have developed the experience and skills that the company wants. Promotions from inside the company may be perceived as safer than senior appointments from outside the organization. People promoted from inside the organization are known and will understand the cultural structure of organization. A key requirement of training and career development plans is not only to fit people in the firm to their existing jobs, but also to the roles that they may be called upon to fulfil in the next few years. The identification of people for promotion, and the early training and development of such people, is known as succession planning. Where gaps occur either for specific high level roles where succession potential is not available, or to fill gaps left by loss or promotion at lower levels, recruitment is necessary.

One global feedback mechanism for the success of human resource plans is to monitor the staff turnover. Does our firm lose more people than other comparable firms? A sensitive test is to get a respected person to interview leaving staff to gain some idea for their motivation. People may leave for good personal reasons, but if a significant number of people are leaving because they feel 'career blocked', this may indicate some serious issues that need management attention. This is, of course, rather late in the day and many firms will employ external consultants from time to time who (on a confidential basis to the interviewed individuals) will survey people in the organization and determine their attitudes and feelings towards the company and their roles within the organization. The appraisal system, with the training programme evaluation, can provide a consistent feedback of the effectiveness of existing policies. Over the next sections of this chapter these issues will be considered in some detail.

## 11.3 JOB DESIGN

To recruit a person without knowing the objectives is like placing a brief with an advertising agency without understanding the communications objectives. The temptation for the inexperienced manager is to design a detailed organizational structure in much the same way as one would design a computer network. All you need is a certain number of file servers, terminals peripherals and away you go. In Chapter Four, we understood that we are more complex than file servers, people have social and emotional needs. If management does not take account of these elements of personality and personal satisfaction, the result will be dissatisfaction and under-performance of the workforce. In times of recession, this problem may be masked by the fear of job loss. However, when job markets are more buoyant, not only will there be a loss of effectiveness and efficiency but also an actual increase in labour turnover (the number of people who leave and have to be replaced). The key issues and action areas will be identified here. Further leading references are given at the end of this chapter.

From our motivational theory, we can appreciate that people like to be recognized, to be perceived to have made a meaningful contribution to the organization to their own and others' satisfaction. The so-called 'scientific' management movement, with its heavy emphasis on mechanistic time and motion studies and efficiency of physical operations, tended to break down operations to small units below human dimensions. People could be trained to perform some small unit operation in a few days. If they should leave, another could be trained at little cost and modest impact. The paradox of this situation was that complex assembly lines were manned by inflexible, low skilled people, without any real motivations, apart from fear and money, to perform. Another problem was that such work did not develop people's potential so a division occurred between those who could see some career progression and those who could only see more of the same for the rest of their working lives. Apart from the ethical and human issues involved in this type of working, in the end its apparent tidiness concealed that people are complex and to get them to perform to their maximum potential requires more flexible and imaginative solutions.

In constructing roles within a new organizational structure, the manager should consider the nature of the people to be involved and consider that the jobs should be of appropriate dimensions. Just in the way that a firm may have forwards and backwards integration and may diversify horizontally, the same is true of roles. A major problem in the 60s movement towards equal opportunity and equal pay was the 'all female [low] grade job'. Below the roles of an old style typist in the typing pool is compared with the role of administrative assistant in the context of a quality assurance department.

---

### ROLE OF 60s TYPIST IN A TYPING POOL

**Contact with customers**   None, work submitted with a cover document either hand written or on tape. Note that in this context customer is taken to be both internal and external customers.

**Technology**   Electro-mechanical typewriter, little if any, error correction capability. Little communications capability. Audio typing considered high technology.

**Understanding of work**   None, operator required to type what was written without any discretion or understanding of the content or technology.

**Performance criteria**   Numbers of errors and amount of work requiring retyping. Appraisal simple and mechanistic.

**Career development opportunity**   None, trapped by the all female grade with no chance to develop skills to make a larger contribution to the firm.

**Time span of discretion**   Discretion limited to possibly selecting the order of the day's work and when to change the ribbon on the typewriter.

**Training needed**   Considerable physical skill needed to reach high speeds, but little intellectual content. One or two years' day release for RSA and little further training needed.

**Satisfaction**   Mixed, for those interested in work zero. Many people were happy in this system as the group developed its own social structure and people developed their work satisfaction from the social interaction in the work group, rather than the work itself.

## ROLE OF 90s ADMINISTRATION ASSISTANT

**Contact with customers**   Expected to be proactive, visiting other departments to resolve issues, in direct contact (E-mail, telephone, fax) with other locations and with customers.

**Technology**   Wide range of high technology equipment (computers, printers, communications) with wide range of specialist and advanced software.

**Understanding of work**   Not only required to understand the wide range of technology, but also the context of contribution and be able to make discretionary inputs (such as corrections of errors). Expected to make a full contribution to the development of the department with suggestions and improvements to customer service.

**Performance criteria**   Complex and depends on diffuse criteria, such as effectiveness (doing the right things) as well as efficiency (doing them in a resource efficient way) and intangible elements associated with higher level jobs, such as initiative and customer satisfaction.

**Career development opportunity**   Range and depth of experience gives scope to move into other areas, such as marketing.

**Time span of discretion**   Considerable, given great scope for own innovation, has control of ordering own work schedule within limits but can also make changes to the way in which the work is done (within prescribed limits).

**Training needed**   Large, involving not only the skills to use a wide range of ever-changing equipment and software, but expected to be involved in the business with product and market knowledge (so as to be able to assist both internal and external customers). Would be seen as a key person for training in activities such as quality awareness programmes as in direct 'moment of truth' contact with customers. Training seen as an on-going and never ending process.

**Satisfaction**   Wider, more open, range of social contacts in the organization. However, need to be much more self-reliant, self-assured and assertive. High levels of satisfaction to those who can accept the challenge. Threatening and isolating for those who do not have the higher level of capability required.

---

The implementation of an organization structure requires immense skill and understanding of the detail and complexity involved in jobs in competitive and technology rich turbulent industries. Job satisfaction does not mean that every person wants or needs to become, for their own self-fulfilment, managing director. People's need for new challenges can be met by appropriate job design and movement. To start another job at the same level within the same organization is a broadening experience and prevents a feeling of being trapped. This job rotation also brings an advantage to the firm in terms of people's broader understanding and commitment to the firm's activities.

## 11.4 ROLE DEFINITION

A role definition is required to provide the manager and the individual with some shared identification of the role. The personnel department can use such a definition to decide the appropriate level of pay by a process of job evaluation. Other departments and people can see how roles link. The role definition is the starting point for the appraisal process, in recruitment it is necessary to define the nature of the position that needs to be filled.

There is no single framework for the role specification or job description. One framework is presented which contains all the major elements common to most systems, however, deviations from organization to organization in the detail are to be expected.

---

### JOB DESCRIPTION

*Job title*   A short meaningful title for the job.

*Department*   In a major company this would include information of site, SBU and department.

*Organization structure*   Who the person reports to, who reports to the person. Links with other departments.

*Purpose*   Key reasons for the role, 'to provide customers with quality assurance documentation'.

*Dimensions*   Annual budget the person is responsible for. Expenditure limits, numbers and nature of subordinate staff. Size of the business operation serviced. Range, diversity and capital value of equipment used.

*Authority limits*   Limits of authority such as scope for disciplining subordinate staff.

*Scope of role*   A focused expansion of the nature of the duties, responsibilities, outputs, actions and inputs required of the individual. Will contain specific references to responsibilities for safety in the workplace and training responsibilities for subordinate staff.

*Qualifications required*   Some roles require formal qualifications. In a safety critical area, only a chartered engineer may be an acceptable signature authority for a permit to work in a potential hazardous environment.

*Contacts*   Some high level jobs may have rather small dimensions in some of the other areas (such as a buyer), but have considerable impact on the organization through contacts more outside the organization than within.

*Key accountabilities* Those specific areas that will form objectives for the appraisal discussions. Will contain explicit requirements for keeping expenses within budget, performance levels in terms of volume and quality, as appropriate to the role.

## 11.5 RECRUITMENT

Recruitment is part of the implementation strategy of the firm. Just as a firm should not continue to attend an annual trade show each year as a matter of custom, so when a vacancy occurs it should not necessarily involve recruitment. It should be regarded as an opportunity to re-examine the way work is done, how roles may be restructured or redefined. In many cases the resulting management appraisal will involve such changes and the recruitment of a person for a redefined role that did not exist before the management analysis. Figure 11.2 shows the basic recruitment process.

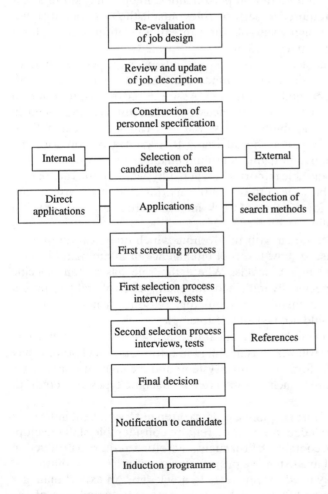

**Figure 11.2** Selection process

In the previous sections, we considered the process of job design and the conversion of this into a role definition or job description. From the job description, we can then draw up the 'profile' or specification of the range of acceptable parameters we require of the person for the role that has been defined. These should be classified as essential and desirable. The perfect person does not exist, to a greater or lesser extent any given candidate will deviate from the ideal profile. This identification of the ideal profile and the noting of deviation is important as it starts to define the key points to be covered in the selected candidate's induction programme.

Typical points that might be covered in a personnel specification are:

1. *Physical*  May not be critical for many roles, but serious consideration should always be given to this question. It is often not remembered that in the electronics industry, colour blindness is a serious problem and it might be wise to cover this issue if selecting a person for a role where colour codes are important. As part of the selection process there should be a medical examination.

2. *Personality*  Different roles require different personalities. People may suffer stress and under perform if they are required to perform roles outside their personality type. An introverted person may be highly suitable for a research position, but not for a sales job with a high customer contact content.

3. *Intelligence*  This model of the selection process extends over the whole range of staff. For certain roles, especially in recession times, the firm may be presented with candidates who have too much capability for the job. As was noted in Chapter Four, to be required to carry out a job below one's capacity is as stressful as being asked to complete a task beyond one's capability. Unless the firm can see a clear path to promote such a person quickly it may be advisable to recruit a person with the appropriate, rather than the maximum, amount of intelligence.

4. *Aptitude*  This can be of considerable importance where physical activities are part of the job, such as scientific glass blowing or the assembly of printed circuit boards. Some people have greater aptitudes for this type of work and are more likely to complete a training programme successfully.

5. *Qualifications*  Care should be taken with this to note which qualification may be included for indicative reasons, to show levels of intelligence or attainment. Typical qualifications in this area will be 'A' levels. Where the role has certain specific requirements these must be specifically indicated, for example, a role may require a chartered engineer or chartered chemist for regulatory reasons. A person without these specific qualifications would not be suitable to employ.

6. *Training*  In today's fast moving industrial context formal qualifications can become out of date very quickly. A person who has qualified in information technology may not have specific training on the firm's operating systems and the high level languages used. Where skills in specific areas such as software and machine types are required, these should be indicated.

7. *Experience*  The possession of formal qualifications is often not a sufficient indication of the capability to apply knowledge. Some roles require considerable skill development rather than just academic content. A firm might, therefore, require a production engineer for a new factory to have extensive project management responsibilities.

8. *Knowledge*  Certain roles may need specific sets of knowledge. An export manager for an electronics company may be required to have extensive knowledge of the

documentation requirements for exports to the USA, for example. Many people have language skills that are not reflected in their formal qualifications. Where language skills are required, the level of proficiency should be indicated rather than a formal qualification. There are many people who have grown up in bilingual environments.

9. *Achievements*   One indicator of the potential to perform in a new role is a record of past achievements in past positions.

10. *Personal circumstances*   If a job requires extensive out of hours work or a lot of overseas travel and secondments, it is wise to check that candidates selected for interview have the personal circumstances which will allow the required working life style.

11. *Odd issues*   Certain other issues may be important from simple ones such as having to hold a full UK driving licence (clean), to more sensitive issues, such as the requirement of being security-cleared and signing the Official Secrets Act before work on Ministry of Defence contracts with security aspects.

The search for suitable candidates is very like marketing. The manager, in consultation with the personnel function, needs to define likely areas where suitable candidates exist. In the real world the ideal candidate does not exist, so the objective at this stage is limited to attracting a reasonable number (perhaps nine to twelve) of suitable candidates with close to ideal specifications. If the firm has enough potential candidates identified from the internal records and 'speculative' applications on file, there may be no need to undertake the time, trouble and expense of any further searching.

---

## OUTLINE JOB DESCRIPTION

### SENIOR FIELD NETWORK INSTALLATION ENGINEER

*Job Title*   Senior Field Network Installation Engineer – UK

*Department*   Customer support

*Organization structure*   Reports to Customer Services Manager, Europe, responsible for 4 Site Installation Engineers and 26 technical installation staff.

*Purpose*   Installation of equipment into customer's premises.

*Dimensions*   Operating budget of £950 000. Responsible for the installation of approximately £32 000 000 of equipment a year at contract value. Responsible for 4 graduate and 26 other technical staff working on 4 different customer locations at any one time. Supervising some 55 contracts a year.

*Authority limits*   Responsible for the authorization of field accommodation expenses to an annual budget of £150 000. Responsible for the hire of temporary non-skilled labour as required on specific contracts.

*Scope of role*   To supervise the orderly completion of customer installation contracts of equipment and necessary network cabling. Time critical role, as payment for contract on completion of installation and performance of installed system to specification. Required to ensure correct installation in a wide range of diverse types of customer premises. Responsible for the safe working and discipline of scattered company work force operating on customer premises, where the highest standards of work and behaviour are essential to the company reputation. Must respect the confidentiality of contract information, as may be installing equipment in customer's premises where the customer is in direct competition in their own markets. Role demands a high level of leadership, managerial and organizational skills. A high content of customer involvement is required to minimize disruption during installation and ensuring equipment performs to customer requirements. Customers often need assistance to fully specify their requirements. Good negotiating and a high level of practical and theoretical engineering skills are needed to resolve field problems as they occur.

*Qualifications required* Chartered Engineer, B.Eng. Comms., or Information Technology Engineering.

*Contacts* Internal: Marketing and Sales, Production, Distribution, Development, and Field Service Departments. Needs to agree extra work as required with customer and inform Sales and Accounts. High level of contact with customer's technical and operational staff. Extensive contact with suppliers of computer equipment to customers to ensure correct interfacing to networks.

*Key accountabilities* Completion of contracts to time and on budget. Maintenance of appropriate recording systems for all work conducted. Ensure complete documentation of all installed systems, including updates. Maintenance of good relations with customers and third party suppliers. To ensure the appropriate career development and training of all staff under his/her management control. To ensure the safe installation of all equipment in accordance with any customer or site specific requirements. To ensure the safe working of staff according to legislation, company rules and any specific site and/or customer requirements. To be responsible for the verification and authorization of accommodation expenses of field staff.

---

## OUTLINE PERSONNEL SPECIFICATION FOR COMMUNICATIONS ENGINEER

### SENIOR FIELD NETWORK INSTALLATION ENGINEER

*Physical* Normal requirements for an Electronic Engineer, must not be colour blind. Given the need for extensive travel and installation in adverse environments, must have very good general health.

*Personality* Must be able to motivate and lead staff, must have an assertive, but not arrogant, attitude to ensure that field staff work to schedules. Must have a good outgoing personality to negotiate and liaise with customer's staff.

*Intelligence* Good, but not exceptional, man management and practical problem solving skills more important.

*Aptitude* No specific physical aptitudes are required.

*Qualifications* Chartered Engineer essential, degree can be in communications (with digital options) or information technology.

*Training* Needs to understand all safety requirements, have a good knowledge of system documentation procedures in a BS5750 environment. Must have extensive working knowledge of UNIX systems and network management.

*Experience*   Field experience in network management.

*Knowledge*   Extensive knowledge of UNIX, BS5750 procedures, network management. Given the multinational nature of many of the customers, knowledge of one or more European languages desirable.

*Achievements*   Network or project management at a substantial level with proven track record.

*Personal circumstances*   Must be able to travel and stay away from home base as contracts demand. Must be able to provide assistance with overseas contracts when situation demands.

*Odd issues*   Given the extensive travel must have a full UK driving licence. High customer involvement requires some experience of field support or engineering sales.

---

For many jobs an advertisement in the appropriate journal paper or journal may well be appropriate. However, there are a number of problems. This can be very expensive, copy times may be long and, if the advertisement is not written with care, vast numbers of inappropriate candidates might be attracted. The company may then have the difficult problem of selecting a first short list of 12 from several hundred applications. The advertisement copy should be written with considerable care to attract only the desired types of candidates.

Apart from cost and time, there can be problems of confidentiality. If the company has decided to move into a new software area, it might as well write to its competitors as advertise for design engineers in the new area of competition. Another problem might be when a company has a senior executive who is under performing, say a works manager. It is a little difficult to advertise for a new works manager under such conditions. In these types of situations, the agency or head hunter may be the appropriate mechanism. The advantage of this system is that the list can be brought down to the second selection process by the head hunters or agency (provided they have been given a good brief in terms of personnel specification). At that stage, the candidates may not even know which company is looking for new staff until they are selected for the final selection process. The majority of jobs are not filled by external advertising but by internal promotion or the other methods discussed above. This is why your CV is so important.

The process of first screening should be a simple process if the personnel specification has been well written. Any candidates that do not satisfy the essential criteria are eliminated. The remaining candidates can be grouped according to how closely they satisfy the additional desirable characteristics. The first selection process can involve several approaches. At some stage of almost all job applications it will involve an interview. This is not only a chance for the firm to determine facts about the candidate, but for the candidate to gain more information about the firm and the role under discussion. The purpose of the interview is to attempt to determine parameters that have not come out in the CV or application form and to provide some three-dimensional colour to the bare facts. However, about the only agreement you will find with personnel specialists is the difficulty of using the interview as a sole selection process. Hence, increasingly, major firms are using tests from hand writing through intelligence and aptitude tests and personality tests. Other types of activities may be group working or group discussions under close observation.

In practical terms, any process used at the first selection process can be used at the second selection process. In general, three differences are encountered. During the first selection process, the personnel specialists may complete all the work and the line managers concerned will only be involved when the candidate group has been reduced to a final short list. The more time-intensive selection exercises, such as candidate presentations, are most often reserved to the final selection process, given the heavy management cost implications to the employing organization. Depending on the company policy, medical examination and approaches to referees may take place before or after this second selection process. An offer subject to the last two conditions may leave the firm in a difficult situation in the event that either turn out to be unsatisfactory. Other candidates may have been informed and the company may find that it has to start the whole selection process over again. To cope with this issue, most selection processes will end up with an offer candidate and one or two 'reserves'. Other candidates will be released but the reserves only informed once a definite acceptance has been obtained.

The whole process of selection, interviewing and informing candidates is highly sensitive. All discussions and documents should be treated in the strictest confidence. Great care should be taken to ensure that all requirements of equal opportunity and access are observed where required (as stated before in certain areas such as security employment different rules may apply). The professional and specialist skills of the personnel manager are invaluable in assisting the line manager to complete this process in a professional way and without too much diversion of effort from the front line task, servicing customer needs.

Too often in poorly managed firms, the confirmed offer and acceptance is seen as the end of the selection process. As always, there should be control and feedback. What parts of the selection process yielded useful information, what parts took up management time but contributed little. The person appointed will, in most cases, differ in some ways to the ideal personnel specification in experience, knowledge and skills. The evaluation of this specification gap provides a good pointer to the specific requirements of the induction training programme.

Induction is the preliminary training and orientation that a new employee receives over the first six months of employment. The career development process is ongoing for senior staff and for new graduate entry staff is an especially intensive process for the person's first five to ten years with the organization.

## 11.6 THE CV

For many readers of this book, the job search will be a major activity. This brief section examines the implication of our knowledge of marketing and additional understandings in this chapter to improve your competitiveness in the job search, job application, interview and selection process. The objective from your view is that you do not want a job, you want a *good* job, *the* job. The approach 'gimme a job, I need it' is not what will succeed.

Two key features of the process need to be remembered. Job search is a personal marketing operation, you are the product and the customers are the prospective employers. They have needs, they have a problem (in marketing terms, a benefit need). The whole purpose is to identify attractive opportunities where you will have a competitive advantage. Once you have done this, the next stage is pure and simple marketing communications. The CV must be true, but it is not an information document (any more than an advertisement), it is a personal marketing document intended to move the employer down the path, awareness to interest, interest in this context meaning wanting to interview you. At the interview and selection meetings you can then complete the process to desire and action (offer you a job).

So what type of CV will gain you an interview? From the earlier discussions we know that the employer will have the personnel specification, which details the type of person who will satisfy the firm's needs. The purpose of your letter and CV should be to ensure that you address the employer's issues (not yours, you are marketing not selling) and set these out in an attractive way that will differentiate you from the 90 per cent of potential candidates that do not get selected for interview. There is no single right way to write a CV, the one that is right is the one that gets the interview. The suggestions below are one approach, but you must find the specific framework that you feel is right for you and will convey your skills and capability in a competitive way.

There is considerable debate as to whether a CV should be one page or not. The view suggested is that it should be as long as is needed to convey a good impression of your strengths for the position sought. If it takes three pages, this is fully acceptable and much better than a crowded one page CV in 8 point type with 5mm margins. However, two key points should be remembered. The first reading of a CV by a potential employer is not likely to be a reading but a quick scan, which may well last less than one minute. Therefore, ensure a good structure, with lots of white space and good sub-headings. On the first scan the future employer need almost look no further than the headings, sub-headings and first lines. Having generated interest, the rest of the CV will be read in more detail. In many situations, the front page only of the CV may be photocopied and distributed (hence the suggestion that the CV should be one page only). However, the skill is to ensure that there is a complete outline of your profile on the first page that is self-standing, the development and detail can then be continued on pages two and three as required. The CV and/or application form should be accompanied with a brief covering letter which is linked to the specific application. In this letter you should again link any key skills needed. Thus, in the case considered above for a communications engineer, an applicant might write (based on real experience) '. . . I am a Communications Engineer with practical work experience of digital networks. My final year project was in linking LANs into satellite systems and, coupled with my excellent working knowledge of French gained on my work placement in Paris, I feel I have much to offer and would be pleased to discuss this opportunity with you further . . .'. Below is an outline CV for such a communications engineer with some comments in italics suggesting the reasons for this layout. However, it is not suggested that this is in any sense a model or perfect structure. It is a basis for you to consider how best to present yourself. This CV should be held on disk, modified as required for each specific application and printed out on the best printer that you have available (PostScript Laser is ideal). With regard to fonts, again the selection is a matter of personal choice of what you think will represent you, but do avoid extravagant fonts, if in doubt, Times Roman is a safe bet (widely used, easy to read, proportional type). Note that a proportional type allows you to get more into a given line length without any apparent crowding to the reader.

## Curriculum Vitae

### Alan John Stanley

| **Term address** | **Home address** |
|---|---|
| 25 East Walk, | 76 Old Harbour, |
| University Town, | Home Town, |
| County T86 E52 | County T86 E52 |
| Telephone 095 43575 | Telephone 088 78347 |
| Fax 095 87805 | Fax 088 87484 |

*Ensure that you can be contacted at short notice at all times. You might be on a reserve list, if a candidate withdraws at a late stage, make certain you are the one that can be contacted quickly. If there is a fax facility at the college or if your parents, brother or sister have access to a fax at your home address, why not give it? Remember, if you are applying for an international position, to give the UK international dialling code.*

**A graduate engineer with experience of digital networks**
**Bilingual in English and French**

An honours B.Eng. (Communications) Engineer with work experience in Paris with 'NetWork France' on digital communications systems. Final year project was in interfacing LAN networks via satellite links.

*This brief note gives an instant profile with an invitation to read on, in this case with details of the work experience.*

### Qualifications

B.Eng. Communications Engineering 2.1

*It is probable that the employer will not be familiar with your course. Provide brief details of options taken and core topics. Remember to include other aspects of the course, such as presentation skills and business studies. If the course contained a final year project a few lines about this may well be very appropriate. This shows the ability to integrate theory and practical needs to solve a real problem and to implement and present a solution. Of course, note any special awards or prizes that might have been gained.*

HND / A levels (as appropriate)

*Give the subjects passed with grades, if they are good. Note, as you go back into the past the detail is less important, concentrate on the recent and that relevant to the specific job in question. Do note any prizes or exceptional project work.*

OND, etc. (as appropriate)

*Brief statement is in order, grades unless exceptional are not important, do note any prizes or exceptional project work.*

### Work experience

*Put the most recent and relevant experience first. If you had a good placement and a few odd jobs to earn money in the vacation put your key work experience first. Refer to your vacation work in brief outline only, highlighting any specific points which might be appropriate, such as ability to assume responsibility.*

*The industrial work experience is a most important section as it may be the key place to differentiate yourself from other 2.1 graduate engineers. Again no fixed format is suggested, but four topic areas should be covered briefly:*

### 1. Employer

*Give not only the name of the employer but also some brief statement of the nature of the business. Remember your future employer may not be familiar with the company and/or with a large organization, the simple name might not give much of an indication (IBM could mean almost anything). If you are restricted by requirements such as the Official Secrets Act (working in a Ministry of Defence area or supplier) it might be wise to note this fact and let the potential employer know why you have not been able to put the full detail in. This will be respected.*

### 2. Department and role

*This is to give a brief outline of the situation so that it sets the stage for the next two sections. The key issue to remember is that the employer is not interested in what you did, except as an indication as to what skills and capability you have developed and how this might be transplanted into the interviewing organization. After a few years of industrial experience there should be some reference to the dimensions of the job, number of subordinate staff, operating budgets etc.*

### 3. Outline the transferable skills gained

*This, in some ways, is the key section, so outline the technical skills developed (implementation of UNIX systems, programming languages, etc.), taking great care to consider all the relevant skills, which may include such issues as documentation as well as strict technical skills.*

*Remember to include other areas of skill or knowledge: 'able to construct and give presentations after Company Sales Engineers Presentation Course' etc. Note familiarity with business systems (preparation of budgets, Quality Assurance in BS5750 environment, etc.).*

*This is a most difficult section to write as in your basic CV (to be edited for any specific job application) you need to list all the skills you have acquired for a range of potential employers (you edit down, as needed, later).*

### 4. Outline achievements

*Very often we take our achievements for granted. This is not the place to do this. So, if on your placement you had a some small project to complete, you might have 'completed installation project for xxxx 4 weeks inside schedule and £5000 within budget. Was awarded employee of the month on the Birmingham site for this'. Achievements might be reduction of costs, improvement of quality, acceptance of a design for production, reduction of manufacturing costs, adaptation of some software or hardware etc. If you have any publications or patents these can be referred to here or in a separate section.*

*It is important to note what you are doing in this section. The first stages make it easy for the potential employer to understand the latter two sections. The normal problem with CVs is that not enough information is given in section one and limited information given in section two, often sections three and four are not included. Thus the future employer is left attempting to guess what skills you might have. If there is another CV which does not give this problem, the latter person will be invited for interview. Section three is critical, as it spells out to the future employer specific skills that should be of direct use if you were recruited in your new roles. The importance of section four is that it says to the new employer that you have achieved in your last role and that you will be able to achieve in your new organization.*

### Other skills and/or information

*If you have not listed all your knowledge and experience of computer systems, languages and packages, now is the place to do it. If you have a driving licence, note it. You may have other skills or knowledge, such as foreign languages. Make certain they are included.*

### Professional memberships

*If you are a student member of one of the engineering institutes, note this, with your wish to proceed to full chartered status.*

### Personal interests

*'Like rock music and drinking' is not likely to impress an employer. Nor is 'like reading, music, walking and travel'. Remember the purpose of this section is to give some colour and further indication as to why you might have characteristics that will make you an interesting prospect as an employee. 'Like music, grade 8 Violin, leader of college orchestra' is appropriate. It suggests to the future employer that even in your leisure time you have the ability to succeed and take a substantive interest. It shows a three-dimensional character with the ability to get on with people.*

*The essential point is to show the employer that you are a real person, that you have substantive interests, have a personality and relate not only in a formal work context, but in a social context. Where there are achievements these should be indicated: 'Enjoy sailing, represented England in the 1993 World Championships in the xxxx class'.*

### Referees

*In general, it is appropriate to give two references; one academic and one industrial. However, you should have a collection of three or four potential referees and select the most appropriate for the application in hand. You should not give a name without the agreement of the person concerned. It is also often useful to provide a copy of your CV. This is convenient for the referee as it may make it easier to provide information in references, such as dates, so it is all to hand for them. Take care here to ensure the right title (Dr, Prof.; indicate if a Chartered Engineer), indicate job title (such as Production Director) and give not only the address but fax and telephone numbers. You need to make it as easy as possible for a potential employer to contact your referees when required.*

---

### 11.6.1 Housekeeping points

Do ensure that this document is produced on the best word processing or desktop publishing system you have access to, and use a laser printer if possible. Do use a good, easy to read, proportional font, do not use lots of different font types, some variation in size and the occasional use of italics may well be advantageous. It is suggested that underlining is an old way of drawing attention to a section of text when such documents were typed, now it may be much more appropriate to make a heading two point sizes larger (12 point for the text and 14 point for the headings) and simply bold. Do run the spell check program! If you draft on one printer and then move to a laser for the final version, check for any odd alignment problems. Use only the best quality paper, as this document is a personal statement about you. Keep an updated version on disk at all times in your career, have a back-up copy. You may find that the ideal opportunity appears but the closing date is today. If you have an up-to-date CV, you can complete and fax an impressive application in less than an hour.

Final point to remember, if you can't take trouble over the production of your CV, what indication does the future employer have that you will take trouble over your work for the new organization?

The above is a brief outline only. The production of a CV takes time and trouble but it is one of the most important documents in your life. Once you have a good master version to copy and amend, it is a matter of a few minutes. Do get a few trusted people to read your CV and give you some constructive feedback, to discuss your draft with your referees is often ideal.

The interview will be a period of a little stress. However, view the tension as something to bring out the best in you. Remember the employer has a problem, they need a member of staff and you are their potential solution. To increase your confidence, do some market research, check for any press reports on the company in the recent past, check the business section of your library, there may well be a copy of the annual report. If not, just ring up the personnel department and ask if they can send you one. If attending an interview at a distant location in a strange town, leave plenty of time to ensure that you can arrive at the appointment without rushing. If you are driving make certain that you will be able to park.

## 11.7 APPRAISAL

Any management system must have a feedback and control system. A cornerstone of feedback and control in human resource management is the appraisal system. In a well-managed company, this is not the substitute for the day-to-day and periodic formal and informal discussion of performance between a manager and his/her staff. This continual process is essential to the effective management and motivation of the individual teams, but there needs to be a coordinating and integrating formal scheme which overlays this, the formal appraisal system

The objective of the appraisal interview is for the manager and the member of staff to review progress over the last year against the objectives that were agreed at the last appraisal. At this stage of the interview, an open ended discussion may be initiated as to how the job has developed, how the role definition and job description may need amendment and the problems that may have needed to be overcome to meet (or prevented) attainment of the objectives. This discussion needs the greatest amount of skill on the part of the appraising manager or else it can be perceived as a confrontational, judgemental exercise and aggressive and defensive responses can be induced. For the process to be successful, the interview has to take place in an atmosphere of openness and trust. This is not easy as there has to be an element of role conflict between the role of counselling and managing (the employee is expected to share with the manager, who will decide pay levels later, ways in which the appraised may have performed less well than ideal). On the basis of this review of performance against objectives, the manager can consider with the appraised member of staff their strengths and weaknesses and provide feedback on performance.

Such reviews can touch on such sensitive issues as underperformance that have been identified, which may be related to an employee's personal problems (the individual's health, drink or drug problems, marital breakdown, bereavement, financial problems). Here the manager may well have to be involved in the counselling and may need to make reference to specialist support from the personnel function.

Having reviewed the past, the future needs to be addressed with objectives to be set for the next period. This requires a process of assertive negotiation on both sides. Objectives may not be imposed on a person. If the objectives are not accepted as challenging and realistic but impossible, the person will not even attempt to try to attain them. The appraisal process will then be seen as some political paper exercise to set people up for later criticism for under-performance.

If the appraisal process has been well conducted, with weaknesses and objectives well identified and agreed, the manager and the subordinate member of staff will understand the skill and career development needed to enable and empower that person to meet the next objectives. This can be translated into an outline agreed action programme of formal training (new qualifications to work for, internal or external courses and informal training (structured work experience, visits to other departments, customers etc.). Again, the training needs and outline programme, should be a shared and agreed outcome from the discussion.

After all this discussion, the firm's appraisal documentation will need completion. In most organizations, this documentation will have been completed during the appraisal process from pre-prepared notes. After completion of the appraisal the manager, in most systems, will be required to ask the member of staff to record his/her comments and agreement to the appraisal record. If all has gone well, the documentation will be reviewed by the appropriate senior line manager (the boss of the appraising manager) and then forwarded to the central personnel department.

The personnel department has a number of important formal roles. One important role is to manage the situation in the event that the manager and the member of staff are unable to agree the appraisal. The appraisal document will record the person's dissent to the appraisal and the personnel department will have then to ensure that an appropriate appeals system is in operation and works. In most organizations such a situation will be referred to the appraising manager's manager—the manager once removed—for a second appraisal discussion (if this still does not resolve the problem, resort is often made to the firm's grievance procedure). To prevent this happening without good cause, the personnel department will ensure that all appraising managers have been properly trained (this is a difficult and sensitive management role) and that staff to be appraised have been properly briefed as to what to expect and the procedures to be used (Trade Unions and staff representatives should be involved where such agreements exist). The personnel department will also be looking for its own feedback and control and will evaluate the quality of appraisals returned from managers (also ensure that all staff have been appraised). The personnel department will be responsible for ensuring a reasonable time scale for the completion of appraisals and ensuring that all the appropriate documentation is in place. The human resources management role of the personnel function now comes into play. The process will not only have identified some people who need support to do their present jobs better, but also the 'high flyers' whose abilities are not being used to the full. The personnel function will be looking to the firm's global human resource needs and will need to consider if such a person should be moved into a new, more demanding and challenging role, possibly with some training to assist. This is, of course, not easy. A manager may not be too happy to see one of the best staff being lost for training with the end purpose of moving this valued and contributing member on and out. In Chapter Four, we considered the problems of not fully using people's capacity and the human resources specialists need to ensure that managers know that under using people soon leads to demotivation. Such career moves are in the best interests of the individuals, the firm and even the manager suffering the loss, in the long term.

The personnel department now have an overview of the succession needs and potential of the company to feed into the manpower planning programme discussed earlier in this chapter (succession planning). There is also an overview of the complete training needs and the most cost effective mechanisms and implementation plans can be made for the next round of training programmes.

For the individual manager involved with the appraisal process for the first time:

1. Ensure that you know the systems and have the required skills.
2. Prepare for the interview. Check what were the agreed objectives. Arrange a suitable time and place for the discussion (no telephones, no interruptions and not across a desk), inform the member of staff and give them time to prepare for the appraisal. To check performance, the manager will often need to talk to customer departments and the other people that the person works with. This type of information gathering needs to be done with tact and discretion. Where the system requires prior completion of the documentation this should be done in good time.
3. Conduct the session, review the performance, note the areas of under-performance, negotiate objectives for the next period and agree training action programme. During the interview process be alert for 'special' issues such as hidden personal problems.
4. Complete the documentation and review overall results of the programme with personnel function and senior managers.
5. Agree and implement action programme, transfers, training programmes, revise job descriptions.
6. In some firms this appraisal process is linked to performance related pay elements. It is right that performance should be rewarded and that to do this there must be a framework of assessment. However, this can detract from the open and trusting atmosphere needed for an employee to share his/her weaknesses and under-performance with the manager.

The appraisal interview is difficult for any member of staff the first time. However, it is a most difficult time for the young manager, when he/she has not to be appraised but to give appraisals to subordinate staff. Some of these may well be technical, non-graduate staff, who have been with the firm longer than the young graduate manager has been alive. Such appraisals need to be conducted with considerable tact.

## 11.8 CAREER DEVELOPMENT PLANS AND TRAINING

The appraisal process will identify areas of weakness and the integration of the sum totality of individual's performance assessments into the global, strategic human resource development programme for the firm. However, the identification of training needs and the selection of the training methods needs some skill.

For the practising manager, a simple and effective process of training needs is to perform a 'task analysis'. This process may not only be appropriate to the training of staff, but also for developing training modules for customers buying new complex technical equipment. The first stage of task analysis is to list the major tasks or responsibilities that a person has to complete to perform a role. To illustrate the basic process we will consider the task analysis of a sales person in an engineering company. The process appears simple; accept sales call from the customer, determine customer needs, enter appropriate order onto computer, check customer credit status, check production and inventory situation, inform customer of price and delivery time. This looks rather easy and we should be able to take the first, half-intelligent person off the street and have them trained in a few days, no problem. Of course, life is more difficult and some considerable skill and knowledge is needed.

---

## OUTLINE TASK ANALYSIS

## INTERNATIONAL ENGINEERING COMPANY EUROPEAN TELEPHONE SALES

*Good telephone skill*  Is a major contact with customer, needs a good telephone manner, able to be polite but get required information quickly without appearing to rush the customer. Given the international nature of the business, a sound working knowledge of several European languages needed.

*Customer needs*  Very often the customer does not know the technical implications of their requirements. A customer ordering a power supply might not know that the number of phases, voltage and frequency needs to be specified. Thus the sales person must have both product range and customer market need knowledge. This is why sales systems are often grouped either by market or by product. This reduces the amount of knowledge that any single sales person will need and reduces the training time.

*Enter order onto computer*  Person needs to be fully trained on firm's computer system and have specific detailed knowledge of the order entry system.

*Check customer credit*  Needs to be able to link into the accountancy system to check customer's current credit level against agreed limits, or whether it is possible to accept orders that would take the customer above agreed limits. Needs to know what action to take if customer would exceed agreed limits.

*Check inventory situation*  Needs to be able to access and interpret materials resource planning system. Needs to know what action to take in the event of an exceptional order that is outside forecast and may require changes to production programme or take stocks down to low levels.

*Inform customer price*  Needs to know discount structures and what effects methods of delivery (air, sea) and terms of sale (FOB (free on board), CIF (cost insurance freight)), possible effects of duty, exchange rate cover costs and current exchange rates.

*Delivery time*  Needs a good working knowledge of timing of various delivery methods, air, rail, roll on–roll off ferry etc.

---

From the above, it can be seen that even for what appears to be a simple job, a wide variety of skills and knowledge are required. Some elements are easy to provide, for example, the company training manager will have a range of 'off the peg' short telephone skill courses. In the selection process, it should be possible to select a person with the appropriate language skills. Given the technical area, some additional training in the specific technical terms will be needed but this will not come ready made from some language course. A possible solution is to get the field sales people to spend some time with the new employee on their visits to the head office, or alternatively to send the new person out on field trips. This would familiarize them with the technical language and also create some understanding of the customer's market needs and the questions that need to be asked to ensure the customer gets what they require. Remember, this may not be what they ask for, as they may not fully understand the technology.

An engineer involved in a materials resource planning system may spend a significant part of the implementation time in training staff. The success of the system may well depend as much on the quality of this programme, as the skill with which the system has been networked, structured and programmed.

## 11.9  TRAINING

All engineers will become involved in training in various contexts, training of subordinate staff (later when you have Chartered status, you in your turn will be responsible for structured experience for new engineers) and customers. In the industrial context, the process of learning is called training rather than education. The difference between these is one of emphasis. Education is for life, training is for working life. In a later section the skills needed for group and team leadership are presented, here the total capacity and personality of the person has to be developed, not just the acquisition of knowledge. Figure 11.3 gives a structure to the complexity of training and learning.

In the industrial context, the starting place should be the task analysis for the job, or the future job, of the individual. From this, a list of structured objectives can be constructed to list the skills in a hierarchy of detail. For the European Telephone Sales job part of the analysis is shown below.

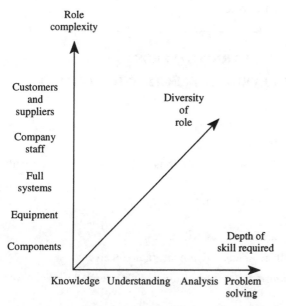

**Figure 11.3**   Complexity of training and learning

## PARTIAL TRAINING OBJECTIVES
## NEW EUROPEAN TELEPHONE SALES PERSON

*Telephone Skills*   Must be able to reply to a call in a polite, helpful, effective and efficient way. Many senior directors make a practice of telephoning in, when away from the firm, to check how the call is handled and the response time. A good telephone manner is critical as, for many customers, this will represent the firm.

There will be many international calls, so the telephone sales person:

a. Must know the more important national dialling codes.
b. Must understand the meanings of the various international tones.
c. Must know the time zone differences for the international calls.
d. Must know the time bands for peak rate and lower rate calls to make longer non-urgent calls at less expensive time of the day.

Basic telephone skills are required, such as being:

a. Able to redirect a call;
b. Able to enter and recall frequently used numbers from memory;
c. Able to implement call diversion when away from desk;
d. Able to effect 'call back' calls.

*Order entry skills*   Each major task needs to be listed and the specific skill elements identified. These are then the training objectives for the training module.

---

The same technique can be extended to how to service a nuclear reactor, only the complexity is much greater.

Complexity is important as it affects the length of time, the innate capacity needed by the individual to learn the skills, and the length of time needed to develop full proficiency. In the training of an engineer, three vectors can be recognized; depth of skill needed, complexity of the role and the diversity of the role.

---

## COMPLEXITY OF LEARNING NEEDS
## EXAMPLES OF COMPLEXITY LEVELS IN ELECTRONIC CONTEXT

**Depth of skill**

*Knowledge*   Simple knowledge, such as resistor colour code.

*Understanding*   Full understanding of how a transistor works.

*Analysis*   Given a defective circuit the individual can perform standard diagnostic tests and rectify the fault.

*Problem solving*   Complete design of a circuit to meet a specific need.

**Complexity of role**

*Components*   Understanding of single components such as disk drives.

*Equipment*   Understanding and working with complete equipment, radio receiver.

*Full systems*   Understanding and working with a full system. Responsibility for full network with computers, vision, sound.

*Internal staff*   No matter how complex the equipment used, the involvement and responsibility for staff considerably increases the complexity of the role. People and their interactions are complex and one 1.44 Mb disk is close to identical to another. Two members of staff will not be identical although the firm may require them to perform similar roles.

External staff   The complexity and skill is extended when interactions are required with external people, the same level of direct authority may not be used, much more negotiation is needed and the cultural diversity of the people will be much larger. A communications engineer may find dealing with people in a hospital, is far different when working the next day, for example, in a bank.

*Role diversity*   As an engineer's responsibility level grows, the range of skills that have to be spanned increases. The production engineer has to span the technology of the equipment being made, the technology of the production process and other skills, such as materials resource planning and distribution logistics. The diversity of the role becomes greatest for the engineer in a multinational company with a wide span of technologies, business skills and diversity of organizational and national cultures.

---

The task analysis process can be viewed as the normal business process of setting the objectives. The same requirement exists to set standards and time scales. For a production worker this could be specified in terms of 'must be able to assemble a Type 3 contact module in three minutes with no errors within two weeks working on the line'. After the task analysis of the role and an appraisal of the skill profile of the individual, the next element in the business planning process is the implementation strategy; in this context the training and learning programme.

Where specific knowledge skills are needed, the computer training packages can be of considerable use. For many common skills, such as keyboard skills, commercial packages are available at low cost and, where the company has a significant number of staff, internal packages can be written. The tutorial packages sold with most word processing and desktop publishing packages are an excellent example of this type of teaching method. It has the advantage to the firm that it is not too expensive as once the package is written, it does not require too much instructor time, knowledge checks can be built in as 'self-assessment questions' and the person can progress at a pace suited to their individual capability and learning speed.

In the engineering context, many physical skills are needed, such as how to use a test instrument, how to solder. One of the most frequent causes of time loss accidents is poor lifting technique, resulting in back injury. A technique known as 'kinetic handling' can greatly reduce the risk of injury and all people who work in production environments should be trained in this technique as part of the induction programme. This includes the office, as a person is just as likely to injure themselves moving a laser printer as a metal casting. To develop such skills, a practical involvement is necessary, with a show, tell, demonstrate and do type of instruction process. The trainee can be given an introduction, shown a video of the technique and various situations that may be encountered, then the trainer demonstrates the technique. Finally, under the supervision of the trainer, the trainee is taken through a set of graduated exercises to develop the necessary skills, judgements and required self-assurance.

In the training of managers, case study analysis is widely used and highly effective. Outlines are given of real business situations and are presented to individuals or groups. Case studies develop the powers of analysis, the ability to generate possible solutions, select from the most appropriate and then consider implementation strategies. These are higher order skills. The extensions to the case study are the business game and computer simulations of the real world, the ultimate limit being flight simulators for the training of pilots.

This still does not represent the full nature of complexity that faces the manager or supervisor where the additional complexity of people and emotions need to be introduced. Role play simulations can be used to develop these personal interaction skills. These can be used for a wide variety of situations. A telephone sales person can be given simulated calls. The analysis of the recordings can enable the person to step outside themselves and gain more insight into how they behave. In the training of managers the technique can be used to develop skills such as appraisal and disciplinary hearings. Again, the use of video recordings provides additional insight for the individual. A major problem in training for these higher order and interpersonal skills is that it is difficult for the individual or management to measure the absolute level of skill attained. The references at the end of the book provide additional detail on training methods.

## 11.10 MANAGEMENT OF GROUPS

Very few roles in engineering involve just one person, almost all work is done in groups or teams. The team may be a formal part of the organizational structure, a specific unit: research laboratory, design team, marketing group etc. 'Team' is not just a label to assign to a number of people who happen to work in the same area or have similar responsibilities. Team members must have a sense of team identity, recognize and understand the other members of the group, and comprehend how they as an individual relate to these other personalities. There is not a single magic number, but clearly this degree of intimate understanding may not take place in large groups of a hundred or more. The maximum size of a group is about twelve to fifteen people. The right size of the group depends to some extent on the nature of the task. Where high levels of personal professional interdependence are required, such as a research team, the complexity of the relationships and time needed to develop them fully, results in a smaller team size. People belong to more than one group or team. An individual will be a member of their own family group and may be a member of the darts team out of work. In work, a person might work in disk drive production (a work group), be a member of the Quality Improvement Task Force (temporary project team) and a staff representative.

The steps (selection, forming, storming, norming and performing) in the formation of a team are shown below. To be effective, a team has to be more than a collection of people.

### 11.10.1 Stages in team formation

1. *Team Selection*   Purpose and mission for the team should be defined with the senior management and with the proposed team leader. The team should be selected on the basis of appropriate skills, experience and personalities.
2. *Forming*   Team leader shares with a collection of people the mission, aims and objectives of the team and attempts to set out the rules, culture and method of operation.
3. *Storming*   The role perceptions of individuals will, to some extent, be at variance with the ideal assumptions built into the above two steps. Individuals will not know and trust

each other. As the problem is better defined mission, aims and objectives must be renegotiated. Role conflicts are confronted but not resolved.

4. *Norming* The group know each other and role conflicts are resolved. In extreme cases, leadership of the group may change. Trust and understanding are built and a framework of mission, aims, objectives are agreed and accepted by team members, strategies are agreed and team cultural norms established.

5. *Performing* The team has, within its frame of operation, a sense of shared values, communication is open and there is a shared sense of purpose. This is sometimes referred to as the 3 Cs—Communication, Consensus, Commitment. However, the term consensus is not entirely appropriate as it suggests a democratic operation of the team. In many industrial situations, decisions are not reached by consensus in the area of difficult, close decisions. Individuals have the right to fully state their view, the team, and in particular the team leader, has to acknowledge the value of the contribution. However, in industrial situations, the team leader often has to make the decision and will be held accountable for it. Thus the team has to accept the quality and integrity of the team leader's leadership decisions. This is not quite the same as team consensus with its implication of a group vote on all decisions.

An effective team has a sense of identity, a sense of purpose and direction which needs to be built on a sense of shared values. Teams do not happen, they have to be assembled. At Stage 1 the team is a collection of people who might make an effective team. Having assembled the individuals a process of team building is required and, once the team is established, a modest effort is required to maintain the relationships.

From this model, it can be seen that if we are selecting members of a team we have to do so not only on the basis of the skill contributions (hardware engineer, computer programmer . . .) but also on the complementary personalities and team roles, the Belbin types (see Chapter 4) being a useful approach. People do not, however, introduce themselves at a team meeting as 'Hi, I am your introverted "plant" (*Belbin team type*) and I am going to programme your system'. Team leadership requires the ability to analyse the team members and to recognize potential areas of role conflict.

The process of 'storming' needs to be managed. If this stage is not recognized, the conflict can become intense and destructive, with people leaving the team or the company. One option widely used in industry is to recognize the difficulty and intensity of Stages 2 (Forming) and 3 (Storming), and provide exercises, such as team building weekends off site, where such conflicts can be resolved in a less formal and less threatening context. Only modest effort is required to maintain a team once these steps have been completed, except when a new member enters the team when, on a reduced scale, the whole operation has to be completed as the new individual accepts and is accepted by the team. Central to performance is the leadership quality of the team leader. The recognition of legitimate power is important, acceptance of leadership in an area is acceptance of legitimate power (mature teams devolve leadership for certain aspects of the task). Some common forms of power are given below:

*Expert power* The power that comes from knowledge and experience, not only in the technologies but also in the proven solution of the process used in solving past problems.

An engineering team with a mixture of skills will not have any problems with the perceived most senior and skilled engineer assuming the leadership role, even if the formal discipline may not be the most central to the project. Often, however, a person without technical skills will not be acceptable to a technical team, they will consider that the person 'does not understand the problems'. For research and technical teams this is the most often and widely accepted form of power.

*Position power* In certain organization cultures (religious, military, police) the position of authority confers power. In the most frequent situation with expert engineers, however, a team leader who relies on appointment as team leader as the power base for team leadership is likely to be a poor leader. This form of power is accepted in the 'forming' stage of the group but will be challenged in technical expert teams if the appointed team leader cannot demonstrate more legitimate power bases later (in effect, the team gives the new leader a honeymoon period to demonstrate what the team considers to be real power). A particular problem occurs where a new leader has to be appointed, especially if that leader has to be drawn from outside the team.

*Resource power* People who have the ability to control resources equipment and laboratory time, etc., have power. In engineering technical contexts, overuse of this power base can cause considerable conflict. A person using this form of power in a team context might well be called upon to justify the decision.

*Personal power* In Chapter Four, it was noted that certain personality types are more likely to want and be prepared to assume power and leadership. Personal power is effective when it is recognized and accepted by the team. It is one of the most frequent sources of conflict during the storming process, one or more individuals may wish to assume a personal power base and the non-acceptance of this by the team can cause intense rivalry.

*Physical power* Not relevant in the normal expert engineering context but in certain group contexts the ability to 'drink others under the table' or effect the highest level of physical performance (sporting team) may confer power. In the latter context it may be regarded as related to expert power.

*Destructive power* Often the most difficult power to recognize and the most important to remove. The group leader must make decisions and if there is not acceptance (this is different to agreement) and real leadership then the active or passive 'why not' obstruction may come into play. A member of the team with some resource power may use it in a negative and non-legitimate way. The most extreme type of such power is deliberate sabotage, destruction of equipment or insertion of a virus on to a computer system.

In these discussions the need for expert advice, central resources, and adequate personnel records have been outlined. These areas, with certain legal obligations, are the responsibility of the personnel function.

## 11.11 FORMAL RESPONSIBILITIES OF THE PERSONNEL FUNCTION

### 11.11.1 Strategy formation

In the analysis of the external and internal environments the 7's' model was largely concerned with human resource issues. One of the key support issues in the value chain analysis is human resources. In the evaluation of a change in direction, such as vertical integration or product diversification, there will be major human resource issues. Staff may need to be recruited, they may not exist in new skill areas where demand far exceeds supply. In the General Electric matrix, evaluation of the opportunity may present an analysis where there is an attractive business proposition but a weak competitive position, as the firm does not have the necessary expertise.

Apart from a very direct and legitimate role in the formation of corporate policy, the personnel function has, like the marketing department, a large role in preparing the company for the future. A proactive role in creating the skills and capabilities not only for the present situation and businesses but for changed circumstances and different business directions. Succession planning is not only about maintaining the position but strengthening the firm's competitive position.

In certain areas of the firm's undertakings the personnel function has the leading role in the formulation of policy and strategies, consistent with the broad corporate mission and objectives. The strategic framework of industrial relations and rewards systems needs to be constructed by experts.

### 11.11.2  Operational

In the earlier section on the recruitment process, a range of personnel function responsibilities were considered, one of which was to assist the line manager in drawing up a full job definition (job description). The translation of this into an accurate personnel specification also requires expert assistance. The line manager will have to recruit a few people a year and will need to rely on the personnel function for an adequate candidate search, including appropriate use of head hunters, agencies and advertising. The recruitment for the Graduate Development Programme may be seen as a strategic responsibility of the personnel function, recruiting young engineers not for the present business, but for where the business is expected to be in three or four years. The whole appraisal, training and career development plan for individuals needs the expert assistance and coordination of the personnel function. There is, however, a key strategic integrative role for the personnel function. There is a real danger that the simple mechanical administration may be a whole set of career development plans for individuals, which when integrated does not match the future demands of the company. The personnel function may need to follow the feedback and control loop to ensure that development plans will prepare people for roles that will exist. There is no more certain way to ensure high staff turnover and poor motivation than to develop people's capability and then underuse it.

The personnel function will have operational day-to-day responsibility for the provision of support services, possibly security (may be an operations responsibility), safety (safety specialists, such as medical experts and specialist training resources), medical (company doctor and counselling services), payroll (construction of pay schedules, implementation may be contracted out or an accounts function), staff services (canteen may be run by personnel or contract supervised by this function), pension arrangements, staff communications (general communication channels, such as company house journal and newsletters, supervision of social activities, such as insurance for company social club etc.), staff sales (many firms who make consumer goods make them available to staff at preferential rates), administration of training rooms (will be used by individual managers for their own briefing and training sessions). In some large organizations it may be difficult to place certain administrative functions such as cleaning, reception and the telephone operators and sometimes the personnel function can be operating in some operational areas.

### 11.11.3 Recording and legal responsibilities

The personnel function is, if anything, a more complex and demanding role than the accountant's, as the span of requirements is vast. Given the ever-changing framework of law, only some of the more important topics are covered in outline. This is an area where specific advice from a professional fully aware of all the current requirements is essential.

### 11.11.4 Health and safety

The requirements are all pervasive. Specific responsibility must be with the line manager who has the direct accountability for the operations under his/her managerial control. The average engineer is not likely to know how many wash basins and toilets must be provided when the work force is increased or the detailed provisions for meal breaks for extended working or shift operation. The personnel specialist will have all the key information to hand and can prevent costly errors being made or, in extreme cases, stopping the company from committing an offence. All managers must have an appropriate system of safety but, like total quality management, the personnel function will frequently have the responsibility for constructing the detailed overall quality policy document and ensuring that this is reflected in the appropriate operating policy statements in each department. Just as with TQM, the function will have the role of internal audit to supervise periodic safety audits and checks. The personnel function will have responsibility to ensure that the full safety records are kept regarding accidents, dangerous occurrences and tracking employee health (statistical checks to see if certain occupations give specific health problems that were not suspected). Given the legal implications, the function will be involved in the preparation of statutory safety and accident reports. Each and every accident must be subjected to a full and exhaustive investigation, involving not only the operational department but the personnel function (where responsible for the corporate safety function) as the internal audit. The correlation and statistical analysis of incidents may identify specific training needs. The procedures for this are a legal necessity, the firm needs to prove that, not only on legal grounds but also for ethical reasons, it makes all reasonable attempts and implements the appropriate procedures to ensure the safety of its employees.

### 11.11.5 Discipline

In all large organizations some people will behave in a way that is not acceptable. This can be a minor offence such as taking an extended break, but will involve all possibilities up to theft and assault. The role of the personnel function is to see that every effort is made to establish the true facts, that the facts have been properly recorded and that the procedures have been implemented in a consistent way. The latter is important as inconsistency in disciplinary treatment may find the company facing legal action for unfair treatment. Particular care must be taken by the young engineer in issuing formal verbal warnings to staff. In most companies these must be given under specific conditions (possibly involving the member of staff to be warned having rights of representation) and with prescribed recording procedures (the individual may well have to be given a copy of the notice of the warning which in most cases will be held on personnel records for a limited time). It should be noted that under-performance or disciplinary matters must be considered as separate to redundancy. The redundancy legislation does not allow the selection of staff on this type of basis.

### 11.11.6  Statistical returns

The firm is required to provide many statistical returns such as notification of industrial disputes. The health and safety issues have been covered above. Firms are required to implement equal opportunity policies, records should be maintained so that this type of information can be extracted without difficulty when required.

### 11.11.7  Employment contract

This is a most complex area where expert advice is always necessary. The employee is entitled to a statement of his/her contract of employment, length of notice and expected hours of work and normal duties. The precise framework and detail that need to be given is affected by ever-changing legislation and case law. Only the professional specialist has the skill and the time to keep updated. One critical area of specific concern to the young engineer is the trial period. If a person is recruited it can be made subject to satisfactory performance and dismissal under this trial period may be made without the full complexity and difficulties of the disciplinary procedures. Many young managers have failed to keep track of marginal performance and have let this situation pass by default, allowing an under-performing person to pass from the trial period; such a manager has created major problems by inaction.

### 11.11.8  Reward systems and job evaluation

In Herzberg terms pay is a 'hygiene factor'. In the long term, not a motivator, but perceived low pay is a very powerful demotivator. A company has to take immense care over this. A person who may be well paid and getting the 'rate for the job' may perceive themselves to be badly paid if they see some other employee receiving higher rewards for what appears to be the same level of responsibility and contribution. In any substantial organization there needs to be a formal framework to arrive at a fair structure of payment and for the process to be seen to operate in a equitable way.

   The obvious difficulty is that people have very different ways and the system has to be seen to be able to compare the skills, levels of responsibility and contribution of roles as different as a design engineer and a cost accountant. A common way to manage this problem is to break up a person's pay into a number of elements:

1. *A rate for the job*   This is arrived at by a process of job evaluation. The job description must be written within a prescribed framework which then enables a well trained panel to benchmark the role against many others, to assess against weighting factors such as size of the job (resources managed, budget responsibilities), depth of knowledge and experience required, impact on the business etc. This weighted score can then be translated into a target or normal pay for a job of this dimension. Such frameworks are offered by consulting companies who train the panel. This has the advantage to the firm

that it is able, in confidence, to benchmark its pay levels with other equivalent roles in other organizations, to assess if the company is paying about the market rate.

2. *Performance related pay*   A person newly promoted to an enlarged role will not perform at the full capacity for that level of responsibility and so most organizations weight the person's basic actual pay by a performance and experience factor. This performance decision is based on the appraisal and objective measures, the meeting of specific objects (attainment of production targets within prescribed budget levels would be obvious measures for a production engineer).

3. *Special allowances*   If a person is required to work shifts, be away from home or required to work in an expensive location (inner London), special elements (shift allowance, London weighting) will be added into the pay. These pay elements will be withdrawn when the condition no longer applies.

4. *Overtime*   For less senior staff significant additional hours of work will be paid on an overtime scale. This may have various weightings for normal overtime, call outs, Saturday, Sunday or Bank Holiday working.

5. *Market rate*   It is a very difficult issue for the firm when a job, through the job evaluation procedure, arrives at a pay level which is not high enough to attract people with certain specific skills. Then the firm will have to pay a market loading to attract the candidate that is required. This can be a source of considerable resentment to other staff performing equivalent work, without a market scarcity valuation.

6. *Job rotation and redeployment*   To achieve organizational flexibility the firm may wish staff to move around the business. Such movements may not always be to jobs of greater size and usually a company seeking this type of flexibility from its staff will allow the individual to carry on their old pay if it is higher than the nominal target pay for the new role. This may be for a limited period of a few years only.


**REVIEW**

The primary role of human resource management must be with the line managers who are in day-to-day contact with people. The personnel function has a critical role in the formulation of strategic policy and in supporting the line managers with effective training programmes and specialist help, such as recruitment. It is important to reflect the needs of the firm into the job design. All jobs should have a full job description so that individuals know what is expected of them. Role definition and personal profiles aid the selection process and before submitting your CV, it is useful to check what the firm may be seeking and highlighting those key points about your ability that are of particular relevance. The CV is a personal marketing document, and its purpose is to get you an interview.

After recruitment staff should have a preliminary induction programme. However, career development does not stop there and a critical part of the feedback and control system for the human resources management of an organization is the appraisal interview, where an individual discusses past performance, career development needs and future objectives for the next review period.

The management of teams is an important process as substantive projects need a group of people and a range of skills. Teams do not just happen, the team leader must take positive action with the selection of the team members, if possible, and then manage the team building process. Teams do not work in a vacuum and both within the team, and in the company in general, the issues of power and authority are important. Power does not simply come from position—it can come from other sources, such as position power or knowledge-based power.

Although the operational manager has the front line role in human resources management, the personnel function has certain key responsibilities, such as maintaining adequate personnel records, ensuring the disciplinary procedures are fair and, in an increasingly regulated environment, legal. Great problems will be caused if the company does not use, and be seen to be using, consistent reward systems for staff in differing functions. Where there are deviations, for example, shift working, then the reasons for the different reward package must be clearly understood, both by the employees receiving the incentive and those who do not.

In many organizations the largest single cost is the staff costs and in any company the future is in the hands of its staff. Failure to manage human resources effectively is to fail to manage the corporate strategy. Policy may not be implemented except through motivated staff.

---

## KEY CONCEPTS AND TECHNIQUES

**Appraisal**   Periodic formal discussion between an individual and his/her manager to review past performance, discuss training needs and set future objectives.

**CV**   The personal marketing document which demonstrates to a future employer that you have the characteristics to satisfy their personnel specification.

**Job design**   The techniques of fitting the individual and the company needs with a job of the right dimensions and character.

**Personnel specification**   The outline of the characteristics required of the ideal person for a role, often split between desirable and essential.

**Role definition**   Links with job design. The formal expression of the individual's role in the organization.

**Task analysis**   The process of breaking a job down to basic elements, tasks that the person has to do. It is then possible to decide the skills needed and the training that may be required.

---

## CASE STUDY

### TAMAR DEFENCE LTD

Consider this case in the role of new business development manager, you are a Chartered Engineer who then did an MBA.

**Head up displays**   Tamar Defence make advanced 'head up' display units for fighter aircraft. Your design team have come up with some electronic systems that have proved it is economic and possible to adapt these to 'head up' display the instruments in cars. There have been successful trials with a major car manufacturer who is very interested in fitting this system to the next, top of the range, car to be launched in 18 months. A company factory is completing an existing contract but will become free when this contract ends in nine months' time. This has a work force of some 200 people who are experienced in small lot defence manufacture.

The selection and formation of the new venture implementation team will be your responsibility. The team will have to complete the development of the selected product, establish a volume production line using new consumer-type electronics production methods and market the new product.

You have been asked to indicate the number and nature of people you will need in the new venture management team. What issues would you consider? How many people would you have in the team and what skills would you include? What actions will you need to take to build the team up?

It has been accepted that you may have to recruit a manager skilled in volume production and a marketing manager with knowledge of the car industry. Outline the personnel specifications for these people.

The company has a no redundancy policy to date and you will have to use the existing work force in the factory. What are the key human resource issues you will need to address in the production area?

---

## QUESTIONS

1. Draft out your CV in full, on a suitable word processing or desktop publishing system.

2. As the general manager of a company, you are to launch an item of fire protection equipment in a year's time. The product exists in prototype form at the moment, but full design has yet to be completed. You have decided to set up a project team to ensure the launch of this product is on time and within budget. The new production line will use new manufacturing technology which will require retraining of staff.

   What departments would need to be represented on this team to ensure effective coordination of this project? Why would they need to be involved?

   Apart from departments (such as production) and disciplines (such as engineering), what other human resource issues would you need to take into account when forming this team? What would be the problems if this was not done?

## FURTHER READING

Beach, D.S. (1985) *The Management of People at Work*, 5th Edition, Macmillan.
Bennett, R. (1991) *Organisational Behaviour*, Longman.
Hunt, J.W. (1986) *Managing People at Work: a Manager's Guide to Behaviour in Organisations*, 2nd Edition, McGraw-Hill.
Katz, R. (ed.) (1988) *Managing Professionals in Innovative Organisations, a Collection of Readings*, Ballinger.
McBeath, G. (1992) *The Handbook of Human Resource Planning, Practical Manpower Analysis Techniques for the HR Professionals*, Blackwell.

# TWELVE

## THE ENGINEER AS CHANGE AGENT

### 12.1 INTRODUCTION—CHANGE AND THE ENGINEER

In Chapter One, we defined an engineer as a person who wished to improve the world through technology, taking a situation from one state to another, better state, that is to say, through the process of change. The design engineer will do this by the creation of new products, the production engineer by the continual development of improved manufacturing technologies and methods. Even the engineer with a marketing role can benefit from an appreciation of this change process as, when marketing and selling advanced equipment (digital communications, robotics, etc.), they are injecting change into the customer organization. Without an understanding of the change process the marketing engineer will not appreciate how the dynamics of change influence the key people in the customer decision making unit.

Our approach considers how the process of change from one stable state to another stable state takes place and the roles needed to accomplish this change process. It is a fact of life that most often change is resisted and the reasons for this resistance are discussed. Finally, the skills and techniques needed to manage change are reviewed.

### 12.2 RATIONAL DECISION MAKING

Figure 12.1 shows the rational decision-making process. This can be considered to have six elements; disturbance, a decision to act, definition of the problem, solution search, application of the preferred solution and feedback and control.

The disturbance can come from any aspect of the organization or its environment. In earlier chapters, the techniques of PEST, Porter 5 forces, value chain analysis and McKinsey 7's' analysis were discussed. These techniques are important for large scale policy decisions of the organization, what new products to make, which technologies to employ. Clearly, disturbances can come in other forms; in TQM it could be an increase in defect rate, Cu-Sum techniques and identification of causes, measles diagrams and Pareto analysis. The managing engineer must be prepared to use any or all of the techniques outlined in the earlier texts to detect and identify disturbances, changes to the organization's operations and operating conditions.

A critical activity is that of deciding if and where action is required. For the larger decisions, the SWOT analysis process will allow the focusing of the explosive range of the internal and external analysis. Pareto analysis and fishbone diagrams etc. will assist in the identification of changes which are relevant in the more normal day-to-day problems. This is the first stage of '*what* is going on?' The next stage is, of course, '*why?*', and 'What is the assignable cause or causes?' It is convenient to remember the key questions:

- What?
- Where?
- Why?
- When?
- Who?
- How?
- By how much?
- How often?

The identification of the change and the decision to act does not give a full definition of the problem; this requires insight and creativity. A common mistake is to define the issue in too narrow a scope. In the manufacture of a product, the production of sub-standard units may be traced back to a delivery of defective components. The simple definition and solution is to complain to the supplier and obtain replacement units and possibly to start a liability claim. However, the incident may well be a specific example of a more general issue, the failure of TQM and poor supplier selection and audit. In the previous discussion of materials resource planning the use of optimum lot size was discussed and we noted that the simple acceptance of set-up costs obscured the key management action needed, to reduce set-up costs and the possible move to a more JIT based environment.

If the definition of the problem needs creativity and judgement, the solution search has an even greater demand. The process requires both lateral thinking and convergent analytical thinking. In a production layout problem it may take creativity to produce a modified floorplan and movement of materials to provide the product or service. The analytical techniques, such as queuing and network theory, can then assist in the analytic determination and modelling of the alternative solutions generated by the more free ranging thinking. The process of problem definition and solution search should involve the participation of all the interested people and, in particular, it must involve the grass roots staff who will be responsible for running the system in the future. Failure to do this will

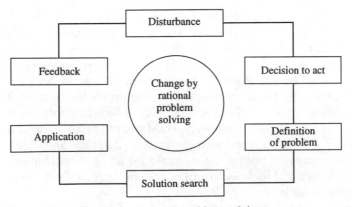

**Figure 12.1**    Change by rational problem solving
*Reprinted from 'The 1985 Annual: Developing Human Resources', eds. L.D. Goodstein and J.W. Pfeiffer, Pfeiffer and Company, 1985, San Diego, USA. Used with permission.*

mean that many inputs, ideas and solutions will be lost and the outcome may well be less good than that which was easily possible.

The involvement of the total workforce is not only essential for the solution search but also most important for its application and implementation. Apart from the fact that the best solution may not have been found, the change process will involve alterations which may be uncomfortable. If people have not been involved the 'not invented here' reaction will surface. The solution will not work as the people who have to make it work will not have the conviction with no sense of ownership of the process. Application not only requires clear logical thinking using techniques such as critical path analysis, but also the ability to lead and motivate people, often people that the engineer may not have direct operation management responsibility for. In the next section we shall consider the types of roles that need to be performed to make this process work.

## 12.3 THE CHANGE PROCESS AND THE ROLES OF CHANGE AGENTS

In Fig. 12.2 the change process discussed in the last section is shown in the inner circle. Around this circle of the rational decision-making process the model identifies five key roles for the effective implementation of the change process: the catalyser, the process helper, the solution giver, the resource linker and the stabilizer. It is possible that one person may fulfil more than one of these roles but, when considering a change process, it is an advantage to ensure that there are people performing each of these roles. If any of these roles are not being performed then there is a high likelihood of project degradation, late delivery, system under-performance for a service or even a complete system failure. It is estimated that 80 per cent of computer systems do not meet the full expectations of the business and complete failures are far from unknown. This is because the system

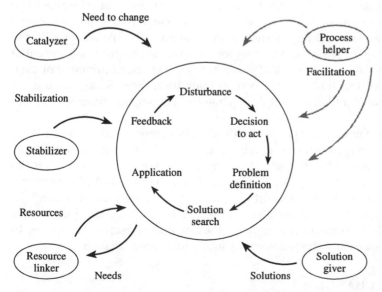

**Figure 12.2**    Roles in management of change process
*Reprinted from 'The 1985 Annual: Developing Human Resources', eds. L.D. Goodstein and J.W. Pfeiffer, Pfeiffer and Company, 1985, San Diego, USA. Used with permission.*

implementers failed to realize that not only were they implementing technology but that they were also agents of change.

The word 'catalyser' is taken from chemistry where a catalyst is a material which is not consumed in the course of a reaction but is directly involved and speeds up the process. The catalyser may often be a difficult, creative, person as this role involves the first perception that there is an issue or a problem. In many circumstances, this will not be regarded as good news. The suggestion that the competition's products have superior technology or that the manufacturing process needs completely changing can be expected to be greeted with the attitudes of 'This is the way we have done it for 10 years so why should we have to change?' or 'It has worked in the past so why will it not work in the future?'.

The process helper is essential to all parts of the change process and as support to all the roles. In the case of the catalyser, the role is particularly important as it is easy to bury a problem for too long, resulting in the competitive edge being lost beyond redemption. The process helper must ensure that the catalyser gains the recognition, even if that is not reassuring and is uncomfortable. The person who fulfils this role must be perceived to be a person of stature and respect, it can be a consultant, but in many engineering organizations it will be a mature professional who has seen more than one complete change of technology.

The first reaction to this change process model is that the solution giver will be the catalyser. This may be the case but is not essential. The solution giver may well be the intellectual squirrel who creatively links seemingly disparate technology, procedures and information into an entirely new package. The second key factor is that this person does not only have to formulate this solution but then communicate and market it within the organization. A solution is not of the slightest use unless it is recognized and valued.

The implementation of a new technology or system of working may need new resources or access to resources not normally available to that group. Somebody must be able to go and fight for new capital equipment, so the engineer must be able to justify the commercial value of the new expense, with techniques such as discounted cash flow analysis. In the early stages, resources may be required on a temporary basis just to prove the potential and the resource linker will need a network of contacts to loan special equipment or even get people with special skills seconded to the project team for a time. Resources are not limited to money, equipment and computer access but also encompass management and technical skills.

Often, the type of person who can perform the role of catalyser or solution giver will not be the type who enjoys, or has an interest in, administration. The role of the stabilizer is critical as only when the change has become 'The way we do things around here', is the change fully implemented. This role, again, not only needs engineering and administrative skills but also good interpersonal skills. The fully implemented change is one where all the people concerned have taken ownership of the new steady state. A key part of this consolidation process will be to win over and overcome any final resistance to change. In the next section, we shall consider the reasons why individuals resist change.

## 12.4 RESISTANCE TO CHANGE

The resistance to change may be both rational; 'I may lose my job', or irrational; 'I do not like computers'. The first and most important element for the engineer as an agent of

**Table 12.1**  Individual's resistance to change

- Change (threat) to rewards
- Fear of unknown
- Change (threat) to security
- Change (threat) to group and personal role relationships
- Change (threat) to status
- Change (threat) to values
- Change (threat) to power
- Change (threat) to skills

change is to understand and respect other people's reasons for wanting to resist change, as only then is it possible to manage the situation. This is not to say that the painful decisions have to be avoided, but rather that the process of resolution should have been seen to be complete and fair, even when it may involve an individual's loss of job. The others still in the organization must understand and respect the decision as appropriate.

Table 12.1 gives a simple model of possible sources of fear and resistance to change. In considering these sources of opposition the theories given in Chapter Four, in particular, the theories of motivation, Maslow and Herzberg, are important. One of the most important sources of stress is not to know, the fear of the unknown. To suspect that one may be made redundant may be much more stressful than the actual redundancy, which can be perceived as a release from the uncertainty. The threat of the unknown and changes to perceived security (such as a transfer to an unknown department or site) moves people right down the Maslow hierarchy of needs. There is no point in talking about the recognition that the new job could bring until the engineering manager has addressed the first Maslow need, the all-important issue to the individual: security.

Maslow also tells us that people have a great need to belong, the work group is not a mechanical assembly of skills with as much relationship as a group of lathes. It is a social entity, a team within which people have social and work relationships that are important to them. Changes in work patterns can disrupt these social structures and without an understanding of the reason for the resistance, the engineering manager may think the resistance is irrational and/or simply destructive.

In a fast moving world of changing technology, even an engineer can find that the skill base becomes outdated. The craftsmen may feel that the introduction of new computer-controlled machine and robots de-skills them to the point that the individual feels that they are just a machine minder and loses self-esteem, the skills for which the individual had achieved recognition (Maslow hierarchy) having become, seemingly, merely part of some mechanical computer code that any person could operate.

Within the work groups there is a social and a formal power system of direct and indirect authority. When work practices are changed then power structures are changed. The individual who perceives that his/her power base is being eroded will feel threatened and insecure. A move to JIT production with zero inspection may well induce this feeling in a quality control inspector who will find that the role, if indeed it still exists, will be that of a facilitator and not the direct exercise of line authority, the responsibility for quality having been delegated to the production area rather than being inspected in an autocratic fashion. This consideration also interacts with status. A simple change from a staff and works canteen to a single status employee restaurant may gain intense adverse reaction out of all proportion to the apparent magnitude of the change. This is because, in Maslow terms, people see the change as a shift in the recognition they receive. On this basis, the reaction can at least be rationalized.

In Chapter Five, the difference between the production and the market-driven company was outlined. In the production company simple production efficiency is the culture, in the marketing company satisfaction of the customer benefit needs in an efficient and effective way requires a different and more flexible culture. Culture change is one of the most difficult management changes to effect.

The threat to rewards should not just be interpreted as financial rewards. Herzberg's theory tells us that financial rewards are a hygiene factor and that a change to a lower pay structure will produce an intense negative reaction. This simple and direct reaction is to be expected; however, more subtle effects can also come into play. Pay is not only a method of financial reward but also may be seen as part of the recognition of the individual. Thus even a small loss of pay, which may not pose a real threat to the individual's standard of living, may induce a strong reaction because of the perceived loss of recognition. Rewards may, of course, be non-financial and an engineer who in the past was able to publish papers may when moved to a role where this is no longer possible consider this loss a major disincentive.

People are territorial in their behaviour, both in the physical sense and in the work sense. The individual has space which they perceive to be their own and this decays in an exponential fashion to total lack of interest in events that are remote. A move of desk and/or change of job is of great interest to the individual. If it is a change for the person working a few yards away, it is still of considerable interest but in the next department it will merely rate a few comments over lunch. If this type of change is affecting somebody on another site it will probably not even rate a comment. It is useful to remember that the individual's perception of the size of the change will not only depend on the actual size of the change but, just like perspective, also on the individual's distance from the change.

## 12.5 MANAGEMENT OF CHANGE—COMMUNICATION

The engineer involved with change has four key objectives to achieve; consultation, communication to gain consensus and commitment. The first stage must be the careful consideration of all the issues with the collection of the relevant facts and analysis of the problem. These aspects of the management of change have been covered in the earlier parts of this chapter. To gain the ultimate objectives of consensus and commitment, a fully motivated team, clear and persuasive communication is essential. The engineer is marketing ideas and policies within the organization and the techniques of marketing outlined in Chapter 5 apply. Using the techniques given earlier in this chapter the key issues that will concern the various publics (stakeholders) within the organization can be identified and this guides the manager in deciding what needs to be communicated.

The starting point of any effective presentation is the audience. The issues that are to be presented must be relevant to the audience and the language and presentation style in keeping with their level of understanding. Most people find that the formal presentation is not easy, in that all suffer to a greater or lesser extent with nerves. There is little point in attempting to deny this. The most useful technique to overcome this is to use the increased level of awareness to channel energy and excitement to the audience. Many expert presenters say that if they do not feel nervous beforehand, they do not have the vital extra presence that makes a good presentation.

Having decided what the content of the presentation needs to be the next stage is to structure it. The opening and closing are vital as key moments that stay in people's minds. Often much of the detail of what goes in the middle will not be recalled next day, but it does prepare the ground for the acceptance of the key points. Consider the case of an engineer making a presentation to senior managers for the purchase of advanced test equipment that will allow product quality to be improved and costs cut. If the engineer starts with 'Proposal for the Purchase of a Fourier Transform Signal Analyser' it is not likely that this will excite many members of the audience, who are unlikely to be engineers. A more positive introduction, 'How Signal Analysers can save us £100 000 next year', is much more likely to gain universal attention. It is useful to prepare the audience for the content to follow, so a very brief introduction and overview should be given. The body of the structured material can then be given. At the end of the presentation the urge is to think 'Good, I have survived' and end with something like 'and that concludes my presentation'. This has lost that vital chance to make that high attention point pay off. A stronger ending would be 'and that is how we will save £100 000'.

All you need to do to give a good presentation is to remember those good points of the lectures you attended and the styles that sent you to sleep. Other people's attention span is not any longer than yours, so, in a longer presentation, you need to introduce some change of pace, or some element of excitement to lift the attention every 10 to 15 minutes. To maintain attention, the voice should be strong (not shouting), animated, with variation of pace and tone and pauses for emphasis. If you are not well-skilled at presentation do take notes with you, but remember that to take a complete script in and just read it can give a long drone which will send people off to sleep in five minutes. It is better to take your key points in on a set of prompt cards, having numbered them so that if they should be dropped they can be reassembled without difficulty (some presenters punch the top left corner and tag the cards together to prevent this possibility). For most people, this provides the right balance of support, enough to keep you confident but not so much that you spend all your time reading the notes.

The object of a presentation is communication and three points are important for this to be effective; *contact* must be made with the audience to build a *relationship*, and there must be *feedback*. If you are looking at your notes, you lose a key mechanism of audience building, eye contact. Eye contact should be made periodically with all members of the audience, not just the two keen ones in the front row. Each and every member of the audience should feel that you are talking to them. This process of eye contact enables you to pick up audience reaction, letting you know when people are losing interest or do not understand. A marketing lecture to computer engineers got off to a difficult start when the lecturer started talking about PLCs. The lecturer saw the blank expressions and lack of understanding in the audience and asked what they understood by the term PLC. The answer was 'Programmable Logic Controller'. The lecture was on 'Product Life Cycle'. Without audience contact the gap in understanding would not have been perceived.

Sound is only one of the senses with which we can communicate. Vision is another powerful way and one can increase the amount of communication and the impact of a presentation by the use of appropriate visual aids. For the large scale presentation slides may be appropriate, for the very small, intimate, presentation a flip chart may be all that is required. For the more usual mid range presentation the overhead projector is the most convenient tool. Most WP, graphics and desk top publishing packages have a wide range of options and, with a laser printer printing directly onto the acetate film, professional quality slides can be produced at very little cost. If a colour plotter is available then the impact can be even further enhanced. There are a number of simple rules to follow in the preparation of a slide. Do not put too much information on a single slide, keep the text size up to a level that is easy to read (18 point is usually satisfactory), use a proportional type, such as Times Roman, as it allows more information to be included and is easy to read. All upper case is difficult to read so use mixed case. If you have several points to make from one slide, cover the later points with a piece of paper (weight it with a small coin to stop it falling off) and reveal each point as you come to it, giving added impact. With 'clip art' on computer packages, drawings and diagrams can be enhanced. Cartoons can be enlarged with photo enlarging photocopiers and projected to provide variation of pace and light relief. If you have large amounts of numerical information to project try not to project spreadsheets, give them as handouts and present the information in graphical form. Many untechnical people simply cannot relate to figures, so graphs, bar and pie charts are much more effective. A common error is to not allow enough time for people to read the information. A second error is for the presenter to turn his/her back to the audience to point or read the information. Pointing is good as it provides movement and emphasis but keep it brief or else eye contact with the audience is lost. If you need to point to something for longer, then rest a pen or pencil on the OHP so you can still maintain full eye contact with the audience.

Any other media may be used when appropriate; demonstrations, models, films and computer animations. However, there is one golden rule; keep it simple, as things *will* go wrong. To minimize this danger and to gain confidence, the presentation should be rehearsed once or twice or, for a major presentation, three or four times. Do not over-rehearse though, you will become bored and this will be communicated to your audience. If the room is unknown to you, go and check the layout and make sure that you know where light and power switches are before the presentation. Make sure that there is somewhere to put your notes and that all you need will be to hand.

Presentation skills are essential for the engineer, whether selling a new business plan, a product or a service to a customer or briefing the work group on the new design programme. Having examined the tools of management in the last chapter, we will next consider how a complete business plan is designed and implemented.


**REVIEW**

The main reason for the employment of an engineer is either to create change by research and development or to implement change in operations. The organization needs to recognize the need to change, decide that action is necessary and define the problem. Once the problem is defined the solution search can be completed, which is a creative process. The solutions need to be applied and then consolidated in to the company systems. The new state must become the new normality. The Myron Chartier model of change identifies a number of key roles in the change process: the process helper who facilitates the entire change process, the solution giver, the resource linker, the stabilizer and the catalyser.

Earlier in the book, techniques such as PEST and Porter analysis have given us the tools to detect changes in the environment. Statistical tools such as time series analysis and Cu-Sums aid the engineering manager in the detection of changes from the anticipated situation. Financial investigation and control with ratio analysis, actual against planned budget with variance analysis can indicate where cost structures may be other than expected. The marketing systems and tools and the techniques of operations give us methods to improve the firm's activities and our understanding of the nature of staff as three-dimensional people with emotions and personality indicates the need to motivate and lead staff to implement new solutions once found.

Individuals and groups may resist change as it may be seen as a threat to skills, security, power, values or role relationships. It is essential to manage the resistance to change and not ignore it. People's resistance to the change is proportional to its perceived magnitude, and so, if the change is at some distance, then it is not of much concern. This is important in communications as people want to know what is going to affect them, not the strategy for Siberia. To manage change communications is essential and the engineer must develop the skills needed to give an effective presentation to a group.

## KEY CONCEPTS AND TECHNIQUES

**Chartier model**    A model for evaluating the stages and roles needed in effective change management.

## CASE STUDY

Regional Gas supplies gas to some 1.5 million homes and 25 000 industrial customers, over an area 80 miles along the M99 and 20 miles either side of the motorway. On privatization, the initial emphasis was on increasing both the efficiency of the distribution network and the number of highly profitable industrial users. You are in the role of Ossie Daniels, a project engineer. You have been very successful in bringing about the improvements to the distribution network on time and within budget.

On the domestic side, Regional Gas has a complicated and old system. There are four regional service centres for the fitters to work from to install and service customers' appliances. There are twelve shops and there were four regional accounts offices (not located with the regional service centres). In the first few years all the regional accounts offices were closed and a central computer system was installed at the new head office site, about midway within the region, just off the M99. This office was built on the reclaimed old gas works and there is still three acres of reclaimed but vacant land on this site.

Regional Gas came under severe criticism from its consumer group six months ago for very poor performance with customer field service. The marketing department were asked to complete a survey of customers and drew the following conclusions: field staff were unhelpful and on 25 per cent of occasions failed to keep the booking. This created customer resentment as only the day was indicated to the householder, not a fixed appointment time. The staff were seen as being unprofessional and frequently left a mess after they had completed their work. Twenty per cent of calls required a second visit as the fitter did not have the required parts.

The marketing department also interviewed a selection of the fitters and drew these conclusions. On 30 per cent of the calls, the customer was not there, the reason was most often that 'they had forgotten as it was over a week ago that they had booked the call'. All calls were booked for the same length of time even though different jobs were known to take different times. Moreover, there was a standard travel time allowance for each job. On some days this resulted in a fitter completing his work several hours early. In other cases, by the end of the day a fitter could have two or three calls outstanding. On average, travelling time was 30 minutes (there was considerable variation as addresses appeared to be assigned without regard to travel implications) and each call needed, on average, 55 minutes on the customer's premises. The fitters were required to cover both industrial and consumer products and it was apparent that they did not know enough about the full range of appliances as there were so many. Another problem was parts. These were issued for each job but often small, low cost, parts (such as washers and gaskets) needed replacing but were not in the 'job pack'. Often a part would not be in the regional service centre and the stock controller would have to ring other centres to find one that did have the part. This took time a long time as people had to check the large number of stock cards. There was one man working full-time delivering parts etc. between the four sites.

The managing director is concerned, having resolved other problems in the business, that service to customers should be improved. The level of capital investment is fully acceptable, provided it can be justified in reduced operating costs and/or improved customer service.

In the role of Ossie Daniels what do you see as the key problems? What solutions would you consider? What information would you need to finalize your solution plans? What resistance could you foresee to these plans and how would you overcome it? How would you go about implementing these plans?

---

## QUESTIONS

1. The senior engineer is concerned with improving the management of organizations and this involves the management of change. From the viewpoint of a production engineer implementing a TQM programme, consider the management of change issues in a move from quality control inspection to automated online testing under the control of production.

   What are the essential roles in the model of organizational change?

   With specific reference to the quality control inspectors in the above situation, what resistance to the proposed change might you expect?

## FURTHER READING

Chartier, M.R. (L.D. Goodstein and J.W. Pfeiffer Eds.), *The 1985 Annual: Developing Human Resources*, Pfeiffer.

CHAPTER

# THIRTEEN

# MISSION

## 13.1 OVERVIEW OF THE BUSINESS PLANNING PROCESS

Figure 13.1 shows the overall structure of the business planning process. The organization needs some overall sense of direction. If we do not know where we are going, how do we know if we are on the right course and when we have succeeded? At this stage, the firm will also have more fully detailed aims and specific objectives, such as desired profit levels. Before you can decide on which direction you need to move in and how far you need to travel, you have to know where you are. In Chapter Two, we outlined the tools of external analysis (PEST and Porter's 5 Force analysis) and internal analysis (Porter's value chain and McKinsey 7's'). With the additional understandings from Chapter Five, with concepts such as PLC, benefits, segmentation and the marketing mix we can conduct this analysis in a customer orientated context. From our consideration of operations (Chapter Six) and human resource management (Chapter Eleven) we can complete this audit with a rich diversity of powerful tools. At this stage of the process, a lot of creative and lateral thinking should have taken place and there is a danger of losing the sense of direction and focus under the wealth of detailed insight. The need is to see both the wood *and* the trees, when required. To order, pattern and determine the key issues the internal and external analysis needs to be refocused with a SWOT (Strengths, Weaknesses, Opportunities, Threats) analysis.

In any activity we do, we make assumptions, and these need to be noted in the business planning process as, often, through the planning period, some of these assumptions may, in the event, prove to be in error. It is essential that the plan should be re-evaluated in the light of the changes. If the assumptions are not noted, it is easy to continue with the plan without realizing that a key foundation has shifted. At this stage, it is possible to evaluate the probable outcome of existing policies. In most cases this will result in the achievement of results which do not live up to the desired expectations, that profits will not be as high as wanted. This is the 'strategic planning gap'. The firm has a whole series of strategy options, market penetration, market development, product and technology development, diversification, backwards forwards integration and operational technologies. The need is to evaluate which options provide a good fit between the firm's capability, the environment and the target levels of performance. Techniques of portfolio analysis (GE matrix) and the key parameters of business attractiveness and the firm's competitive advantages need to be addressed.

The strategic engineering manager can then formulate this into specific objectives, such

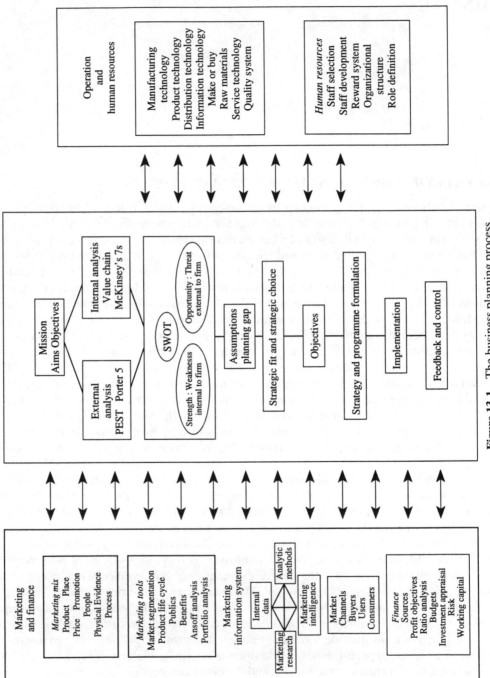

**Figure 13.1**  The business planning process

as to launch a new product. The detailed strategy and operational programmes need to be formulated and the implementation conducted on a day-by-day basis. The only certain thing about a business plan is that it will not work precisely as expected, not least of all because of the impossibility of fully predicting competitive responses. So, control mechanisms must be put into the plan to measure performance and to exercise control where deviations occur. As described above, this appears a very linear process with a single pass, but at each stage there may be a need to feed back insights from a latter stage and reconsider some issues. Business planning is not a single action but a philosophy of management. Most companies will operate a rolling five year plan with a complete revision every year. Having looked at the broad perspectives we can consider the elements and the process in detail.

## 13.2 MISSION, AIMS, OBJECTIVES, STRATEGIES

As the newly elected editor of a college magazine you might have a whole number of things to consider. You would have some central understanding of why the magazine should exist and what the students gain from it. Under this core feeling of what the magazine should be, you would have some distinct issues that it should address. You would have some firm targets for its operations and some schemes to get to those targets. For each edition you would need a detailed publication framework. As in any business venture you would have:

*Mission*    All the student news they will not print elsewhere.

*Aims*
1. To inform: key student events;
2. To campaign: better student accommodation;
3. To amuse and entertain: all those in campus jokes.

*Objectives*
1. To break even so publication can continue;
2. To have a circulation of 50 per cent of all students and staff;
3. To have a cover price of no more than 25 pence;
4. To publish every two weeks.

*Strategies*
1. Gain advertising and sponsorship from banks etc. so as to be able to keep cover cost down;
2. To use student volunteers to 'desk top' publish so as to keep production costs down;
3. To ensure sale points in all faculty coffee rooms and Student Union areas;
4. To have posters for each edition to attract interest and encourage purchase;
5. To have special editions: near vacation with special sections on cheap, interesting holidays.

A firm is faced with the same set of issues.

### 13.2.1 Mission

**Nature of the mission**    The mission is a short statement of what the firm is, rather than

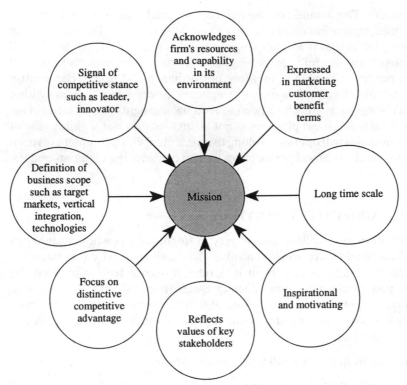

**Figure 13.2**  The structure of mission

simply what it does. It is an expression of just why it exists. Although the mission is short, it does take some thought to formulate. Figure 13.2 shows the nature of the mission statement. A common mistake is to focus on what the firm does rather than how customers view the product. In fact, customers do not buy a product, they, in marketing terms, buy benefits. When you go out to buy a floppy disk, do you want a floppy disk? In benefit terms, the answer is no! You do not want to hang it on the wall to look at it, you want to store data. The value of considering the customers and their benefits is that you can concentrate on what really matters. The customer is not concerned about the floppy disk technology if he can obtain his data storage needs in a way which is more convenient. In business, love the customer not the product.

---

A software engineer had written a superb set of programs for expert analysis of statistical data and pattern recognition. This was easy to use and required little understanding from the user as the 'expert system' would prompt the user to use the appropriate techniques. To do this, the engineer had used advanced programming techniques he had developed from his PhD research. In presenting this package to a potential major customer he explained just 'how state of the art' was the programming and how very complex problems had been overcome.

The engineer did not win the contract. The user could not believe that such a 'complex, state of the art' system could be easy to use. The engineer was in love with the product, not the customer. He presented the product and not the benefits.

---

Uninterruptible power supplies are important for many computer applications. Phase distortion, voltage spikes, drop-outs and brown-outs can cause a whole set of problems, including data corruption. The temptation is to design a high technology system which will take care of all of the problems. An engineer doing report writing at home may not be too concerned if he should lose power for an hour, as long as his data is not corrupted. A modest, plug-in board which would give power for a safe powerdown with appropriate file closures and programme exits might be all that is required. All the other features may not give this person any real additional benefits and may merely make the device so expensive that it is not bought. A supermarket with laser checkouts will not be able to operate if there is no power. There may be financial justification for some significant provision of more protection. The complex computer systems used for air traffic control can never go down. If they did, the resulting chaos could put many lives at risk. This situation calls for the highest levels of protection.

At first sight there appears to be one product need. On analysis of the customer benefits, and the valuations that a customer might put on these benefits, there are considerable differences in performance requirements. In marketing terms, there is segmentation of the market. The mission should indicate the benefits and segments that the firm regards as its business. For such a company providing uninterruptible power supplies to life critical applications, you might have a one line mission statement and its development as follows.

---

### PLYMOUTH POWER
**Technology you can trust, ceaseless power for life**

We aim to provide our worldwide customers with the most appropriate technology for the most secure uninterruptible power supplies that can be economically produced.

We aim to provide the best design and system advice with unsurpassable service for our systems which function in life critical situations.

We aim to provide our systems in the most cost-effective way to meet our customers' needs and to provide a fair return on investment to our owners.

We aim to provide employees with secure employment which enables them to make a maximum contribution to society and fully develops their potential. We are an equal opportunity employer.

We recognize in all our activities our responsibility to society and will conduct all our affairs in compliance with all national laws, with the highest standards of corporate ethics and with due regard to the environmental impact of our actions.

---

To arrive at such a statement the firm's senior managers must consider a number of issues. It is, first and foremost, a statement about the life values of the senior management and how these are reflected into their business. This is a statement of people who care about life and believe in a product which they consider brings benefits to people. It recognizes some implicit history of the company and its existing capability. They have, from their prior skills, developed the capacity to design and manufacture such systems and have the resource to continue to do so. However, it recognizes the specific focus. Although the geography is world wide, it excludes the vast markets for other types of uninterruptible power supplies and so, whilst taking account of the firm's strengths, it also takes note of its limitations. It is an expression of this firm's distinctive competence and its distinctive values.

**Definition of business scope**  The served markets are important to the definition of the business scope. In the above example of power supplies, the benefit segmentation has been considered. This is one way of defining market segments that the business will want to use. In Chapter Five, other forms of market segmentation were discussed. A company might wish to use any of these in the development of its mission focus. Defining the geography of the firm has to be part of the mission process. Should 'Plymouth Power' be interested in the UK market, the complete European market or the total world market? 'Plymouth Power' needs to take a view on this as it will affect all its operations. Within the EC only a restricted range of electrical regulations would apply, for the global market place, a wider range of regulations will have to be considered and incorporated into the design of the equipment.

The served markets is one dimension of the business scope. Another dimension is to define the vertical scope of the company. For an electronics company this could be a total chain, from the fabrication of components and boards at one extreme to simply marketing with the product subcontracted to another firm for manufacture. A major company can be fully integrated back to the primary sources of its raw materials. A chemical or steel company may integrate back to the mines for its primary input materials such as phosphate rock, coal etc. A paper company may own the forests to produce the wood for its pulping operations. At the consumer end, a pharmaceutical company, such as Boots, may consider that the ownership of the retail outlets is important. Consumer electronics companies may opt for selling via high street shops and out of town discount warehouses. If such a company wanted total control, however, it could opt to have its own retail outlets.

Technology can be another dimension that the firm may need to define its scope. A firm may be engaged in the transport of people across the English Channel. Possible options are a tunnel, ship, hovercraft, and air. Many firms may not wish to work in all possible technologies that might serve their market benefit needs, but restrict themselves to those technologies where they consider that they can deliver the benefit with some special extra skill. They instead choose to work in a way in which the firm considers it can maintain a special distinctive competence and competitive advantage.

**Competitive stance**  Information technology, aerospace, and pharmaceuticals are examples of industries where many major companies place a great emphasis on technical innovation and leadership as a strategy for marketing and financial success. If that is the company mission then the mission statement must reflect that. However, although these leader companies are major employers of scientists, technologists and engineers with their emphasis on R and D, this does not represent the only possible strategy. In the pharmaceutical industry Fisons and Glaxo will lead the market but other companies will seek to use low cost 'me too' technology to supply generic drug alternatives once patent protection has expired.

**Firm's capability**    For people to believe the mission, it has to be realistic. 'Plymouth Power' could not enter power generation and supply, it does not have the financial resources or the technology. The mission should be a realistic but challenging aspiration for the firm. It should be relevant to the internal situation and reality of the company and take due account of the pressures in the environment, including the activities of the firm's competitors.

**Values of key stakeholders**    In Chapter Two, the role of the various stakeholders in a company was reviewed. The mission will reflect the values of the firm's most intimate stakeholders. The senior managers who draft the statement, the owners who they must satisfy and the employees who will have to implement the mission. However, the mission will also reflect the values of the other stakeholders in such areas as the environment, and politically and socially sensitive areas, such as equal opportunity.

**Time scale**    Mission statements change, but not with the seasons. The value of mission is to give some continuity to the organization. Major insurance companies have had the mission 'personal financial security for the individual' for over 100 years. New interpretations have become necessary with increasing complexity of life and financial services but the core benefit has remained constant.

**Distinctive competitive advantage**    All the above considerations have been made to define and set the firm's own view of that special area where the organization considers it will have greater skills, more focused resources and better benefits to offer its served markets than its competitors. Without this the company enters a David and Goliath contest, with the small problem that they forgot to bring the sling along.

**Motivation**    Without the aspect of motivation all this discussion amounts to is where we should dig the next hole. A key difference between the successful firm and the deceased brand name is commitment, communication, coordination and community. The mission statement is the written expression of the core concepts and values of the firm around which these ingredients of success can be built.

### 13.2.2  Factors affecting the formation of mission and strategy

The firm is an organic entity which is constantly renewing and growing. For both the multinational and the small high technology company, the process is a feedback loop. Within the loop, the people making the decisions must consider what the alternatives are and then decide which are the right ones for their organization to exploit. This process

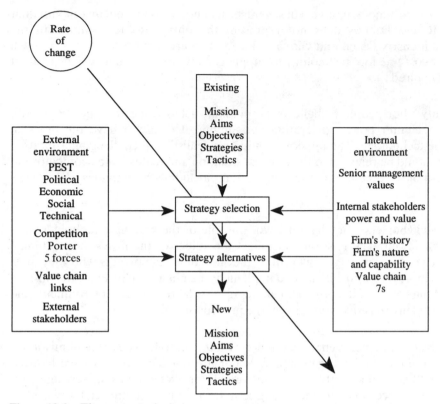

**Figure 13.3**  The context of mission

takes place in a context that conditions the possibilities and the outcomes, this is shown in Fig. 13.3.

Differing industries and technologies have vastly varying change scales. The fashion industry will produce a range of clothes for a single season of a few months. Primary utilities (gas, water, electricity), infrastructure (roads) and heavy primary industry (chemicals, metal extraction) may have construction times of five years for individual facilities. Total investments will be many billions of pounds. Of necessity, change is slower. It is essential for the firm to be sensitive and react to the time scale of change relevant to its industry.

The firm does not exist in a vacuum. In designing an amplifier, a different product will be needed for an air-conditioned office in Europe than for field service for the military in tropical forests. The PEST analysis considers the political issues (such as privatization of electrical supply has considerable impact on the economics of heat and power generation); the economic trends (such as higher personal incomes allowing more spending on consumer electronics); social trends (for example, more professional women buying their own cars demands a product focused on their specific benefit demands) and technical (such as communication and IT making banking from the home possible).

The firm needs to take account of competition and the possible competitive responses to its actions. The use of Porter's 5 forces of competition (existing direct competition, supplier power, buyer power, new competitors and substitute products) allows the firm to evaluate this environment. The firm exists in an integrated context, and consideration of the organization's value chain links will establish just how well the company is structured into this framework. For example, a computer company must be well linked into the technical developments in new components or it will design computers on yesterday's technology.

In the previous discussions, we have implicitly covered the interests of a number of the firm's stakeholders, the senior managers, the employees, the customers, and the suppliers. However, other stakeholders may have considerable power (for example, the environmental publics who may disapprove of the resources to be consumed or environmental impact of the firm's proposed actions).

The whole process of audit, strategy search, selection and implementation will be coloured by the values of the people who are involved. The senior managers may be very innovative or, conversely, they may be followers of change rather than leaders. Other possible dimensions are consultative or power centred, or, high risk takers or don't take a chance. The owners may want a quick killing with short term profits or they may wish to build for the future and accept lower returns in the short term. The way that the company has reached its position may well condition its way into the future. A firm has to take account of its history. The reality of the firm's nature and capability is a major factor. Value chain analysis gives insight into this. The evaluation of the firm's capability and its impact on mission, possible strategy options and strategy selection can be completed by consideration of the McKinsey 7's' (Structure, Systems, Style, Staff, Skills, Strategy and Shared Values).

---

## FLY BY WIRE

During the Second World War and into the 70s, aircraft were controlled by hydraulic systems activating flaps etc. Modern aircraft are computer controlled and companies in these markets had to develop new skills and technologies.

---

## 13.3 RELATIONSHIP BETWEEN MISSION, AIMS, OBJECTIVES, STRATEGY AND TACTICS

Mission statements are broad statements of company philosophy and do change with time but are not to be changed every year. Missions give a long term sense of direction and purpose to an organization. Mission statements do not give enough sense of performance to provide for effective management action. This additional dimension is given by aims and objectives.

The difference between an aim and an objective is that an aim expresses a desire and an objective takes this one stage further, to provide a target and a time scale of achievement.

'Plymouth Power' might consider that it should be possible, with advanced diagnostic boards and communications technology, to run remote early preventative maintenance checks from a world service centre.

Their key mission statement is: *'We aim to provide the best design and system advice with unsurpassable service for our systems, which function in life critical situations.'*

Their aim may be to *'provide remote diagnostics for early preventative maintenance'*.

Their objective may be *'to have a proven product for sales launch in two years'*.

---

Objectives help to define the organization in the environment, they help in the coordination of decisions and decision-makers; we are all working to defined goals. Objectives provide a standard for assessing the performance, both at the company level and also at the personal level when considering a person's contribution to the organization at an appraisal discussion. Mission statements are the broad direction but objectives are more tangible and provide the reality that is required for focus and motivation. A financial aim might be to improve profitability, its reflection in an objective might be to increase the return on net assets to 15 per cent in two years. In marketing, the aim is to improve the market position and a firm objective would be to increase market share in the UK to 25 per cent within one year. Sometimes a quantitative objective is not possible, but some qualitative measure of attainment can be substituted. So, an aim to offer customers quality products might have to gain BS5750 approval within one year as its objective.

A large organization does not simply have one mission and one set of objectives. There is a cascade of mission, objectives and lower level mission. The overall mission for the large organization will set objectives for each specific business unit. A telecommunications company will have a broad mission but a specific unit, such as customer appliance sales, will need to take its objective from the parent company and formulate this into a local mission statement which will then need further amplification into the detailed objectives for the single business. The whole process will require repeating for each significant operational area. So, each department should have defined its very specific local mission and have its quite particular targets and objectives. The same process should apply to the new product development project with the project having its own family of mission, objectives and strategies, all, of course, in harmony with the global mission and objectives.

At the initial stage of the business planning process we will have tentative objectives or extensions of past objectives. At this stage we may well not know if these are attainable or not. We need to refocus all this analysis with the SWOT analysis.

## 13.4 SWOT (STRENGTHS, WEAKNESSES, OPPORTUNITIES AND THREATS)

We need to determine what issues we consider are key to the future as a link from in-depth analysis to judged purposeful action. Strengths are elements of the firms's resources or value chain links which when considered in the context of the external environment gives, or might give a distinctive competitive advantage. A shop which processes films in three hours might consider this a strength, at first. However, if other shops can do it in one hour then it is not a strength. Although strengths are internal to the organization, they have to be measured relative to the external environment. Weaknesses are the simple reverse, elements of the firm's resources or linkages which when considered with the external environment gives or might give a competitive disadvantage. An opportunity is an attractive area for the firm's development where it would enjoy a competitive advantage. A threat is a challenge posed by an unfavourable trend, including competition, that would lead, in the absence of purposeful action, to the erosion of the firm's position. Although this appears simple, it is in fact a powerful tool to gain the critical insight and focus to arrive at a situation where we can say 'this is the position which means this and we must do . . .'. It is the link between analysis and the move to considered action.

## OUTLINE SWOT FOR PLYMOUTH POWER

| **Strengths** | **Opportunities** |
| --- | --- |
| Innovative products | Exports |
| New remote diagnosis board | Diversification |

| **Weaknesses** | **Threats** |
| --- | --- |
| Narrow product base | Competition |
| | New imports |

## 13.5 THE STRATEGIC PLANNING GAP

In life, there is often a gap between what are our desires and what, given our continuing actions, are our realistic expectations. The need is to bridge the gap to bring the realistic expectations into line with the desires. In some circumstances, it may be that we have to reduce the level of our desires and reduce our objectives to those that are attainable. However, most often, in business we are concerned in how we can improve the situation to move expectation into line with aspirations, Fig. 13.4 shows the 'strategic planning gap'. Ansoff analysis allows us to generate and evaluate the four generic marketing strategies; market penetration, product development, market development and diversification. In the general business context, other options are possible; the firm can integrate forwards or

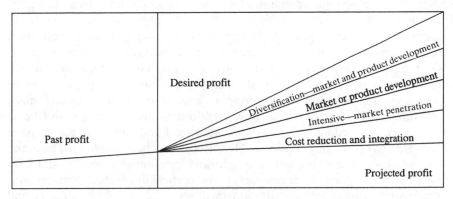

Figure 13.4   The strategic planning gap

backwards to gain more of the added value in the total chain from raw materials to delivery of customer satisfaction. The firm may be able to reduce costs with added value (improved quality) and/or reduce costs by using new materials and/or manufacturing technologies. All the techniques given in Chapter Five and Chapter Six, may assist in this process.

Having said that most organizations seek to follow expansion strategies, brief mention needs be made of the two alternative generic strategies of consolidation (stability) strategies and retrenchment strategies. In major businesses, differing SBUs will require differing strategies. In a mature market it may be necessary for one SBU to pursue a strategy of consolidation. Where the SBU's products are in decline the optimal policy for the parent organization will be a retrenchment strategy and the management of the decline to maximize the remaining profitability of the unit. A key feature of business policy is that rapid and effective action may be necessary. If an SBU is in a shrinking market the effective policy is often a rapid retrenchment (with considerable pain and job losses) to scale back to a sustainable level of operations, to reduce overheads and, most importantly, to recover as much as possible of the working capital. To just continue to fight the lost cause will produce escalating losses and even bankruptcy for the firm.

Within the above strategies, various options exist to gain competitive advantage. Many large organizations will opt for cost leadership. Quality is, in general, not a parameter that can be reduced. This policy is not simply a high risk 'cutting corners' cheap and cheerful policy but a determined attack to reduce overheads and achieve economies of scale whilst maintaining quality and service. The firm may seek to differentiate its products, to provide added benefits. This area has become important in the sphere of information technology, where manufacturers of systems may have to provide field customer support as a means to sustain their competitive advantage. In such application areas it is as important for the systems company to understand the customer's markets and operational needs as to be able to manufacture good hardware and write efficient computer code. As discussed in Chapter Five, in marketing strategy terms the firm may decide that rather than advance on a broad front, with attacks on several market segments, a focused approach on a specific market segment and an in-depth penetration on a narrow front may be best. Many small software houses adopt this strategy with highly tailored packages for specific end user groups (solicitors, chemists etc.).

If we consider the music industry, we can see various operations exploiting all these generic strategies. Major electronic companies have become studio owners as they have defined their mission as home entertainment and without the films and music they are in strategic weakness (competitive response to Porter supplier power). On the introduction of CD recording technology, a number of companies went into Eastern Europe to record large amounts of the classical repertoire at a fraction of the cost that such recordings would have cost using Western concert halls and artists, a cost leadership strategy. Many record houses exist with specialist offerings just offering a depth of music to a specific music group, and sometimes this is not restricted to records but to broadcasting with Classic Gold; a focus strategy. Recording technology has advanced and some companies have focused on state of the art recording facilities. All options have been exploited, from the virtual company which owns nothing but copyright and gets music recorded and CDs manufactured and distributed, all under contract, to the vertical integrated company with its own studios, manufacturing and distribution facilities. The possibility of a virtual company operating in this market allows strong competition in terms of product offerings as the cost of entry is restricted to the marketing costs. Of course, the basic costs of a CD's production does not change, but the consumer's benefit valuation does, from £3.00 for a recording of a classic by an unknown artist to £20 for specialist imported recordings.

As the above industry example shows, a firm should have a whole range of options, existing business to expand or contract and new businesses to enter. What is needed is the optimal portfolio that matches the mission. The portfolio analysis, with evaluation of the attractiveness of the business (profitability, growth, etc.) and the firm's competitive position (market share, cost structures) provides the broad strategy selection.

## 13.6  STRATEGIC FIT AND STRATEGIC CHOICE

The techniques of portfolio analysis, the Boston matrix and the GE matrix were introduced in Chapter Five. At this level of analysis we should reject the Boston matrix as too simplistic; market share and market growth are important but are far from the only parameters that are important. The two key factors are market attractiveness and competitive advantage. The firm has to find opportunities in areas that are attractive and where it will enjoy some distinctive competitive advantage.

In the above section, we have discussed some of the sources of competitive advantage: technological leadership, cost leadership, vertical integration, market focus and/or high market share (market share is the Boston matrix factor). Other sources of potential strength are strength of product line and if the company has a strong product range and depth these may support it is a move into a related market, especially if the firm should have a strong brand image. A market will be attractive if it is growing (the Boston matrix factor), has many customers, is large and profitable, and with a restricted range of competition. The techniques of financial analysis (see Chapter Nine) allow us to estimate the returns and, given some estimates of risk distributions, to even estimate probable payoffs. Having decided what businesses to back and the generic strategy to advance the businesses, the firm now has to implement the strategy. All strategic planning is of no value without a sound and flexible implementation. Flexibility is a key success factor. Apart from a fast moving PEST environment, no firm can totally predict the competitive responses from all five Porter sources of competitive pressures. Flexible adaptation and contingency options are necessary.

### 13.6.1  Implementation strategy

A strategy is the set of plans and actions through which we will be able to achieve our objectives, satisfy our aims and fulfil our mission. When 'Plymouth Power' have designed and tested the new remote diagnostics system they will need a strategy to let their customers and people who influence the purchase know about the system, gain their interest to evaluate the system and then purchase. In marketing terms, as part of the overall strategies 'Plymouth Power' would require a marketing communications strategy.

---

### PLYMOUTH POWER

**Remote fault detection system**

**Outline marketing communications strategy**

**Publicity**   Get the product exampled as state of the art technology on science and technology programmes on radio and TV. Provide good press releases so the product gets reported in the trade and technical magazines. Emphasis on the extra measure of safety the system will provide to the general public.

**Advertising**   Feature the product in a very few, select, key technical magazines read by engineers and design consultants.

**Direct mail**   Send a feature brochure to the engineers on all sites with suitable 'Plymouth Power' supplies to make them aware of the product for new installations and how their existing equipment can be retro-fitted. Mail technical staff in equipment manufacturers to continue to get their endorsement of 'Plymouth Power' equipment: 'We recommend Plymouth Power supply systems for use with our computers'.

**Personal selling**   Specific engineering sales calls to key customers and key specifiers, such as design consultants.

---

Tactics is the detailed level of all the actions which we need to take to work our strategy. On a month-to-month basis, we need to look at how things have been working, how things may have changed in our business environment and decide what set of actions we can best take. 'Plymouth Power' would have a set of tactics for their marketing communications programme. This would involve details such as the first customer groups to target and the actual visit lists. In greater detail, it would involve the precise nature of each sales presentation, which would have to be tailored to each specific customer's needs and benefits.

Two vital facets have to be kept in mind, the imperative aspect of financial control at every stage and the time factor. It is all too easy in implementation to run out of both time and money. The implementation plan must cover all of the necessary aspects, a marketing plan, a technical plan for innovation, an operations plan on how the product or service is to be provided (including the procurement plan), all within the framework of the planning budget. The key element has so far been neglected; these plans will not work without people and resources (money is not the only resource needed for the complete implementation of a plan). The mission aims and objectives having been decided the team has to be selected (where this is possible, where this is not possible the probable lack of fit needs to be taken into account). The human resources need to be structured, the reporting relationships defined and established. It is one thing to write a set of reporting relationships in an organizational structure and complement these with the most detailed job descriptions but, without understanding the interactions of people (Belbin types), personality and motivational issues, even the best organizational structures will not work. The diversity of implementation is so vast it is not possible to be prescriptive. Any of the techniques outlined in the previous chapters will apply to certain situations, the skill of management is the selection of the right techniques (being effective, doing the right thing) and then applying them with skill (being efficient, doing it right). To control you have to measure and feedback and control is mandatory to any long term success.

## 13.7 FEEDBACK AND CONTROL

There is one universal law which applies to both to science, engineering, technology and business:

*If it can go wrong, it will, at the most dangerous time.*

No part of the operational plan can be without its monitoring system and the normal rules of feedback and control apply. The detection systems must be sensitive (without giving too much noise or false signals to overload the control system), the operating characteristics of the measurement and control system must not distort the control signal and, where distortion may be suspected, the sources and nature of distortion must be allowed for. Unlike physical control systems the distortion will often come from the people elements of the system. It is not possible to complete an objective PEST analysis, we all bring our personality, experience and a perspective which, in fact, implies a personal distortion of the reality. To guard against this the skilled managing engineer will be sensitive enough to listen and take account of other people's views, giving a perspective which can remove some of the distortions, in particular to listen to views which may be uncomfortable and challenge the accepted truth. This is not to say that the manager should be blown off course with every slight change in the environmental winds, but when a gale is about to descend it is in order to shorten sail quickly before the complete plan is dismasted. The two most critical elements are to monitor the plan spend against actual, account for variances and take corrective action, in particular to take great care with working capital. Time is the one management resource which is finite and may not be changed, once the day has passed it may not be regained. In production, marketing or project management, it is also essential to ensure that schedules are monitored and milestones achieved. Throughout this text the techniques have been outlined. The MkIS (Marketing Information System) provides the information for monitoring the external environment, the PEST and competition, the effectiveness and efficiency of our marketing mix implementations. TQM and the MkIS system provide the tools to monitor the internal environment and the value chain links (for example, to suppliers) and the effective and efficient conduct of the firm's operations. Above all the techniques of human resource management (such as appraisal) enable the engineering manager to manage, motivate and lead the team.

One final word must be said about feedback and control; when things have gone right, the reasons for this should be evaluated. However, much more importantly, the reasons for failure must be analysed, often this will indicate a failure in the feedback and control system. This is far from easy, as unless the environment is supportive and open, people will seek to minimize and conceal failure 'the punishment of the innocent' problem. In this environment, the real problems will not be detected and the next errors and failures will become inevitable. If a person succeeds, both the member of staff and manager should share in the success (the individual has succeeded, the manager created the framework for the individual to prosper), when there is trouble the manager must not just head for the hills and punish the subordinate. If a subordinate has got into trouble it must imply that there may have been some failure in the selection, training process or support process. All the feedback systems in the world are without value if there is no control. The manager is not receiving this information for interest but action. The precise action required will depend on the deviation from plan and the options for corrective action.

## REVIEW

The mission, aims, objectives, strategy and tactics framework is entirely natural and applies to personal life as well as to the firm. A young student might have this chain between the mission; 'I want freedom to purchase a car'.

*Mission*   I want freedom and self-expression.

*Aim*   Mobility.

*Objective*   To buy a car by the end of the year.

*Strategy*   Buy a second hand car from a good outlet with an 18 months/18 000 miles warranty, that is less than 2 years old.

*Tactics*   The detailed selection of outlets, car model, year and features; ideas on how to get the price down.

---

The overall effect of this process is to define the firm's role in the greater business world and to motivate people. The objectives help coordinate people's activities and provide standards that they all share and expect to achieve. Within this framework, all the detailed tactics can be developed in a coherent way, so that people do not fall over each other and the firm, in effect, does not shoot itself in the foot.

After this divergent process, it is necessary to refocus the attention with the SWOT, analysis. This gives a firm framework to move from analysis to well-considered action, based on what the manager perceives as the key issues. In most cases the SWOT analysis will throw up a mismatch between the desired objectives, such as profits, and the projected performance if policies and strategies are not changed. The manager will consider the generic strategy options and seek those areas where the firm has a good strategic fit and potential to create a competitive position in an attractive market area. The process of portfolio analysis can be used as a means of strategic choice. Strategy selection is not restricted to deciding in which market areas the company should be active in but other parameters, such as the degree of vertical integration.

There is no simple model for implementation strategy, given the vast range of options and conditions. All the techniques of marketing, operations and human resources management should be applied and the techniques of financial analysis provides the tools to evaluate the probable monetary outcomes of these strategic and tactical policies. The monitoring of the plan against actual with the MkIS and MIS systems provides the feedback system to evaluate the deviations from the desired path before the business plan comes off the rails. However, this feedback is of no avail if the management look at it with interest, feedback needs to be converted into purposeful corrective action. Any management plan must contain provision for some margin of error and even some specific contingency plans, even if this is the allocation of some budget for unexpected problems. The key to business success is the determined, flexible, implementation of a sound mission in a well-informed context with a motivated and well-trained workforce.

---

## KEY CONCEPTS AND TECHNIQUES

**Aims**   The development of the mission into broad intents. Aims may be modified more frequently than mission and are usually examined on an annual basis. Aims may be referred to as open objectives by some.

**Feedback and control**    The process of monitoring actual performance against budget with variance analysis, MkIS systems; the feedback systems. Contingency planning and corrective action are needed to return the action programme to the planned course.

**Mission**    The one page statement of what the firm is and its position in business from a customer benefit orientated viewpoint. Subject to rare changes when a major change of direction or firm's philosophy is required.

**Objectives**    Objectives are the specific targets. An objective has a standard of achievement and a timescale for its attainment. It provides the specific focus that is lacking in mission and aims. Most often reviewed on an annual basis.

**Strategic choice**    The business planning process will suggest many options for the development of the business, it is necessary to select. Portfolio analysis is one tool for this process. The manager is looking for competitive advantage in attractive areas, a strategic fit.

**Strategic gap**    The strategic planning gap is the gap between the desired objectives and the best estimate of the likely outcome of existing policies and strategies. Mechanisms of bridging the gap include marketing strategies of market penetration, market development, product development and diversifications. Other options involve strategic options of vertical integrations and operational technologies.

**Strategy**    The set of plans and actions to achieve the objectives. Usually developed at the same time as the objectives are formulated.

**SWOT**    Strengths, Weaknesses, Opportunities, Threats, analysis, a way to refocus all the internal and external analysis into key issues for the direction of management action.

**Tactics**    The detailed month by month actions and sub-plans to make the strategies work. Frequently needs to be formulated, adapted and changed as the major strategies are implemented. Often in response to changes in the environment, such as competition response to a strategy.

---

## CASE STUDY

## FASTCHECK

**Recent history**    You are a member of a multi-disciplinary development team in a major multi-national who has a subsidiary making a range of advanced scientific instruments using state of the art technology. Within the team there are various scientists (biological, chemical and physical, mathematical), engineers (mechanical and electronic) and technologists (food, etc., who develop the application methods for the specific customer markets). Over the last year a group of you have collaborated in the conception and prototyping of a new instrument. The parent company has taken out a master patent on the breakthrough technology on a world wide basis.

**The concept**    The initial idea came from a problem in microbiological analysis. The traditional method of microbiological assay is to serial dilute the sample (such as a food product) and then to introduce a known volume of various dilutions onto an agar plate with nutrient media. The plate is then incubated for three to five days to allow the single organisms to develop colonies which can be counted and identified.

There are various problems with these traditional techniques. Considerable insight can be gained by the use of special media, staining dyes, and microscopic techniques. However, this requires very high skills which are often difficult to recruit, train and hold in industry. The length of time is a severe problem, moreover, both in industry and in the diagnosis of infections in the medical area.

Some time ago it was realized that the growth of micro-organisms produced materials (so-called 'metabolites') that changed the electrical properties of the nutrient media in very small, but with modern state of the art electronics and computer technology, measurable ways. A first generation of instruments was developed on this basis. However, although the reporting time could be reduced to a matter of hours, considerable skill was needed.

The measurement of the electrical properties gave only a broad measure of the total number of organisms and identification was only possible by multiple testing in various differing media. A skilled and labour intensive process.

Your development team have come up with an innovative solution to all these problems using advanced technologies from all your disciplines. The heart of the instrument is an innovative detector for the changes in properties. By bonding a number of modified enzymes onto a specially developed polymer electrode, a large number of individual bio-electrodes (at present 10 to 20, but potentially in excess of 100) can be incorporated into a single cell. This allows a number of specific metabolized materials to be detected and estimated. The mode of detection is by the development of small potentials at the micro-electrode. The highly specific nature of the bio-electrodes giving different potentials to differing metabolized materials.

Very advanced mechanical and electronic engineering is required due to the size of the electrode area (technology from microchip manufacture had been modified), small potentials and very high impedances. Advanced information processing software has been written to process the information and resolve mixed (confounded) responses so that, with a single measurement, the instrument can not only give an accurate estimate of the number of the organisms but an analysis of their types and distribution.

Key problems on the instrument have been resolved with custom chips for analogue to digital conversion of the very small potentials, even with the high impedance, and full development of the software with extensive statistical validation of the accuracy of the method. The instrument would only be viable if the cell could be made cheap enough to be disposable so that the instrument could be used by much less skilled staff than in the past.

**Application areas**  The ability not to only count but to analyse the types of micro-organisms appear to your group to have applications in the following general areas:

- Food industries
- Agriculture
- Medical
- Environmental
- Public health

Even at the prototype stage, however, the group can see further exciting developments. With the use of different enzymes, metals can be detected, even at very low levels. With the use of enzymes produced by genetic manipulation it has proved possible to produce custom electrode combinations for the detection and estimation of given organic compounds. Thus, the instrument could be used for analysis of products, in the bio-technology industry, for example.

The highly specific nature of the multi-dimensional electrodes, with the advanced software, has removed the need for the very extensive, time consuming and expensive sample preparation associated with established techniques. The group are very excited, as the multi-disciplinary concept appeared to have produced an instrument whose versatility and application is only bounded by imagination.

**The present situation**  There have been major problems with the other divisions of the multi-national. Given the small size of the present instrument operations with no distinctive advantages the head offices have suggested that the instrument division should be closed, with the multinational concentrating on their core activities. They have not been impressed with the information given above as they consider the project to be too risky and speculative, with no extensive operations analysis of how to produce the instrument or any realistic market potential analysis.

The group operate enlightened employment policies and have given three months' notice of their intention. Generous severance payments have been proposed. After the initial shock the development group decided that they had not fully developed the business plan for the instrument. However, they decided that they could gain the skills to do this. The embryonic board of the new company met with the senior management to propose that they would buy out the division and market the instrument. The multinational is sensitive to the public image crisis on this decision and has given an undertaking to the group that, if they can find the necessary finance, they may buy the division with all rights to patents taken out for the instrument. Moreover, as part of the restructuring they could buy not only the small development centre laboratories and workshops, but also the general product distribution unit that was adjacent to the development centre. It will take three months for the company to transfer the operations from this centre. The company have agreed that the nominal board of the proposed company can use their period of notice to prepare their business plan, find finance and make an offer for a management buyout.

What do you think are the issues that should be considered by FastCheck in drafting their provisional mission statement? Draft out what you consider the mission statement should be for FastCheck. Complete an environmental audit for FastCheck and focus into a SWOT analysis. What are the strategy alternatives for FastCheck? What further information would you need to decide the most viable option for FastCheck's development?

## QUESTIONS

1. Consider an organization you have worked for, or your present college, and draft out a mission statement.

2. In this chapter, the music industry was used as an example of possible generic strategy options. Consider this industry from the point of view of a musician, a recording company and a distributor. Outline the possible generic strategies. Select named examples and compare and contrast their strategies with the options you have outlined. If you were in their position, would you change anything and why? What do you consider are the keys for future success of these organizations?

## FURTHER READING

Jauch, L.R. and W.F. Glueck (1988) *Strategic Management and Business Policy*, 3rd Edition, McGraw-Hill.
Johnson, G.J. and K. Scoles (1988) *Exploring Corporate Strategy*, 2nd Edition, Prentice Hall.
Kotler, P. (1991) *Marketing Management; Analysis, Planning, Implementation and Control*, 7th Edition, Prentice-Hall.

# INDEX